PAKISTAN INSIGHTS 2020

PAKISTA

INSIGHT

2020

PAKISTAN INSIGHTS 2020

Editor

Tilak Devasher

Vivekananda International Foundation
New Delhi

PENTAGON PRESS LLP

Pakistan Insights 2020
Editor: Tilak Devasher

ISBN 978-93-90095-18-6

First Published in 2021

Published by
PENTAGON PRESS LLP
206, Peacock Lane, Shahpur Jat,
New Delhi-110049
Phones: 011-64706243, 26491568
Telefax: 011-26490600
email: rajan@pentagonpress.in
website: www.pentagonpress.in

Printed at Aegean Offset Printers, Greater Noida, U.P.

PAKISTAN
Political Map
KHYBER PAKHTUNKHWA
Mingora
Mansehra
Mardan
Abbottabad
Parachinar
Peshawar
ISLAMABAD
Kohat
Rawalpindi
Bannu
Kundian
Gujrat
Sialkot
AFGHANISTAN
Sargodha
Gujranwala
Dera Ismail Khan
Sheikhupura
Chiniot
Lahore
Zhob
Jhang
Faisalabad
Kasur
Chaman
PUNJAB
Sahiwal
Okara
Quetta
Multan
Dera Ghazi Khan
Bahawalpur
Nasirabad
BALOCHISTAN
Sadiqabad
Rahim Yar Khan
Jacobabad
Sukkur
Larkana
IRAN
INDIA
SINDH
Nawabshah
Turbat
Mirpur Khas
Gwadar
Hyderabad
Karachi
LEGEND
International Boundary
Province Boundary
National Capital
Province Capital
Major City
Arabian Sea
0 50 100 Miles
0 50 100 Kilometers
Copyright © 2019 www.mapsofworld.com

Contents

Pakistan at a Glance

Area

Total (Land and Water): 881,889 sq km

Province-wise Area

Balochistan: 347,190 sq km

Punjab: 205,345 sq km

Sindh: 140,914 sq km

Khyber Pakhtunkhwa (including erstwhile Federally Administered Tribal Agencies): 101,741 sq km

International Borders

Afghanistan: 2,670 km

China: 438 km (via Pakistan Occupied Kashmir)

India: 3,190 km

Iran: 959 km

Length of Coastline

1,046 km

Energy

Production of Crude Oil: 2,652,217 barrels

Number of Oilfields: 167 (July 2018)

Production of Natural Gas: 123,749 cubic feet

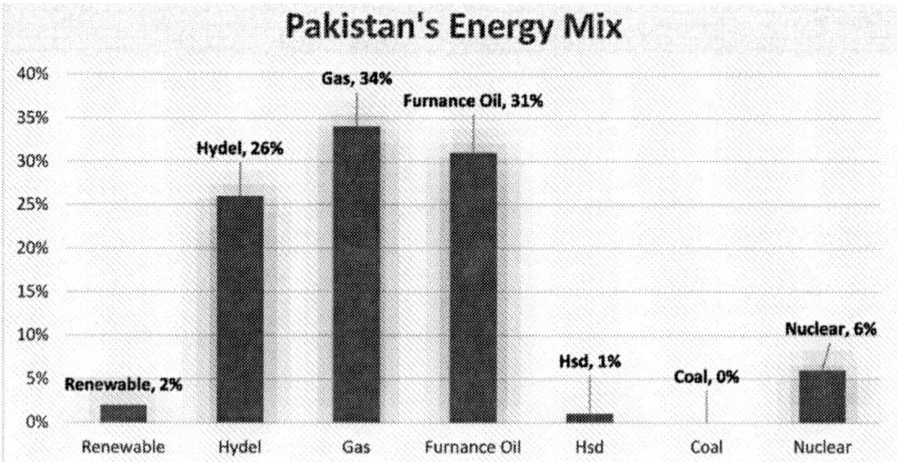

Source: https://en.dailypakistan.com.pk/featured/a-primer-on-pakistans-energy-mix/ (Hsd: High Speed Diesel)

Number of Gas Fields: 181 (July 2018)

Electricity Generation: 15,139 GWh (July 2018), 2017-18: 134,995 GWh (PBS)

DEMOGRAPHIC BASE

Population

207,862,518 (2017)

Population Density

242.9 per sq km (Britannica)

Human Development Index (HDI) (2019)

0.560, Rank 152 (UNDP)

Province-wise Demography

Punjab: 53 per cent

Sindh: 23 per cent

Khyber Pakhtunkhwa (including FATA): 17 per cent

Balochistan: 6 per cent

(*Source:* Census 2017)

Religion

Muslims: 97 per cent (Sunni 77 per cent, Shia 20 per cent)

Christians, Hindus and Others: 3 per cent

ECONOMIC PROFILE

Economy-General

Basic Economic Parameters

Criteria	*Values*
GDP (billion $) 2019 [2]	278. 222
GDP growth (annual %) [2]	1 %
Inflation (July-April 2020) [3]	11.2 %
Agriculture (% of GDP) [1]	19.31 %
Industry (% of GDP) [1]	19.29 %
Services (% of GDP) [1]	61.40 %
Exports of goods and services (% of GDP) [2]	10.1 %
Imports of goods and services (% of GDP) [2]	20.33%
Gross capital formation (% of GDP) [2]	15.611 %
Urban population growth (annual %) [2]	2.7
Energy use (kg of oil equivalent per capita) [2]	484.44
Electric power consumption (kWh per capita) [2]	471.04
Tax revenue (% of GDP) [3]	11.8
Personal remittances received (billion $) [2]	22.322
Foreign direct investment (billion $) (2019-20)	2.1
Net official development assistance received (current US$) (millions) [2]	3,005.15

[1] PBS; [2] World Bank Data; [3] Pakistan Economic Survey 2019-2020.

INFRASTRUCTURE PROFILE (Pakistan Economic Survey 2019-2020)

Infrastructure

Road Network: 263,775 km

National Highways of Pakistan: 13,000 km

Railways (Track Length)

11,811 km

MILITARY PROFILE (MILITARY BALANCE 2020, IISS)

Defence Budget (US $)

2016	*2017*	*2018*	*2019*	*2020*
9.19 bn	9.72 bn	1.11 tr	1.40 tr	1.48 tr

Force Levels

Active: 653,800 (Army 560,000; Navy 23,800; Air Force 70,000; Paramilitary 282,000)

Strategic Forces

Army Strategic Forces Command: 12,000-15,000

Air: 1-2 sqn of F-16 A/B or Mirage 5 may be assigned a nuclear-strike role

Coast Guard

5 Patrol and Coastal combatants

List of Contributors

Dr. Arvind Gupta is the Director of the Vivekananda Foundation, New Delhi. He was the Deputy National Security Adviser and Secretary, National Security Council, Government of India, during 2014-17. Prior to that, he was Director-General of the Institute for Defence Studies and Analyses, Ministry of Defence, New Delhi, during 2012-2014. He is a former career diplomat and has served in the Ministry of External Affairs and Indian missions abroad. Author of four books, his last book *How India Manages Its National Security* was published by Penguin in 2018. He has edited several books. In 2020, Sage India published a co-edited (with Anil Wadhwa) volume titled *India's Foreign Policy: Surviving in a Turbulent World.* He also co-edited with Arpita Mitra a volume titled *Vasudhaiva Kutumbakam: The Relevance of India's Ancient Thinking to Contemporary Strategic Reality,* (Aryan International, New Delhi).

Rana Banerji is a former officer of the Indian Administrative Services (IAS-1972, Assam-Meghalaya cadre). He retired as Special Secretary, Cabinet Secretariat, in October 2009. After retirement, Banerji headed a Task Force on Intelligence Reforms at the Institute for Defence Studies & Analyses (IDSA). He participates in the UN Human Rights Commission Privacy Rights Rapporteur's annual meetings on Accountability & Intelligence Reforms. He has participated in several Track II & Track 1.5 interactions on Indo-Pak relations, Indo-US Security Relations and Indo-Pak-Afghan Tripartite Dialogue (2010-2015). His focus area of expertise pertains to Pakistan, Afghanistan and Islamic Terrorism.

Tilak Devasher is a Consultant with the Vivekananda International Foundation. He is a former Special Secretary, Cabinet Secretariat, Government of India. During his professional career, Tilak specialized in security issues, especially pertaining to India's neighbourhood. He is the author of '*Pakistan: Courting the Abyss*' (December 2016) and '*Pakistan: At the Helm*' (June 2018) and '*Pakistan: The Balochistan Conundrum*'. All the books have been published by Harper Collins India. He is currently a member of the National Security Advisory Board (NSAB).

Prateek Joshi is a PhD candidate at the University of Oxford. Earlier, he was Researcher/Associate with Vivekananda International Foundation. He was working on Trans-Himalayan Geopolitics, Pakistani Politics and Sino-Indian Conflict. Prior to joining VIF, he was working on a project with the Institute of Defence Studies and Analysis, New Delhi. Some of his writings have appeared in and *South China Morning Post.*

V. Srinivas, IAS, serves as the Additional Secretary to Government of India in the Ministry of Personnel, Public Grievances and Pensions with additional charge of Director General, National Centre for Good Governance. He served as the Advisor to Executive Director (India) in the International Monetary Fund from 2003 to 2006 and is the author of "*India's Relations with the International Monetary Fund 1991-2016: 25 Years in Perspective*" with a fellowship from the Indian Council of World Affairs published in 2019. His second book, "*Towards a New India: Governance Transformed – 2014-2019*" was published in 2019. He has authored 156 papers/articles.

Aakriti Vinayak is a Research Associate at Vivekananda International Foundation, New Delhi. She has completed her Masters in International Relations from Jawaharlal Nehru University and Bachelors in History from Jesus and Mary College, University of Delhi. She has also completed her MPhil from Department of Political Science, University of Delhi. Her research interests are primarily Pakistani Politics, India's Neighbourhood and China, Soft Power and Cultural Diplomacy. Prior to joining VIF she has worked with Institute of Chinese Studies, *The Times of India* and Indian National Trust for Art and Cultural Heritage (INTACH).

Brig. Rahul K. Bhonsle (R) is an army veteran with over three decades of active service. He is an independent consultant on research and knowledge management in defence and security issues in the Indo Asia Pacific Asia and Director, Security Risks Asia, a Risk and Knowledge Management Consultancy, based in Delhi.

Amb. D. P. Srivastava is Distinguished Fellow at Vivekananda International Foundation. A former diplomat, he was Indian Ambassador to Iran, the Czech Republic, Libya and India's High Commissioner to Malta. During his tenure in Iran, he led negotiations on Indian participation in Chabahar Port. The author has also served in Karachi. After retirement, he served as Senior Advisor to ONGC Videsh Ltd. for a year (2015-16), and on the Board of Directors of GAIL (2017-20). He holds post-graduate degree in Political Science and Governance.

Dr. Shalini Chawla is Distinguished Fellow at the Centre for Air Power Studies (CAPS), New Delhi. She joined CAPS in 2006 and has published widely in national and international journals on a wide range of issues relating to Pakistan and Afghanistan. She lectures regularly at leading establishments of the Indian Armed Forces and universities. She has authored four books titled *Pakistan's Military and Its Strategy* (2009), *Nuclear Pakistan* (2012), (co-author) *India's Sentinel: Select Writings of Air Commodore Jasjit Singh* (2014) and (co-author) *Strategic Advantage of Air Power* (2019).

Dr. Gulshan Rai was the first National Cyber Security Coordinator, Government of India in the Office of the Prime Minister. Prior to that, he was Director General, CERT-In (Indian Computer Emergency Response Team) and headed E-Security & Cyber Law Division, STQC and other divisions in the Ministry of Electronics & Information Technology. He has led the team to put in the first Cyber Technological Legislation, "The Information Technology Act, 2000". Such legislation led to other legislations. He was a member of the Data Protection Committee that drafted the Data Protection Law. He has also led the team to set up a National Watch and Alert System in the country as part of cyber security initiative and Computer Emergency Team. He led Government teams to the United Nations to negotiate "norms of behaviour in Cyber Space, Internet domain and WTO".

Amb. Satish Chandra joined the Indian Foreign Service in 1965 and till 1989 was posted in various capacities in Indian missions in Vienna, Karachi, Washington D.C., Algiers, and Dhaka as well as at headquarters. Subsequently, served as India's Ambassador to the Philippines (1989-1992), its Permanent Representative to the UN Offices in Geneva (1992-1995) and its High Commissioner to Pakistan (1995-1998). He set up the NSCS in 1999 and headed it as Secretary till demission from office in February 2005 concurrently holding the post of Deputy National Security Advisor from February 2002. Apart from representing India at a variety of multilateral fora such as the IAEA, WHO, ILO, the UN Human Rights Commission, the Disarmament Commission, etc., he served as the President of the Conference on Disarmament during his assignment in Geneva. He was President of the Association of Indian Diplomats in 2010. He has been associated with Vivekananda International Foundation since its inception in 2009 and is currently the Vice Chairman of its Board of Trustees.

Amb. T.C.A. Raghavan is a former diplomat. He has served as the Indian High Commissioner to Singapore and Pakistan. He is currently Director General of the Indian Council of World Affairs. He is the author of "*The People Next Door: The Curious History of India's Relations with Pakistan*". (New Delhi, 2017)

Lt. General S. A. Hasnain, PVSM, UYSM, AVSM, SM, VSM and Bar (Retd) is a former Corps Commander of the Srinagar-based 15 Corps which is responsible for the security of Kashmir. He spent much of his service in J&K, both on the Line of Control, Siachen Glacier and in counter-terror operations. He is Chancellor, Central University of Kashmir. He is also Member, National Disaster Management Authority.

Sushant Sareen is a Senior Fellow at the Observer Research Foundation and associated with its Neighbourhood Initiatives program. Before joining ORF, he worked in various capacities with the Vivekananda International Foundation (VIF), Institute for Defence Studies and Analyses (IDSA), Public Opinion Trends and southasianmedia.net. He is the author of: "The Jihad Factory - Pakistan's Islamic Revolution in the Making". He has also authored a number of monographs including on the China-Pakistan Economic Corridor, the insurgency in Balochistan and Operation Zarb-e-Azb. In addition he has contributed chapters for edited volumes and written papers on the situation in Pakistan and on India-Pakistan peace process for academic journals and newspapers. He appears frequently on TV programmes.

Dr. Yatharth Kachiar is a Research Associate at the Vivekananda International Foundation. She is a Ph.D. from the Centre for West Asian Studies, Jawaharlal Nehru University, New Delhi. Her doctoral thesis was on "Soft power in Turkish foreign policy in West Asia and North Africa, 2002-2013". Her area of interest includes the Afghanistan-Pakistan region, West Asia, India and the neighbourhood.

Amb. Gautam Mukhopadhaya (IFS 1980) has served in Indian embassies in Mexico, France, Cuba, the Permanent Mission of India, New York, and Ministry of External Affairs, India; as well as on deputation with the ministries of Culture and Defence of India, Consultant on Social Development at the UN, New York, and Visiting Fellow at the Carnegie Endowment for International Peace, Washington DC. He graduated from the National Defence College (NDC) and re-opened the Indian Embassy in Kabul in November 2001 after the ouster of the Taliban. He then served as India's Ambassador to Syria, Afghanistan and Myanmar before retiring from service in May 2016. He is presently affiliated to the Centre for Policy Research as a Senior Visiting Fellow focusing on Afghanistan, Myanmar, India's Act East policy, the Indo-Pacific and the North East of India.

Lt. General R. K. Sawhney, PVSM, AVSM (Retd) is Centre Head & Senior Fellow, National Security and Strategic Studies & Internal Security Studies, Vivekananda International Foundation. He is a former Deputy Chief of the Army Staff and a former Director of Military Intelligence. He is a post-graduate in Defence and Security Planning from the Royal College of Defence Studies, London. Post retirement, he was deputed by the Government of India to monitor the situation in Afghanistan, a country that he has visited almost every year since 2002.

Amb. Amar Sinha served as India's Ambassador to Afghanistan (2013-2016) and retired in 2017 as Secretary in the Ministry of External Affairs. During his 35 years as a member of the Indian Foreign Service, he served in Indian missions in Algeria, Argentina, the USA, Indonesia, Belgium and the EU, Tajikistan and Afghanistan. Currently, he is a member of the National Security Advisory Board and a distinguished fellow at RIS, a Delhi-based think tank focussed on economic and developmental issues.

Editor's Note

Following the setting up of the Pakistan Study Group (PSG) in the Vivekananda International Foundation (VIF) in February 2018 and its success in bringing out *Pakistan Insights 2019*, it was decided to continue with the Insight series, making it an annual feature.

During the past year, the PSG has continued to discuss and debate issues relating to Pakistan in a holistic manner, going beyond the headlines. Given the constraints imposed by COVID-19, the PSG has met virtually and as before, the discussions have been candid and enriching.

Dr. Arvind Gupta kick-starts the discussions with an overview of developments in Pakistan in 2019-20. His broad thrust is that despite heavy odds and less than satisfactory performance, Imran Khan has survived because the Army was satisfied with their protégé and there was no visible challenger.

In two articles, Rana Banerji looks at the internal developments in Pakistan and civil-military relations. While discussing the entire gamut of internal developments, he asserts that the 'unholy alliance' between Imran Khan and the army was accompanied by diminishing constitutional rights and encroachment on autonomies of civil society. He examines in detail the extension saga of the army chief and its various dimensions and notes that the balance of power between civilians and the army is likely to remain heavily tilted in favour of the latter in the foreseeable future.

Tilak Devasher looks at the COVID-19 phenomenon in Pakistan and notes how there was a sudden turnaround in the number of positive cases and fatalities from about mid June. At one stage, the virus was galloping across Pakistan and then suddenly the brakes seem to have been applied. Whether this was a genuine turnaround or due to drastic reduction in testing, time will tell. However, Pakistan could well have to brace itself for a potential second wave.

Three articles—by Prateek Joshi, V. Srinivas and Aakriti Vinayak—look at the various dimensions, some overlapping, of the Pakistan economy. Prateek explains the economic situation inherited by the Imran Khan government and how it had to go into fire-fighting mode immediately, shed its pre-election rhetoric and make a U-turn by seeking a bail-out from the IMF. V. Srinivas notes that as Imran Khan completes two years in office, there exist enormous economic challenges and meeting public expectations remains an uphill task. He analyzes how an IMF programme was inevitable and goes into details of the programme. Aakriti looks at the complicated relationship between the IMF and Pakistan and assesses that while the IMF programme has provided a breather for Pakistan, it has differing consequences on the economy. She also delineates the impact of COVID-19 on the Pak economy.

Brig. (R) Rahul Bhonsle reviews the terrorism landscape in Pakistan that he calls the 'continued crisis of strategic identity'. He quotes a Pak-based think tank according to which there is continued resistance of the state to undertake structural changes in the socio-political, religious, administrative and constitutional spheres that can overcome fundamental support factors of terror.

While the focus of attention has been on J&K, Amb. Dinkar Srivastava turns the spotlight on the part of Kashmir illegally occupied by Pakistan—POK and GB. He traces the history of these areas and the contradictions in Pakistan's stance of supporting a 'liberation struggle' across the LOC and repression at home. He underlines how Pakistan has brutally used sectarianism to keep the Shia-majority GB under control and used Islamisation to compensate for the absence of democracy. The 5 August 2019 developments in J&K allowed both Imran Khan and the so-called PM of POK for grandstanding and using the opportunity to burnish their poor governance track records.

Nuclear weapons remain integral to Pakistan's overall strategic positioning against India, writes Dr. Shalini Chawla on Pakistan's nuclear brinkmanship. She underlines that Pakistan acquired nuclear weapons for war prevention and to conduct the policy of sub-conventional warfare through terrorism without fear of Indian military retaliation. This explicitly explains Pakistan's nuclear positioning which relies on a first-use doctrine projecting a low nuclear threshold and an element of uncertainty. Another element behind Pakistan's nuclear programme is the desire to be visualized as the leader of the Islamic word. Though Pakistan does not have an officially announced doctrine, the basic elements as enunciated by Pak leaders are Indo-centricity, credible minimum deterrence, strategic restraint and first use. Additionally, it boasts about TNWs and full spectrum deterrence.

In another chapter, Dr. Chawla writes about Pakistan's developing indigenous capability in defence production. Starting from establishing an ordinance factory to manufacturing .303-inch calibre rifles and ammunition in the 1950s, Pakistan has embarked upon modernization in the last two decades due to its strategic relationship with China. Today there are over 20 public sector and 100 private sector units engaged in the manufacture of defence-related products. The key among these is the Pakistan Ordinance Factories (POF), Wah, that comprise a cluster of 14 factories geared to conventional weapons production. Others include Heavy Industries, Taxila, Pakistan Aeronautical Complex, Heavy Mechanical Complex, Air Weapons Complex, Karachi Shipyard and Engineering Works (KSEW), National Development Complex (NDC), etc. Interestingly, a majority of the defence production units are established for servicing Chinese equipment and to assemble/co-manufacture and produce Chinese equipment. Despite this, Pakistan's defence industry has yet to come up with an indigenous design and development of weapons systems.

Given the growing importance of the cyber world, Dr. Gulshan Rai takes an in-depth look at the digital landscape of Pakistan during the last ten years and notes that it has registered a significant surge. New technologies are getting integrated into developmental strategies in the country and the utilization of cyberspace has become a useful and important tool. However, Pakistan has a long way to go in enhancing the resilience and security of cyber infrastructure and implementation of robust technology architecture, cyber security strategy and legislation. In fact, Pakistan has invested more resources in developing its cyber operations than on investment in enhancing resilience of its cyber infrastructure. State actors that are units of the defence forces, run these operations working under the overall guidance and supervision of the Inter-Services Cyber Command. These groups are also connected with a large number of non-state actors. According to Rai, Pakistan's offensive postured cyber policy is counter-productive since it would invite retaliation. Instead, he advocates that Pakistan should invest its resources in implementing fast and secure digitalization that would go a long way in socio-economic development and delivering citizen-centric services.

In a *tour-de-force,* Ambassador Satish Chandra reviews the entire gamut of Indo-Pak relations under Imran Khan including the Kartarpur Sahib Corridor, the Pulwama attack and the Balakote air strike. He concludes that since Imran Khan's assumption of office of PM, the relations have been at the lowest, leaving aside periods of actual military conflict and are unlikely to see any improvement for the foreseeable future. He notes that even at the worst of times in the past, a certain level of civility and courtesy had been maintained between the leadership. Imran Khan and Shah Mahmood Qureshi have jettisoned this. One reason is that despite impressions to the contrary, Imran Khan has never been soft on India even in his cricketing avatar when he saw cricketing encounters with India as a jihad. The 5 August 2019 developments have raised Pakistan's visceral antipathy towards India to fever pitch and it has remained there due to Pakistan's failure to sway the international community to its point of view.

Continuing with Indo-Pak relations, Amb. T. C. A. Raghavan reflects on what he calls the India-Pakistan binary and de-securitization. According to him, the India-Pakistan binary of 'Engagement-Disengagement' has intensified in both directions over time: the greater the intensity of engagement, equally significant and fraught has been the disengagement that followed. Thus, one view is that it is lunacy to embark on engagement knowing that disengagement following a breakdown is inevitable. He notes that political initiatives ended repeatedly on the anvil of political and institutional instability in Pakistan or when civil-military tensions in Pakistan moved up a few notches. Complicating matters, according to Raghavan, is the fact that the relationship has always been part of a wider context of regional and international forces and such influences cannot be underestimated. He also explores the impact that COVID-19 could potentially have on the possibilities of de-securitized elements being introduced in the India-Pakistan agenda.

Lt. Gen. Ata Hasnain (R) discusses the impact of the 5 August 2019 developments in J&K, i.e., removing its special status and creating two Union Territories. He focuses on the international and diplomatic dimensions, external and internal security situation on the LOC, governance and attitude of the people. One of the negative factors he identifies was the weakness in the Indian effort to reach out to international think tanks and media to explain its narrative. He calls for the Indian narrative to be better packaged and disseminated. On the security front, he notes that since 5 August 2019, the separatists have been isolated and their hold over the system weakened due to the strong convergence on counter-infiltration and Intelligence-based operations. Narrowing the space for overground workers (OGWs) to operate has assisted the process. He, however, warns that failure to trigger instability may lead Pakistan to resort to spectacular terrorist attacks like Pulwama and also points to possible Pak-China collusion in Ladakh. Ata also underlines the need for better governance and restoration of political activity in J&K.

Sushant Sareen has an interesting take on China-Pakistan relations that he calls the 'Paradox of Asymmetry' where, despite being the stronger side, China is often seen to be leaning backwards to accommodate the weaker Pakistan. Yet, China isn't giving a free lunch to Pakistan and finds enough strategic benefit and economic returns to justify its engagement with Islamabad. He notes that the setting up of the CPEC authority is perhaps the most egregious example of Chinese clout in Pakistan. He points to the mutual good-fit Pakistan believes that the more China is invested in Pakistan, the less chance there is of the latter losing interest. The Chinese believe the more they invest in Pakistan, the closer they pull it into their sphere of influence. Despite some instances of a few blips, the bilateral relationship will only deepen and go forward because neither can afford to walk away.

In another paper, Lt. Gen. Ata Hasnain (R) sheds light on the complexities of the triangular Pak-Saudi-Iran relationship delving into Pakistan's individual linkages with these two countries and into the larger geopolitical game of Islamic and international politics. He evaluates that the triangle is faced with challenging times of rapid and unpredictable change in the world order based upon emerging dynamics and a new balance of power.

Dr. Yatharth Kachiar looks at another triangular relationship—that of Pakistan-Turkey and Malaysia—together with the OIC. She holds that the primary force that binds the three countries together is the pre-eminence of Islamic issues in their foreign policies and by focusing on these issues they aim to forge a space for themselves in the Islamic world and strengthen their support base at home. In the process, the troika aspires to dethrone Saudi Arabia as the established leader of the Islamic world. However, she aptly notes that the lack of economic and military strength would pose a major challenge to them in their endeavours.

In another paper, unlike the 'all-weather' China-Pak relationship, the Pak-Russia relationship is tentative, coming out of the Cold War bipolarity, writes Dr. Yatharth Kachiar. She notes that relations improved gradually with the end of the Cold War and have picked up pace more recently. Developments in Afghanistan, especially, brought the two closer with Russian concerns centred upon the growing presence of the Islamic State Khorasan Province (ISKP), instability, terrorism and drug-trafficking spilling over from Afghanistan into the Central Asian countries. Pakistan thus became a crucial country in the Russian strategic imagination. A contributing factor was India moving closer to the USA. Despite this, as of now, the military and economic bilateral ties are at a nascent level though the minuscule transfer of military equipment has significant political symbolism.

Two chapters are devoted to Pakistan and the Afghan peace process and Pakistan's role in Afghanistan. The first is by Amb. Gautam Mukhopadhaya and the second by Lt. Gen. Ravi Sawhney and Amb. Amar Sinha. According to Gautam, though motivated by its own narrow interests, the US-led direct talks facilitated by Pakistan leading to the US-Taliban agreement in Doha on 29 February 2020 have generated hopes of peace in the absence of any alternative to a continued military stalemate. The prospects, however, are not very bright because the Afghan people have not been part of a peace process in which the Taliban are seeking victory and that the terms of the agreement are seriously imbalanced and favours the Taliban. In a nutshell, the peace agreement that he examines in detail is flawed, driven by US, Pakistani and other foreign interests. Pakistan sees in the peace process an opportunity to regain strategic depth, influence and control in Afghanistan that was lost with the ouster of the Taliban in 2001. Gautam also delineates the scenarios that could emerge as and when the intra-Afghan talks get underway.

Lt. Gen. Sawhney and Amb. Sinha look at the internal developments in Afghanistan closely, especially levels of violence in 2019-20, US policy and its impact and elections in Afghanistan. They also provide a perspective on the US-Taliban agreement of February 2020 that they term as resembling a stillborn baby refusing to kick or wail. However, they note that despite its flaws, the agreement is the closest Afghanistan has come to start intra-Afghan negotiations and the national mood favours giving it a good shot. While there is no clarity if the Taliban as a whole were willing to peacefully re-integrate in a power-sharing agreement, they have continued to attack every fibre of Afghan society. Worryingly, the recently-released prisoners were back in the battlefield. The authors acknowledge that Pak-US relations were marked by wild swings: from pubic accusations and castigation to the USA acknowledging Pakistan's role in facilitating the deal with the Taliban. However, Pakistan may have misread Afghan weariness with war as their willingness to get the Taliban back or acceptance of the ideology of the Taliban. In reality, the continuing violence has made the Afghans treasure the gains since 2001 even more. Their prognosis of whether Afghanistan will see peace or degenerate into more bloodshed would depend on the Taliban (and their Pakistan backers) showing signs of change.

In conclusion, the Editor tries to do some crystal-ball gazing to predict the future trajectory of Pakistan.

Members of the Pakistan Study Group are:

Dr. Arvind Gupta—*Director VIF*
General N. C. Vij
Amb. Satish Chandra
Amb. G. Parthasarathy
C.D. Sahay
Lt. Gen. Ravi Sawhney
Lt. Gen. Ata Hasnain
Rana Banerji
Amb. Arun Kumar Singh
Amb. T.C.A. Raghavan
Amb. D. P. Srivastava
Rahul Bhonsle
Dr. Shalini Chawla
Sushant Sareen
Yatharth Kachiar
Aakriti Vinayak
Tilak Devasher—*Convenor*

Tilak Devasher
Consultant VIF
Member, National Security Advisory Board

New Delhi, 18 September 2020

Introduction
Developments in Pakistan: An Overview

Arvind Gupta

In the rocky politics of Pakistan, there is always a danger to the stability of the Imran Khan-led Government, which has a thin majority in the parliament. However, despite the heavy odds, the government has survived the turbulence. This is because the Army is presently satisfied with their protégé, Imran Khan. Even though he has no visible challenger at the moment, his performance on most governance issues has been less than satisfactory. Further, the coalition government will always be vulnerable to political machinations. Therefore, Imran Khan has to be careful not to antagonize the Army. Not surprisingly, therefore, he has let the Army run the country's security policy fully and has kept himself confined to the domestic agenda and diplomacy.

Politics

In 2019, Chief of Jamiat Ulema-e-Islam (F) Maulana Fazlur Rahman did try to mount a challenge to Imran Khan by organizing an 'Azadi march' of his supporters to Islamabad. Citing rigging and fraud in the elections of 2018, he demanded the resignation of the prime minister. Nothing came of the march. It fizzled out because the opposition parties were not fully on board with the Maulana because of their own compulsions. Imran Khan emerged unharmed.

Imran Khan has played his cards well. He ensured that he did not ruffle the Army. He gave a three-year extension to Army Chief Bajwa, thus securing his support. The Pakistan Supreme Court challenged the extension but the potentially destabilizing storm dissipated as the government quickly got the Army Act amended thus legalizing and legitimizing the Army Chief's extension post-facto. Thanks to the continued support of the Army, Imran Khan's government looks stable at present despite its uninspiring two years in the saddle,

Imran Khan has been ruthless on the opposition. He has used the National Accountability Bureau (NAB) and the anti-corruption drive to keep opponents on their toes. A seriously ill Nawaz Sharif is in London and a struggle has broken out in the PML (N) for the leadership. The opposition parties complain of oppression but are unable to do much. The opposition has been vocal in opposing Imran Khan but also ineffective. A weakened PPP, confined mostly to Sindh, is careful not to do anything to anger the Army.

In order to survive, Imran Khan was compelled to make several concessions to fundamentalist parties, particularly the Tehrik-e-Labaiq Party (TLP), on the Asia Bibi blasphemy case. The court absolved Asia Bibi of the charges of blasphemy. This angered the fundamentalist elements. She was allowed to escape to the West. Imran Khan, fearful of the wrath of the fundamentalist elements in the country, had to retract on some of the high-level appointments he had made because the appointees were Ahmadiyyas, who are regarded as non-Muslims. Imran Khan appears weak in front of the fundamentalists.

Imran Khan would have to worry on yet another front. Originating in South Waziristan, the popularity of the *Pashtun Tahaffuz Movement* (PTM) is growing despite state repression, censorship, and intimidation. Led by young Pashtun leaders, the PTM has been demanding the stoppage of repression of the Pashtuns and accountability for missing Pashtun youth. They speak openly against enforced disappearances and the extrajudicial killings during the military's fight in South Waziristan.[1] They have also been raising anti-Army slogans because it is the Army, which over the years has launched military campaigns in the Pashtun areas where devastation has been caused and a large number of innocents have been killed or displaced. The movement has support from fellow Afghans in Afghanistan too. The PTM movement has been peaceful so far. It has the potential of becoming a major headache for the government in the times to come.

In the 2018 elections, two of the PTM's top leaders, Mohsin Dawar and Ali Wazir, were elected to parliament from North and South Waziristan, respectively, as independents. In January 2020, Manzoor Pashteen, the young charismatic leader of the PTM, was taken into custody and accused of sedition and criminal conspiracy. This is the first time that he has been arrested. Pashteen has often led huge rallies in which the slogan "Yeh jo dehshat gardi hai, isske peeche wardi hai!" i.e., "This terrorism, the military is behind it!" has been chanted regularly. Blaming the military directly for terrorism is a novel development in Pakistan. The Army cannot take this challenge lightly.

Balochistan is Pakistan's largest province but also the smallest by way of population. Rich in mineral resources, it is a complex region where nationalistic and separatist feelings are the strongest. It is also the poorest of the provinces. Insurgency has persisted in various phases since 1948. But things are changing. Islamist tendencies are growing. Nationalistic groups are clashing with religious groups. Zikris, an Islamic sect distinct from the Sunnis, are facing persecution. Half of the province is populated by Pashtuns. Madrassahs are growing rapidly. Tribal structures and the traditional Sardari system are weakening. The Iran-Balochistan border is restive. The China Pakistan Economic Corridor (CPEC) has introduced fresh complexities in the regional dynamics.[2] Discontentment in Balochistan can be expected to grow in the future.

Balochistan's traditional social and tribal structures are changing rapidly with the onset of modernization, urbanization and the growth of the middle-class. Nomadism has almost vanished. The middle class is increasingly taking up the leadership role in place of the tribal elders. Yet, the insurgency thrives. Pakistan's repression has grown as Balochistan's geopolitical significance grows. The province's enormous resources are now in the crosshairs of the Chinese whose eyes are on the resources. The CPEC road to Gwadar passes through Balochistan.

The Chinese face the hostility of the locals in Balochistan, who fear that China will siphon off their resources. There have been repeated attacks against Chinese engineers and personnel. China and Pakistan have been coordinating their efforts to deal with the Balochi resistance. Pakistan has raised a 15,000-strong paramilitary force to provide security for the CPEC assets. Under Pakistan's pressure, the USA has designated the Baloch Liberation Army (BLA) as a global terrorist organization. This will be a setback to the insurgents. Yet the Baloch insurgency continues to simmer.

Economy

Getting the IMF to sanction a USD 6 billion loan to shore up the sinking economy can be counted as a major achievement of the Imran Khan Government. The loan will provide temporary relief but will come at the cost of severe austerity measures, which are already beginning to bite. Economic growth is likely to fall to 2-3 per cent per annum. Imran Khan also lobbied heavily with Saudi Arabia, the UAE, and China to get financial assistance. He had some success in this regard. About USD 6 billion were placed in Pakistan's treasury. Oil payments were also deferred.

The fact is that despite these band-aid measures, Pakistan's economy is slipping. It suffers from long-term structural problems such as low tax-to-GDP ratio, low savings rate, stagnating exports, double-digit inflation, circular debts, etc. After paying for debt servicing and defence, little money is left for other purposes. The government has little space for spending on socio-economic development. Under the IMF-imposed austerity conditions, Pakistan's manoeuvrability to spend has been restricted. Prices of utilities have gone up, placing an unbreakable burden on low-income groups. Imran Khan's promise to build a "Naya Pakistan", a welfare state modelled on the Prophet's ideal state in Medina, looks to be a pipedream.

The economic ground reality is tough. Several sectors are in trouble; for example, the government has not been able to resolve the circular debt problem, which has plagued the power sector for years. According to official figures, the overall circular debt was Rs. 1.78 trillion at the end of 2019, reflecting a 34 per cent increase from Rs. 1.33 trillion since September 2018 when the PTI government came to power. The Power Division and National Electric Power Regulatory Authority (NEPRA) differ with each other on the true scale of the circular debt problem. Net receivables of energy companies increased by 27 per cent in 18 months.[3] Despite this, the fact is that electricity rates have been increased by nearly 40 per cent in the last two years.

Pakistan hosts the scourge of terror groups on its soil. These groups, often patronized by state agencies, finance their activities through dubious means. Pakistan's financial system is too weak and compromised to deal with terror financing. The Financial Action Task Force (FATF) has continued to maintain Pakistan on its grey list despite Pakistan's best efforts to wriggle out of it. The government has not been able to satisfy the FATF on the implementation of the latter's recommendations to curb terror financing and money laundering. The consequences for Pakistan's economy will be disastrous if the country is moved to the blacklist of the FATF.

Socio-economic Challenges

Amidst political and economic chaos, the challenges in Pakistan are being ignored. Sherry Rehman, a PPP leader, in her article "Three Tsunamis for Pakistan" sounds a warning that "Pakistan is on the verge of multiple development crashes, magnified on the rocks of low economic growth."[4] According to her, the imminent challenges of unchecked population growth, climate change, and food and water security have been neglected in Pakistan

Pakistan's population growth rate is 2.4 per cent per annum, which matches with the 2.4 per cent GDP growth rate of the economy. Pakistan's population has grown by 57 per cent since 1998. The growing population has put tremendous pressure on scarce resources, which have shrunk due to recurrent financial crises. Pakistan is perhaps the only country where the literacy rate has fallen in the last two years from 58 to 56 per cent. Over a million young people are entering the job market every year. A stagnant economy cannot accommodate so many young people.

Water

Thanks to the growing population and mismanagement of resources, water is also a highly sensitive issue between the provinces and in India-Pakistan relations. Water scarcity has emerged as a serious crisis in Pakistan. Pakistan's per capita consumption of water in the agriculture sector is the highest in the world. On the seriousness of the water issue, *Dawn* pointed out the inability of the government to deal with it. *Dawn* wrote[5]:

> 'The scale of the water sector is so large, and the number of problems that need simultaneous attention so vast, that the prime minister would be well advised to adopt a more systematic approach to pursuing his priorities in this area. In doing this, it would be a sensible move to consult water sector experts outside the water bureaucracy, and even beyond the donor agencies. It will take a monumental effort to build the coalitions he needs to generate a positive outcome in the water sector, and one can only wish him all the best in this endeavour."

Climate change is making the problem even more complex. In the last two years, Pakistan has moved from the world's seventh most affected country by climate change to the fifth. Sherry Rehman writes, "At this point, only 20 per cent of Pakistan has access to clean drinking water, while the rest consume faecal and industrially contaminated toxins. Lead and arsenic are now endemic to the Indus plain, while our per capita usage of water is, wait for this, the highest in the world."[6]

Foreign Policy

Imran Khan has followed an activist foreign policy. He reckons himself to be a statesman in the mould of Jinnah whom he frequently invokes in his speeches. Pakistan was facing international isolationism when Imran Khan took over. To ease international pressure on multiple fronts, Imran Khan has made some deft moves. He has reached out to the Islamic countries including Saudi Arabia, UAE, Turkey, Malaysia and Iran and not neglected the USA while deepening its engagement with Russia. China, however, remains the cornerstone of Imran Khan's foreign policy.

Imran Khan's main efforts have been to secure external assistance for Pakistan's beleaguered economy, end the country's isolation, rally the international community against India on Kashmir and build solidarity with the Islamic world. His diplomacy has yielded mixed results. He has been able to get some assistance for the crisis-ridden economy from Pakistan's friends. He has also managed to get supportive statements from Malaysia and Turkey on Kashmir. He has left no stone unturned to launch a virulent anti-India, anti-Modi, anti-BJP and anti-RSS campaign around the world, including at the United Nations. He has repeatedly pleaded with the international community to intervene in Kashmir. Knowing Pakistan's true nature, the international community has been largely cold to Imran Khan's entreaties. But the situation can change. The international community is notoriously fickle. China, despite its profession of good relations with India, helped Pakistan's cause by arranging an informal closed-door meeting of the UN Security Council on Kashmir. This was a big setback to India.

China and the CPEC

During his election campaign, Imran Khan was highly critical of the China-Pakistan Economic Corridor (CPEC). However, after he became the Prime Minister and visited China, he changed his tune rapidly. The CPEC has emerged as the central pillar of China-Pakistan relations. According to Sherry Rehman,[7] "With an opportunity pipeline estimated at over $ 62 billion in investments in infrastructure, energy, communications, and industry, CPEC stands for more than just an investment platform. It is not a resource-channel Pakistan can afford to miss." With the CPEC, the importance of China for Pakistan has grown manifold, overtaking that of the USA for Pakistan. The CPEC is the biggest piece of China's Belt and Road Initiative (BRI), which is the signature initiative of President Xi. It helps in China's projection as a great power.

The CPEC's ambit is vast. It is not a mere economic corridor; it will change the regional geopolitics. China is seeking an outlet to the Arabian Sea. It has built a port at Gwadar (Balochistan) and building another one nearby in Jiwani. These ports are commercially unviable and yet China is spending a huge amount of money on building them. In due course, these ports are likely to be used as naval bases. Gwadar port allows China to escape the Malacca dilemma, reach out to the Middle East and Africa, bring it close to the Persian Gulf and put pressure on India.

Besides infrastructure construction, the CPEC also encompasses digital connectivity. As the Jinnah Institute report notes, "(The) 6,299-km long underwater line will extend from the Gwadar port stretching across the Indian Ocean to Djibouti connecting Asia with Africa. China will be controlling the reins of this network and all countries participating in the BRI will have to rely upon Beijing for their internet freedom and face the risk of being surveilled (under surveillance)."[8]

For Pakistan, the USD 62 billion CPEC offers both opportunities and challenges. Pakistan would gain with the construction of power projects, railway lines, roads, telecommunication links, and other infrastructure projects. Early harvest projects worth USD 18 billion have been reported. However, the long-term impact of these measures is doubtful. Many of them are not economically viable. Pakistan's ability to absorb CPEC projects is questionable. Furthermore, the CPEC has resulted in rising hostility towards China in Sindh and Balochistan. Several Chinese engineers have been abducted and attacked in the last few years. Pakistan will have to bear the heavy burden of meeting the cost of the 15,000-strong paramilitary forces raised to protect the CPEC.

The lack of transparency in CPEC projects is a major negative for Pakistan. No one knows how many projects have been implemented, what were their terms and conditions and how have they been funded. The likely debt trap in which Pakistan can fall causes major anxiety. The example of Sri Lanka's experience with Chinese loans in the construction of the Hambantota port is often cited. When Sri Lanka could not pay back the debts incurred on the construction of the economically unviable Hambantota port, China took custody of the port and 15,000 ha of surrounding land on a 99-year lease. Such things can happen to Pakistan as well. Will Pakistan be able to pay the debt it is incurring on CPEC projects? Will China seize Pakistani assets in case of non-payment of debts?

While these are genuine worries, many people in Pakistan argue that Pakistan's CPEC debts constitute only 6 per cent of Pakistan's external debt of nearly USD 100 billion. According to official Chinese statements, early harvest projects worth USD 18.9 billion in investments are made up of USD 6 billion in government loans with a 2 per cent interest rate and private investments in the form of equity worth USD 3 billion and USD 9.8 billion in commercial loans with a 5 per cent interest rate. So far, the government of Pakistan only needs to repay USD 6 billion over 20-25 years."[9] This can be managed if the country's balance of trade situation is favourable.

But that is where the catch lies. Pakistan's ability to earn foreign exchange is severely limited. Pakistan's exports are not doing well. Beyond textiles and Basmati rice, it exports little else. Having signed Phase-2 of the Free Trade Agreement with China, the balance of trade has become more adverse for Pakistan. Even though China has offered ASEAN duty rates to Pakistani exports, Pakistan can hardly take advantage of the concessions on offer as it has little to export to China. Pakistani analysts note that China has rescheduled debts worth USD 50 billion to other countries rather than going for asset seizure in each case. Thus, the risk of falling into a debt trap and consequent asset seizure is underplayed in Pakistan.[10] The fact is that irrespective of the pros and cons of the CPEC, Pakistan cannot get out of it now because this is the signature project for China. It will have to bear the costs of the projects if they turn unviable.

USA

President Trump had stopped US assistance to Pakistan. However, the USA realized that Pakistan's cooperation would be necessary for arriving at any deal with the Taliban. Although the USA is fully aware of Pakistan's complicity in terrorism, it went ahead to curry favour with it to make the Taliban deal possible. The USA will continue to rely on Pakistan until the deal, which, inter alia, involves Taliban commitment not to attack US troops, US troop withdrawal and intra-Afghan dialogue is implemented. The deal may even be unravelling. Much has been made in Pakistan of Trump's public offer to mediate between India and Pakistan on Kashmir. Pakistan's jubilation is misplaced. Trump's offer is a non-starter because India will never agree to US mediation. Trump knows it. That is why he kept silent on this while visiting India. It also interpreted President Trump's remarks on Kashmir during his visit to India in February as being in favour of mediation while the exact opposite was the case.

It is unlikely that US-Pakistan relations will return to their earlier close status any time soon. The USA is withdrawing from Afghanistan. It is aware that Pakistan is completely under the influence of China whom it regards as its main rival. In the meanwhile, the USA's relationship with India is strengthening and has become a comprehensive global partnership. Trump's visit to India was a big success. The USA is now supplying advanced weapons to India. Despite differences on trade issues, bilateral trade is showing a healthy rise. This trend will strengthen in the future. The growing Indo-US partnership will make the Pakistanis even more sceptical of the USA.

Afghanistan

Pakistan has welcomed the US-Taliban deal signed on 29 February 2020. The US-Taliban deal will pave the way for the eventual return of the latter to power. Pakistan will benefit from this development. At the same time, it has warned that 'spoilers' could sabotage the deal. The reference is to India. Pakistan continues to shelter the Taliban top brass on whom it wields considerable influence. It has taken full advantage of Trump's desire to leave Afghanistan. Taking advantage of US difficulties in Afghanistan, Pakistan was quick to take credit for the US-Taliban deal.

Islamic World

Pakistan prides itself as being the leader of the Islamic world because of its large Muslim population, geostrategic location, a strong Army, the possession of nuclear weapons and the fact that it is the only country, which was created, based on religion. It maintains close relations with the Gulf countries where work a large number of Pakistani expatriates who remit large sums, which are critical for the Pakistani economy. Therefore, it is highly sensitive to India's relations with the Islamic countries. Of late, Pakistan has been disturbed that India has made inroads into the Gulf by building close and strategic relationships with important countries like Saudi Arabia, UAE, Oman, Kuwait, Qatar, and even Iran. When UAE invited the Indian Foreign Minister Sushma Swaraj as a special guest to the Organisation of Islamic Cooperation (OIC) meeting in 2019, a peeved Pakistan declined to attend the meeting to express its displeasure. Pakistan is also the chairperson of the OIC contact group on Kashmir. It has tried to use the OIC, with some success, to have a resolution passed on Kashmir in every meeting. It has also hosted the Secretary-General of the OIC on a visit to Pakistani-occupied Kashmir. For Pakistan, OIC support on Kashmir is very important. Given Prime Minister Imran Khan's pronounced Islamic leanings, Pakistan exploiting the OIC and the Islamic world for anti-India propaganda cannot be ruled out.

Pakistan's relations with the OIC countries, however, are not exactly smooth. The Islamic world itself is divided on a host of issues. Pakistan is compelled to do tightrope walking between Saudi Arabia, the acknowledged leader of the OIC, and Shia Iran. In 2020, Prime Minister Imran Khan, under Saudi pressure, cancelled his visit to Kuala Lumpur where Malaysian Prime Minister Mahathir had organised a summit meeting of Islamic countries. The meeting was attended by several leaders like those from Iran, Turkey, Qatar, etc. Saudi Arabia suspected that Malaysia was trying to build an alternative grouping of Islamic countries.

Pakistan had to do some delicate diplomacy not to ruffle Malaysia's and Saudi Arabia's feathers. Pakistan is caught between the rival Islamic blocs. Notes a Pakistani analyst, "Pakistan is caught in a dilemma where its heart is in the Malaysian-Turkish bloc, which has been openly supporting Pakistan's Kashmir cause, but its mind is with the Saudi-led bloc, which has money and political influence that Pakistan needs for its struggling economy".[11]

India

Imran Khan has used the India bogey to deflect attention from the pressing problems he faces at home. He began his tenure as prime minister with the assertion that he wanted peace with neighbours including India. He has ended up by saying that he sees no point in talking to India. The fact is that Pakistan's support for terrorism against India had never diminished. Cross-border terrorism into India has continued. The Pulwama terror attack by the Pak-based Jaish-e-Mohammad in February 2019, the Balakot airstrikes by the Indian Air force that followed and the attempted counter-attack by the Pakistani Air Force on Indian targets have changed Indo-Pakistan dynamics completely. The two countries withdrew their High Commissioners and Pakistan suspended trade with India after the Balakot strikes. Analysts, however, believe that Pakistan is continuing to trade with India through third countries. According to Pakistan's official figures quoted in *Dawn*,[12] Pakistan's exports to India dropped by almost 97 per cent to USD 8 million during the July-Feb period from USD 246 million a year ago while imports from India dropped by 69 per cent to USD 318.25 million from USD 1.03 billion over the last year. However, Islamabad has allowed the import of medicines and pharmaceutical raw materials from New Delhi.

The nullification of the temporary Article 370 of the Indian Constitution on Jammu and Kashmir by the Indian Parliament has proved to be the last straw for Imran Khan. He feels that India has changed the status quo undermining the UN resolutions on Kashmir. He has built a narrative for the international community that by nullifying Article 370, India has undermined the UN resolutions on Kashmir. Imran Khan has been quick to use the anti-CAA protests in India to portray that Muslim minorities are in danger. He has repeatedly lobbied with the Islamic countries that Muslims are being turned into second-class citizens in India. One can expect that Pakistani propaganda will continue in this direction in the foreseeable future.

Pakistan is rapidly building its nuclear and military arsenal. It has repeatedly tested the short-range, nuclear capable Haft missiles. China is helping Pakistan build new frigates. The former head of Pakistan's strategic planning department, Lt. Gen. (retired) Khalid Kidwai, in a lecture at the International Institute for Strategic Studies (IISS) at London, publicly warned India that Pakistan now has Full Spectrum Deterrence and that India should not think that its actions would go unpunished in future.[13] On numerous occasions, Imran Khan has himself issued thinly veiled nuclear threats against India. This way, he hopes to invite the attention of the international community to the Kashmir issue. He has frequently implored them to intervene in India-Pakistan issues. Such irresponsible statements are designed to create panic and uncertainty in the mind of the international community so that they can put pressure on India.

It is interesting that despite the new low in India-Pakistan relations, the two countries have gone ahead and inaugurated the Kartarpur Sahib Corridor, which provides access to Indian Sikh pilgrims to the holy shrine of Nankana Sahib Gurudwara in Pakistan. The Pakistanis have sought to gain brownie points by hailing the step as Pakistan's love towards the minorities in contrast to India's alleged intolerance towards its minorities. India will have to be cautious that the Kartarpur Sahib Corridor is not misused by Pakistan for pro-Khalistan, anti-India propaganda and inciting Sikh pilgrims.

Conclusion

Pakistan is likely to remain vulnerable to internal and external shocks. Be it the economy, socio-economic conditions, or terrorism, there is little that Imran Khan has done to resolve Pakistan's structural problems. He is a populist leader who is playing the Islamic card all the time. He uses incendiary Islamic rhetoric to garner support amongst Muslim countries. Pakistani rulers assess that Pakistan is too big and too important a country to be allowed to fail by the international community. The grant of the USD 6 billion IMF loan to Pakistan is a case in point. The USA, Japan and China favoured the granting of the loan. Given its growing stakes in the country, China is emerging as a helper of last resort. An emboldened Pakistan is not going to give up the use of the cross-border terrorism card against India. With China's help, Pakistan is also building its nuclear and military potential and trying to narrow the gap with India. Anti-Indianism has strengthened under Imran Khan's rule. Pakistan has launched a high decibel propaganda war against India. India-Pakistan relations have deteriorated steadily with little hope of improvement.

NOTES

1. https://www.aljazeera.com/news/2020/01/pakistan-pashtun-movement-attack-200128085744910.html. Accessed on 8.3.2020.
2. Muhammad Amir Rana, "Religion, Nationalism and Insurgency in Balochistan", 14 July, 2019, https://www.dawn.com/news/1493929. Accessed on 8.3.2020.
3. https://www.dawn.com/news/1537657/our-messed-up-power-sector. Accessed on 8 March 2020.
4. Sherry Rehman, "Three Tsunamis for Pakistan", Jinnah Institute info@jinnah-institute.org via icontactmail3.com, 4 March 2020.
5. *Dawn,* 28 September, 2018.
6. Sherry Rehman, "Three Tsunamis for Pakistan", Jinnah Institute info@jinnah-institute.org via icontactmail3.com, 4 March 2020.
7. Sherry Rehman, *CPEC 2.0: The Promise and The Peril,* A report by Jinnah Institute, Islamabad, 2020.
8. Ibid.
9. Ibid.
10. Sherry Rehman Report on CPEC.
11. Muhammad Amir Rana, "As Muslim world is divided, Pak caught between two blocs", February 10, 2020, https://www.asianage.com/opinion/oped/100220/as-muslim-world-is-divided-pak-caught-between-two-blocs.html Accessed on 9.3.2020.
12. https://www.dawn.com/news/1539214/govt-working-to-increase-exports-says-commerce-ministry. Accessed on 8.3.2020.
13. Keynote Address and Discussion Session with Lieutenant General (Retd) Khalid Kidwai, 7th IISS–CISS, *South Asian Strategic Stability: Deterrence, Nuclear Weapons And Arms Control Workshop*, https://www.iiss.org/events/2020/02/7th-iiss-and-ciss-south-asian-strategic-stability-workshop. Accessed on 9.3.2020.

INTERNAL

1

Internal Situation 2019-2020

Rana Banerji

Efforts of the military establishment in Pakistan to consolidate a docile democratic façade during the year came up against a severe economic crisis, civilian incompetence to handle it, one-sided accountability and ineffectiveness of political institutions to stem the rot. Pakistan seemed headed once again towards a possible rejection by the common masses of the 'unholy alliance' between the Army and Imran Khan's Pakistan Tehrik-e-Insaf (PTI). This has been accompanied by diminishing constitutional rights and encroachment on the autonomies of civil society, media and the judiciary.

Persisting Economic Dilemmas

Imran Khan inherited an economy in crisis, with a heavy debt burden and repayment commitments to international lending organizations. Pakistan's current account deficit was around $ 15 billion in 2016-2017. It increased by 43 per cent to $ 18 billion in June 2018 while the fiscal deficit ballooned by 68 per cent. Pakistan has met its debt servicing requirements **only by borrowing more**. In August 2016, the State Bank of Pakistan held $ 18.1 billion in net foreign exchange reserves, just after it completed a three-year IMF program. Within two years, net foreign exchange reserves halved. The 2018-2019 Economic Survey revealed that the GDP growth rate had slowed down to 3.3 per cent.

The surge in imports has been driven by the growing volume and cost of energy imports. Pakistan imports about 80 per cent of its oil needs, constituting around 20 to 30 per cent of the total imports. The country tends to find itself in a balance-of-payments crisis whenever oil prices rise. As a net energy importer and as a country that has comparatively expensive energy and electric power rates, liabilities in the electricity and energy sector exceed $ 10 billion. Electricity economics has caused persistent headaches because it was being sold at a price lower than the cost it was being generated. Circular debts were written off in the past, but proved to be temporary relief.[1] Its exports are less competitive.

Pakistan's central bank devalued the rupee four times since December 2018, weakening it by more than 20 per cent, amid efforts to avert a balance-of-payments crisis in the $ 305 billion economy. Inflation stood at 9.4 per cent in March 2019. Measured through the Consumer Price Index (CPI), it was recorded at 11.53 per cent in March 2020.

All these issues figured in several painful rounds of negotiations with the International Monetary Fund (IMF) in 2019. The IMF insisted not only on structural reforms, but also on measures requiring spending cuts to reduce the fiscal deficit. Agreeing to provide approximately a $ 6 billion bailout under its Extended Funding Facility, the IMF recommended raising of electricity and fuel tariffs, general sales tax and a free-floating Pakistani rupee.[2]

Only 1 per cent of the population pays income tax in Pakistan. Many loopholes exist in the taxation structure, which has enabled the rural rich and corporate bigwigs to evade the tax net. Efforts to implement the IMF conditions caused a rise in prices of essential commodities. Traders, hurt by the increase in taxes, ran to the Army Chief, seeking exemptions. However, they were told the tax collection effort would continue with no let up. A press release issued by Inter Services Public Relations (ISPR) shortly after the meeting indicated that businessmen "will cooperate in implementation of government reforms and also play their part by paying taxes and investing in a socially and economically responsible manner".[3]

An initially gung-ho Finance Minister, Asad Umar, a close personal friend of the PM and son of a former General, raised unduly optimistic expectations of combating the self-perpetuating IMF aid cycle[4] but he was unceremoniously removed from the Finance portfolio, only to bring back erstwhile military-approved economic administrators closely associated with earlier IMF bailouts.

Towards the year-end, the IMF released its first tranche of approximately $ 900 million. An agreement of another tranche of $ 450 million was announced, to be made available soon into the New Year.

One-sided Accountability

A spate of investigations were revived by the PTI government in old cases against leaders of the two mainstream Opposition parties, the Pakistan People's Party

(PPP) and the Pakistan Muslim League (Nawaz) (PML-N). This is being implemented through the National Accountability Bureau (NAB) headed by former Justice Javed Iqbal, which bent backwards to oblige the ruling regime.

This approach caused considerable political bitterness. Prominent politicians of the PML (N) like former PM, Shahid Khaqan Abbasi and Punjab Law Minister, Rana Sanaullah were incarcerated on the flimsiest of grounds, sans evidence. Judges of lower courts were found complicit in cooking up false charges.

Imran Khan seemed determined to fulfil a campaign pledge to punish corrupt politicians who had ostensibly plundered national wealth. However, the perception deepened in civil society about the accountability process not being just or even-handed, turning instead into a tool of crass political victimization.

Judicial ire

Shortly before his retirement on December 20, 2019, the Chief Justice of Pakistan, Asif Saeed Khosa, minced no words pointing out "that the growing perception of accountability being pursued at present is lopsided" and is seen as "a part of political engineering, a dangerous perception, which needs to be remedied, to remain credible".[5] Under pressure, National Accountability Bureau (NAB) Chairman Justice (retd) Javed Iqbal had to point out that `winds of change' would be seen soon in the pending cases! His assurances lacked credibility.

The Election Commission too was urged to expedite decisions on long-pending cases against ruling PTI functionaries but it remained in limbo, with disagreement persisting between the ruling party and the opposition about appointing new members as terms of the Chief Election Commissioner, Justice (retd) Sardar Mohd Khan and other members ran out.

The Chief Justice took umbrage at PM Imran Khan's remarks made while inaugurating construction of a new highway connecting Hazarazat areas in Khyber Pakhtunkhwa (KP), (November 18). Imran had alleged that 'the powerful and corrupt were bribing highest levels of the Judiciary'.[6] Khosa urged Imran to' be more careful', and not cite instances of the past, as the judiciary was quite independent after 2009. It had ruled impartially, disregarding who was 'high' or 'low'. This led a perceptive observer to remark, 'Unwilling to see ominous signs on the horizon, Imran had become prisoner of his own rhetoric'.[7]

The tenure of Chief Justice Khosa in the Supreme Court was marked by careful reticence to move away from exercise of suo moto jurisdiction, under Art. 194 of the Constitution, for all manner of actions so extensively used by his predecessor, Justice Saqib Nisar, to promote populist interventionist programs.

Khosa's verdicts in the Mumtaz Qadri execution appeal and the Aasia Bibi case, exonerating her of charges of blasphemy, represented bold, fearless and upright upholding of principles of sound jurisprudence. He also tried to seriously address the issue of high pendency of old cases and focused on reducing adjournments sought by advocates on flimsy grounds.

The Army Chief's Extension

One issue, above all, muddied the waters in the latter half of 2019; the matter of extension in the tenure of the Army Chief, General Qamar Javed Bajwa.[8] His term was otherwise to have ended on November 29, 2019. It was extended for three years on August 19, 2019 through a terse order from the Prime Minister's office, justifying it on grounds 'of the regional security environment', a thinly veiled reference to the situation in Kashmir and the ongoing Afghan peace talks between the USA and the Taliban.[9] Normally a Presidential notification signed by President Arif Alvi should have confirmed this step but there was no clarity on whether this was done.

On November 25, Chief Justice Khosa set the cat among the pigeons by suspending the extension and not allowing withdrawal of a petition filed by Riaz Hanif Rahi, a habitual legal maverick representing the so-called Jurists Foundation, challenging it. Two days of frenetic discussions ensued in court during which CJ Khosa questioned the modalities of the PM passing an order on the extension, on August 21, after only 11 out of 15 Cabinet members had approved it. This forced the Cabinet to hold an emergency meeting the same day to amend Rule 255 of the Army Regulations, and provide for "extension in tenure", besides "suspension/ limitation of retirement". A new summary was produced in court after approval by the PM and the President but it did not satisfy the CJ, who exclaimed that 'the whole process had been turned upside down'.[10] Ultimately, Khosa relented (November 28), allowing Bajwa's extension as COAS for six months, after being assured that suitable legislative amendments would be brought in, within six months, to determine the Army Chief's tenure and other terms and conditions of service.'[11]

Legislation to amend the Army Act was quickly drafted, on January 7, 2020, to provide for a three-year extension to serving defence force heads and the Chairman, Joint Chiefs of Staff Committee (CJCSC), under the discretionary powers of the PM, with a ceiling age of 64 years. Consensus emerged as quickly (in the New Year, 2020), between the ruling party and the main opposition parties to approve it.

Maulana's March

The political ante was upped in October 2019 with Maulana Fazlur Rehman, Jamiat Ulema–e–Islam (JuI-Fazlur) leader, announcing that he would hold an 'Azadi March', seeking deliverance from 'a rigged election' (in 2018). He also demanded ouster of the 'selected' Prime Minister.

Starting on October 27 from outlying provinces, huge crowds of disciplined JuI (F) marchers descended on the capital, Islamabad, congregating at the city outskirts (Peshawar Mor). Though begun as a solo flight and with initial foot-dragging by other mainstream political parties, the sheer enthusiasm and disciplined progress of JuI(F)'s marchers moving through the main cities of Sindh and Punjab built pressure on leaders of the PPP and PML (N) to share the podium with the Maulana, albeit briefly. Secular Pashtun nationalists, Mehmood Khan Achakzai (Pakhtunkhwa Milli Awami Party- PKMAP) and Mian Iftikhar Hussain (Awami National Party-ANP) also joined, though the Pashtun Tahaffuz Movement (PTM) refrained.

Even though it ended rather abruptly on November 13, emboldening pro-government protagonists to claim it had turned out to be a damp squib, discerning analysts saw the Maulana winning back political space lost in the 2018 election defeat in his traditional Dera Ismail Khan bastion. The Maulana claimed afterwards that he had been offered various bribes to call off the march, such as re-election from Dera Ismail Khan, chairmanship of the Senate and leadership of the provincial government in Balochistan, which he 'rejected'.[12]

The 'Azadi March' had become a demonstration of downtrodden people, predominantly from Khyber Pakhtunkhwa and Baluchistan and partly also from Sindh and southern Punjab—bringing to the fore 'the frustration of toiling masses, representing moderate, conservative Deobandis', against 'deprivations and the illusion of a false consciousness'. This could serve as a possible 'catalyst for contradictory processes'...'in a precarious civil-military equation, regardless of religious overtones.'[13] It exposed weaknesses in the PTI government's political management.[14] It was even alleged that the march signified 'an indirect approach', whose true motive was to undermine the military leadership that had "selected" Imran as PM.[15]

PTI and the Politics of Provincial Satraps

Part of Imran Khan's problem has stemmed from the perception of ineffective governance in the provinces, especially in Punjab. The PTI won a narrow majority of 181 seats in the 371-member Punjab Assembly with Opposition contender,

PML (N), getting 174 seats . The PML (Quaid-e-Azam) led by former CM Pervez Elahi with 10 seats, supported the PTI government.

There were several contenders for the post of Punjab CM, including Jehangir Tareen, a close confidant of the PM, who was disqualified to hold political office under Art. 63 of the Constitution. Yet he continues to have access to the PM and is often able to influence policy decisions and administrative transfers and postings in the province. The Governor, Chaudhary Ghulam Sarwar came back from the UK and joined the PTI. As another aspirant for political office in the province, he also operates as a centre of power, as does Pervez Elahi in his role as Speaker of the Punjab Assembly.

Usman Buzdar, a Baloch tribal leader from Dera Ghazi Khan district was PM Imran Khan's surprise choice for the post of Chief Minister, despite having no previous administrative experience and a record of frequent change of political affiliations, from the PML (Q) to the PML(N) and now, just before the 2018 elections, to the PTI, as part of the disgruntled group of politicians aspiring for a 'separate South Punjab suba (province)'.

He inherited this mantle from Shahbaz Sharif, who had built up a good reputation as an efficient administrator. Usman Buzdar's administrative inexperience has stood out in sharp contrast to the acumen displayed by his predecessor.

The main burden of these pulls and pressures has fallen on the Punjab bureaucracy, which even otherwise, is supposed to have built up strong kinship (biradari) and political loyalties in the past. These connections were cited in frequent chopping and changes of posts, both in the civil administration and the police set up, resulting in the reluctance of bureaucrats to stick their neck out while taking firm or quick decisions to help ameliorate the plight of the common masses.

The 'Pinky Peer' Phenomenon

Bushra Riaz Wattoo, 46-year-old third wife of PM Imran Khan, otherwise known as 'Pinky Peer', is a follower of a Sufi saint, Baba Farid, whose shrine in Pakpattan is venerated by feudals and the common masses in Punjab. Imran reportedly met her while visiting the Baba Farid shrine. Her first husband, Khawar Maneka, who was a Customs department bureaucrat, belonged to this district and had wide political connections. Bushra built on these connections. She is believed to dabble in Sufism and claimed to have occult powers to forecast political developments.

As First Lady, she unexpectedly recommended Usman Buzdar for the post of Chief Minister. Despite complaints of non-performance against him, she has remained his staunch supporter, influencing the PM to ward off calls for a mid-term in-house change in the provincial leadership of the party.

Squabbling in Khyber Pakhtunkhwa (KP)

Mahmood Khan, who represents the Matta constituency of Swat, was chosen Chief Minister of KP despite being a comparative political lightweight, disregarding the claims of the current National Assembly Speaker, Asad Qaiser, and other contenders like Atif Khan, Shah Farman and some others. Former KP CM, Pervez Khattak, currently Defence Minister in the Federal cabinet continues to interfere in provincial politics and decision-making, as a result of which administrative management has suffered. There are complaints of financial scams, especially in regard to the incomplete Peshawar rapid bus transit project, started during Khattak's tenure.

PML (N)

After the '*Dawn* leaks' case of October 2016 failed to restore civilian supremacy over the military, the July, 2018 elections witnessed a deliberate crafting of a result which ensured that Nawaz Sharif and his PML (N) could not come back to power. Anything but a level playing field was manipulated to benefit Imran Khan's Pakistan Tehrik-e-Insaf (PTI). Several feudal 'electable' candidates from South Punjab were made to switch allegiance to Imran Khan's PTI on the promise of making South Punjab a separate province.[16]

The PML (N) could win only 85 seats in the 342-member National Assembly compared to the Pakistan Tehrik-e-Insaf (PTI)'s 156 seats. The verdict in the Punjab Provincial Assembly was closer, with PML (N) getting 174 seats in the 371-member House, against PTI's 181 seats.[17]

Nevertheless, in an extraordinary display of personal courage and political astuteness, Nawaz Sharif resisted efforts to emasculate him politically. He refused to give up plans for a street protest against the 'rigged' 2018 elections. He came back from London leaving ailing wife, Kulsoom on her deathbed to face incarceration in the NAB's 'Accountability cases'.[18]

After becoming PML-N president, Shahbaz Sharif gradually distanced himself from the erstwhile party hardline and flouted the instructions of Nawaz Sharif to resist the military establishment in an uncompromising manner. He may have resorted to this stratagem, not only to get some concessions for the medical treatment abroad of his critically ill brother, as also possibly to push his own candidature/acceptability before the military establishment for an in-house political change later.

Nawaz Sharif's Health

While serving a prison sentence in the NAB cases, Nawaz Sharif suffered a serious health setback, with his platelet counts falling to dangerously low levels. Proper diagnosis could not be made. Eventually, the Lahore High Court gave him bail on medical grounds.

The PTI government cussedly dragged its feet in lifting Exit Control restrictions before Sharif's departure, demanding exorbitant indemnity bonds for a 'one-time' let up for a 'convicted' offender. The Lahore High Court suspended the indemnity bond requirement on challenge by the PML (N). Nawaz Sharif finally left Lahore on November 19, for treatment in the UK. He would probably need heart surgery again before seeking remedial facilities for platelet disorder at the Sloan Kettering Hospital in the USA.

Maryam Nawaz, Sharif's combative daughter and designated political heir, was prevailed upon to adopt a low profile and accept the Shahbaz Sharif line of no confrontation with the Establishment during this period. This did not prevent ruling party politicians from averring that they would not allow Maryam to leave the country to be besides her ailing father.

The PML (N)'s political revival remains linked to Nawaz Sharif's health. If he recovers, he has an outside chance of staging a comeback.[19] For the moment, though, as 2019 drew to a close, the Army remained in no mood to allow the PML (N) to resurge, despite its rising impatience about the PTI's inept handling of day-to-day governance.[20]

Pakistan People's Party (PPP)

Former President Asif Zardari faced a similar dilemma, going to jail on charges of illegal money laundering. He complained of adverse discrimination as his adverse heart condition did not get the same compassionate attention. Eventually, the courts did grant him bail but he has not, so far, left the country for medical treatment abroad.

His son and anointed political heir, Bilawal Bhutto Zardari, displayed improved maturity and adroitness in the minefield of Pakistani politics, drawing large crowds in Sindh and Gilgit Baltistan, talking effectively about the plight of the common masses on bread-and-butter issues, as also on the hypocritical 'double standards' of the ruling dispensation.

Administratively, the PPP's provincial government under Chief Minister Murad Ali Shah held its own, rebuffing attempts by PTI leaders, including President Arif Alvi, to destabilize or hamper its functioning in myriad ways. However, PPP's national resurgence remained a distant goal and can result only from a revival in Punjab, as it currently has a rump presence in Sindh.

A 'rudderless' MQM?

Meanwhile, even as the noose tightened on their exiled 'Imam', Altaf Hussain, for criminal and financial misdemeanours in the United Kingdom, various factions of the Mohajir Quami Movement (MQM), some in alliance with the PTI Federal government, failed to significantly challenge the PPP as an urban political force in the greater Karachi urban agglomeration.

PPP's Bilawal Bhutto went as far as to offer MQM a share in power in the provincial government if they gave up its alliance with the PTI at the centre.

On January 12, 2020 MQM's Khalid Maqbool Siddiqui announced he was withdrawing from the Federal Cabinet as the PTI government had failed to address the development of Karachi. However, he clarified that the party would continue to support the government.

The MQM has 7 seats in the National Assembly. If they withdraw support, the PTI would still retain a slender majority of 3 (175 seats) in the 342-member House. However, if Akhtar Mengal's Baluchistan National Party (BNP-M) and PML(Q) also withdraw support or intensify bargaining for Cabinet berths, the PTI government's stability would be threatened.

These developments have created a sense of fragility though the military establishment may not be ready to signal the uprooting of the PTI government just yet.

Ethnocentric Faultlines

Pakistan continued to face ethnic discontent in different areas. Conditions in both Balochistan and Sindh remained deplorable in terms of human development. Several cases of abduction of Hindu minority girls by Sindhi feudals were reported, with the usual ineffectual remedial law and order measures promised by the provincial authorities afterwards.

Agitations by different factions of Baloch nationalists continue to simmer.

Balochistan remains the most under-reported province, due to strict censorship and control over travel. Within Balochistan, the tiny Hazara Shia community is the most targeted, attacked and fast-diminishing ethnic minority.[21]

In June 2020, the Baluchistan National Party-Mengal withdrew support from the Federal government as none of its demands made in the accord with PTI had been met. Its 4 MNAs started sitting separately in the National Assembly though they have not voted against the government so far.

After the 'Zarb-e Azb' and 'Radd ul Fasaad' military operations in the Federally Administered Tribal Areas (FATA), many residents were displaced. Pashtun nationalists belonging to the Pashtun Tahaffuz Movement (PTM) came out in direct confrontation against the Army and Frontier Corps, protesting against the targeting of Pashtuns in these operations.[22]

Barelvi Resurgence

In the post-2018 election scene, the rise of Khadim Rizvi's Tehrik-e-Labaik Pakistan (TLP) represented three strands—a strong sense of Barelvi victimhood (despite being the numerically preponderant Islamic sect in Pakistan), a growing disenchantment with the direction and linkages of Deobandi and Wahabi groups with terrorism within the country and a potential to erode grassroots support from PML (N) and emerge as a political force in Punjab, which could play a balancing role in facilitating the Army's claimed mainstreaming of hardline Islamic radical elements.[23]

However, after the Supreme Court declared Aasia Bibi not guilty of blasphemy in October 2018, the TLP's bravado and capacity to disrupt normal economic and business activity in the country seemed to have been curbed through firm State action.

Financial Action Task Force (FATF)

The Pakistani establishment remained under pressure from the Financial Action Task Force (FATF) set up in 1989 after a G-7 resolution. On FATF's 'grey list', Pakistan has been found to have strategic deficiencies in its anti-money laundering regime (AML/CFT). Though some curbs have been placed on leaders of the Jamaat-ud-Daawa/Lashkar-e-Taiba and Jaish-e-Mohammed, these may be cosmetic and short-lived. International pressure would need to be kept up to make these curbs meaningful.[24]

The Youth Bulge

There is a pronounced "youth bulge" in Pakistan, with potential to be channelled in directions positive or negative. Young Pakistanis remain patriotic, though their religious identity is highly conservative, aware of sectarian and ethnic lineage but not necessarily extremist, which may sometimes supersede their affinity for country. They display a desire for upward mobility and partiality to emigrate, yet seem paradoxically optimistic about their future.[25] The year 2019 saw more discontent among youth, adding huge numbers to those already unemployed and remaining with inadequate access to good avenues of education.

In overall terms, looking at Pakistan in its domestic context, the future does not present a very stable scenario.

The military leadership's impatience with the PTI government's bumbling administrative competence was palpably evident, yet Army Chief General Bajwa cast his lot with them, especially on the issue of extension of his term. This did not make him very popular with his peers, the influential collegiate group of three-star Generals.

When the Army Chief's extension was being berated by judges of the Supreme Court, rumours and conspiracy theories sprung up in Pakistan, suggesting portends of 2020 being a 'year of political change'. Yet, measures to defuse political confrontation between mainstream parties seemed to have been set in motion after the detailed judgment of Justice Khosa in the Army Chief's extension case.

This could well provide a new lease of life to the current centre-right government to hang on to power for a while where a strong military and a weak civilian puppet remain on 'the same page', though persona at the helm may change. It will keep promising milder Islamic values of a utopian Medina, protection of national sovereignty and partial deference to the West. Economic constraints will be sought to be managed through a renewed strategic partnership with the USA, with Chinese and Saudi largesse providing occasional, if inadequate, temporary relief.

This would nevertheless be accompanied by deep political, economic and social disparities that could have a destabilizing impact. Pakistan will be more fractious in 2020, and remain dependent on external financial aid.

NOTES

1. Arif Rafiq, President, Vizier Consulting: Pakistan's Economic Turmoil: Strategic Challenges, Consequences, and Contingencies: The Stimson Center, Washington, USA, October 2, 2018:

https://www.stimson.org/content/pakistan-economic-turmoil-strategic-challengesconsequences-and-contingencies.

2. Shahbaz Rana : Asad Umar discloses IMF demands for loan package: *Express Tribune*, June 21, 2019.
3. Khurram Hussain: 'Chief & the tycoons': *Dawn*, 10.10.2019.
4. Shahbaz Rana : Asad Umar discloses IMF demands for loan package: *Express Tribune* June 21, 2019.
5. Ahmer Bilal Mehboob: 'Credibility of Accountability': *Dawn*, November 10, 2019.
6. Dawn.com, November 2018.
7. Zahed Hussain, 'Act two, Scene one': Dawn: https://www.dawn.com/news/1517712, November 20, 2019.
8. Najam Sethi, 'Two Narratives': *The Friday Times*, November 1, 2019.
9. Article by Author: Rediff.com, August 19, 2019; https://www.rediff.com/news/column/What-pak-army-chiefs-3-year-extension-means-for-j-k.
10. *Dawn*, November 25, 2019.
11. *Dawn*, November 29, 2019.
12. *The News*: November 23, 2019.
13. Imtiaz Alam: 'Azadi March: A Catalyst For Democratic Change or Contradictory Processes?': *The Wire*, November 11, 2019.
14. Saleem Safi: 'Geo TV interview with Chaudhry, Pervaiz Elahi, Speaker, Punjab Assembly': *The News*, November 16, 2019.
15. Najam Sethi: 'Failed Experiment': *The Friday Times*, November 22, 2019.
16. Ajay Darshan Behera: 'Pakistan General Elections 2018: Clear Signs of a Guided Democracy': *Sage journals*; https://journals.sagepub.com, doi September 28, 2018.
17. Election Commission of Pakistan: July 25, 2018: https://ecp.gov.pk/AllResults.aspx
18. Najam Sethi: Two Narratives: TFT, 01.11.2019.
19. Najam Sethi: 'Waiting for Godot': *The Friday Times*: March 29, 2019.
20. Article by Author: 'Whither PML (N) after Nawaz Sharif ouster': (Chapter 7): *Pakistan Insights*: Publishers: Vivekananda International Foundation/Pentagon Press, 2019.
21. Tahira Abdullah: 'Human Rights in an imperfect democracy'; Jinnah Institute, www.jinnah-institute.org;10.12.2019.
22. Junaid Roshan Tanoli and Jawad Falak: Pakistan's New Rising Ethno-nationalist Fault lines: Centre for Strategic & Contemporary Research, Islamabad, Pakistan: May, 2017.
23. T.C.A. Raghavan: Barelvi assertion & TLP: Chapter 5, *Pakistan Insights*, VIF 2019.
24. Arvind Gupta: 'Pakistan &FATF': Chapter 10: *Pakistan Insights*, VIF, 2019.
25. Moeed Yusuf: in Stephen Cohen's '*Future of Pakistan*: Brookings Institution, 2011: http//www.brookings.edu/papers/2010/09 bellagio conference papers.aspx

2

Civil-Military Relations

Rana Banerji

Civilian-military relations in Pakistan carry the baggage of 34 years of military rule under four serving generals who assumed the office of President, abrogating the Constitution and fundamental human rights. Gen. Zia-ul-Haq mutilated it beyond recognition via the 8th Amendment in 1985. Its theocracy-leaning components are still intact, despite the 18th constitutional amendment. Though the right to political participation and party-based electoral politics stand restored and Pakistan's 'parliamentary democracy' can no longer be considered "fledgling", it still struggles against illiberal and non-democratic forces, severe polarization, turncoats and "electables", feudal/tribal mindsets, and a paucity of civility in political interactions, within and outside its legislature.[1]

The July 2018 elections were held against this backdrop. The military leadership was ensuring that three-time Prime Minister Nawaz Sharif who had tried to assert civilian supremacy could not come back to power. Anything but a level playing field was created to benefit Imran Khan's Pakistan Tehrik-e-Insaf (PTI), against Sharif's Pakistan Muslim League (PML-N). Several feudal 'electable' candidates from South Punjab were made to switch allegiance to the PTI on the promise of making South Punjab a separate province. The PTI won 156 seats compared to the PML (N)'s 85 in the 342-member National Assembly.

This was Imran Khan's moment. He had struggled in politics for twenty-two years with single-minded determination to achieve this pinnacle. Not all his tactics were consistent or met his own professed ideological standards. Many were opposed to the PTI's street agitation in 2014, its efforts to have the election results altered or get the Nawaz government ousted by 'extra-constitutional' means. Yet, Imran gave hope to millions of people across a cynical electorate with his agenda of 'Naya Pakistan', promising to rid the country of corruption and working for a compassionate Islamic welfare state, focused on the felt needs of the poor.

Much was made throughout the rest of 2018 and 2019 about the Army and the 'elected' civilian government being 'on the same page', beginning a new chapter of harmonious governance and gilt-edged development of the country under this new dispensation.

Army Chief's Extension

Though anticipated for a while, the timing of Pakistan's current Army Chief Gen Qamar Javed Bajwa's three-year extension announced in a terse order from Prime Minister Imran Khan's office on August 19 came as a surprise. The order was justified on grounds 'of the regional security environment', a thinly-veiled reference to the situation in Kashmir and the ongoing Afghan talks.

After the 2018 election results, it was payback time for the Prime Minister and Imran Khan readily obliged, but the order issued almost four months before Bajwa's tenure as Army Chief was slated to end on November 29, 2019. It was not immediately clear whether it had received President Arif Alvi's concurrence, as required under Art. 243 of the 1973 Constitution.[2]

Bajwa is the sixth Army Chief whose term was extended, after Gen. Ashfaq Pervez Kayani (2007-2013). Four other Chiefs (Ayub, Yahya, Zia and Musharraf) imposed Martial Law, abrogated the Constitution of the day and usurped the Presidency.

The real motives of dictators and army chiefs, who did and did not get an extension, have always been domestic. It is no different this time around. Generals Ayub Khan and Yahya Khan lost both wars and territory. General Zia-ul-Haq lost territory in Siachen but scored a pyrrhic victory in Afghanistan, with a jihadist blowback so severe that Pakistan is still reeling under it. Pervez Musharraf got egg on his face in Kargil and struggled afterwards, during the lawyers' agitation. In periods between direct military rule, the Pakistan army has wielded power from behind a civilian façade. After Musharraf, the army under Gen. Kayani opted to rule from behind the scenes. Gen. Bajwa has persisted with this pattern.[3]

Yet some decidedly curious developments clouded Bajwa's extension, giving rise to conspiracy theories about whether the civilians and the military remained 'on the same page' after all!

When in mid-September 2019 a journalist asked President Arif Alvi whether he had signed any notification on the subject, his reply was ambiguous, "Although a decision has been taken to extend Gen. Bajwa's tenure, the file has not yet been sent up to me for signing."[4]

New Judicial Activism?

On November 25, Chief Justice Khosa set the cat among the pigeons by suspending the extension, not allowing withdrawal of a petition challenging it filed by an advocate, Riaz Hanif Rahi, of the so-called Jurists Foundation. Questioning the modality of the PM's order, Khosa forced a new summary to be produced in court, which did not satisfy him. During proceedings before the three-member bench, he observed that 'the whole process had been turned upside down'.[5] Ultimately, he relented (November 28), allowing Bajwa's extension as COAS for six months only, after being assured that suitable amendments would be brought in through new legislation within six months.[6]

Though Khosa claimed his intervention was an exercise of 'judicial restraint', the proceedings shook up a complacent, even incompetent, PTI government.

Imran Khan's immediate response after the judgment was to issue an aggressive tweet, alleging that internal mafias and external forces seeking to cause instability and friction between institutions would now be disappointed!

Opinion in Pakistan was not unanimous regarding the verdict. Former Senate Chairman Waseem Sajjad opined that tenure of the Army Chief was deliberately left vague as the Constitution makers did not want to curtail civilian supremacy. Barrister Aitzaz Ahsan felt this was very much a matter within the Prime Minister's discretion.

Even as Islamabad remained agog over this controversy, the PTI government announced (November 19) the promotion and appointment of Lt. Gen. Nadeem Raza, Chief of General Staff, as the next Chairman, Joint Chiefs of Staff Committee (CJCSC) with effect from November 27, 2019, vice Gen. Zubair Mohd Hayat, who stood retired. This was very much an endorsement of Bajwa's choice, by a rubber stamp PM and President.

An officer of the Sindh regiment, Gen. Raza had served stints in the Military Operations Directorate, Training faculties and as Corps Commander, 10 Corps, Rawalpindi. He **was not, however, the senior-most Lieutenant General** ascending to this four star post. He superseded Lt. Gen. Sarfaraz Sattar, Director General, Strategic Plans Division (SPD).

Detailed Judgment

The detailed order of the three-judge bench came almost a month later, on December 16, shortly before Khosa's retirement as Chief Justice on December 20, 2019. It was full of rather tongue-in-cheek aspersions about the proclivity of Pakistan's generals to disparage civilian competence.

Emphasizing the need to provide "certainty and predictability" to the post of Army Chief for all times to come, and noting that in Pakistan's "peculiar historical context", the Army Chief "holds a powerful position in ways more than one", it pointed out that "unbridled power or position, like unstructured discretion", could be dangerous.

Rubbing in the irony of past behaviour of Pakistan's generals, the Chief Justice wrote, "In the backdrop of the last three scores and 12 years of our history, I may observe with hope and optimism that framing of a law by the Parliament regulating the terms and conditions of the office of [the army chief] may go a long way in rectifying multiple historical wrongs and in asserting sovereign authority of the chosen representatives of the people besides making exercise of judicial power of the courts all pervasive. It is now for the people of Pakistan and their chosen representatives in the Parliament to come up with a law that will provide certainty and predictability to the post of COAS, remembering that in strengthening institutions, nations prosper."[7]

The judgment clarified that in case the federal government remained unable to bring a law within six months, Bajwa's retirement "shall stand enforced" and the President shall have to appoint a serving General as the new COAS, on the advice of the Prime Minister.

After this order, if no legislation could be effected before April 28, 2020, the senior-most cohort of generals would then include Lt. Gen. Humayun Aziz, 5 Corps Commander, Karachi; Lt. Gen. Naeem Ashraf, 2 Corps Commander, Multan and four others, who were otherwise slated to retire only in December 2020.

Apart from causing a few flutters among ambitious generals hoping to replace Bajwa at the last minute, the judges' observations during hearings of the bench (November 26 to November 28, 2019) caused considerable humiliation to the military as an institution.

Review Petition Filed

Though traditions of jurisprudence in the subcontinent militate against the success of review petitions, the PTI government felt constrained enough to file one on

December 26, just before the one-month deadline for its admissibility expired. Brazenly enough, Bajwa himself became party to the petition.

Apart from referring to somewhat extraneous issues of Pakistan allegedly facing 'a fifth generation war against enemies of Pakistan' (read India) and the unfinished 'war against terror', the review petition raised several questions of law against the judgment while pleading for "preservation of two leading institutions" and a "healthy democracy".[8] It insisted it had been filed "in the interest of public good" and asked for in-camera hearings.[9] It sought to flag "legal and constitutional faults" in the judgment,[10] as apparently, the apex court had 'stepped into the shoes of the executive, substituting its opinion, though there 'was nothing in the Constitution which empowers the Supreme Court to settle the tenure or terms and conditions of the COAS.'

As the Supreme Court had already proceeded on its scheduled vacation, there was no immediate word on its response to the review petition.

Reactions within the Army

The decision to give Gen. Bajwa a three-year extension did not go down very well with other Generals and simmering discontent persisted within the senior echelons of the Pakistan Army.

If the three-year extension prevailed, as many as twenty-two Lieutenant Generals would stand retired before Bajwa hung up his boots.[11] Though superseded by Raza's elevation as CJCSC, Lt. Gen Sattar, otherwise slated to retire only in December 2020, did not follow convention by putting in his papers as DG, SPD though another Lieutenant General was appointed to this post. This complicated matters as he remained without any post. In such circumstances, Army Chief General Bajwa may have had no choice but to have the Ministry of Defence issue Sattar a severance notice. Some senior serving officers believed this created a needless negative impasse.[12]

Even as Bajwa reshuffled his officers while his extension was still being discussed by the Supreme Court's three-judge bench, resentment intensified because of the unceremonious dumping of erstwhile favourites like Lt. Gen. Bilal Akbar, who was banished from the prestigious Rawalpindi 10 Corps command to the Pakistan Ordnance Factory, Wah, and Lt. Gen. Asim Munir Shah, who was eased out even earlier, to the backwater 30 Corps, Gujranwala from the Inter-Services Intelligence Directorate (ISI), within ten months of being posted there.

Government Drafts Bill to Introduce Required Legislation in Parliament[13]

On January 2, 2020, in a rare show of consensus, the government and the major political parties in the Opposition—the PML (N) and the People's Party of Pakistan (PPP)—agreed to amend the Pakistan Army Act to regularize Gen. Bajwa's extension.

A bill titled Pakistan Army (Amendment) Act 2020, and two similar bills for the Navy and Air Chiefs, were tabled in the National Assembly on January 7, 2020 and quickly passed the same day. Despite being an Opposition-dominated house, the Senate passed the bill equally quickly, (in twenty minutes!) on January 8.[14]

According to the bill, Section 8-A, B, C, D, E, F will be inserted in the Army Act. The new bill clarifies that retirement age and service limits prescribed for a general, under the rules and regulations made under this Act, shall not be applicable to the Chief of the Army Staff, during his tenure of appointment, reappointment or extension, subject to a maximum age of sixty-four (64) years. A similar provision has been made for the post of Chairman, Joint Chiefs of Staff Committee (CJCSC).

The PM would have discretion to extend tenures of Defence Service Chiefs and this advice 'shall' be binding on the President. However, in the case of the CJCSC, the term used in the bill is 'may' (instead of 'shall'). This will provide some scope for exercise of discretion by the President.

Why the PTI government left open this lacuna in respect of the CJCSC is not immediately clear. It leaves open leeway for differences between the President and the PM, particularly if they belong to different parties, as also between civilians and the defence services in future.

Under Section 8 B (2), these amendments cannot be challenged in courts of law "on any ground whatsoever." According to some Pakistani analysts, the last word in this regard may not have been said just yet, as reasons for giving extension have to be recorded in writing, reasonability of which could come under the scope of judicial review if challenged before higher courts.[15]

In what seemed an effort to ingratiate themselves further with the Army and to put pressure on the new Chief Justice of the Supreme Court, Gulzar Ahmed, after passing the bills in the National Assembly, the PTI government did not withdraw its review petition on the Khosa judgment from the Supreme Court.

The resolution of Bajwa's extension in this manner underscored all over again the irony of Pakistan's prevailing political ethos, wherein the silent threat of military disapproval can help dissolve chronic antagonisms despite senseless persecution of civilian political opponents by those temporarily in power.

Grass-roots workers of the PML (N) were quite disappointed and felt that Nawaz Sharif's 'brave' agenda of 'giving respect to the vote' had been jettisoned. PPP leader Bilawal Bhutto did not even attend the National Assembly session on January 7. Only leaders of some small parties like Hasil Bijenzo of the National Party of Pakistan opposed it 'in principle', though its representative in the Senate, Dr. Ashok Kumar voted in its favour!

A seasoned political journalist who had seen it all opined, 'Sadly, the argument that institution-building is the best strategy for a stronger Pakistan has been indefinitely deferred'.[16]

The Musharraf Treason Case Judgment

On December 17, 2019, a special court composed of Chief Justice of the Peshawar High Court (PHC), Waqar Ahmed Seth, Nazar Akbar of the Sindh High Court (SHC), and Shahid Karim of the Lahore High Court (LHC), found former President, Gen. (retd) Musharraf guilty of high treason and sentenced him to death. The judgment had one dissenting note, on the aspect of its execution.

It may be recalled that in July 2009 a 14-judge bench of the Supreme Court of Pakistan found Gen. Pervez Musharraf's declaration of emergency in November 2007 illegal and unconstitutional in the Provisional Constitution Order (PCO) Judges case.

On 5 April 2013, the Supreme Court accepted a petition filed against Musharraf that accused him of committing treason under Article 6 of the Constitution. A three-member bench headed by Chief Justice Iftikhar Mohammad Chaudhry was constituted to hear the case. However, Chaudhry recused himself from the bench. A two-member bench led by Justice Jawwad S. Khawaja dealt with it thereafter and put Musharraf's name on the Exit Control List (ECL).

In June 2013, Prime Minister Nawaz Sharif told the National Assembly of Pakistan that his government had filed a written request before the Supreme Court to put Musharraf on trial for treason. In November 2013, the Supreme Court accepted the Sharif government's request to set up a Special Court to try Musharraf.

Ironically enough, the initiative to punish an Army General for abrogating constitutional provisions was being taken by a civilian Prime Minister who had originally emerged in Pakistani politics as the chosen protégé of a military dictator. He subsequently graduated into a mass-based politician but was ousted in another military coup. Indeed, Nawaz Sharif had to learn his lessons the hard way, being hauled with chains to solitary confinement in jail, during an earlier brush with his chosen Army Chief.

These developments were not to the liking of the Army. Gen. Kayani did not put out his neck to save Musharraf though he advised him not to return to the country to face trial or contest elections. After Kayani's retirement, Gen. Raheel Sharif was selected by PM Nawaz Sharif as the new Army Chief though he was number three in the Army's seniority or pecking order. Raheel did not openly object but there was no doubt that the Army was reluctant to endorse the zeal of the civilian leadership to punish Musharraf.

On 2 January 2014, as Musharraf was on the way to attend proceedings of the special court, his convoy was suddenly diverted and taken to the Armed Forces Institute of Cardiology (AFIC) in Rawalpindi. On 7 January 2014, the AFIC submitted a medical report to the special court stating that Musharraf was suffering from triple-vessel coronary artery disease.

Musharraf finally appeared in court after avoiding twenty-two consecutive hearings only on 18 February 2014, but no charges were framed against him. On 21 February 2014, the court dismissed Musharraf's plea challenging the special court's jurisdiction and asking that his treason trial be held in a military court. On 31 March 2014, Musharraf was indicted for high treason.

It seemed at this juncture that the higher judiciary had its own axe to grind against the military and was still smarting over the manner in which Chief Justice Iftikhar Chaudhry had been treated by Musharraf in 2007.

Yet it was reluctant to go the whole hog.

In March 2016, Musharraf moved an application before the Supreme Court seeking one-time permission to go abroad for medical treatment. On 16 March 2016, the Supreme Court upheld a 2014 Sindh High Court ruling that ordered the removal of Musharraf's name from the ECL. Subsequently, on 18 March 2016, Musharraf left the country for Dubai, United Arab Emirates.

He remains in hospital there, apparently quite ill due to undiagnosed ailments or causes not made public so far.

Though the case languished for a while after Justice Khosa became Chief Justice, it acquired momentum again. A Special Court was constituted afresh and a new public prosecutor appointed. This was challenged by Musharraf's counsel in both the Lahore and Islamabad high courts, to little avail.

Issuing a 169-page judgment on December 17, 2019, Justice Waqar Seth, the presiding judge, went as far as to direct 'the law enforcement agencies to strive their level best to apprehend the fugitive/convict (Musharraf) to ensure that the punishment is inflicted as per law and if found dead, his corpse be dragged to the D-Chowk, Islamabad, Pakistan and be hanged for 03 days.'

Musharraf's lawyer, Salman Safdar, announced in a press conference the same evening (December 17) that they would challenge the verdict in the Supreme Court, though Musharraf is unlikely to be fit or willing to return to the country any time soon.

Caustic Army Reaction

Following the verdict, the ISPR issued a strong statement saying the "decision given by special court has been received with lot of pain and anguish by rank and file of Pakistan Armed Forces".[17] It further specified, "An ex-Army Chief, Chairman Joint Chief of Staff Committee and President of Pakistan, who has served the country for over 40 years, fought wars for the defence of the country can surely never be a traitor".

The DG ISPR also disclosed that the army chief had held a detailed conversation with the PM and exchanged views on how to take the situation forward after the verdict, keeping in view the "sentiments of the armed forces" and of patriotic Pakistanis.

PTI's Law Minister, Farogh Naseem, said on December 19 that the government would ask the Supreme Judicial Council, a forum which deals with accountability of judges, to remove the leader of the three-judge panel that sentenced Musharraf.[18]

The Musharraf verdict will likely remain un-implementable, not least because of uncertainty regarding his health. However, in the current civil society ambience, recourse to unconstitutional measures by a recalcitrant general may become that much more difficult in the future.

The judgment may have helped Gen. Bajwa to recoup lost ground in terms of the discontent generated within the Army on his extension. Reports from Pakistan indicated that senior officers in the Army had started rallying around him, even if they had reservations earlier about his extension. Now, they wanted him to have his full three years in addition, if only to show the country who is boss![19]

Lahore High Court Invalidates Judgment[20]

On January 13, 2020, a three-judge bench of the Lahore High Court declared the Special Court verdict unconstitutional, on grounds both of its wrongful constitution, without Cabinet approval then, and the amended article 6 of the Constitution being inapplicable as it was 'ex post facto'.

This judgment is unlikely to be appealed against by the PTI government and suits the military establishment as well.

Other Developments within Pakistan Army

In a significant set of changes effected on November 22, 2019, Gen. Bajwa brought in Lt. Gen. Sahir Shamshad Mirza, Adjutant General, as his new Chief of General Staff (CGS). An officer of the Sind Regiment, Mirza has had a brilliant career so far. He served earlier as Director General, Military Operations. He would be the senior-most officer in the cohort of those eligible to become Army Chief after Bajwa retires in 2022, ahead of the current DG, ISI, Faiz Hamid.

Lt. Gen. Nadeem Zaki Manj, Armoured Corps, moved from I Corps, Mangla as Director General, Strategic Plans Division (SPD). Another Armoured Corps officer, Lt. Gen. Shaheen Mazhar Mehmood goes to I Corps, Mangla from XI Corps, Peshawar. His place in Peshawar was taken by Lt. Gen. Nauman Mahmood, Baloch Regiment. Lt .Gen. Muhammad Amir, Artillery was appointed Adjutant General.[21]

Professional considerations seemed to have dictated most of these changes.

The Army currently has some 177 generals in fighting arms (this does not include doctors, engineers and other technical services). Two are four-star generals, 28 three-star generals, of whom 9 corps commanders and 19 principal staff officers are key advisors to the Chief. Another 148 are two-star major generals. Some of those would have moved up a notch if the Chief had retired on time. Forty-three major generals have already been superseded. They will go home regardless.

The Army's Reform Agenda[22]

Well-informed Pakistani military analysts believe, the extension could offer Gen. Bajwa an opportunity to reform Pakistan's upper Defence command structure, to better administer its three armed services under a single Chief of Defence Staff (CDS) or empowered JCSC Chairman. With an extension under his belt, the COAS could involve civilian and retired military experts to streamline the set-up to better provide a single point of advice to the Prime Minister. Currently, the Army Chief does that anyway but this bypasses the seniority ladder since the Joint Chiefs Chairman is out of the loop, more often than not.

Regional Commands

Pakistan has taken tentative steps towards regional commands but it needs to devolve operational powers to their heads, perhaps elevating them to four-star rank, reporting to the CDS or Joint Chiefs Chairman. There seemed to be a need for a clearer line of command in manning the war room at the PM's Office, to coordinate service operations.

Simultaneously, the government could press for an updating of war directives. This could yield fresh doctrines from all the three services. This needs to be done on a regular basis, setting a clear vision for the next five years or so, reviving the institution of regular quadrennial or quinquennial reviews, so that the civil and military leaderships can jointly set their defence targets. If General Bajwa can set Pakistan on this path, his extension will have been well earned.

A pitfall Bajwa could best avoid is not to depute Army officers to civilian jobs. In what was a popular move after Musharraf's departure in 2008, Kayani withdrew mid-level officers from civilian posts. However, on November 27, 2019, recently retired 12 Corps commander, Balochistan and erstwhile DG, ISPR, Lt. Gen. (retd) Asim Bajwa was appointed head of a newly-constituted China-Pakistan Economic Corridor (CPEC) Authority, ostensibly to oversee timely completion of projects.

In September, 2019, PM Imran Khan appointed Moeed Yusuf, a civilian academic, who had spent long years at the US Institute of Peace (USIP), as his Strategic Policy Planning adviser. On December 24, 2019, this designation seems to have been changed to Special Assistant to PM. It may be recalled that in October, 2019, a US academic, Dr. Christine Fair, had questioned the credentials of Moeed Yusuf, dubbing him 'a Pakistani agent', which allegations were promptly denied by the USIP. It is a matter of conjecture if he would be associated in any of the above tasks connected to the Army reform agenda. It seems highly unlikely.

Conclusion

Civil–military disunity may have been temporarily patched up over the imbroglio pertaining to the Army Chief's extension.

Both the PTI government and a Army Chief seemingly wanting to hang on to power gathered considerable egg on their faces while the highest court in the land deliberated on the issue and cast aspersions on the motives of Army generals.

Conspiracy theories abounded about whether at all the civilians were happy with Bajwa's extension or fell in line with motions related to the extension out of fear.

The balance of power between civilians and the Army is likely to remain heavily tilted in favour of the latter in the foreseeable future. Only time will tell whether the Army and its 'selected' protégé, Imran Khan, will continue to 'remain on the same page' and for how long, or how other aspiring political wannabees would want to step in as the proverbial 'King's party', to provide a continuing façade of an imperfect and struggling democracy.

NOTES

1. Tahira Abdullah: Human Rights in an imperfect democracy; Jinnah Institute; www.jinah-institute.org: 10.12.2019.
2. Article by Author: 'Pakistan: What Pak Army Chief's 3-year extension means for Kashmir': Rediff.com, August 20,2019.
3. Mohd Taqi: Domestic, Regional Implications of Pakistani Army Chief's Term Extension: www. thewire.com: 23.8.2019.
4. Najam Sethi: 'Two Narratives': *The Friday Times,* November 1, 2011.
5. *Dawn,* November 25.
6. *Dawn,* November 29.
7. Haseeb Bhatti:'Ball in Parliament's court to provide certainty to Army Chief's post with new law': *Dawn*: December 16, 2019.
8. Hasnat Malik: 'Govt challenges SC verdict on army chief's extension'; *Express Tribune*: December 26, 2019.
9. *Dawn*: December 26, 2019.
10. Hasnat Malik: Statement of Firdaus Ashiq Awan, Information Minister quoted; Op cit: *Express Tribune*.
11. Article by Author: 'Resentment over Pak Army Chief's extension': Rediff.com, November 22, 2019 https://www.rediff.com/news/column/resentment-over-pak-army-chiefs-extension/20191122.htm
12. Article by Author: ' Pakistan: Discontent simmers in Pakistan Army; Rediff.com: December 25, 2019.
13. Syed Irfan Raza:'Rare political accord on changes to Army Act': *Dawn*: 03.01.2020.
14. *Express Tribune*: 'Services Chiefs tenure bills clear last hurdle': January 9, 2020.
15. Najam Sethi show: You Tube: January 7, 2020.
16. Zahed Hussain: 'Legislation on COAS's tenure': *Dawn*: 8.01.2020.
17. https://dailytimes.com.pk/523775/dg-ispr-terms-treason-case-judgment-as-unethical-and-inhumane;
18. Radio Free Europe/Radio Liberty: December 20, 2019.
19. Article by Author: 'Pakistan: Discontent simmers in Pakistan Army': Rediff.com: 25.12.2019.
20. *The News*: January 13, 2020.
21. Article by Author: 'The man who could succeed Pak army chief:' Rediff.com: November, 26, 2019.
22. Shuja Nawaz blog: 'The man who could succeed Pak army chief:' August 26, 2019; https://shujanawaz.com/category/blog/

3

The Great COVID-19 Mystery

Tilak Devasher

The corona virus pandemic has presented an unprecedented challenge to the global community. While it will ultimately wane, at the time of writing, the world is still grappling with the crisis. However, in Pakistan, as per official figures, there appears to have been a sudden turnaround since mid-June 2020 for reasons that are not readily understood or explained. If genuine, this reversal of the pandemic would no doubt be remarkable. While there are lingering doubts about the figures, and fears of a second wave, Pakistan's handling of the pandemic itself has thrown up several elements that showed how not to deal with a crisis of such magnitude. Most importantly, it revealed paucity of leadership that was not able to get its act together because of which the people had to suffer both medically and economically.

This chapter delineates Pakistan's handling of the crisis and looks at the turnaround, as per official figures.

The Turnaround

The first confirmed case of corona virus was reported in Pakistan on 26 February 2020 in Karachi of a student returning from pilgrimage in Iran. Pilgrims returning from Iran formed the first major cluster of imported infections. The second major cluster was of locally transmitted infections from the Tableeghi Jamaat's annual ijtema (congregation) from 11 March at Raiwind. Though it was cancelled on 12 March, by then an estimated 100,000 believers, including around 3,000 foreigners, had already set up camp together in close quarters. They dispersed to their home towns without being tested or isolated. As a result, major transmission in Punjab and Sindh was traced to the Tableeghi Jamaat ijtama.[1]

As the Minister for Planning and Head of National Command and Operation Centre (NCOC), Asad Umar warned on 5 April that corona virus cases were expected to touch the limit of the health system in the next few weeks despite the low spread of the virus.[2] Imran Khan has also warned that the outbreak could take a turn for the worse by the end of April that will put more pressure on hospitals.[3] Such a situation was largely the result of woeful investment in the health sector for decades by successive governments.

Thereafter, the virus quickly spread to all parts of Pakistan. By 31 March, the government estimated that about 27 per cent of the corona virus cases were the result of local transmission.[4] This figure of local transmission went up to 58 per cent by mid-April[5] and to over 96 per cent by June, as per the data of the Ministry of National Health.[6]

The COVID-19 virus proliferated rapidly in Pakistan. On 22 May, the number of confirmed positive cases totalled 50,694. This figure nearly doubled to 98,943 on 7 June—i.e., an addition of nearly 50,000 cases in a period of 16 days. The tally swelled by another 50,000 cases or so, but in half the number of days (eight), standing at 146,254 as of 15 June. This showed a little less than 200 per cent increase in 24 days. The rate at which the virus was mushrooming took Pakistan to the sixth rank among countries with the highest number of new cases.[7] The government's frustration in its inability to control the spread was apparent when the Punjab Health Minister, Dr. Yasmin Rashid, accused the citizens of Lahore of being "jahil" (illiterate) for not taking the corona virus seriously, adding that "few nations are more jahil than Pakistanis".[8]

From about late June-early July onwards, the positive cases started diminishing rapidly, first in official figures, then from news reports and finally from the imagination of the people. Similarly, reported deaths due to the virus dipped sharply while conversely there was a big uptick in the recovery rate.

Official figures are revealing. On 13 June, there were officially declared 6,825 new positive cases, though many believe this to be an underestimate due to low testing (discussed below). By early August, such cases had declined to just above 600. By early September, the corona virus infections had dwindled to 200-300 a day. The deaths declined from about 150 in mid June to less than ten in early August.

By 2 August, Pakistan had around 280,200 registered cases and close to 6,000 deaths, ranking thirteenth among the COVID-19 affected countries globally (in terms of total cases). According to official statistics, the daily number of confirmed cases had declined considerably since early July.

This remarkable turnaround happened against the backdrop of three developments that make these figures highly suspect. First, by mid-June, the government had restored almost all business activities in order to jump-start the economy. Second, media reports indicated that even at the best of times, taking precautionary measures like wearing masks and social distancing were weak; after mid-June, such measures were almost totally given up. Third, attributes of normality like crowded shopping centres, opening of marriage halls, etc., were visible in most places.

Hence, the critical question is how did the turnaround occur against such a backdrop?

Till the time of writing, no realistic scientific answer has been provided. People have speculated that heat and strong sunlight could have led to the virus slowing down.

The government, on the other hand, took credit for the decline in the number of new cases due to its 'smart lockdown' strategy whereby it imposed a strict curfew-like lockdown only on those parts of a city where there was an increasing number of cases and removing restrictions in specific areas where the positive rates were low. However, the problem with such a strategy was that poor data and low testing rates hampered efforts to "track, trace and quarantine". This involved identifying and isolating virus carriers and their contacts and placing hot spots under quarantine; this was essential to curb the virus.[9] It was assessed that in densely populated cities like Karachi, Lahore and Peshawar, restrictions in some areas were unlikely to prevent the spread of the virus. As an expert put it: 'Let's not fool ourselves with economist-led 'smart' lockdowns. All Pakistani cities are now too infested to avoid full lockdown. With population densities of more than 4,000 persons per square kilometre, this was inevitable. This is the only way to restrict further spread of the contagion to the rural areas.'[10]

Media reports provided different answers. According to *The Nation*, for the past few days, Pakistan's corona virus cases had shockingly been recorded as falling. It quoted the Health Ministry stating that 3,892 cases were confirmed across the country on 25 June that marked a fall of almost 3,000 cases from the record high of 6,895 reached on 13 June. The figures were 6,604 on 19 June, 4,951 on 20 June, 4,471 on 21 June, and 3,946 on 22 June.[11]

Dawn was blunter when it stated: 'Reports that COVID-19 cases in Pakistan have been falling in recent days should be viewed with caution.' It quoted data released by the NCOC showing that the past few days witnessed between 4,000 to 5,000 daily cases as compared to mid-June that saw between 5,000 and 7,000 cases. Though looking promising, the *Dawn* pointed out that the same period in which corona virus cases supposedly declined also witnessed a sharp reduction in testing. Where the authorities had conducted more than 31,000 tests in a single day around mid-June, in the past few days the numbers had fallen to below 25,000. In fact, according to one NCOC press release on 25 June, the total number of tests was below 22,000. Not surprisingly, *Dawn* held that one likely factor behind the fewer positive cases was that fewer people were being tested. It advocated that the focus of the authorities should not be on the number of people testing positive, but rather on the number of tests being done and the percentage of total tests versus total positive cases in a single day. This percentage in mid-June was between 18 per cent and 22 per cent, which meant that 18 to 22 out of every 100 persons tested were COVID-19 positive. It noted that thereafter that percentage has been recorded at between 16 to 20 per cent—a mere 2 per cent reduction that could hardly be claimed as a victory when testing had been reduced by a third.[12]

According to the *Daily Times*, 'it would not be going too far to fear that the ruling party might be in denial about how its handling of the most important problem confronting the country is turning out. Regrettably, it does not seem that the government is in any mood to accept that it might need to correct its course of action.'[13]

Leadership and Tackling the Crisis

True leadership is tested during times of national emergencies like the corona virus pandemic when people look up to their leader to chart the path out of danger. In such extraordinary situations, leaders have to realistically understand the various dimensions of the peril, adopt a decisive policy after all-round consultations, sink internal differences so that the country can unitedly deal with the situation and create a national will and confidence to overcome the crisis. The COVID-19 crisis thus was an opportunity for Imran Khan to prove his mettle. However, he failed to measure up. To start with, his understanding of the crisis was limited as evidenced by his initial assertions that the virus was like the flu; that 97 per cent of those infected would recover and only the old and sick were in danger.[14] This was incorrect and even contradicted by the PM's former special assistant on health, Dr. Zafar Mirza, who said a majority of the confirmed cases in Pakistan were of young people. In fact, 84 per cent of the confirmed cases were found to be between the ages of 20 and 64 years.[15] Moreover, Imran Khan clearly failed to factor the scale of 3 per cent in a country with a population of 220 million. Then, of course, he sought to justify not imposing a lockdown by blatantly lying that the Indian PM had to apologise for doing so. The fact was that PM Modi had apologised for the hardships that the people had to face during the lockdown, while emphasising that it was necessary.

Though Imran Khan claimed that his government had swung into action as early as 15 January, much before the first case was even reported in Pakistan, in reality, the National Security Committee (NSC) only met on 13 March to discuss the pandemic. By this time, there were already two dozen cases in Pakistan, infected pilgrims were streaming in from Iran via Taftan in Balochistan and the massive Tablighi Jamaat congregation had taken place in Raiwind, Punjab. Imran Khan's government simply failed to assess the magnitude of the developing problem.

His poor leadership led the NSC to constitute a National Coordination Committee (NCC) chaired by the Prime Minister and including the Army Chief, the four provincial chief ministers and senior military officers to evaluate the pandemic situation. The NCC set up a National Command and Operations Centre (NCOC) to act as its implementation arm. Not surprisingly, a serving army general was made the convener.

Understanding apart, Imran Khan's approach towards tackling the crisis was tentative and lacked decisiveness. Ignoring the view of medical experts that without physical distancing, the infection was likely to spread exponentially, he rejected a national lockdown but then vacillated between this decision and imposing a 'partial' or 'smart' lockdown . Even the timing of easing restrictions came under severe criticism.

The strategy could still have worked if the provinces had followed suit. However, ignoring the PM, on 23 March the Sindh CM took the initiative for a province-wise lockdown. Warning of the health dangers, the provincial government urged the centre to devise a national strategy, including through robust shutdown measures. Punjab, KPK and Balochistan belatedly followed suit, though not calling it a 'lockdown' in deference to the federal government and resorting to flexible restrictions. The army chipped in by saying it would enforce the lockdown. Imran Khan was thus left red-faced. The uncoordinated manner of 'locking' down of different provinces made the situation even more chaotic especially because there was very little inter-provincial coordination.

Imran Khan was also found wanting on other counts. Even in this hour of crisis, he was unable to show leadership to unify the country. Instead, he chose to continue to follow the path of political victimisation of opponents and demonstrated a belligerent attitude towards them. Thus, after addressing a video-conference of parliamentary leaders, he chose to go offline instead of listening to their views. He thereby signalled that he was not interested in their opinions on dealing with the crisis. This hostility was again amply demonstrated during the special session of the National Assembly called exclusively to discuss the COVID-19 situation. Instead of formulating a united response, the opposition and treasury hurled charges at each other. He continued with his policy of trying to weaken the opposition using state institutions to target top leaders on corruption charges leading to the imprisonment of several of them. Not surprisingly, the country remained bitterly divided at a time when unity was critical. The onus for failing to develop a national consensus on the way forward and intensifying political polarisation must lie squarely with the leadership.

In dealing with the crisis, Imran Khan depended on his unelected/ unaccountable friends and technocrat advisers and special assistants rather than elected parliamentarians. It is suspected that they had advised against a full lockdown for the sake of their personal fortunes that would have been affected in case factories were closed.

Another indicator of his inadequate leadership was evident in the timing of the decision to relax the lockdown even though by his own assertions there was no lockdown to begin with. Though Pakistan had not suffered from a massive spread in May, there was consensus that the peak had yet to come. Thus, the relaxation was done at a time when the number of cases and fatalities were rising, there was very little testing and it was against the advice of medical professionals. Moreover, while social distancing was prescribed, there was very little enforcement. The SOPs were being honoured only in the breach and the scenes at markets and in mosques were like the pre-COVID-19 days.

The one initiative that Imran Khan took was the formation of a Corona Relief Tiger Force, comprising young volunteers to help the government in its relief efforts. He also put together a 'relief package'. The efficacy of both these was hotly contested. The Tiger Force, set up with much fanfare, did not bother to perform the task it was set up to perform in the first place—to assist the government during the lockdown, mainly by keeping people at home by helping them with the chores that took them outside, like paying bills, getting groceries and other supplies, and withdrawing money from banks. Instead, now the Force, which fell flat on the above tasks was asked to keep an eye on government offices, educational institutions, markets and police stations, not to forget land record offices and kutcheries, and report public complaints.[16] Quite likely, this force would act as PTI's own informal troopers who would be very effective during the elections.

Lockdown

Imran Khan's rejection of a lockdown was based on the argument that it would ruin the economy adversely affecting the 25 per cent poor who would lose their livelihood and sustenance. Addressing the nation on 23 March, Imran Khan, who himself held the federal health portfolio, initially ruled out a countrywide closure, saying it would adversely affect the poor and working class. The argument had merit, except for the fact that in case the virus spread due to no lockdown, the poor would be the first to suffer due to the lack of medical facilities. Instead of a full lockdown, he appealed to the people to self-quarantine themselves while closing educational institutions, sporting events, etc. However, the construction industry and some other sectors like tourism were to be opened in phases.

On 14 April, Prime Minister Khan extended the restricted lockdown until 30 April but also relaxed restrictions. Several non-essential industries, including construction, reopened. His justification for doing so were that continuation of even a restricted lockdown was taking a toll on the poor and impacting the economy. Yet, signs of economic recovery since the lockdown was lifted were few and the virus did threaten to overwhelm the precarious health systems.[17]

On 9 May, the lockdown was lifted. Though Khan insisted that the decision was consensual, taken with the consent of the provinces, the Sindh chief minister disagreed, accusing Islamabad of forcing the decision. The Punjab and Balochistan governments too were unhappy with the lifting of restrictions.

As result of the lifting, there was a surge in cases and Pakistan found itself among the top twelve pandemic-affected countries worldwide. By 9 May, when the lockdown was lifted, the total number of cases was around 29,000 and the death toll was 637. About six weeks later, the total number of cases was more than 180,000; the death toll stood at over 3,000.[18]

In early June, the Pakistan head of the World Health Organisation recommended imposing targeted and intermittent two-weeks-on, two-weeks-off lockdowns. In a letter to the Punjab health minister, he noted that Pakistan did not meet any of the prerequisites for fully lifting restrictions.[19] The Prime Minister's health adviser, however, rejected the recommendation asserting that the WHO had assessed Pakistan's situation through a "health lens" but the government had "to make tough policy choices to strike a balance between lives and livelihoods".[20]

Dawn summed it up well when it held: 'In a move that flies in the face of ominous data, Prime Minister Imran Khan has decided to further ease lockdown restrictions across the country and to reopen almost all sectors of industry—an unfortunate decision that will see a greater surge in corona virus infections.... It is almost as if the top leadership does not read the news or the alarming COVID-19 data.'[21]

Or, as a scribe put it: 'It was a surreal moment listening to the prime minister as he warned the nation of more corona virus deaths while removing restrictions that could contain the spread of the deadly infection. His latest words highlight the recklessness that defines the federal government's approach while dealing with an existential crisis. With almost all restrictions on movement gone, it has now been left to the people to save themselves from the fast-spreading disease. The state has virtually abdicated its responsibility of protecting the people.' He added that because of the confusion in policy, Pakistan could neither contain the disease nor create conditions for the quick revival of the economy. Most amusing were the claims of some federal ministers that the entire world was now following the 'vision' of their great leader. What they did not want to understand, he wrote, was that the spread of the disease would not only have serious consequences for public health but also for quicker economic recovery.[22]

According to another scribe, 'Not only did the government impose the initial lockdown half-heartedly but in prematurely reopening the economy—and tourism—it exposed the country to the risk of an exponential spread of the virus. This unfortunately is what is happening now'.[23]

Messaging

An ominous feature of the situation was the fact that many people in Pakistan were unaware of the risks of contracting the potentially fatal virus. The reason for this was the government's confused messaging and its inability to convince the public of its danger since it did not launch a public awareness campaign. This was promoted by the belief that COVID-19 would not affect people in countries with warm temperatures or that the BCG vaccine provided protection against it. The government's message that the virus could be fatal and, pending a vaccine, the only protection was social distancing should have been unequivocal. On the contrary, the government demonstrated a casual attitude towards the lockdown and enforcing social distancing as also an undue haste lift it so diluting the message about the pandemic's seriousness.

For example, in early June, Imran Khan announced that people should take care, try to stay indoors and then paradoxically announced at the same time the reopening of tourism so that people in large numbers could start going to tourist areas like Murree, Swat, Kaghan, Naran, etc. This prompted a scribe to write: 'I have not seen a government abdicate all responsibility to safeguard its citizens from clear and present danger so comprehensively as this government has just done.'[24] Such a step would lead to the virus spreading to areas that were already too ill-equipped to handle the situation. Then again, on several occasions, like during his visit to the ISI hqrs, Imran Khan was seen without a mask. Such careless messaging and casual attitude on the part of the leadership raised the obvious question of how would the public follow safety norms if their leaders were not doing so.

The government's mixed messaging and misinformation from some religious leaders meant that many Pakistanis disregarded public health advice. The federal government's easing of lockdown measures, despite warnings by the political opposition and medical professionals that transmissions would surge, and the further lifting of the lockdown, on 9 May, encouraged public complacency.

Poor messaging also included the people being told that the strain of corona in Pakistan was milder than the one in other parts of the world and that there would therefore be far fewer infections and deaths; SOPs were announced without making any effort to enforce them; the government first eased the lockdown and then lifted it entirely. This led the public to take the virus lightly and the people continued the festivities after Eid.[25]

According to a social media analytics report, the government's public awareness messages on the pandemic and the precautions to be taken failed to reach a large portion of the population. Information regarding the deadly virus was reaching the public via local news channels and private sector companies with only a meagre 5 per cent recalling government messages. Only 38 per cent could correctly name the official helpline (1166) to report COVID-19 symptoms.[26]

Given the mixed messaging, it was not surprising that, according to a survey by Gallup Pakistan, 55 per cent of Pakistanis believed that the threat of the corona virus was exaggerated. As a nation, Pakistan was fourth on the list of those most likely to believe that the pandemic's effect had been overplayed.[27]

As *The News* put it: 'First, there were reassurances that it is nothing but some sort of flu that is not going to affect many. Then there was reluctance in imposing a lockdown on the pretext of a failing economy, which was declining anyway much before the corona virus hit the country. Advisers and ministers were taking it lightly, some even going so far as comparing the casualties in road accidents with corona deaths.'[28]

Testing

What made the figures of positive cases even more alarming was that the number of tests conducted in the country was only 39,183 till 7 April with the then testing capacity standing at 3,088 per 24 hours. Of those tested, nearly 10 per cent had been positive.[29] According to Dr. Zafar Mirza, testing capability would be enhanced by the end of April. He said: "Earlier around 800 tests were being conducted daily but for the last few days we are conducting 2,500 to 3,000 tests a day. By the end of this month, we will hold up to 25,000 tests daily."[30] However, even by the end of May just about half of this capacity had been achieved. Strangely, in the last week of April, barring Sindh, the other provinces reduced testing leading to suspicions that this was deliberately done to show fewer positive cases.[31]

Meanwhile, urging authorities to ramp up testing, Dr. Ma Minghui, the deputy director general of the Xinjiang Uygur Autonomous Region Medical Products Administration and the head of the Chinese medical team that visited Pakistan, told the media that "In Pakistan, one out of every 10 person tested for COVID-19 up till now has returned a positive report. This is much higher than Xinjiang, where only one in 100 people tested for the virus reported positive." She also warned that the possibility of the outbreak in Pakistan could be far bigger than the confirmed numbers show. "Unfortunately, Pakistani authorities are fighting this virus in the dark right now...the shortage of testing kits and reluctance of citizens to come forward for testing may be masking true numbers. And you cannot contain COVID-19 until you have a clear picture.[32]

According to data released by the NCOC on 21 May, 15,346 tests of COVID-19 were conducted during the last 24 hours—6,164 in Sindh, 5,439 in Punjab, 1,644 in Khyber Pakhtunkhwa and 1,331 in Islamabad. Overall, 429,600 tests had been conducted by then.[33] On June 10, 2020, tests conducted were 23,799.

In June, the minister overseeing the pandemic response had said that authorities would increase daily testing capacity to 100,000 by July.[34] According to the NCOC, testing capacity had increased to over 70,000 by early July.[35] Yet, less than one-third of that capacity was used.

The World Health Organisation (WHO) had advised the government to enhance its daily testing capacity to 50,000 to assess the actual prevalence of the corona virus across the country. The government did enhance the tests to 30,000 in mid-June, only to bring them down subsequently for unknown reasons. Calling for increased testing, a doctors' forum said that the government's figures of confirmed cases were "not representative of the actual ground situation".[36]

There was a lot of scepticism about the government figures in the media and political circles. Thus, according to *The News*: 'The number of newly infected people has been kept in check not by following precautionary measures, but by not conducting as many screening tests as we should have done. The WHO recommends that around 50,000 tests should be carried out per day. Pakistan's figures have been, to say the least, baffling.'[37]

According to the *Pakistan Today*, 'The country's ability to deal with the epidemic, to absorb the shock it is administering, is being compromised, rather than enhanced, by the government's attempt to avoid testing, which is an essential part of managing the pandemic, whether it is through 'smart lockdowns' or contact tracing.... It is more important to keep its citizens alive than provide the WHO and other international bodies doctored figures.[38]

The PMLN too was critical of the low testing rates, asserting that the number of corona virus cases was high in Punjab but the number of tests was low.[39] An All Parties Conference (APC) of Punjab convened by the Pakistan People's Party alleged that the government was hiding the actual number of deaths caused by COVID-19, and that the situation was horrible in Punjab. It further added that Punjab had 60 per cent population of the whole country but had conducted less than 30 per cent tests out of the total conducted in Pakistan.[40]

Fatalities

Strangely, if official statistics were to be believed, the number of deaths in the first five months of 2020 was lower than the corresponding period of the previous year. Such a calculation does raise questions about the integrity of the data on COVID-19 fatalities.

In Lahore, for example, there were 906 graveyards; the number of deaths from January to May 2020 was lower than the corresponding period in the previous year. In May this year, 1,748 deaths were recorded by graveyards of the entire city compared with 5,015 in May last year. This was quite an unbelievable drop. In contrast, there was not much difference in the figures of January 2020 (2,557 deaths) and that of January 2019 (2,595 deaths). The same was in the case of February.[41]

In Karachi, the situation was the reverse with a spike in the number of dead or near dead being brought to hospitals and graveyards. According to one report, a total of 3,265 dead bodies were brought to 30 graveyards of Karachi between 20 February and 9 April (49 days). This raised fears that the number of COVID-19 fatalities could be much higher than being reported. However, there was no official confirmation and no hospital was reported to have conducted tests to ascertain whether the real cause of death was COVID-19 or not.[42]

According to another report, 200-odd deaths in Karachi, in two weeks' time were just about normal. However, the figure had risen. During a TV interview, Dr. Seemi Jamali, Director of Jinnah Post-Graduate Medical Centre (JPMC), Karachi's biggest public-sector hospital, said that over the last 15 days in April, there was a 21 per cent increase in year-on-year in the total number of patients either brought dead or dying within hours after arrival. Most of these patients were suffering from 'pneumonia-like symptoms'. His account was substantiated by the Edhi Foundation stating that the number of bodies received at their mortuaries in Karachi between April 1 and 13 was 388 as against 230 bodies received during the same period last year. This showed a significant increase of 158 deaths. The cause of death of those brought dead or expiring within hours of arrival at the JPMC hospital, however, remained officially unknown since no post-mortem was reported.

While the official corona virus death toll across the country stood at over 200 on 21 April, the number of deaths by unknown causes did raise a big question mark on the authenticity of the official figures. The only way the issue could have been resolved was if all the hospitals across the country tested patients who were brought to them dead or nearly dead in order that the actual number of deaths from the pandemic could be ascertained.[15]

This situation in Karachi led Murad Ali Shah, the chief minister of Sindh, to state that he feared that the actual number of deaths in the province was probably much higher than what was being reported. His suspicion was that many cases with "pneumonia-like symptoms" were simply going undetected.[43]

By the third week of June, the government claimed that Pakistan's mortality rate was just 1.93 per cent, which was nothing worse than the common flu. However, analysts pointed out that these numbers did not reflect the ground reality. In effect, reduction in testing and insufficient testing kept the numbers low giving a false assurance.[44]

The death toll was likely under-counted since many families, fearing the religious and social stigma of the disease, were not reporting infections or seeking treatment. The Khyber Pakhtunkhwa government, for instance, was investigating declining mortality figures, to check if patients were dying unrecorded at home.

One main reason for this is that according to a recent Gallup International survey carried out in March 2020 as many as 43 per cent of all Pakistanis had not taken any precautionary measures to protect themselves from corona virus. The survey declared this as the highest percentage of citizens among the 28 nations that took part in the poll.[45] According to another survey carried out by the Aga Khan University (AKU), less than one in 10 rural residents correctly identified being in crowded areas as a factor for getting infected. Moreover, 74 per cent of the rural sample incorrectly believed mosquito bites to be a cause of the global pandemic.[46]

Reports

Contrary to official figures showing a remarkable turnaround, several reports had pointed to an impending crisis of grave proportions.

The Punjab government's smart sampling data analysis of COVID-19 prevalence in Lahore in May 2020 estimated 670,800 actual new cases, which was six per cent of the city's population of 11.18 million. The study revealed that the results of the tests from Lahore showed that six per cent of all those tested were positive with a few towns showing positivity as high as 14.7 per cent. The study, which was sent to the chief minister on 15 May 2020, was kept secret for over two weeks despite startling findings vis-à-vis the high prevalence of corona virus in the provincial capital, calling for urgent action to contain the spread of virus.[47] The Punjab government also declined to follow the recommendations of the health authorities to apply a 30-day complete lockdown two weeks after being presented with the disturbing picture of Lahore resulting from local transmission of corona virus.[48]

The Punjab government report was followed by the President of the Punjab chapter of Pakistan Medical Association (PMA) claiming at a press conference in Lahore that there were no less than 3.5 million corona virus cases in Lahore and 20 million in Punjab. According to him, cases remain under-reported because of the government's failure to conduct sufficient tests. The government, he said, decided to ease the lockdown when it should have further strengthened it.[49]

The Sindh Health Minister, Dr. Azra Fazal Pechuho, told the Sindh Assembly in early June that with the lockdown eased off countrywide, the COVID-19 pandemic situation in Pakistan had become out of control to the extent that patients of the viral disease were likely to emerge from every house, after which the hospitals would not have spare beds and ventilators to deal with the health crisis. She said there had been an exponential rise in the corona virus cases in the country since the lifting of the lockdown by the middle of the last month. Had there been continuity in the lockdown, the ongoing health crisis would not have become so grim, she remarked.[50]

Dr. Saleem Abro, Director General Health, Balochistan, warned at a press conference in mid-June that cases in Balochistan could increase to over 100,000 within the next few months. According to him, about 40 per cent of the population in the province was currently infected and people were not informing the government about infected patients and deaths occurring in various parts of Balochistan. He expected cases to peak from July to September when the situation could become dangerous. He lamented the fact that even though health authorities had recommended a complete lockdown, their warnings were ignored with the lockdown converted to a "smart" lockdown.[51]

Figures revealed by an Imperial College London simulation were even more startling, as they modelled the worst-case scenarios for tens of countries: the UK data simulated that, in the extreme event that no action was taken to curb the spread, 2.2 million people could die of COVID-19 in Pakistan between February 2020 and June 2021. The same analysis suggested that, with interventions and mitigation, deaths could be lowered by at least 40 per cent.[52] All these reports about the rapid increase in the number of corona patients put a question mark over official data especially due to lack of facilities to test all virus suspects and a deliberate drastic reduction in testing.

The opposition PPP in fact warned the federal government to come out of its illusions, stop downplaying the threat and act to prevent a serious health crisis. PPP parliamentary leader in the Senate Sherry Rehman told the Senate, "Of all people being tested in Pakistan, 20 per cent are reporting positive, which is the third highest ratio in the world" adding "Pakistan has the fifth fastest outbreak in the world [where the virus is] accelerating beyond the point of containment.[53]

Economy

There are various estimates about the impact of the virus on the economy that was in dire straits even before COVID-19. The pandemic exacerbated the economic crisis.

In April, the World Bank had warned that Pakistan's economy could show negative growth of between 1.3 per cent to 2.2 per cent in the current fiscal year whereas the IMF's projected a negative growth of 1.5 per cent.[54] In a subsequent World Bank report, *Global Economic Prospects*, of early June, Pakistan's economy was likely to have a negative GDP growth of negative 2.6 per cent for the fiscal year 2019-20 and negative 0.2 per cent during 2020-21. All other major economies in the region—India, Bangladesh, Nepal and Bhutan—would remain in the growth mode during fiscal 2019-20, even though all would suffer from the pandemic's impact.[55]

According to the Economic Survey 2019-20, at least another 10 million people were expected to slip below the poverty line as a consequence of the corona virus pandemic and the number of people living below the poverty line could rise from the existing figure of 50 million to 60 million.[56] The government estimates were that the GDP would contract by 0.38 per cent for the fiscal year 2019-2020. According to the Federal Minister for Planning, as a result of the crisis, 20 to 70 million people could fall below the poverty line, 18 million people could become unemployed due to the lockdown and around one million small entities may close down permanently.[57]

A recent UNDP report stated that Pakistan had one of the lowest levels of preparedness because of its limited human development, poor health infrastructure, and related issues.[58]

Pakistan was vulnerable not only because of its inadequate health infrastructure but also because of the situation of food security. The Household Integrated Economic Survey (HIES), 2018-19 revealed that 16 per cent of the population was experiencing moderate or severe food insecurity. The incidence was twice as high among the rural population, 20 per cent, as among the urban, 9.2 per cent. Shockingly, three out of five households, 61 per cent, among the lowest two income quintiles in the survey, were experiencing food insecurity. According to the World Food Program (WFP) 2020, over three million people in the country were experiencing severe food insecurity, mainly in the drought-affected districts of Balochistan and Sindh. Over half a million people in these provinces were described as in emergency conditions.

In such a bleak scenario coupled with the impact of the pandemic, swarms of desert locusts had arrived to attack crops and damage rural livelihoods, particularly in Balochistan, Sindh and South Punjab.[59] The situation was still unfolding and could further deteriorate. The Food and Agriculture Organization (FAO) had warned that the magnitude of damage to the crops posed a severe threat to food security and livelihood of affected communities. It forecast economic losses of over $ 5.1 billion, depending on the scale of damage to the crops.[60]

If the government's goal in lifting the lockdown was to get the economy moving, little suggests that this happened. Indeed, it was clear that economic growth depended on curbing the virus. On 22 April, days after the lockdown was first eased, the World Health Organisation's Director-General had warned,

"Without effective interventions [in Pakistan], there could be an estimated 200K+ cases by mid-July. The impact on the economy could be devastating, doubling the number of people living in poverty".[61]

The government provided emergency assistance to families in need, including food subsidies and support, but for many this aid was barely enough. The Ehsaas emergency cash program (earlier the Benazir Income Support Program) provided financial assistance to an estimated twelve million families that fell under the poverty line. Islamabad began the scheme on 9 April and extended it the following month to provide a similar amount to four million unemployed workers.[62] Yet the lump sum cash transfer of approximately $ 75 to cover four months of expenses hardly covered food costs. Such support could well be critical for months. According to Imran Khan, the cash disbursement program could only be a temporary solution, which was why the lockdown was lifted. "There's no way the government can give out handouts to feed people for that long".[63] Yet with the pandemic continuing to hinder any economic recovery, the need for state assistance appeared likely to increase further. A prominent public health expert and demographer noted: "There is no choice but to provide the essentials like food, water and health care for the poorest 20 per cent of the population for the next few months....[t]he counterfactual is skyrocketing poverty, malnutrition and deaths of key household members that will be difficult to repair financially and emotionally".[64]

The government was to receive $ 1.5 to $ 2 billion in temporary debt relief from G20 member-countries; the International Monetary Fund allocated $ 1.4 billion through its Rapid Financing Instrument, to mitigate the economic impact of the pandemic; the World Bank restored Pakistan's budgetary support and granted a $ 500 million loan for pandemic-related health care and social safety nets; the Asian Development Bank approved a $ 500 million loan for the government's health and economic response, including social protection for the poor. Bilateral donors such as Germany have also extended assistance, with Berlin providing 0.5 million Euros to help Pakistan overcome the pandemic's socio-economic impact at the local level. All this aid would have greatly helped to mitigate the impact of the pandemic on the poorer sections of society.

The Religious Dimension

A major complicating factor for Pakistan was that it believed that it was the last bastion of Islam. Despite other Islamic countries like Saudi Arabia and Iran banning all religious gatherings, Imran Khan took the position that Pakistan was an independent country and allowed congregational prayers in mosques. While the provinces restricted congregations in mosques to five or less, Sindh went ahead and declared a curfew from 12 to 3 pm on Fridays to prevent large congregations. Despite this, there were violations all over the country. Most notable was the controversial Lal Masjid cleric, Maulana Abdul Aziz, in Islamabad who directly challenged the government by not only holding large congregations at almost every prayer but also declared brazenly that he would continue to lead the prayers. Full capacity pictures from inside Lal Masjid in Islamabad during the lockdown were shocking, though the government did not take action against him.

Moreover, initially on 14 April, prominent ulemas rejected any restrictions on mosques declaring that daily prayers would be held as usual. One of the ulemas even insisted that the best way to get rid of the virus was to increase the attendance in mosques.[65]

The situation was especially fraught with danger because of Ramzan and the get-togethers for *Sehri* and *Iftar* as also for special prayers *taraweeh* and *aitekaf.* To avoid a confrontation, the President of Pakistan, Dr. Alvi, met prominent ulemas and worked out a so-called 20-point compromise agreement on 18 April, without consulting provincial governments. Under this, all the demands of the clerics for opening mosques nationwide and holding daily congregational and *taraweeh* prayers during the month of Ramazan were accepted with certain precautionary measures for social distancing. However, the clerics declined to take any responsibility related to the enforcement of these precautionary measures.[66] As a result, thousands prayed in packed mosques, ignoring health measures and creating new hot-spots of viral infection.[67] Many clerics appear to have told worshippers to demonstrate piety by praying shoulder to shoulder, warning that the pandemic was a punishment for sins of erring Muslims, arguing that the faithful were immune and that life and death were in God's hands alone.[68] As a result, many who regularly attended mosques either believed they would not contract the virus or that prayer would protect them.[69] Many also chose not to get tested or treated due to religious and social stigma attached to the disease.[70]

In effect, by ignoring the safer course adopted by countries like Saudi Arabia, Iran, Turkey, Egypt and Jordan not to allow congregational prayers in mosques, Pakistan took a huge risk. Enforcing and monitoring social distancing norms was an impossible task since there were tens of thousands of mosques all over the country. In such a scenario, allowing daily congregational prayers for a whole month could well have facilitated the corona virus pandemic to spread far and wide leading to a major increase in infections and casualties that was witnessed later.

The Tableeghi Jamaat congregation in Raiwind in March that led to a spike in COVID-19 cases had provided strong evidence of what happens when social distancing was not observed during religious events. Despite this example, for the government to have allowed congregational prayers during Ramazan showed that it buckled under the pressure of the clerics with Imran Khan once again failing to exercise strong leadership in a crisis.[71]

Judiciary

The judiciary, too, played its part in the COVID-19 saga in Pakistan. First, in mid-April in a suo moto (on its own volition) hearing, the Supreme Court chief justice calling for a uniform policy, warned the Sindh provincial government not to close businesses and services that generated revenue for the federation. This led to the Sindh government falling in line with the centre.[72] Again, on 19 May, the Supreme Court noted that provinces were constitutionally bound to follow Islamabad's directives.[73]

In an important but strange development, a full bench of the Supreme Court on 18 May ordered the provincial governments to open all shopping malls. It also set aside the federal government's decision to close shops, markets and businesses on Saturdays and Sundays, saying it reflected no justifiable rationale. The court held that the virus "apparently is not a pandemic in Pakistan" and questioned why fighting it was "swallowing so much money".[74] Though impinging on executive authority, the PTI government saw this as a vindication of its position that a lockdown was not needed.

The court's observation about there being no pandemic in Pakistan was contrary to the WHO's declaration of COVID-19 being a global pandemic and the reality of hundreds of thousands who had already died and millions who had been infected world-wide. Pakistan was in danger of having the unique but dubious distinction of being perhaps the only country that was in denial about the pandemic.

Conclusion

Pakistan, like the rest of the world, was faced with a huge calamity. Whether the pandemic overwhelmed a country or not depended largely on the ability or otherwise of the government to provide leadership, unify the country and take the hard measures required. On this account, despite the official figures, Imran Khan showed a paucity of leadership traits. Imran Khan needed to heed the warning of the Chinese medical team in Pakistan that the outbreak could be far bigger than the confirmed numbers showed, since shortage of testing kits was masking true numbers. One Pakistani doctor summed it up best when she told the media: "We're likely to have a very big outbreak, no matter what we do now. And we will not be equipped to handle the numbers. There will be breakdowns at many levels. Better border controls and quarantine measures should have been instituted a lot earlier, but I think the cat's now out of the bag."[75]

Given its poor medical infrastructure, poorer social distancing measures, lack of leadership, an economy on the brink and a polarized polity, Pakistan could potentially face a public health disaster that under-reporting positive cases would not resolve. Even with the official numbers, the potential second wave could serve to shake the government from its complacency.

NOTES

1. International Crisis Group, 'Pakistan's COVID-19 Crisis' 7 August 2020, https://www.crisisgroup.org/asia/south-asia/pakistan/b162-pakistans-COVID-19-crisis
2. COVID-19 : Umar hints at health sector's inability to deal with rising cases, *Business Recorder*, 6 April 2020, https://epaper.brecorder.com/2020/04/06/10-page/832633-news.html
3. PM sees outbreak taking turn for the worse by month's end, *Daily Times*, 10 April. 2020, https://dailytimes.com.pk/592886/pm-sees-outbreak-taking-turn-for-the-worse-by-months-end/
4. 27pc cases due to local transmission, *Daily Times*, 31 March 2020, https://dailytimes.com.pk/586031/27pc-cases-due-to-local-transmission/
5. '58% of Pakistan's corona virus cases locally transmitted', *Daily Times*, 17 April 2020, https://dailytimes.com.pk/597163/58-of-pakistans-coronavirus-cases-locally-transmitted/
6. 'PTI govt guilty if death toll multiplies: Sherry', *Dawn*, 24 June 2020, https://www.dawn.com/news/1564831/pti-govt-guilty-if-death-toll-multiplies-sherry
7. 'On a rampage', *The Express Tribune*, 16 June 2020, https://tribune.com.pk/story/2243216/on-a-rampage
8. Maleeha Lodhi, 'Reaping a bitter harvest', *Dawn*, 22 June 2020, https://dawn.com/news/3000974/reaping-a-bitter-harvest
9. International Crisis Group, 'Pakistan's COVID-19 Crisis', 7 August 2020, https://www.crisisgroup.org/asia/south-asia/pakistan/b162-pakistans-COVID-19-crisis
10. Zeba Sattar, "Lives not worth saving", *Dawn*, 13 June 2020, https://www.dawn.com/news/1563196
11. 'Some Hope', *The Nation*, 26 June 2020, https://nation.com.pk/26-Jun-2020/some-hope
12. 'Premature optimism', *Dawn*, 26 June 2020, https://www.dawn.com/news/1565272/premature-optimism
13. 'No confusion?' *Daily Times*, 26 June 2020, https://dailytimes.com.pk/631989/no-confusion/
14. International Crisis Group, 'Pakistan's COVID-19 Crisis', 7 August 2020, https://www.crisisgroup.org/asia/south-asia/pakistan/b162-pakistans-COVID-19-crisis
15. 'Pakistan recording 1,000 new virus cases on average daily: WHO', *Pakistan Today*, 7 May 2020, https://www.pakistantoday.com.pk/2020/05/07/pakistan-recording-1000-new-virus-cases-average-daily/

16. 'Force without direction', *Pakistan Today*, 28 August 2020. www.pakistantoday.com.pk/2020/08/27/force-without-direction/
17. International Crisis Group, 'Pakistan's COVID-19 Crisis' 7 August 2020, https://www.crisisgroup.org/asia/south-asia/pakistan/b162-pakistans-COVID-19-crisis
18. Pakistan reports 4,471 cases of COVID-19 in a day, *The Nation*, 22 June 2020, https://nation.com.pk/22-Jun-2020/pakistan-reports-89-deaths-by-coronavirus-4-471-cases-in-a-day
19. 'WHO recommends 'intermittent, targeted' lockdowns in Pakistan', *The Express Tribune*, 9 June 2020, https://tribune.com.pk/story/2239223/1-recommends-intermittent-lockdown-punjab
20. Corona killing four an hour in Pakistan, *The News*, 11 June 2020, https://www.thenews.com.pk/print/670728-corona-killing-four-an-hour-in-pakistan
21. 'An alarming decision', *Dawn*, 3 June 2020, https://www.dawn.com/news/1560989/an-alarming-decision
22. Zahid Hussain, 'Blundering into disaster', *Dawn*, 3 June 2020, https://www.dawn.com/news/1560990/blundering-into-disaster
23. Maleeha Lodhi, 'Flight from reality', *Dawn*, 8 June 2020, www.dawn.com/news/1562090/flight-from-reality
24. Khurram Husain, 'Losing without a fight', *Dawn*, 4 June 2020, https://www.dawn.com/news/1561161
25. 'A belated realisation', *Pakistan Today*, 17 June 2020, https://www.pakistantoday.com.pk/2020/06/16/a-belated-realisation/
26. 'Survey shows whopping majority thinks inhaling steam, ablution wards off COVID-19', *The News*, 12 April 2020, https://www.thenews.com.pk/latest/643399-survey-shows-whopping-majority-thinks-inhaling-steam-ablution-wards-of-COVID-19
27. 'Perception and the pandemic', *The News*, 23 June 2020, https://www.thenews.com.pk/print/676293-perception-and-the-pandemic
28. 'Talking lockdowns', *The News*, 16 June 2020, https://www.thenews.com.pk/print/673126-talking-lockdowns
29. 'Spike in cases', *The Express Tribune*, 9 April 2020, https://tribune.com.pk/story/2193729/6-spike-in-cases/
30. Ikram Junaidi, ''Pakistan virus cases cross 5,000 mark, *Dawn*, 12 April 2020, https://www.dawn.com/news/1548527/pakistan-virus-cases-cross-5000-mark
31. Ikram Junaidi, 'Number of virus tests drops across country except in Sindh', *Dawn*, 29 April 2020, https://www.dawn.com/news/1553087
32. Usman Hanif, 'COVID-19 detection higher in Pakistan than Xinjiang: Chinese doctor', *The Express Tribune*, 09 April 2020, https://tribune.com.pk/story/2193693/1-COVID-19-detection-higher-pakistan-xinjiang-chinese-doctor/
33. Ikram Junaidi, 'COVID-19 cases may increase by 15-20pc next week', *Dawn*, 22 May 2020
34. 'Just in a month: Pakistan faced 242pc surge in deaths', *The News*, 15 June 2020, https://www.thenews.com.pk/print/672682-from-may-14-to-june-14-pakistan-faced-242pc-surge-in-deaths
35. 'COVID-19: Data shows Pakistan utilising only a third of its testing capacity', *The News*, 08 July 2020, https://www.thenews.com.pk/latest/683849-COVID-19-data-shows-pakistan-utilising-only-a-third-of-its-testing-capacity
36. Doctors' forum stresses need to enhance COVID-19 testing in Pakistan, *The Nation*, 13 July, 2020, https://nation.com.pk/13-Jul-2020/doctors-forum-stresses-need-to-enhance-COVID-19-testing-in-pakistan

37. 'Covid by numbers', *The News,* 3 July 2020, https://www.thenews.com.pk/print/681094-covid-by-numbers.
38. 'The pandemic rages on', *Pakistan Today,* 29 June 2020, https://www.pakistantoday.com.pk/2020/06/28/the-pandemic-rages-on/
39. 'PML-N states low COVID-19 test rate', *Dawn,* 21 May 2020.
40. Hassaan Ahmed, 'APC accuses Punjab govt of concealing actual number of COVID-19 deaths' *Daily Times,* 8 June 2020, https://dailytimes.com.pk/623516/apc-accuses-punjab-govt-of-concealing-actual-number-of-COVID-19-deaths/
41. Umar Cheema, 'How authentic is official death count?' *The News,* 18 June 2020, www.thenews.com.pk/print/674346-how-authentic-is-official-death-count
42. Tufail Ahmed, '3,265 bodies brought to 30 graveyards of Karachi in 49 days, data reveals', *The Express Tribune,* 17 April 2020, https://tribune.com.pk/story/2199754/1-3265-bodies-brought-30-graveyards-karachi-49-days-data-reveals/
43. Omer Farooq Khan, 'In Pak, fears that COVID-19 deaths may be higher than reported', *Times of India,* https://timesofindia.indiatimes.com/world/pakistan/in-pak-fears-that-COVID-19-deaths-may-be-higher-than-reported/articleshow/75188698.cms
44. Muhammad Hassan Ayub, 'Foolish optimism or wise pessimism?', *Pakistan Today,* 24 June 2020, https://www.pakistantoday.com.pk/2020/06/23/foolish-optimism-or-wise-pessimism/
45. 'Nearly 50% Pakistanis yet to take precautionary steps against coronavirus', *The Express Tribune,* 01 April 2020, https://tribune.com.pk/story/2188169/1-nearly-50-pakistanis-yet-take-precautionary-steps-coronavirus/
46. Tufail Ahmed, 'Half of Pakistanis unaware of common risk factors for coronavirus', *The Express Tribune,* 16 April 2020, https://tribune.com.pk/story/2198770/1-half-pakistanis-unaware-common-risk-factors-coronavirus/
47. Amer Malik, '670,800 feared infected, no Lahore locality virus-free', *The News,* 2 June 2020. www.thenews.com.pk/print/666800-670-800-feared-infected-no-lahore-locality-virus-free
48. Asif Chaudhry, 'Punjab ignores dire warning over asymptomatic patients', *Dawn,* 2 June 2020. www.dawn.com/news/1560664/punjab-ignores-dire-warning-over-asymptomatic-patients
49. 'Playing politics with pandemic figures', *Pakistan Today,* 09 June 2020, https://www.pakistantoday.com.pk/2020/06/08/playing-politics-with-pandemic-figures/
50. Azeem Samar, 'COVID-19 patients will soon emerge from every home as epidemic out of control, PA told', *The News,* 05 June 2020. www.thenews.com.pk/print/668039-COVID-19-patients-will-soon-emerge-from-every-home-as-epidemic-out-of-control-pa-told
51. 'Number of Covid patients in Balochistan may reach 100,000 soon', *Dawn,* 14 June 2020, https://www.dawn.com/news/1563429/number-of-covid-patients-in-balochistan-may-reach-100000-soon-official
52. 'Troubling projections', *Dawn,* 16 June 2020, https://www.dawn.com/news/1563859/troubling-projections
53. 'PTI govt guilty if death toll multiplies: Sherry', *Dawn,* 24 June 2020, https://www.dawn.com/news/1564831/pti-govt-guilty-if-death-toll-multiplies-sherry
54. Haris Ahmed, 'Pakistan's economy in deep trouble', *The Express Tribune,* 27 April 2020, https://tribune.com.pk/story/2207551/2-pakistans-economy-deep-trouble/
55. Khaleeq Kiani, 'Economy to contract even more than estimated earlier: WB', *Dawn,* 9 June 2020. www.dawn.com/news/1562327/economy-to-contract-even-more-than-estimated-earlier-wb
56. Iftikhar A. Khan 'Another 10m likely to slip below poverty line', *Dawn,* 12 June 2020,

https://www.dawn.com/news/1562982/another-10m-likely-to-slip-below-poverty-line

57. Amumtaz Alvi, '1m small entities to shut for good: 18 million people may lose job, says Asad Umar', *The News*, 4 May 2020, https://www.thenews.com.pk/print/653670-18-million-people-may-lose-job-asad-umar
58. 'Covid disparities', *The News*, 6 May 2020, https://www.thenews.com.pk/print/654523-covid-disparities
59. 'Centre, Sindh undecided over impending locust menace', *The Express Tribune*, 3 May 2020, https://tribune.com.pk/story/2213354/1-centre-sindh-undecided-impending-locust-menace/
60. Hari Lohano, 'Food insecurity and hunger in Pakistan', *The Express Tribune*, 24 June 2020, https://tribune.com.pk/story/2249020/6-food-insecurity-hunger-pakistan/
61. Pakistan's coronavirus cases can rise to 200,000 by mid July sans 'effective interventions': WHO, GEO TV, 23 April 2020, https://www.geo.tv/latest/284567-pakistans-coronavirus-cases-can-rise-to-200000-by-mid-july-sans-effective-measures-who
62. 'PM launches cash disbursal program for workers today', *Dawn*, 18 May 2020, https://www.dawn.com/news/1557911
63. Kirti Joshi, 'Millions would have starved if lockdown wasn't lifted: PM Khan', Inshorts, 21 May 2020, https://inshorts.com/en/news/millions-wouldve-starved-if-covid19-lockdown-in-pak-wasnt-eased-imran-1590032597633.
64. Zeba Sattar, "Lives not worth saving", *Dawn*, 13 June 2020, https://www.dawn.com/news/1563196
65. 'A risky concession', *Pakistan Today*, 19 April 2020, https://www.pakistantoday.com.pk/2020/04/18/a-risky-concession/
66. Kalbe Ali, 'Govt accepts most demands of clerics', *Dawn*, 19 April 2020, https://www.dawn.com/news/1550419/govt-accepts-most-demands-of-clerics
67. Manzoor Ali, 'Violations of SOPs for mosques aggravates situation in KP,' *Dawn*, 6 May 2020, https://www.dawn.com/news/1554899
68. ICG Report.
69. 'Survey shows whopping majority thinks inhaling steam, ablution wards off COVID-19', *The News*, 12 April 2020, https://www.thenews.com.pk/latest/643399-survey-shows-whopping-majority-thinks-inhaling-steam-ablution-wards-of-COVID-19
70. Crisis Group telephone interviews, health professionals, Karachi, Islamabad, May 2020.
71. For a detailed look at Imran Khan's leadership in the crisis see the author's article 'Imran Khan fails to deliver, *The Tribune*, 20 April, 2020, https://www.tribuneindia.com/news/comment/imran-khan-fails-to-deliver-73534
72. 'Sindh can't close entities paying taxes to centre: SC', *The Express Tribune*, 04 May 2020, https://tribune.com.pk/story/2214213/sindh-cant-close-entities-paying-taxes-centre-sc
73. 'Provinces are bound to follow Centre's directives: SC', *The Express Tribune*, 19 May 2020, https://tribune.com.pk/story/2224700/1-people-not-taking-COVID-19-seriously-scs-remarks-ag-tells-court
74. Nasir Iqbal, 'SC orders opening of all shopping malls', *Dawn*,19 May 2020, https://www.dawn.com/news/1558179.
75. 'Coronavirus exposes underfunded health infrastructure', *Dawn*, 24 March 2020, https://www.dawn.com/news/1543298/coronavirus-exposes-underfunded-health-infrastructure

4

Economy in 2019: Trends and Challenges

Prateek Joshi

Introduction

The year 2019 began with a sombre projection for Pakistan's economy after the high expectations from the China Pakistan Economic Corridor (CPEC) and Imran Khan's leadership skills crumbled beneath the structural inefficiencies that have ailed the Pakistani economy for a long time. After enjoying a consumption-driven growth bubble financed by massive borrowings during former Prime Minister Nawaz Sharif's last term, the macroeconomic situation became unsustainable by the time Imran Khan took charge as the current Prime Minister in 2018. The situation gave the ruling party an alibi to cover its own limitations and justify its decision to approach the International Monetary Fund (IMF), after much dithering, for a bailout. The Budget for the Fiscal Year (FY) 2019-20 estimated a growth rate at 2.4 per cent (the lowest in a decade) and the Fiscal Deficit at 7.2 per cent of GDP.[1] The falling growth outlook, combined with depleting foreign exchange reserves, once again forced Islamabad to seek external support, ranging from its traditional allies to the International Monetary Fund. The challenges also resulted in the replacement of erstwhile Finance Minister Asad Umar with a former World Bank technocrat, Hafeez Sheikh, with a new designation as Advisor to the Prime Minister on Finance and Revenue. This chapter looks at Pakistan's turbulent economic trajectory in the year 2019 in the context of its structural deficiencies and the political economy of external bailouts that have tied its fiscal fate with the IMF's conditionalities tighter than ever before. This, in turn, adversely affects the ruling Pakistan Tehreek-e-Insaf's (PTI's) political capital as the gap between promise and delivery continues to widen on multiple fronts.

Naya Pakistan and the Road to IMF

Besides promising a rejuvenated ideological narrative for Pakistan, the *Naya Pakistan* election manifesto of the PTI single-stepped solutions on restructuring the economy by rectifying wrongs committed by the previous regimes. Soon after taking charge, however, the limits of this rhetoric became obvious and the government resorted to fire-fighting to prevent a crisis. In a nutshell, stagnating growth rate, rising domestic-cum-external debt, rising circular debt and a narrow Tax-to-GDP ratio have defined Pakistan's economic performance in the last few years.

To begin with, the economic indicators of FY 2018-19 would help to comprehend the challenges that have shaped the performance of the subsequent year. Pakistan achieved a GDP growth rate of 3.29 per cent in FY 2018-9, much less than the anticipated official projections of 6 per cent. Fiscal Deficit rose to 5 per cent of the GDP, up from 4.3 per cent in the preceding financial year. The growth rate in the agricultural and industrial sectors remained dismally low at 0.8 per cent and 1.4 per cent, respectively, as against the targets of 3.8 per cent and 7.6 per cent. Overall, the agricultural sector registered a negative growth rate in major crops like rice, cotton and sugarcane (with total crop production falling by 4.4 per cent compared to the previous year). In the industrial sector, mining and quarrying declined by 1.96 per cent, and large-scale manufacturing registered a 2.09 per cent decline. According to the Pakistan Economic Survey (PES) 2018-19, the reasons cited for the subdued industrial activity included "lower PSDP expenditures compared to last year, muted private sector construction activities and lower consumer spending on durable goods amongst others". The PES recorded that during the July-March 2019 phase, "total revenue registered zero growth, while growth in total expenditures was 8.7 per cent", resulting in higher Fiscal Deficit.

Between July 2018 and March 2019, Pakistan's "total debt and liabilities went up by PKR 6 trillion, increasing from PKR 28.879 trillion in June 2018 to PKR 35.094 trillion", amounting to 91.2 per cent of the nation's GDP.[2] By end of FY 2018-19, circular debt reached PKR 1.5 trillion, up from PKR 1.03 trillion in the preceding year.[3]

External debt rose to USD 105.8 billion by the first quarter of 2019, up by USD 9.9 billion "in the fourth quarter of 2018".[4] Some relief was noted in the

Current Account Deficit (CAD), which fell by 27 per cent during July-March 2019 and stood at 4.1 per cent of the GDP. According to the Pakistan Economic Survey 2018-19, the fall in CAD resulted from the relatively higher decline in the imports compared to exports in the above-mentioned time frame.

The new government exhausted the available options in order to shore up its depleting foreign exchange reserves and to address fiscal challenges in order to avoid the IMF route, as evident in the former Finance Minister's speech while introducing the second mini-budget, wherein he stated that "his aim had been to eliminate all factors that necessitate a return to the International Monetary Fund for a bailout package by successive regimes."[5]

Within the first six months of taking charge, the government came out with two mini-budgets with a dichotomous policy entailing expenditure cuts, accompanied with the easing of the tax/duty structures and other quick-fix solutions aimed at stimulating industrial activity. For instance, Public Sector Development Expenditure was reduced by PKR 250 billion compared to the previous year in the first mini-budget. Some highlights of the later efforts included a reduction in taxes levied on small and medium scale enterprises, reduction in interest rate charged on agricultural loans, relaxations in taxes/duties associated with the renewable energy sector (to reduce dependence on energy imports), etcetera.

In a reversal of the Pakistan Muslim League-Nawaz led government's approach, the exchange rate was deregulated with the dual aim of signalling the IMF of Pakistan's amenability to adjust to its rule book as well as making exports competitive to check CAD. Even though the IMF route was eventually availed, Pakistan managed to stave off the crisis for the short to mid-term time period by exploiting its traditional alliances with China and the Middle East. The PES gives a breakup of approximately USD 9.2 billion it secured in FY 2018-19 to shore up its forex reserves, of which Saudi Arabia gave "USD 3 billion in short loan and USD 3 billion in the shape of deferred payment on oil imports. Similarly, the UAE government provided USD 1 billion, whereas China has given USD 2.2 billion."[6] However, the data does not match with the details of the agreement with Saudi Arabia. During Prince Salman's visit to Pakistan in February 2019, it was reported that Saudi Arabia and Pakistan signed a three-year agreement in which Pakistan would receive oil supplies on deferred payments worth USD 275 million per month from July 2019 onwards, according to which Pakistan secured approximately USD 9.9 billion for three years.[7]

Simultaneously, Pakistan worked on two key pre-requisites for the bailout by allowing its currency to adjust to market forces and raising the price of basic utilities that otherwise consumed a substantial part of non-capital expenditure. The State Bank of Pakistan changed its earlier policy of managed float (where the government intervenes time to time to stabilize the exchange rate) to the IMF-directed policy of market-based float system.

Only a few days before the IMF formally assented to the bailout program, the exchange rate (which was well below 150 rupees to a dollar till mid 2019) crossed the 160 mark, depreciating by as much as 7 rupees on one single day in June 2019.[8] Between May and June—a crucial phase between IMF's in-principle approval and formalization of the agreement—the rupee depreciated by almost twenty rupees, indicating Pakistan's adherence to the IMF's pre-conditions.

Roughly, two months after taking charge, the new government sought the 13th bailout from the IMF while maintaining an ambiguous stance given its populist orientation and Imran Khan's long history of criticism of international financial institutions. At the same time, the then Finance Minister continued to deny reports of any engagement with the IMF. In reality, the government not only exhausted all avenues that would reduce the amount sought to a feasible scale but also agreed to carry out reforms to speed up the process. Imran Khan, meanwhile, attempted to hard-balance his populist agenda, which was reflected in the form of tax reliefs in the mini budget and a massive low-cost housing scheme, among many others, the limitations of which were soon to be realised. An IMF team visited Pakistan in October 2018, followed by IMF Chief Christine Lagard's visit in March 2019.

In April 2019, the government released a reported titled 'Road map to Stability, Growth and Productive Employment', wherein it identified the structural problems and its willingness to carry out wide-ranging reforms, from proposing tax reforms, power sector reforms, restructuring public sector enterprises and other stringent accountability measures to narrowing of the revenue expenditure gap.[9]

The negotiations phase also gave rise to many speculations as Asad Umar was forced to step down in the midst of the talks. One strong theory doing the rounds was to do with IMF's insistence to cut defence expenditure as part of the Government's fiscal consolidation efforts. While it would be naive to believe that Umar must have agreed to this during the course of negotiations, the fact that the issue came up in the discussions with the IMF might have prompted the Army into action. Even if a cut in defence expenditure was not forthcoming,

Umar's removal put an end to the debate on a potential compromise with defence expenditure. This is corroborated by the appointment of Dr. Hafeez Sheikh who replaced Umar as the Financial Advisor to the Prime Minister. Sheikh has been associated with the World Bank and has long experience of working with international financial institutions. He served as Privatisation Minister during the Musharraf era and during his term as the Finance Minister in the last Pakistan People's Party (PPP) government, he unsuccessfully led the negotiations with the IMF. Pakistan eventually secured the bailout in 2013, but only after the PML-N came to power. For reasons best known to the establishment, the appointment of an economist with a history of unsuccessful negotiations with the IMF did not make sense at that critical juncture. Further, Umar had not been on good terms with Jahangir Tareen who happened to be the PTI's other power centre and a close confidante of Imran Khan. In the ongoing austerity drive, it is believed that he had planned on cutting the massive sugar subsidies, which put the powerful sugar lobby in action against him. Jahangir Tareen himself is a sugar baron, which might have prompted him to act against Umar.

Finally, in May 2019, the IMF gave an in-principle approval for the bailout and its Executive Board approved a USD6 billion loan request in July 2019. The disbursement would be spread over a period of 39 months. In lieu, Pakistan has been subjected to a spectrum of conditions, namely:[10]

1. Flexible exchange rate and tightening of monetary policy (to increase interest rates and attract foreign exchange inflows) with the aim of "correcting imbalances, rebuilding reserves, and keeping inflation low including freeing of exchange rate controls."
2. To make fiscal consolidation sustainable, increasing "revenue mobilization by 4 to 5 per cent of GDP at the federal and the provincial level" during the phase of the present program.
3. "Depoliticizing gas and power tariff setting and over the program period, gradually bringing the sector to cost recovery".
4. Finally, the fact that the IMF agreed to the program only after a thorough examination of the CPEC conditionalities also accounts for much of its strictness out of America's fear that the amount could be diverted to repay loans to China.

The Budget 2019-20 was unveiled amidst this backdrop.

Budget 2019-20: Unrealistic Ambitions

The total estimated expenditure in the budget was PKR 7.022 trillion, along with an outlay of PKR 8.24 trillion with a current expenditure (non-asset generating expenditure) of PKR 7.29 trillion. Estimated current expenditure registered an alarming rise of 75 per cent over the FY 2018-19 figure (PKR 4.7 trillion) with the largest increase coming from a rise in domestic and foreign debt servicing from PKR 1.9 to PKR 2.8 trillion (almost 48 per cent). Since the government could not do much about cutting the current expenditure, consisting of payments on loans, interests and other day-to-day governance expenditures, as compensation, it cut development expenditure by 17.4 per cent, from PKR 1.15 trillion to PKR 950 billion (of which PKR 700 billion is allocated to the Public Sector Development Plan (PSDP). For the provincial share of the PSDP, the government allocated PKR 917 billion.

The socio-economic sector registered serious expenditure cuts. The Education Budget stood at PKR 77 billion, a reduction of PKR 20 billion from the amount allocated in FY 2018-19. Allocation under the head of Economic Affairs (spending on agriculture, mining, manufacturing, construction and communication) registered a steep cut from the PKR 142 billion last year to PKR 84 billion in the present budget (almost 70 per cent reduction). It is not clear what led to such a reduced allocation to this head for FY 2019-20, especially when actual allocation (PKR 142 billion) rose by 80 per cent over the proposed allocation (PKR 80 billion) in FY 2018-19.

Gross Revenue target was estimated at PKR 6.71 trillion, which is 25 per cent higher than the collection during FY 2018-19 (PKR 5.031 trillion). Given the pressure to raise revenues, an ambitious tax revenue target of PKR 5.55 trillion was projected, almost 35 per cent higher than the amount raised last year (PKR 4.15 trillion). One of the main goals is to raise direct taxes by 25 per cent to PKR 2.09 trillion and indirect taxes by a staggering 39 per cent to PKR 3.4 trillion. The budget even proposed a 40 per cent hike in the non-tax revenue to PKR 894 billion.

Such ambitious targets against the backdrop of the challenges faced by the Pakistani economy naturally raises questions about Pakistan's ability to raise revenue. In the domain of direct taxes, the government took the unpopular route of reducing income tax slabs from Rs. 12 lakh per annum to Rs. 6 lakh per annum, a move that has not gone down well with the middle class. Given the poor history of tax collection and rampant tax evasion, Pakistan has one of the lowest tax-to-GDP ratios in the world at below 11 per cent. Only two million people file income tax returns—out of which 600,000 are employees in the organized sector. Nearly 380 companies account for 80 per cent of the total tax.

There are over 341,000 electricity and gas connections, but only 40,000 (less than 10 per cent) are registered with sales tax. Only 1.4 million out of 3.1 million commercial consumers pay tax. Out of 50 million bank accounts, only 10 per cent pay tax. Out of 100,000 companies registered with the Security and Exchange Commission of Pakistan, only half pay tax. Pakistan's revenue collection target in all their budgets has been ambitious; the last five years' record shows a shortfall in actually meeting targets in the revised estimates. For FY 2018-19 too, the net revenue receipts were 17 per cent lower than the target estimate. Given these challenges, the benchmarks set by the budget are not only ambitious but also risk eroding the PTI's political capital.

Conclusion

Shedding its pre-election rhetoric, the PTI not only approached the IMF, but also appeared more than willing to take unpopular decisions to align its economic policies with the IMF's directives. At the time of writing this chapter, the course correction has yielded some results, a development that can be described as a combination of policy planning and inadvertent developments. For instance, the CAD contracted to USD 1.54 billion in the first quarter of FY20 compared to USD 4.28 billion in the same quarter of last year following the Central Bank's decision to depreciate the currency and increase the benchmark interest rates, thereby raising the dollar value of remittances and discouraging imports. Lately, the Current Account Surplus figure of $424 million in July 2020 has been a matter of celebration, but it resulted from higher remittances and a decline in imports in the pandemic phase.

By January 2020, the total debt rose only by 4 per cent to PKR 33 billion over a period of seven months, a development initially dubbed as an improvement but it soared further to PKR 36.3 billion by the end of June 2020.[11] Also, massive depreciation of the rupee made energy imports relatively expensive, which spilled over as higher fuel prices and power tariff. Much of the hike in the power tariff came from higher capacity charges in 2019, or "charges paid to power producers for unused electricity (that constitute the bulk of power tariffs in Pakistan)", which rose by 60 per cent.[12] The marginal improvements notwithstanding, it is too early to predict whether they could contribute to the larger goal of restructuring the economy and controlling the rising debt figures. In the light of the reduced allocation towards Development Expenditure in the FY 2019-20 Budget, the present challenges could even exacerbate if the targets of raising revenues and institutional capacity building are not balanced by a concomitant allocation to the productive sectors of the economy. Last, but not the least, the federal structure in Pakistan has come under duress as the Federal Government increasingly targets the provinces for slowing down the desired pace needed to restructure the overall economy. In its annual report, the State Bank of Pakistan targeted the provincial governments for their "lack of institutional capacity" and inability to carry out the reforms necessary for capacity building, which resulted in "lower revenue collection that contributed less to tax-to-GDP ratio and fiscal consolidation efforts".[13] This has been interpreted as an attack on the 18th Constitutional Amendment (of 2010), which, besides restoring parliamentary powers, also granted substantial autonomy to the provinces. The politicization of the matter threatens to re-ignite the regional tendencies, mainly in Sindh and Balochistan, which have witnessed varying forms of identity assertions. These challenges also explain why the Pakistan Army's top leadership (including the Army Chief himself) has stepped in to discuss the prevailing economic situation and potential solutions.

Lastly, as the regional geopolitical environment shifts gears, in the absence of any major economic restructuring, Pakistan is preoccupied in revaluating its international economic partnerships considering its recurring aid/loan dependencies from external sources. Despite the preponderance of economics in determining the present-day international clout of any nation, Pakistan's obsession with Kashmir and its attempts to forge newer transnational religious alliances put it at the crossroads with Riyadh whose discomfort resulted in deferment of the oil supply agreement that provided a major cushion to the Pakistani economy. The vacuum is being filled by Beijing, as demonstrated by its swift transfer of $ 1 billion to Islamabad after Riyadh urgently demanded the repayment of an oil purchase loan to Pakistan. While the government appears more committed to embark on major economic reforms, the visible constants appear to be manifesting in the form of an ever-increasing dependence on Chinese largesse (with potential strings attached), both for the CPEC and the economy at large.

The author is a PhD candidate at the University of Oxford.

NOTES

1. Hufsa Chaudhry, "Budget 2020: Govt predicts 2.4pc growth, Rs7 trillion in expenditures", *Dawn*, Islamabad, June 12, 2019.
2. Mehtab Haider, "Pakistan's total debt, liabilities rise to Rs35tr", *The News International*, Karachi, May 21, 2019.
3. Khalid Mustafa, "Power sector circular debt soars to Rs1,032b", *The News International*, Karachi, July 11, 2018.

4. Panos Mourdoukoutas, "IMF Won't Stop China From Turning Pakistan Into The Next Sri Lanka", *Forbes*, New Jersey, July 4, 2019.
5. "Finance Minister Asad Umar presents third finance bill for fiscal 2019 amidst loud protests", *Dawn*, Islamabad, January 23, 2019.
6. Pakistan Economic Survey, Government of Pakistan.
7. Saudi oil supply to Pakistan on deferred payment begins, *Radio Pakistan*, Islamabad, July 1, 2019.
8. Talqeen Zubairi, "Dollar continues climb against rupee", *Dawn*, Islamabad, June 27, 2019.
9. "Road map to Stability, Growth and Productive Employment", Government of Pakistan, Finance Division, Islamabad, April 8, 2019.
10. IMF Executive Board Approves US$6 billion 39-Month EFF Arrangement for Pakistan, *IMF*, July 3, 2019. Link: https://www.imf.org/en/News/Articles/2019/07/03/pr19264-pakistan-imf-executive-board-approves-39-month-eff-arrangement
11. Shahbaz Rana, "Govt debt rises only 4% to Rs33tr by end-January", *The Express Tribune*, Karachi, March 11, 2020.
12. Capacity payments swell 60pc to Rs 664bln in FY2019, *The News International*, Karachi, July 17, 2019.
13. Dr. Ikramul Haq & Huzaima Bukhari, "Pakistan's fiscal dilemma", *The News International*, Karachi, November 17, 2019.

5

Pakistan's Economy under Imran Khan

V. Srinivas, IAS

Abstract: *Prime Minister Imran Khan promised a growth rate of 6 per cent; in his tenure, Pakistan recorded growth rates of 3.3 per cent in 2018-19 and 2.4 per cent in 2019-20. Development Expenditures are currently below 2018 levels and external debt has risen from USD 95 billion to USD 106 billion. In 2020, Prime Minister Imran Khan will be completing two years of his electoral tenure in August 2020. There exist enormous challenges on the economic front and meeting public expectations remains an uphill task.*

Introduction

Imran Khan assumed office as the 22nd Prime Minister of Pakistan on 18 August 2018. The PTI reform agenda envisaged driving Pakistan's economy on a path to sustainable high growth. According to the PTI, the crux of the problem lay in flawed energy policies, spiralling fiscal deficit, grossly inadequate tax-to-GDP ratio, multiple bailouts by international agencies and under-investment in education, health and skills sectors. The PTI also identified antiquated governance, all-pervasive corruption and lack of political leadership as reasons for the long-term decline in the economy. The PTI said that a business as usual is not sustainable, as Pakistan will become the "poor man of the 21st century" with per capita debt of PKR 1,45,000 per Pakistani.

The PTI economic reform program envisaged creation of a fiscal space of 9 per cent of GDP with a 5 per cent increase in tax collections, 2 per cent reduction in wasteful expenditure and 2 per cent reduction in losses of PSE's. Further, the economic reforms vision projected a growth rate of 6 per cent, inflation to be brought down to 7 per cent, fiscal deficit to be brought down to 4.5 per cent, tax revenues to be raised by 15 per cent and a four-fold increase in welfare spending.

Structural reforms were envisaged in the energy sector, expenditure reform, revenue collection and human capital development. The Railway Ministry was to be abolished and replaced by a Railway Board, a fully autonomous board to manage the PSE similar to Malaysia's Khazanah. An expenditure emergency was to be announced with all Governor houses and PM house being converted to places of public use and expenses of the President to be cut by half. The number of federal ministries was to be reduced to 17 from 37, no development funds for parliamentarians and elimination of all discretionary funds.

It was clear that the Imran Khan Government faced formidable macroeconomic challenges. Current account deficits were widening, there were fiscal slippages, and an accommodative monetary policy stance. Foreign exchange reserves had declined to 2.3 months of import cover and debt-related vulnerabilities had increased. The foremost challenge the economy faced was to achieve higher growth rates without corresponding resources to support it. To address the severe macroeconomic instability, Pakistan needed to adopt policy measures with the objective of maintaining fiscal discipline, contain losses of public sector enterprises and adopt structural reforms, in addition to a tighter monetary policy stance.

In his first address to the nation, Prime Minister Imran Khan emphasized on cutting government expenditures as part of the cost-cutting initiative and several austerity measures were announced. The PTI Government banned the discretionary use of state funds and first-class air travel by officials and leaders, including the President and Prime Minister. Shortly thereafter, the PTI Government announced the sale of 100 luxury cars of the Prime Minister's House under the austerity drive. The sale was held on the lawns of PM House. The PTI Government hoped to get US$ 16 million from the sale but managed to make only US$ 600,000 from the sale of 70 cars. It was not easy to make the expenditure cuts that were necessary—cuts in defence spending, additional allocations to education were not feasible. The media criticized the PTI Government's U-turns on converting PM House into a research university named Islamabad National University and the failure to make any headway with the proposed education reforms or health care reforms. Quite clearly, the challenges of macroeconomic stabilization had taken precedence over the issues of growth.

The Quest for Energy and CPEC

Pakistan embarked on a massive investment program in energy and infrastructure to mitigate the chronic shortages, diversify the country's fuel mix and improve trade connectivity. The China–Pakistan Economic Corridor (CPEC), which is a large package of investment projects, totalling about US$ 55 billion (20 per cent of GDP) over a decadal period. There are 19 CPEC projects—US$ 17.7 billion in energy sector, US$ 5.9 billion in infrastructure, which are in the advanced stages of planning and implementation. The CPEC infrastructure and transport projects are financed by long-term concessional government borrowing from China, while the CPEC energy sector projects involved foreign direct investment and commercial borrowing from Chinese financial institutions. CPEC projects were expected to add about US$ 13 billion to the Pakistan economy over a decadal period. At the same time, Pakistan faced long-term payment outflows in the form of loan repayment, profit repatriation and imports of input fuel. The repayments are expected to rise every year reaching a peak of US$ 3.5–$ 4.5 billion by financial year 2024/25. It is important for Pakistan to build up foreign exchange reserves to cushion the impact of the enhanced payments outflows. This requires a significant amount of fiscal discipline, raising of tax revenues, restructuring of public sector enterprises to ensure cost recoveries and a gradual phasing of new external borrowing commitments.

The Inevitability of another IMF Program

Pakistan had been on an IMF program from 2013 to 2016. The policy agenda despite a prolonged IMF program had remained incomplete, requiring continued efforts for macroeconomic stability and growth supporting structural reforms. The IMF's discussions with Pakistani authorities in 2018 highlighted the risks of Pakistan's medium-term capacity to repay the IMF loans with the rising burden of Fund repayments in the years 2019-2024. Pakistan's repayments to the IMF were to commence at SDR 243 million in 2018 and peak at SDR 820 million in 2021, with a gradually declining schedule until 2026. The repayments amounted to 22 per cent of the foreign exchange reserves in 2022. Further, external imbalances had widened, international exchange reserves had declined and market confidence had eroded. The restructuring of Pakistan International Airlines, Pakistan Steel Mills and Pakistan Railways had not progressed and financial losses continued to accrue and the energy sector companies continued to incur new payment arrears. There were also external repayment obligations on account of CPEC investments. Quite clearly, Pakistan's capacity to make repayments was already fraught with high risks. It was in this scenario that Pakistan needed to approach the International Monetary Fund for the 22nd time.

On June 19, 2019, Reza Baqir, Governor of the State Bank of Pakistan, wrote to the Managing Director IMF seeking IMF assistance under the Extended

Fund Facility (EFF), on grounds that international reserves had reached critically low levels, balance of payments gap was still large in an environment of limited market access. The situation was grim and extremely worrisome. Macroeconomic vulnerabilities had increased on the back of weak policies, with pro-cyclical fiscal policies leading to a surge in fiscal deficit and an accommodative monetary policy resulting in a significant current account deficit. Fiscal deficit widened to 7.3 per cent for the second year and current account deficit, which stood at 6.3 per cent in 2018-19 narrowed on the back of 19 per cent rupee depreciation.

Reza Baqir said that although significant measures had been undertaken to meet the macroeconomic challenges, the structural challenges remained unaddressed and institutions had not been strengthened to ensure economic discipline. Further, a less favourable external environment had added to the difficult picture. The gradual policy measures—depreciation of the rupee, some monetary tightening and increase in gas prices were simply not enough to stabilize the economy. Comprehensive reforms became a felt need for fiscal tightening and addressing the maturing debt obligations in the coming years. Economic activity in Pakistan had slowed considerably with the agriculture, manufacturing and construction sectors witnessing considerable contraction owing to reduction in government spending. Economic growth declined to 3.3 per cent in 2019 from 5.5 per cent in 2018 while inflation accelerated to 9.1 per cent from 4.2 per cent in 2018.

Fiscal deficit continued to grow and the deterioration was due to revenue shortfalls, particularly in personal income tax collections. The tax-to-GDP ratio came down to 13 per cent, which is the lowest in South Asia. At the same time, expenditures continued to rise due to higher interest payments, subsidies and defence-related spending. Fiscal deficit was largely financed by increased borrowing from the State Bank of Pakistan. Power sector arrears accumulated in the past two years, and reached close to 4 per cent of GDP as a result of delays in adjusting tariffs, reversal of policies and non-payment of implicit subsidies by the government. Losses were also witnessed in major public sector enterprises like Pakistan International Airlines, Pakistan Steel Mills and Pakistan Railways, all of which amounted to 2 per cent of GDP. The banking sector remained stable but there was a lot of reluctance to lend to the government. Banks maintained the global norms of capital adequacy and non-performing loans in agriculture and SMEs remained high at 15 per cent. Unemployment was 6 per cent and 30 per cent of the population remained below the poverty line.

The external sector was substantially weakened. Exports were flat, the Pakistan rupee had depreciated by 21 per cent in FY 2018/19 and foreign direct investment inflows were weak.

Pakistan's twin deficits—fiscal and current account—had moved into unsustainable territory. Macroeconomic stability was a huge challenge. The overall situation of low savings, low revenue generation and high trade gap painted a grim economic picture, which needed an immediate bailout.

The IMF program 2019-2022

On July 3, 2019, the IMF Executive Board approved a 39-month extended arrangement under the Extended Fund Facility to Pakistan for an amount of USD 6 billion. This represented Pakistan's 22nd program with the IMF since Pakistan's membership of the IMF in 1950. The pace at which Pakistan's IMF program was approved, with low conditionality, indicated strong backing from large shareholders of the IMF—the USA, Japan, and EU member-countries. The IMF projected considerable positive estimation for a decisive turnaround in Pakistan's economy in the program period, which may not happen in the current sluggish global economic environment.

Pakistan's economic reform program supported by the EFF, has two main pillars: (a) macroeconomic stabilization; and (b) strengthen and build institutions. The key elements are the following:

(i) A decisive fiscal consolidation to reduce public debt and build resilience, with an ambitious FY 2020 budget, supported by comprehensive efforts to increase revenue mobilization by 4-5 per cent of GDP;
(ii) Expanding social spending including through the broadening and strengthening of safety nets to support the most vulnerable;
(iii) A flexible market-determined exchange rate, rebuilding of official reserves to provide a buffer against external shocks, monetary policy to shore up confidence and contain inflation;
(iv) Structural reforms through strengthening of institutions, increasing governance and transparency and promoting an investment-friendly environment to ensure sustainable growth.

Pakistan's EFF program that runs from July 3, 2019 to September 2, 2022 for a period of 39 months at 210 per cent of quota, is a frontloaded program with SDR 716 million (35 per cent of quota), the first tranche being released on July 3, 2019. The next four tranches of SDR 328 million (16 per cent of quota) will be due for release between December 6, 2019 and September 4, 2020. The last four tranches of SDR 560 million (28 per cent of quota) are due for release from March 5, 2021 to September 2, 2022. In all, four quarterly and four semi-annual reviews have been scheduled under the program.

Debt Sustainability

Pakistan's current external liabilities stand at USD 85.48 billion which is 43.4 per cent of GDP. External debt to China stands at USD 15.15 billion, to Japan at USD 5.67 billion and to Saudi Arabia at USD 6.41 billion. External debt to China is far more than the entire Paris Club debt. External debt risks remain high though the IMF has projected that external debt will decline after peaking in FY 2021.

Without strong and timely support from official/bilateral lenders, a return to a sustainable debt path is not possible. General Government and government-guaranteed debt stands at 80.5 per cent of GDP and the maturity structure of the public debt has worsened with 57 per cent of the public debt having a maturity of less than a year. The debt management strategy is aimed at lengthening the maturity profile and widening the investor base. Gross Official foreign exchange reserves currently stand at USD 11.2 billion, barely enough to cover two months of imports and are expected to increase to USD 28.1 billion which would be four months of import cover in the program period.

Over the Program period, IMF approval has the potential to unlock around USD 38 billion from Pakistan's international partners.

The expected support from bilateral and multilateral creditors is expected as follows:

1. China	US$ 6.3 billion
2. Saudi Arabia	US$ 6.2 billion
3. UAE	US$ 1 billion
4. World Bank	US$ 1.3 billion
5. Asian Development Bank	US$ 1.6 billion
6. Islamic Development Bank	US$ 1.1 billion

The gross inflows of multilateral and bilateral disbursement would be

July–September 2019	US$ 3 billion
October–December 2019	US$ 5 billion
January–March 2020	US$ 6.5 billion
April–June 2020	US$ 4.8 billion

Debt sustainability is an integral part of the program if these moneys are to materialize.

Fiscal Program

The IMF has said that there is a need to reduce fiscal and quasi-fiscal deficits and build stronger revenue mobilization. Pakistan seeks to increase revenue collection through a broad-based tax policy and bring down fiscal deficit. General Government Debt at 80 per cent of GDP has to be brought down to 67 per cent to create space for investment. Accordingly, the 2019-20 Budget proposed higher revenue measures for 1.7 per cent and power sector subsidies have been budgeted. However, there have not been major cuts in social sector spending with the Benazir Income Support Program (BISP) showing a slight increase in allocations. The BISP program reaches over 5 million families. The BISP program envisages a disbursement of Rs.1,000 to all BISP beneficiaries and launching of "one woman-one account" to bring 6 million women under financial inclusion.

Amongst the major tax policy reforms are measures aimed at removing exemptions and preferential treatment to reduce distortions in the tax systems and broaden the tax base. The first step is increased sales tax on petroleum products. Preferential sales tax rates for sugar, steel, edible oil, medium and large retailers exist. Removal of sales tax exemptions, simplifying filing procedures and increased compliance are proposed. Pakistan also seeks to strengthen the taxation on real estate and agricultural turnover. A shift from sales tax to VAT has been proposed in the coming years. A semi-independent tax authority is to be created and no further tax amnesty will be given. This is a continuous structural benchmark under the IMF program. The income tax threshold has been reduced for salaried and non-salaried individuals. A gift tax has been introduced. Federal excise duties on cigarettes, aerated drinks and cement have been introduced and Customs duty exemptions on LPG have been eliminated.

To increase fiscal discipline, Pakistan adopted a Public Fiscal Management Act, which necessitates Parliamentary approval for budget authorizations.

Monetary Policy Program

Macroeconomic stability remains a key area under the program. For this, the monetary policy needs to be tightened. There has been a cumulative upward revision since 2017 of 450 basis points in the policy rate and the rupee has moved 31 per cent against the dollar. Interest rates have risen above 10 per cent. While the Governors of the State Bank of Pakistan have pressed for a tax-to-GDP ratio of 15 per cent, primary and revenue surplus has remained a mirage with both tax and non-tax revenues well below the target. The State Bank of Pakistan has been pressing for deferred oil payments arrangements and increased government efforts to arrange for financing from China, Saudi Arabia and UAE to give Pakistan some cushion against the headwinds.

Monetary policy has been tightened and the inflation objective of 5-7 per cent has been laid down. One of the important steps envisaged under the program is elimination of the State Bank of Pakistan financing the budget deficit. Fiscal dominance had eliminated every semblance of autonomy of the State Bank of Pakistan (SBP). Hence, the continuous performance criterion under the IMF program sought that the Pakistan Government refrain from new direct financing of budget by the SBP. This is significant for the autonomy of the SBP. Amendments to the SBP Act are proposed to enhance operational independence, governance and the Governor's tenure.

The IMF program does not interfere with the ongoing social sector programs—the national financial inclusion strategy, the long-term financing facility, the export financing scheme, the low-cost housing plan, the SME financing plan and promotion of digital payments. The IMF has said that protecting the most vulnerable from the impact of adjustment policies is an important priority. As poverty reduction and social inclusion are crucial for sustainable growth, an indicative floor on social spending has been prescribed to support the most vulnerable. Pakistan's policy of protecting lower income households from higher energy prices will continue, although there will be a specific upward revision in the gas tariffs.

As with every IMF program, there is an emphasis on structural policies. Eliminating power sector losses on a sustainable basis will require new pricing and improvements in governance and infrastructure. Privatization of seven selected public sector enterprises, audit of Pakistan International Airlines and Pakistan Steel Mills, triage of SOE's and enhancing of SOE legal framework have been prescribed.

The IMF program also entails that Pakistan improves the effectiveness of the Anti Money Laundering (AML)/Combating the Financing of Terrorism (CFT) regime to support its exit from the Financial Action Task Force (FATF) list of jurisdictions owing to shortcomings in effectively addressing terrorist financing risks. The National Executive Committee of FATF is monitoring and coordinating the efforts to implement the FATF action plan.

Pakistan submitted a 500-page report to the Joint Group of the FATF on January 8, 2020, sharing the progress on the 27 points in a bid to come out of the grey list. The FATF in March 2020 has said that Pakistan will have to comply with 13 crucial points by June 2020, including prosecution and conviction of banned outfits and proscribed persons to exit from the grey list. The other points on which the FATF seeks Pakistan's compliance include effectiveness of sanctions to curb terrorist financing, to take action against illegal money or value transfer services, to put in place a sanction regime against cash couriers, to cut off funding of banned outfits and conversion of madrasas to schools and health units. The FATF's review meeting scheduled for June 2020 has been postponed due to the COVID-19 crisis and the review would now be held in October 2020.

Managing Director IMF Meeting with Prime Minister of Pakistan

On July 21, 2019 the Acting Managing Director of IMF, David Lipton, met Imran Khan, Prime Minister of Pakistan. In his discussions, the Acting Managing Director discussed the recent economic developments and the implementation by Pakistan of the economic reform program supported by the IMF. He said that Pakistan needed to mobilize domestic tax revenue now and place debt on a firm downward trend.

On November 8, 2019, the IMF staff and the Pakistan authorities reached an agreement on the policy reforms needed to complete the first review under the program and disburse US$ 450 million, which will unlock significant bilateral and multilateral funding. The IMF noted that the performance criteria were met, while the work was in progress for meeting the structural benchmarks and that progress had been achieved in improving the AML/CFT framework with additional work to be done before March 2020. Five indicative targets for end-September 2019 were missed, including tax revenues collected and power sector arrears. Structural benchmarks were implemented albeit with delays and internal auditors have been selected to conduct audits of Pakistan International Airlines and Pakistan Steel Mills. The IMF noted that international partners remained supportive of Pakistan's reform efforts. The recommendations of the IMF staff were duly ratified by the Executive Board of the IMF on December 19, 2019. The Executive Board has called for faster progress to improve the AML/CFT framework and swift measures to exit all the FATF's list of jurisdictions with AML/CFT deficiencies.

Is Pakistan's EFF Program Viable?

Debt risks are very high in the low conditionality program. The debt ratio in the absence of strong implementation would rise of 83 per cent of GDP by 2024 and financing needs would remain at 26 per cent of GDP. External debt risks are also very high, and from a current high of 37 per cent of GDP are projected to decline after 2021 to a sustainable path. There are significant risks of current account and exchange rate and unless Pakistan's economic program responds to the IMF prescription and financing assurances materialize, a major economic crisis requiring a stronger adjustment program cannot be ruled out. The revenue targets projected are ambitious and even the Army Chief has been nominated to the National Development Council to help the economy that is in doldrums.

It should be noted that Pakistan continues to receive strong financial support from China, Saudi Arabia and UAE who have maintained their exposure to Pakistan by extending new financing in the amount of US$ 700 million from China and US$ 3 billion from Saudi Arabia fully covering the matured loans; the Asian Development Bank has approved a US$ 1 billion new Special Policy Based Loan to further strengthen the balance of payments. For the next 12 months, Pakistan remains fully financed under the IMF program with bilateral and multilateral commitments being realized. Even after this, Pakistan will owe the IMF SDR 6,146 million by September 2022 and debt repayment risks would continue to exist.

Pakistan 2020 under Imran Khan

In 2020, when Prime Minister Imran Khan will be completing two years of his electoral tenure, there exist enormous challenges on the economic front and meeting public expectations remains an uphill task. The Government will have to enhance the use of AML tools to support anti-corruption efforts, ensure independence of the financial intelligence unit and establish a robust asset declaration system for public servants. There is also a need to strengthen the effectiveness of anticorruption institutions in investigating and prosecuting corruption cases.

Prime Minister Imran Khan has rolled back the tax concessions given on petroleum products, telecom services and increase in threshold for income tax collection and lowering of income tax rates for both salaried and non-salaried persons. The excise duty on cement and cigarettes has been increased upwards and power tariffs have been revised upwards. The zero rating regime for export-oriented sectors, textiles, carpets, leather, sports goods and surgical goods has been ended. Large cuts in development expenditures were witnessed in 2019-20. In the financial year 2020, the deceleration in development expenditure has been partially addressed with additional expenditures for National Highway Authority, National Transmission and Dispatch Company and Pakistan Electric Power Company.

On the social sector, Pakistan has said that it intends to transfer the additional one-off disbursement of PRs 1,000 to beneficiaries of the Benazir Income Support Scheme in August 2020, after finalizing the banking contracts for the stipend disbursement. Not many major social sector programs have been launched, although there have been structural modifications in the existing schemes for girls' education like Waseela e-Taleem (WeT) and the affordable housing program in Ehsaas.

One of the clear shifts the IMF program necessitated was enhanced Government commitment for not resorting to deficit monetization. This meant a complete elimination of government borrowing from the State Bank of Pakistan to retire its commercial bank debt. Instead, the Government is borrowing heavily from commercial banks to retire its debt to the State Bank of Pakistan. With interest rates remaining static and heavy government borrowing, there has a slowdown in private sector credit.

The receipt of the first tranche from IMF and bilateral donor support has enabled Pakistan to overcome the pressure on the current account. With subdued global commodity prices, there is likely to be a further contraction in imports. Tepid global growth may also reflect negatively on Pakistan's export earnings and remittances.

REFERENCES

1. PTI Economic Vision, PTI, Pakistan Tehreek-e-Insaf, www.insaf.pk.com
2. Pakistan Economic Survey 2018-19, Ministry of Finance, Government of Pakistan, www.finance.gov.pk
3. "Imran Khan's car sale fails to bring in the moolah", *The Week* dated September 18, 2018, www.theweek.in
4. "How "U-Turn" Khan totally neglected Pakistan's Socio-Economic Development", *The Economic Times*, dated June 26, 2019, www.economictimes.indiatimes.com
5. Pakistan: Staff Report for the 2015 Article IV Consultation, Ninth Review under the Extended Arrangement, Request for Waivers of Non-Observance of Performance Criteria, and Request for Modification of a Performance Criterion – Press Release; Staff Report and Statement by the Executive Director for Pakistan, IMF Country Report No. 16/1, January 2016., www.imf.org
6. Pakistan: 2017 Article IV Consultation – Press Release; Staff Report; Informational Annex; and Statement by Executive Director for Pakistan, IMF Country Report No. 17/212, July 2017, www.imf.org
7. Pakistan: First Post-Program Monitoring Discussions – Press Release; Staff Report; Statement by Staff; and Statement by the Executive Director for Pakistan, IMF Country Report No: 18/78, March 2018, www.imf.org
8. Pakistan: IMF Reaches Staff-level Agreement with Pakistan on the First Review under the Extended Fund Facility, dated November 8, 2019, www.imf.org

9. Pakistan: Executive Board Completes the First Review of Pakistan's Extended Fund Facility, dated December 19, 2019, www.imf.org
10. Pakistan: Request for an Extended Arrangement under the Extended Fund Facility – Press Release; Staff Report and Statement by Executive Director, July 8, 2019, www.imf.org
11. Pakistan: First Review under the Extended Arrangement under the Extended Fund Facility and Request for Modification of Performance Criteria – Press Release; Staff Report; and Statement by the Executive Director for Pakistan, Country Report No. 19/380, December 23, 2019, www.imf.org

6

IMF Developments in Pakistan

Aakriti Vinayak

Pakistan, under the leadership of Imran Khan, is known for taking sweeping U-turns. 2019 saw the biggest and yet the most expected U-turn by Imran Khan in seeking an International Monetary Fund (IMF) bailout. The year 2019 began with Pakistan battling massive twin deficits, deteriorating foreign currency reserves, low exports, diminishing tax revenues, a weak currency, and non-sustainable external debt payments and soaring sovereign debt. The boom-and-bust cycle continued unabated and the persistent economic weakness forced the country to seek the 22nd IMF bailout since Pakistan's membership of the IMF in 1950. On July 3, 2019, the IMF executive board approved a 39-month arrangement under the Extended Fund Facility for Pakistan for an amount of USD 6 billion. It is pertinent to mention that an IMF bailout comes with stringent conditionalities and has "strings attached" with it. The front-loaded conditionalities have a teething impact on Pakistan's troubled economy. The IMF then is a double-edged sword. However, Pakistan has been over-reliant on the IMF for providing short-term relief to its drowning economy. Further the year 2020 has till now seen an unexpected turn of events with the Covid-19 breakout sending shockwaves throughout the world including Pakistan. Pakistan, in this grim situation, has turned desperately to the IMF and other international financial institutions for help.

This chapter deals with this complicated relationship between the IMF and Pakistan and its steady developments in 2019 and looks briefly at the current scenario. The question that hovers large is whether the IMF is a rescue or a trap. Firstly, this chapter will try to understand why Pakistan knocked at the doors of the IMF for the 22nd time. Why did Imran Khan take this U-turn despite being averse to borrowing from international financial institutions? Secondly, this chapter will look at the details of the IMF bailout and what are the conditionalities that needed to be implemented? It will try to grapple with the complexities of the bailout. Thirdly, this chapter will underscore the implications of an IMF bailout on Pakistan's economy and how it impinges on the masses. Lastly, it will try to understand the current dilemmas faced by Pakistan under the Covid-19 crisis.

Knocking at the Doors of IMF Again

Historically, Pakistan has been largely dependent on foreign bailouts to keep its economy afloat.[1] It has knocked at the doors of the IMF 21 times and has been a habitual borrower from the lender of last resort. In fact, Pakistan has had more IMF programmes than all the other South Asian countries combined.[2] Interestingly, 10 programs have been signed under poverty reduction, growth trust and the General Resource Account of the IMF and 12 of these have been bailouts. The current program is the 13th bailout.

Pakistan has a chequered history with the IMF. Out of the 21 programmes with it, only the last programme (2013-2016) was deemed "successful", and that too after the fund allowed more than a dozen waivers on non-observance of performance criteria. In fact, Pakistan is often called as a one-tranche nation, "a veiled reference to the country's track record of taking loans at critical times and then abandoning them prematurely, either because of a crisis of balance of payments or because further disbursements required tough policy actions".[3] The bailouts given to Pakistan have only emboldened it, encouraged it to treat debt as disposable income and when payback time comes, seek more handouts. Being a prolonged user of the IMF, Pakistan has never carried out the structural reforms it recommended. The chart below depicts the complicated relationship between the IMF and Pakistan. It is pertinent to scrutinize the agreement as it was signed after much dilly-dallying and inconclusive talks between the IMF and Imran Khan's "Naya Pakistan".

Imran Khan's Biggest U-turn

Imran Khan before being elected had made tall claims of rooting out corruption, making structural economic reforms and most importantly not to beg and borrow from international financial institutions. He, in fact, provocatively declared, "I would commit suicide rather than extend a begging bowl before the IMF".[4] However, the ground reality of a volatile nation like Pakistan shattered Khan's election promise of building an Islamic welfare state. Imran Khan inherited a

IMF Bond

Pakistan does not withdraw entire amount in most loans with IMF

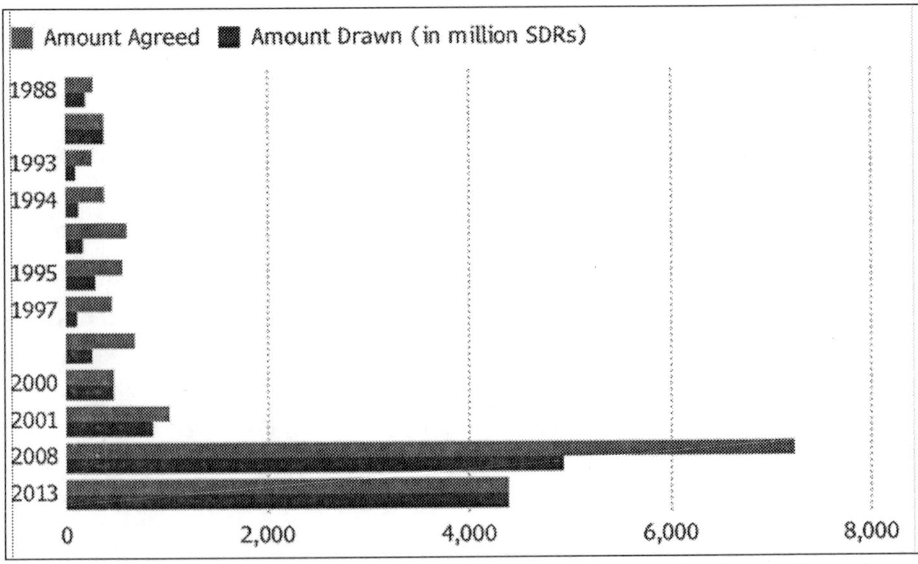

*Special drawing Rights is determined by summing values in US dollars, based on market exchange rates, of a basket of major currencies.

Source: International Monetary Fund; https://www.bloombergquint.com/global-economics/for-pakistan-s-13th-imf-bailout-expect-tougher-conditions

floundering economy, which was going through a structural crisis. There was balance-of-payments crisis, overvalued currency, declining competitiveness and a growing trade deficit. However, Khan, rather than taking any prompt corrective measures and to avoid approaching the IMF (and avert its tough conditionalities), turned desperately to the "friendly countries". Saudi Arabia came to Pakistan's rescue with a US$ 6 billion loan package in October 2018, United Arab Emirates pledged a US$ 3 billion financial support package and reportedly China gave Pakistan US$ 2 billion at the beginning of 2019. However, these were just stopgap measures as the economy continued to be in the doldrums. With inflation climbing to over 8 per cent, the rupee losing a third of its value and with foreign exchange reserves barely enough to cover two months of exports, Pakistan was forced to approach the IMF. On May 12, 2019, after six months delay, dithering talks, changing the finance minister and subsequent adjustments based on IMF's directions (austerity measures, cutting down government expenditure, raising the price of basic utilities) Pakistan and IMF reached a staff level agreement over a $6 billion bailout to be disbursed over a period of three years. Further on July 3, 2019 the executive board of the IMF approved a 39-month extended arrangement under the extended fund facility (EFF) for Pakistan for an amount of SDR 4,268 million (about US$6 billion or 210 per cent of quota) to support the authorities' economic reform program. Imran Khan's frenetic attempts to avoid the stringent conditionalities of IMF failed, as there were no options left to arrest the economic crisis. He stated, "I repeat the reforms are painful...it's like a surgery. When you conduct surgery for a while, the patient suffers, but then improves".[5] The IMF deal came as a political blow to a Pakistani government that had promised to build a new welfare state. The IMF-Pakistan deal also led to criticism amongst the opposition political parties. They denounced the deal as a "complete sell-out". Maryam Nawaz, vice-president of the Pakistan Muslim League-Nawaz (PML-N) party, said the government had led Pakistan to the "brink of economic disaster" in just nine months.[6]

The biggest U-turn by Imran Khan, however, was predictable as an editorial in *Dawn* succinctly summarized why the current government, despite being averse to the IMF, took recourse to it:

> "Of course, much of this is cyclical. Every incoming government in Pakistan has found an economy plagued with massive imbalances requiring emergency support from the IMF. And they have all begun their terms with an IMF programme, while repeating the words 'we inherited a broken economy'. But having done so, they have all been required to take decisive action, as the short-term impact is to stifle growth while laying the groundwork for a revival in the medium term. Of course, they have all failed to implement the long-term structural reforms that are necessary to make this growth sustainable, which is the reason we keep finding ourselves returning to this place repeatedly. And the circle is continued till this government".[7]

While Imran Khan had assured the people that this would be the last time Pakistan would approach the IMF, the assurance cannot be taken seriously, as the deep structural crisis that persists in Pakistan (which has not been fixed meaningfully) pushes the country repeatedly to the IMF.

The IMF Bailout Package

It is critical to understand the complexities of the IMF bailout and the front-loaded conditionalities. The US$ 6 billion loan included an immediate disbursement of US$ 1 billion to help Pakistan address its immediate balance-of-payment crisis. And then, there is an extended period arrangement, which would be phased out over the duration of 39 months. The program is also subject to four quarterly reviews and four semi-annual reviews. The key components of the IMF program are fiscal consolidation, a market-determined exchange rate and elimination of quasi-fiscal losses in the energy sector. In the staff report released by the IMF on July 8, 2019, the key elements are further explained.[8]

- A decisive fiscal consolidation to reduce public debt and build resilience, started with the adoption of an ambitious FY 2020 budget. The adjustment will be supported by comprehensive efforts to drastically increase revenue mobilization by 4 to 5 per cent of GDP at the federal and provincial levels over the program period.
- Expanding social spending, including through the strengthening and broadening of safety nets to support the most vulnerable; a flexible, market determined exchange rate to restore competitiveness, rebuild official reserves and provide a buffer against external shocks. This will be supported by an appropriate monetary policy to shore up confidence and contain inflation, conducted by an independent central bank.
- Energy sector reforms to eliminate quasi-fiscal losses and encourage investment, including the depoliticizing of the gas and power tariff over the program period, gradually bringing the sector to cost recovery, and
- Structural reforms through strengthening institutions, increasing governance and transparency and promoting an investment-friendly environment necessary to improve productivity, entrench lasting reforms and ensure sustainable growth.
- Strong financial assistance by Pakistan's international partners will support the EFF. The Fund-supported program is expected to coalesce broader support from multilateral and bilateral creditors in excess of US$ 38 billion, which is crucial for Pakistan to meet its large financing needs in the coming years.

The report that was released also mentioned a prior condition on terror financing that is strengthening the effectiveness of Pakistan's Anti-Money Laundering and Combating the Financing of Terrorism (AML/CFT) regime to support its exit from the Financial Action Task Force (FATF) list of jurisdictions with serious deficiencies—the so-called Grey List.

Pakistan did work on the lines of the IMF as there was a price hike, steady increase in taxes, severe cuts on government spending and market-led currency reforms. In fact, the budget released on June 11, 2019, was under the looming shadow of the IMF.[9] The highlight was its fixation with maximizing the revenue collection.

However, Pakistan missed some targets set by the IMF. After the completion of the first quarterly review by the Executive Board of the IMF on December 19, 2019, the report that was released mentioned that Pakistan missed some indicative targets like net tax revenues collected by the Federal Board of Revenue (FBR), net accumulation of tax refund arrears and power sector arrears. The report also expounded the lukewarm progress on structural reforms, especially those aimed at strengthening governance of economic institutions.[10] In this regard, it mentioned some progress has been made on AML/CFT deficiencies, but a lot needed to be done as Pakistan still remains on FATF's grey list. Also, it warned that the potential blacklisting by the Financial Action Task Force (FATF) could result in a freeze of capital flows and lower investment to Pakistan

The IMF has been lenient and has provided waivers and slippages to Pakistan. Even after missing some set targets, at the conclusion of the first quarterly review, the IMF had expressed its satisfaction with the programme. In fact, it had adjusted the programme condition to complete the work on AML/CFT from October 2019 to June 2020, since Pakistan was retained on the FATF's grey list.[11] The FBR, which faced a Rs. 211 billion shortfall, requested the IMF for a lower tax target of PKR 5.23 trillion as against the budgetary target of Rs. 5.503 trillion. The IMF cut the FBR tax collection target to 5.238 trillion, that is, a reduction of Rs. 265 billion.

Until now, Pakistan has also been successful in receiving two tranches—the first tranche of USD 991.4 million was released in July 2019 and the second tranche of USD 452.4 million in December 2019. However, Pakistan was going through a tough second quarterly review as the country's fiscal deficit breached 2.3 per cent of GDP in the first half of 2019-20. There were disagreements between the IMF and Pakistan over a mini budget and increase in electricity tariffs. Pakistan also demanded a further reduction in the tax target to PKR 4.8 trillion.

The controversial second review however remains postponed due to the Covid-19 crisis. However, the pressure still remains, as the completion of the review will lead to Pakistan receiving the third tranche of USD 450 million.

IMF Double-edged Sword?—Repercussions on the Economy

The IMF bailout package, which has provided breathing space to Pakistan, however, has differing consequences on the economy. The conditionalities have an important influence in economic decision-making and the way the economy is managed or mismanaged. The moot question that arises is whether the current

IMF bailout has led to any macroeconomic corrections and structural reforms in Pakistan's economy or has it led to further complications?

The economy was recovering slowly albeit briefly under the umbrella of the IMF programme. It had steered the economy to some macroeconomic corrections. Some of the fiscal positives were that in September 2019, Pakistan's current account deficit dropped by 80 per cent to a 41-month low of $ 259 million, with a 111.5 per cent rise in foreign direct investment (FDI) and 194 per cent increase in private investment.[12] Further, in the beginning of 2020, the CAD dropped by 72 per cent to $ 2.654 billion.[13] The foreign exchange levels also reached a safe level. In fact, the Moody Investor Service upgraded Pakistan's economic outlook from negative to stable. However, the economy was still dealing with serious challenges on the fiscal and external fronts. On the fiscal front, due to insufficient revenue generation, the tax revenue target remained elusive. In the first half (July-December 2019, the tax revenue collection fell short of the target by Rs. 290 billion and the fiscal deficit stood around Rs. 995 billion or 2.3 per cent of GDP.[14] As mentioned previously, the FBR had requested the IMF to reset the tax collection target to 5.23 trillion and by February 2020 to 4.8 trillion. On the external front, the export growth rate stood at 3.15 per cent in dollar value in the first half of FY20. The inflation also reached 14.5 per cent, highest in the last ten years.

Another grave issue was that of the circular debt. Circular debt or the power sector arrears described as the cash shortfall within the Central Power Purchasing Agency (CPPA) that it cannot pay to power supply companies remains the critical challenge in Pakistan's power sector.[15] At the time of signing the $6-billion bailout package, the IMF had allowed Pakistan to add only Rs. 39 billion to the circular debt during the July-December period. But it relaxed the limit to Rs. 93 billion in the first review talks after the PTI government added Rs. 77 billion in the first quarter alone, bringing a monthly addition to Rs. 25.7 billion.[16] The gravity of the issue can be ascertained from the fact that as on January 2020, the Pakistan Tehreek-e-Insaf (PTI) government has added about Rs. 565 billion to the circular debt.[17]

The IMF's strict conditions, rather than reforming the economy, had further crippled it. The brunt of the economic mess was felt by the masses. The devaluation in the rupee, rise in interest rates, cutting subsidies and privatizing loss-making state-owned enterprises had a jarring impact on the middle classes. With the high cost of production and complicated taxation mechanism introduced by the FBR as directed by the IMF, there were nationwide strikes by the traders and businessmen as the stock exchange rates plummeted and businesses slowed down. In April 2020, the newly released report of the Human Rights Commission of Pakistan referred to the adverse impact of the IMF bailout by stating that the agreement with the IMF had put Pakistan in a tight economic situation and "Hyperinflation and unprecedented power and energy hikes, coupled with a sharp decline in income among the middle, lower-middle and working classes, brought about extraordinary hardships for ordinary people".[18] There also continues to be massive rise in unemployment, poverty and hunger in Pakistan. Clearly, the magnanimity of the IMF program has not made Pakistan improve and restructure its economy and address the deep-seated problems. In fact, the people have felt the burden of the reforms, leading to distress. However, as the editorial in *Dawn* points out, Pakistan has been repeating the same blunder through the years:

> "Each programme since then has carried these two dimensions: macroeconomic adjustment meaning more taxes, exchange rate depreciation and interest rates hike followed by structural reform. And in each case, the story has played out in the same way: the government takes the money, imposes massive hardships on the population through austerity and 'demand compression', and then reneges on its commitments for structural reform through a patchy implementation, at best. This cycle has repeated itself so often now that if were to add up all the years since 1988 that Pakistan has spent inside an IMF programme, we would find that the country has spent more time inside than outside fund programmes. And now we are gearing up for one more round".[19]

Hence, Pakistan keeps lurching from one crisis to another. However, it is currently dealing with the worst crisis as the Covid-19 pandemic escalates in Pakistan, leaving the economy in shambles. The continued recourse to the IMF seemed inevitable.

Covid-19 Crisis: Pakistan's Recourse to the IMF

The Covid-19 virus that originated in China and later evolved into a pandemic has engulfed the whole world. The world is grappling with the devastating impact of Covid-19 on the economy, as it is not just a health crisis but also a social and economic crisis. Pakistan was already reeling under a grim economic situation and Covid-19 has further exposed the vulnerabilities of the weak state, which now remains at the edge of an economic collapse. The country reported its first case on 26 February, 2020, in Karachi. The Imran Khan government underplayed the situation and the pandemic spread all over the country. In March 2020, the preliminary assessment of losses done by the Asian Development Bank stood at $ 5 billion. Further, as reported by *The News International,* it was predicted that Pakistan might face an initial loss of $ 8.2 billion from the economic effects of the corona virus pandemic. It also stated that "the losses are going to be incurred on account of drop in the GDP growth because of reduction in services sector, including airline business and others, FBR revenue loss, massive decline in imports, exports, reduction in remittances, disruption in food supplies and other fronts".[20] Further, in April 2020, the IMF World Economic Outlook has projected the GDP growth rate at negative 1.5 per cent in 2020. Pakistan is also facing multidimensional challenges, the foremost among which are poverty and unemployment. It is estimated that the poverty headcount will rise from 24.3 per cent to a base of 29 per cent and at least three million people will lose their jobs. The economic situation remains abysmal on all fronts. The economic survey of Pakistan released on June 11, 2020, revealed that the economy has contracted by 0.38 per cent due to the adverse impact of Covid-19.[21] The economic fallout has hit the country hard and exposed the vulnerabilities of a weak state. The unsustainable situation has led Pakistan to desperately take the immediate help of the IMF again.

It was in March 2020 that Pakistan asked the IMF for a low cost, fast-disbursing loan under its Rapid Financing Instrument (RFI) to deal with the disastrous economic impact of Covid-19. The RFI provides quick financial assistance, which is available to all member-countries that exhibit urgent balance-of-payment needs. RFI replaced the IMF's previous policy that covered Emergency Natural Disaster Assistance (ENDA) and Emergency Post-Conflict Assistance (EPCA). On April 16, the IMF approved a loan of $ 1.4 billion for Pakistan for its urgent balance of payment requirements and assist it in dealing with the socio-economic impact of the crisis.[22] The IMF has also paused the discussions with Pakistan on the second review of the three-year extended fund facility program. The temporary relief provided by the IMF has made Pakistan's survival possible; however. the uncertainty still looms large. .Pakistan's over-reliance on international assistance has made the country shun its responsibilities to initiate structural reforms. As stated by Husain Haqqani, Pakistan instead of reforming the country's policies has sought debt restructuring and waivers on account of the pandemic, just as it previously sought international assistance as a reward for fighting terrorism.[23]

Conclusion

Pakistan is teetering on a potential economic disaster. With exports stagnant, inelastic revenue collection, widening fiscal deficit and astronomical external debt, Pakistan's economy remains in a crisis. Further, Covid-19 comes as a stark reminder of the hollowness of a weak state's economy. Recourse to the IMF has only provided a temporary relief to the tottering economy. In fact, the strict conditionalities has led to enormous hardships for the people

However, the question arises, how long can an economy sustain itself on bailouts and external assistance? As noted by Tilak Devasher, "the basic reason for the inconsistent performance of the economy is the structural weaknesses that have been not rectified over the decades" and he further mentions that it will not be rectified by ad-hoc, band-aid type of solutions".[24] The IMF bailout has put Pakistan on a ventilator, keeping it going but without the heft to implement structural changes needed to resuscitate the economy on a long-term basis.[25] At best, the IMF only provides a quick fix rather than an in-depth restructuring of the frail economy. Hence, unless the structural problems of the economy in the form of savings-investment deficit, the expenditure-revenue deficit and the import-export deficit are tackled, it will continue to be in the doldrums. Pakistan should acknowledge the trouble and start working from scratch; otherwise, it is heading for a collapse.

NOTES

1. Tilak Devasher (2016), *Pakistan: Courting the Abyss*, Harper Collins, Noida, pp. 248.
2. Khurram Hussain, "Pakistan and IMF: The ties that bind", *Dawn*, Islamabad, January 11, 2015.
3. "Pakistan-IMF ties: A chequered history", *The Express Tribune*, Karachi, August 5, 2016.
4. "View From The Neighbourhood: Imran's U-turns", *Indian Express*, April 22, 2019.
5. "In Dubai, Pakistan prime minister warns of 'painful' reforms", *Aljazeera*, February 11, 2019
6. "Explainer: What the IMF bailout package means for Pakistan", SBS Urdu, May 15, 2019
7. "The price of indecision", *Dawn*, Islamabad, May 23, 2019
8. Pakistan: Request for an Extended Arrangement Under The Extended Fund Facility, IMF Middle East and Central Asia Dept., July 8, 2019
9. Prateek Joshi and Riya Sinha, "Pakistan Budget 2019-20- Unrealistic Ambitions", *Vivekananda International Foundation*, Delhi, July 11, 2019
10. First Review Under The Extended Arrangement Under the Extended Fund Facility and Request For Modification of Performance Criteria, IMF Middle East and Central Asia Dept, December 23, 2019
11. Ibid.
12. Kunwar Khuldune Shahid, "Is Pakistan's Economy Recovering", *The Diplomat*, February 7, 2020.
13. Erum Zaidi, "C/A gap narrows 72 pc in July-Jan on improved trade balance", *The News*

International, February 20, 2020.

14. Syed Haris Ahmed, "Pakistan's economy battling a host of challenges", *The Express Tribune*, Karachi, February 10, 2020.
15. Nasir Jamal, "Why circular debt isn't dying away", *Dawn*, Islamabad, January 20, 2020.
16. Shahbaz Rana, "PTI govt adds Rs 565 billion to circular debt", *The Express Tribune*, Karachi, January 16, 2020.
17. Ibid.
18. "HRCP report asks government to reorient the economy", *Business Recorder*, May 2, 2020.
19. "Back to the IMF", *Dawn*, Islamabad, July 5, 2019.
20. Mehtab Haider, "Coronavirus: Pakistan may face initial economic loss of Rs. 1.3 trillion", *The News International*, March 20, 2020.
21. Imran Ali Kundi, "All economic targets missed", *The Nation*, Lahore, June 12, 2020.
22. "Covid19: IMF approves nearly $1.4 billion to meet balance of payment crisis", *Economic Times*, April 17, 2020.
23. Hussain Haqqani, "Pakistan discovers the high cost of Chinese investment", *The Diplomat*, May 18, 2020.
24. Tilak Devasher (2016), *Pakistan: Courting the Abyss*, Harper Collins, Noida, p. 245.
25. Tilak Devasher (ed) (2019), *Pakistan Insights*, Pentagon Press LLP, New Delhi, p. 160.

7

Terrorism in 2019: Continued Crisis of Strategic Identity

Brig (R) Rahul Bhonsle

Preview

Terrorism continued to pose dilemmas for Pakistan's national security in 2019. Pakistan's inability and unwillingness to control extremism—religious and sectarian—was amply highlighted even as violence continued to decline in numbers. Manifestation of Pashtun separatism surfaced to an extent, a phenomenon that the Establishment, the Army and the Inter Services Intelligence (ISI) seem to be either oblivious to or do not want to face it head on. A survey of terrorism in Pakistan in 2019 by at least three think tanks in the country[1] identified continued resistance of the state to undertake structural changes in the socio-political, religious administrative and constitutional spheres that can overcome fundamental support factors of terror even as there was considerable success in controlling violence.[2] Thus, the management of terrorism, rather than transformation, was the main objective and practice in 2019 indicating that there is unlikely to be any recompense in containing terrorism in 2020 as well.

Thus, the State and the people's tryst with terrorism continued in 2019 in Pakistan. The overall matrix of diverse ideologies supporting terrorist groups had multiple trajectories – Islamist extremism, sectarianism and separatist dogmas. A new track of global religious extremist terror linked to the millenarian Islamic State, more commonly known in this part of the world as Daesh or Islamic State of Khorasan Province (ISKP), emerged. The Establishment's propensity to work with terrorist groups as partners in destabilising neighbours—India and Afghanistan—hemmed in programmes to restrain ideologies supporting use of indiscriminate violence in the form of terrorism. State authority to transform tribal areas towards the national mainstream governance system received a fillip in 2019 with the assimilation of Federally Administered Tribal Areas (FATA) in the province of Khyber Pakhtunkhwa (KP). However, this did not affect the supply factor of terror—recruits, bases and funds to terrorist groups operating in this zone for years such as the Tehreek Taliban Pakistan (TTP).

For statistical records, however, there has been a decline in violence which has resulted in a shift from the strike-hard campaigns launched by the Pakistan Armed Forces using indiscriminate air and artillery, internally displacing millions of civilians in this zone in the past half a decade or so to Intelligence-based targeted operations. There are indications of a slow burning Pashtun separatist militancy, which may be taking root despite attempts by the Pakistan Establishment to link the Pashtun Tahafuz Movement [PTM] to support by India and Afghanistan. There was not much progress in the field of financing of terrorism with Pakistan's "friends" continuing to bail out Islamabad from being blacklisted by the Financial Action Task Force (FATF). A detailed review of the activities of terrorist and religious extremist groups in Pakistan in 2019 is carried out in the subsequent paragraphs.

Where was Pakistan in 2018?

In assessing the activities of terrorist groups in Pakistan in 2019, a brief look at where Pakistan was in 2018 may be in order. The US Department of State's Country Report on Terrorism in Pakistan of 2018 states that externally targeted groups such as the Afghan Taliban and the Haqqani Network (HQN) in Afghanistan and the Lashkar e-Tayyiba (LeT) and Jaish-e-Mohammad (JeM) in India continued to operate with impunity with no restrictions on training, recruiting or collection of monies. The LeT front organizations even contested the July 2018 general elections in an attempt to gain legitimacy, which however dismally failed.[3] The State Department observed that while the threat level remained high, there was a downward trend in terms of incidents and their impact—fatalities and injuries. The Tehrik-e-Taliban Pakistan (TTP), Jamaat-ul-Ahrar (JuA), Islamic State Khorasan Province (ISKP), and the sectarian group Lashkar-e-Jhangvi al-Alami (LJA) focused on Islamic including sectarian extremism. Importantly the State Department indicates that the ISKP could be acting in collaboration with some of these groups. Religious and sectarian minorities remained vulnerable. Separatist groups operating in Balochistan and Sindh targeted government as well as diplomatic entities using armed assaults, "IEDs, VBIEDs, suicide bombings, targeted assassinations, and rocket-propelled grenades", in 2018.[4] In the counter-terror domain, apart from operations by the

Armed Forces that were claimed to be Intelligence based, military courts sentenced 104 convicted terrorists to death, 15 more than in 2017.[5]

In a major setback to Pakistan internationally, the FATF placed the country on its "grey list" for a series of deficiencies in the anti-money laundering and countering terrorist financing regimes. Pakistan's failure to fully implement the UN Security Council's sanctions against ISIL (Da'esh) and al-Qa'ida was also cited.[6] To counter violent extremism (CVE), Pakistan operated five de-radicalization camps where the curriculum offered was "corrective religious education", vocational training, counselling, and therapy.[7] However, madrassas continued to support "extremist" doctrine with many failing to register with the government or to provide documentation of funding. [8] In 2019, much the same pattern is evident as outlined in subsequent paras.

Review of 2019

Violence Metrics

A notable development in the counter-terrorist campaign in Pakistan in 2019 was a drop in the overall level of violence of terrorist incidents. 393 people lost their lives, including 150 security forces personnel, 133 civilians and 110 militants in 270 violent incidents (including security forces actions and militant attacks) while 687 people were injured, including 506 civilians and 178 security forces personnel. Suicide attacks were down by 44 per cent compared to 2018, overall militant attacks by 31 per cent and fatalities by 48 per cent. The average militant attacks per month also declined to 13 as opposed to 19 in 2018, 35 in 2017, 43 in 2016, 59 in 2015 and 134 in 2014 as per data compiled by the Pakistan Institute for Conflict and Security Studies, Islamabad (PICSS).[9] Most of the security forces casualties were in Khyber Pakhtunkhwa, followed by Balochistan and Punjab while Sindh recorded five and two security personnel losses.[10] The trend of decline in militant attacks that started after Operation Zarb-e-Azb in 2014 and the National Action Plan at the start of 2015 is evidently continuing. Operation Raddul Fasad has further pushed militancy to lower levels since 2013.[11] Religious extremist groups are believed to be behind 56 per cent of terrorism-related incidents, ethno-nationalists 27 per cent, and sectarian in nature attacks 6.5 per cent, the rest having unidentified roots.[12] The trend of reduction of violence in terrorist incidents in Pakistan has also been confirmed through the database maintained by the South Asia Terrorism Portal (SATP), an independent source.[13]

Provincial Distribution

Balochistan witnessed the highest number of militant attacks in 2019 but there was a reduction as compared to the previous year. In 2018, 99 militant attacks were recorded which dropped to 66 in 2019, a 34 per cent decline in Balochistan. In 2019, in Balochistan, 171 people were killed and 427 injured. Amongst the fatalities, 89 were civilians, 58 security forces personnel and 24 militants and of the injured 354 were civilians, 71 security forces personnel and two militants. FATA also witnessed a 21 per cent decline in anti-State militant attacks except in North Waziristan. In 2019, in 52 attacks, 64 people were killed, including 45 security forces personnel, which is 70 per cent of the total deaths caused by militant attacks in erstwhile FATA region in 2019. Nearly 88 people were injured, including 57 security forces personnel and 33 civilians during the year.[14]

Khyber Pakhtunkhwa (excluding the former FATA region) saw a 25 per cent decline with 30 anti-State violent incidents recorded by PICSS which led to 46 killed and 101 injured. Nearly 26 of the 46 dead were security forces personnel while 16 were civilians. Nearly 79 of the 101 injured were civilians and 21 security forces personnel. Punjab, Pakistan's most populated province, saw five attacks that were the same in number as in 2018 with 13 killed and 42 injured. Sindh saw four attacks as compared with 15 in 2018. One militant attack each was recorded in Pakistan Occupied Kashmir (POK) and Federal Capital Territory of Islamabad killing five and two security forces personnel.[15]

Types of Attacks

Suicide attacks, IEDs and bombs remained a major threat apart from the use of hand grenades and targeted gun attacks. Suicide attacks saw a drop comparable to the years prior to 2007 as the Lal Masjid or Red Mosque incident is said to have been a trigger for the same. There were six suicide attacks in which 45 people were killed including 28 civilians, 11 security forces personnel and 6 militants while 112 people were injured including 101 civilians and 11 security forces personnel. Use of Improvised Explosive Devices or IED was the preferred option with 84 attacks recorded in which 112 people were killed and 441 injured.[16]

Tracking Terrorist Groups

Tehreek-e-Taliban Pakistan (TTP)

The TTP has lost much of the sting of the years when the Mehsud leaders—Baitullah and his successors—controlled the faction. However, PICSS notes that the TTP continued to expand its footprint in the tribal districts (former FATA) as well as in Malakand Division of KP province. Aman or Peace Committees were warned in Bajour, Swat, Dir, Buner and Waziristan not to cooperate with the Pakistani security forces and reports of distribution of pamphlets were evident. The TTP is now reportedly based in areas of Afghanistan adjacent to Waziristan, thus being able to target North and South Waziristan.

Mufti Noor Wali, leader of the TTP, has assumed direct control asserting authority over local commanders. An important development is Wali's call for separation from the Pakistan State for non-implementation of the Sharia and advocacy of Pashtun rights. The PTM has also been espousing the latter. Inclusion of Mufti Noor Wali's name as Specially Designated Global Terrorist in September 2019 by the United Nations Security Council (UNSC) with possible U.S. support was a major boost to counter terrorist forces though the outcome on the ground appears to have been limited. Noor Wali has offered to give up arms if the Deobandi clerics indicate that fighting the state was not permissible under Sharia.

In 2020, the TTP and the Hizbul Ahrar are expected to expand their activities in Bajaur, Mohmand, Khyber and North Waziristan where they have been able to establish a base as well as in the Balochistan areas of Zhob and Loralai. The TTP will continue to pose a major threat to Pakistan as the group can attract radicalised and impoverished sections of the youth in the tribal belt with ease.[17]

Hizbul Ahrar

The second most active group after the TTP in the tribal belt was Hizbul Ahrar, a splinter of the same, initially named as the Jamat-ul-Ahrar. As is usual practice, the group changed its name on August 23, 2019, and the National Counter Terrorism Authority of Pakistan included it in the list of proscribed organizations. PICSS claims that the leader and founder of JuA, Umar Khalid Khorasani, continues to run the outfit but the public face is Mukarram Mohmand, a close relative. HuA also has links with the Baloch rebel groups as per PICSS as it published an attack of the BLA in February on its website.[18] HuA launched a number of operations in the tribal belt and remains active despite proscription by the Pak government.

ISK and AQIS

The ISK launched a major suicide attack in Hazar Ganji area of Quetta on April 12 in which 21 people were killed and 49 injured. The group also indulged in a number of targeted-killings of Taliban commanders in Peshawar and Quetta and one killing of a low-level Shia scholar in Karachi. This is ascribed to the breakup of the group with the Lashkar-e-Jhangvi (LeJ) thus making standalone attacks for the ISK difficult. PICSS indicates the possibility of an alliance between the ISK and the TTP in the future.[19]

Available open-source information now reveals that the ISK could also be aligned to terrorist groups under control of the ISI operating in Jammu and Kashmir such as the Lashkar-e-Taiyyaba and the Jaish-e-Mohammad. Importantly, the Islamabad Policy Institute assesses that the presence of "large disenfranchised segments of society, high level of radicalization and existence of militant groups" could provide the Daesh traction in the year ahead.[20]

The AQIS has carried out small-scale operations in Sindh and Punjab. The CTD Sindh killed AQIS's head for Sindh province, Talat Mehmood alias Yusuf, in an Intelligence-based operation along with two other commanders which considerably influenced the operations of the group.[21]

Baloch Groups

The formation of the Baloch Raaji Aajoi Sangar (BRAS) consisting of Balochistan Liberation Front, Balochistan Republican Guards, Balochistan Republican Army and a faction of Balochistan Liberation Army that had defected from the main group was a key development in Baloch militancy in 2019. BRAS or Baloch National Freedom Front claimed responsibility for a number of attacks including target-killing of 14 Pakistani security forces in the coastal area of Makran near Ormara in April 2019. BRAS will facilitate coordination of activities of the Baloch groups across several districts of Balochistan and sustain some of the groups that had been marginalised. It also provides a larger media presence for the group. Thus, in November 2019, BRAS released its yearly report in which it claimed that attacks were carried out in Tagran, Turbat, Ormara, Panjgur, Zamuran, Mand and Washuk, killing 31 personnel of Pakistani security forces including three officers, 26 pro-government Razakars (militia men) while 12 security forces personnel were injured and eight kidnapped which however remains unverified.[22] On July 2, 2019, BLA was declared a terrorist organization by the US government. This limited the social media outreach of the group as many of its official Twitter and Facebook accounts were blocked after the declaration. BRAS can pose a major challenge in 2020.

Counter-militancy Operations

Counter-terrorist operations designated as Intelligence-Based Operations led by the Army and supported by the Air Force, Special Services Groups, Army Aviation and paramilitary forces like Frontier Corps (FC), were conducted in 2019. The

Pakistan Army established a counter-terrorism grid in the form of company and platoon bases in the tribal belt, which has led to resentment among the locals and is one of the triggers for support of the PTM. Nearly 367 Intelligence-based operations were conducted directed against TTP–22, Daesh-75, Al-Qaeda/Foreign Fighters-44, Afghan Taliban-4, and other militant groups–119.[23] A point to note is that despite the TTP being the most violent terrorist group, the number of IBOs launched is the least amongst the indigenous groups, the reason for which appears unclear at present.

An important factor in counter militancy has been the construction of the border fencing on the Durand Line.[24] Pakistan security forces have thus been able to control the flow of movement of groups to and from the country to Afghanistan. The intention is a one-way movement of elements which are favourable for controlling influence in Afghanistan such as the Afghan Taliban, while preventing Pakistan's banned groups from operating with impunity. Despite this, there are indications that many Pakistan groups are operating in the Nangarhar and Kunar provinces of Afghanistan.

Religious Extremism

Prevalence of state munificence, if not downright collusion with religious extremist groups, continued in 2019, even though it has not been able to make as much public impact as in 2018 and earlier. This could be ascribed to the rude shock of failure of these groups including the Kashmir-centred Lashkar-e-Taiyyaba (LeT) to make gains in the general elections in that year. Blasphemy is a belief that has deep roots and conspiracy theories surrounding the same continue to be a bane against minorities. Violence against minorities has continued as an enraged mob in Ghotki town attacked properties worth millions of rupees and looted several shops belonging to the Hindu community after the owner of a school was accused of blasphemy in September last year. The much vaunted "Naya Pakistan", announced with much fanfare by Prime Minster Imran Khan, has failed to manifest.

The much-touted proposal for madrassa reforms has also lacked an outcome-oriented approach and is thus being carried out by rote per se.[25] With focus on authority over the madrassas including curriculum, there is insufficient attention to reduction of hatred towards other religions and sects. The autonomy that has been given to waqfs [Islamic charitable trusts] due to pressure from the madrassa lobby to outline the syllabus has possibly reduced the overall impact of the reforms and will continue to provide a raison d'être to continue preaching against minorities and sects within Islam.[26]

Hedging at the FATF

Pakistan's perfidy of hedging at the Financial Action Task Force (FATF) continued through 2019. The FATF again placed Pakistan in the, "Jurisdictions under Increased Monitoring" as indicated in the release on 21 February 2020 or the Grey List as it is commonly known indicating seven major deficiencies apart from a general commitment to curb the many manifestations of terror.[27]

Overall Review

There is a general conclusion by think tanks in Pakistan that the decline in numbers does not suggest elimination of terrorism. This is evident from operations by the terrorist groups in the tribal belt as well as in Balochistan. In fact, the Pakistan Institute for Peace Studies (PIPS) concludes that despite an overall decrease in terrorist incidents in the country the situation in Khyber Pakhtunkhwa remained unchanged from the previous year and has warned that North Waziristan has emerged as a major hotspot where over 42 per cent of the total 125 reported attacks have been noted.[28] Slow transition of implementation of the erstwhile FATA's merger in KP, mainly due to multiple bureaucratic, political and legal hurdles, has been identified as a major factor.[29] The Islamabad Policy Institute (IPI) in its annual report for 2019 highlights the danger of terrorism morphing into a long-term threat through new recruitment and alliances between terrorist groups.

A deeper alienation among the Pashtuns is also likely to be caused by the deployment of the Pakistan Army in company nodes amidst civilian population in the tribal areas thus infringing on the much-cherished privacy. The PTM has been highlighting this facet from time to time but neither the Pakistani Establishment nor the think tanks appear to be taking a serious view of the same.

While a number of deradicalization camps have been established and were reported to be functioning, the outcome from them is not clear.[30] PIPS recommends a high-powered national-level truth and reconciliation commission under parliament to undertake a comprehensive review of the ideologies that promote violence and recommend measures to contain them.[31] In the context of Balochistan, the missing persons issue remains a key factor, the resolution of which can act as a confidence-building measure with the local population but is unlikely to be addressed as the core institution, the Pakistan Army, is linked with the maximum cases of disappearances and there are no indications of the State taking up this gigantic challenge soon.

Even in the sphere of policy, the National Internal Security Policy (NISP) in 2014 and the revised version in 2018 has not been given emphasis by the Pakistan Tehreek Insaaf Government as per the IPI. The PTI seems to be content at letting the Pakistan Army handle security challenges. This is a grossly deficient approach which is evident from the peripheral application of conflict management strategies rather than attempts at resolution. The dissolution of military courts following lack of political support to them and with parliament failing to muster the majority to extend the tenure in 2019 has reduced the tools that the military has been using in countering terrorism to some extent, though its impact was not evident during the year.

In the overall context, the IPI summarises the general opinion of think tanks in the country that terrorism continues to pose a substantial challenge to Pakistan in 2020 and may have moved away from the headlines. Yet in the long term, it will have a bearing on State security.[32]

Significantly, the external dimension of this grave threat to regional security which has resulted in instability in Afghanistan for decades and has imposed the cruelty of terror on the people of Jammu and Kashmir is a sequitur which need not be gone into here but a brief look at events in the past three months as per succeeding paragraphs needs mention.

Postscript – circa 2020 – The "Deceitful Establishment"

Recent events in the country indicate how terrorism remains the leitmotif of the Establishment and a strategy against India, Afghanistan and other states while being a tactic against mountain brother China. Castellum.AI, the New York-based regulatory technology company, which specialises in watch list compliance, noticed that Pakistan had removed 4,000 names from the 'proscribed persons list' maintained by its National Counter Terrorism Authority (NACTA). The removal included the name of Zaki-ur-Rehman Lakhvi, the LeT mastermind behind the 2008 Mumbai terror attacks.[33]. Co-founder of the tech firm, Peter Piatetsky, who is a former senior policy adviser for the US Treasury, told the European Foundation for South Asian Studies (EFSAS), an independent organisation based in Brussels, that "Removing close to 4,000 names without a public explanation is unheard of and it raises significant questions about the listing process".[34] The Castellum.AI report was carried by the *Wall Street Journal* which queried the Government of Pakistan. The response was not forthcoming but an explanation in a local newspaper stated, "The list has been bloated up to 7,000 names with multiple inaccuracies such as the names of dead individuals, Afghan nationals, untraceable names without proper identifiers".[35]

The Pakistan Establishment's involvement in supporting the Islamic State of Khorasan targeting the gurdwara in Kabul is another manifestation of what it believes to be a successful strategy to protect national interests in Afghanistan, but refuses to identify as the proverbial snake that bites its own master. An EFSAS Commentary recounts, "[there is] little doubt that it was the Pakistani Inter-Services Intelligence (ISI) that had orchestrated the attack [on the gurdwara in Kabul on 25 March] and had used its terrorist proxies, the Haqqani network and the Lashkar-e-Taibah (LeT), to do the dirty work on its behalf".[36] A follow-up of this incident is the alacrity with which the Pakistan Foreign Office sought the extradition of Abdullah Orakzai alias Aslam Farooqi, a key leader of the Islamic State in Khorasan Province (ISKP), which had organised the gurdwara attack in Kabul.[37]

Terrorism is thus not just a security challenge for Pakistan but a Crisis of Strategic Identity.

NOTES

1. Pakistan Institute for Conflict and Security Studies (PICSS), Islamabad. Pak Institute for Peace Studies (PIPS) and Islamabad Policy Institute (IPI).
2. Pakistan Institute for Conflict and Security Studies (PICSS), Islamabad. 2019. PICSS Annual Security Assessment Report – 2019, https://www.picss.net/product/annual-security-assessment-report/
3. United States Department of State. Country Reports on Terrorism 2018. Pakistan. Available at https://www.state.gov/reports/country-reports-on-terrorism-2018/. Accessed on 11 February 2020.
4. Ibid.
5. Ibid.
6. Ibid.
7. Ibid.
8. Ibid.
9. PICSS, op. cit.
10. Pak Institute For Peace Studies (Pips). Pakistan Security Report 2019. Available at https://www.pakpips.com/product/pakistan-security-report-2019 Accessed on 15 February 2020.
11. PICSS, op. cit.
12. Rizvi, Syed Farhan. Editor. Pakistan Outlook 2020 – Politics, Economy and Security. Islamabad Policy Institute. Islamabad. 2020. Available at https://ipipk.org/pakistan-outlook-2020-politics-economy-and-security/16993/27/01/2020/ Accessed on 23 March 2020.
13. Data Sheet Pakistan. South Asia Terrorism Portal. Available at https://www.satp.org/datasheet-terrorist-attack/fatalities/pakistan accessed on 23 March 2020.
14. PICSS, op. cit.
15. Ibid.
16. Ibid.
17, Rizvi, op. cit.
18, PICSS, op. cit.

19. Ibid.
20. Rizvi, op. cit.
21. PICSS, op. cit.
22. Ibid.
23. Rizvi, op. cit.
24. PICSS, op. cit.
25. Rizvi, op. cit.
26. Ibid.
27. FATF Decision on Pakistan 21 February 2020. Available at https://www.security-risks.com/security-trends-south-asia/pakistan/fatf-decision-on-pakistan-21-february-2020-15195.html. Accessed on 26 April.
28. Pak Institute For Peace Studies (PIPS). Pakistan Security Report 2019. Available at https://www.pakpips.com/product/pakistan-security-report-2019. Accessed on 15 February 2020.
29. Ibid.
30. Ibid.
31. Ibid.
32. Rizvi, op. cit.
33. Pakistan Removes Almost 4,000 From Terrorist Watchlist, Possibly Including Terrorist Leaders. April 20, 2020. Available at https://www.castellum.ai/insights/2020/04/14/pakistan-removes-names. Accessed on 26 April 2020.
34. Ibid.
35. EFSAS Commentary. Why Pakistan poses multifarious challenges for those seeking to curb its sponsorship of Terrorism. 24-04-2020. Available at https://www.efsas.org/commentaries/why-pakistan-poses-multifarious-challenges-for-those-seeking-to-curb-its-sponsorship-of-terrorism/. Accessed on 26 April 2020.
36. EFSAS Commentary. Pakistan's role in the Kabul Gurdwara attack has been established, and its mounting despondency is becoming starkly evident. 10-04-2020. Available at https://www.efsas.org/commentaries/pakistan%E2%80%99s-role-in-the-kabul-gurdwara-attack-has-been-established/. Accessed on 26 April 2020.
37. Pak Supported Kashmiri Terrorist Camp Network in Eastern Afghanistan. Available at https://www.security-risks.com/security-trends-south-asia/afghanistan/pak-supported-kashmiri-terrorist-camp-network-in-eastern-afghanistan-15401.html. Accessed on 26 April.

8

'Azad' Jammu and Kashmir and 'Gilgit-Baltistan'

Dinkar P. Srivastava

There is an irony inherent in the title chosen by Pakistan for the territory illegally occupied by it in 1947. 'Azad' Jammu and Kashmir is not free to reclaim the Northern Areas, which was separated and taken over by Pakistan for direct administration in 1949. The agreement was kept secret because this was a violation of the UN resolutions Pakistan professes to champion. The Northern Areas were 'liberated' by Major Brown by raising the Pakistani flag in Gilgit Agency in November 1947. He described it as a coup d'état against the Maharaja's government in his biography. This is perhaps a unique instance in the annals of world history, where the 'freedom struggle' was waged by representatives of a colonial power. Both 'Azad Jammu and Kashmir' and the Northern Areas, later re-named 'Gilgit-Baltistan', are part of the state of Jammu and Kashmir, which has acceded to India. Pakistan's de-facto control of this region is a violation of UNCIP resolutions that had asked Pakistan to withdraw from the territory.

Pakistan's present constitution adopted in 1973 does not include 'Azad Jammu and Kashmir' and the Northern Areas as part of that country. However, Pakistan claims responsibility for external defence and foreign policy of the two territories. In the classical sense, this can only be described as a colony, which is not part of the territory of the controlling power and yet governed by it.

The contradictions between Pakistan's foreign policy stance of supporting a 'liberation struggle' across the LOC and repression at home do not end here. The constitution of 'Azad Jammu and Kashmir' does not allow the Jammu and Kashmir Liberation Front (JKLF) or other parties espousing the 'independence' option to participate in elections. Their freedom is limited to championing 'Azadi' for the people of Jammu and Kashmir. JKLF was used by Pakistan to initiate the campaign of terror across the LOC in J&K in the early 1990s. At home, the organization continues to be suppressed brutally. In the Valley itself, it was marginalized by pro-Pak terror outfits and its cadres were physically eliminated in many cases.

Pakistan appointed a political agent, Mohammad Alam, to replace Brigadier Ghansara Singh, the Governor of the Northern Areas, after Major Brown staged his coup d'état. The Political Agent was responsible to the Pakistan government; the territory was kept separate from 'AJK' since inception. This was a symbolic act. Neither the Political Agent, nor the Pakistan government, had effective control over the territory at that time. This separation of the territory took place much before Pakistan took over the administration of the Northern Areas directly in 1949 through the Karachi Agreement, which was kept secret for the next three decades.

The separation of the Northern Areas from 'Azad Jammu and Kashmir' resulted in the loss of more than 80 per cent of the territory of 'AJK'. Forty-three years later, when the 'AJK High Court' ordered the restoration of the Northern Areas to 'AJK', its ruling was quickly overturned by the 'AJK' Supreme Court. Surprisingly, the Supreme Court could not find a substantive argument against the High Court's judgment. It had to resort to the purely procedural argument that the High Court lacked jurisdiction on Northern Areas. The 'AJK' Supreme Court stated that the Northern Areas were part of the State of Jammu and Kashmir, but not part of 'Azad Jammu and Kashmir'. The argument was actually a contrived attempt to quash the 'AJK' High Court's order, which had caused Pakistan deep embarrassment. But the Supreme Court's ruling was also an admission that both the 'AJK' and Northern Areas *continue* to be part of the State of Jammu and Kashmir.

Pakistan's control over both the territories was illegal from the beginning. Its rhetoric in the UN emphasized the independence of the 'Azad Government'. On the ground, Pakistan exercised absolute control over 'Azad Kashmir', as well as the Northern Areas or 'Gilgit-Baltistan'. Pakistan adopted methods, which present a stark contrast to the process followed by India. In Jammu and Kashmir, a Constituent Assembly was convened in 1951, which affirmed the State's accession to India in 1956. Pakistan took over control without any consultation with the people. This was true not only of the Northern Areas, but also of 'Azad' Jammu and Kashmir, which was run based on Rules of Business by the Ministry of

Kashmir Affairs and Northern Areas. India's actions were criticized in international forums as a departure from UN resolutions. Pakistan had breached the UN resolutions in 1949 when it changed the territorial status quo of the area expected to undergo plebiscite by separating the Northern Areas. But it escaped censure by keeping the arrangement secret both from the UN and the people of 'Azad Jammu and Kashmir'.

The absence of transparency was not the only difference in the approaches of the two countries. There was no democracy either in 'Azad' Jammu and Kashmir or in Northern Areas. The elections were held in Jammu and Kashmir in 1951 to elect the members of the Constituent Assembly. The first elections based on the adult franchise were held in 'AJK' only in 1970.

Pakistan raised an outcry after India abolished Articles 370 and 35-A in August 2019. These were temporary provisions of the Indian Constitution. Pakistan's Constitution never had any parallel provisions. In fact, Pakistan's present constitution was adopted only in 1973. The earlier two constitutions adopted in 1956 and 1962 had short shelf life. Was the omission of any provision in Pakistan's constitution against demographic change and protection of property rights in 'AJK' and 'Gilgit-Baltistan' purely a coincidence? After all, the constitution adopted in 1973 has a provision to govern territories not part of Pakistan. It could have included a provision to maintain their distinct identity and demography. Of course, by 1973, the demography had already changed in the absence of any legal bar. This creeping change in the composition of the population continues to date. The change has taken place both ways. The Sixties saw large-scale population displacement from 'Azad Jammu and Kashmir' on account of the construction of the Mangla dam. This resulted in the migration of Mirpuris to the UK. The construction of the Karakorum Highway was the beginning of an influx of outsiders from Punjab and Khyber-Pakhtunkhwa. The development of CPEC (China-Pakistan Economic Corridor) has reinforced this process.

The situation is worse for 'Gilgit-Baltistan'. Hamna Tariq cites Prof. Dr. Martin Sökefeld who has aptly described the situation of Gilgit-Baltistan as 'Not Part of Kashmir, but the Kashmir Dispute'. Pakistan has separated it from 'Azad Jammu and Kashmir', but maintains the legal fiction that it is distinct so that it can claim it has not violated UNCIP resolutions. This means that it has neither the freedom to choose its destiny, nor get a 'provincial' status. This arrangement solves Pakistan's problem. 'Gilgit-Baltistan' gets the worst of both the worlds.

Sectarianism

Pakistan uses religion to suppress ethnic identity in 'Azad' Jammu and Kashmir as well as in 'Gilgit-Baltistan'. This reflects a wider trend within its polity. In the Northern Areas, this policy has been given a further twist. Islam was used to promote sectarian division. Pakistan's military establishment favoured minority Sunni organisations and pitted them against the majority Shias. Hamna Tariq cites Izhar Hunzai, the CEO of the Aga Khan Rural Support Program operating in Gilgit-Baltistan '...the surge in sectarian violence was not natural but propagated by the federal government to cause unrest and distress in Gilgit-Baltistan'.[1] The Zia period saw one of the worst massacres of Shias in the Northern Areas. 'His treacherous reign saw the state-sponsored Gilgit Massacre of the region's Shia population in 1988, ingraining ideas of exclusivity based on religious belief'.[2] The results of this policy of divide-and-rule are still being felt in the territory. The policy is reminiscent of what the British did in pre-partition India.

Zia encouraged Islamisation. Faith was used to compensate for absence of democracy. It was also helpful to create a cadre of militants who could be used in jihad in Afghanistan and later in Kashmir. A group of tribals from NWFP carried out an attack in 1988 in which 400 Shias were killed. The locals point out that it was not possible for the tribals to cross over long distances and reach Shia areas, unless they had the sanction of the State. The sectarian clashes have continued since then with increasing regularity.

Musharraf continued Zia's policy after he seized power in 1999. 'In 1999, Islamabad introduced amended textbooks, produced by the government-funded Textbook Board of Pakistan, authored by Sunnis of the Deobandi School.'[3] The ensuing protests by the Shia population were put down brutally. 'GB Shia leader Zia-uddin negotiated with the Education Ministry to revise the biased syllabus for years on end; he was gunned down in 2005 for spearheading the movement against state-sponsored divisive tactics'.[4] The textbook issue showed that the rise of sectarianism was not a local phenomenon, but had State sanction. The initiative for introduction of textbooks based on the majority Sunni sect came from the Federal Ministry of Education. In May 2012, scores of Shia travellers were killed by unknown assailants in Kohistan'.[5]

China-Pakistan Economic Corridor (CPEC)

The China-Pakistan Economic Corridor (CPEC) was initially announced at the end of 2013. The value of projects under the programme has gone up from 46 billion dollars to more than 60 billion dollars. The former Prime Minister, Nawaz

Sharif, saw it as an answer to Pakistan's infra-structure deficit. Imran Khan, when in the opposition, was critical of the programme. After becoming Prime Minister, he accepted it. Pakistan needed Chinese help to meet its debt and foreign exchange crises. For China, CPEC is an expression of geo-politics.

Domestic critics of CPEC point to the absence of consultation with stakeholders. 'CPEC's Long-Term Plan (2017-2030) was formulated by the centre with little input from local leaders, business or civil society actors.'[6] CPEC also led to the demand for security from Chinese contractors and engineers. This increased military presence, particularly in Gilgit-Baltistan in the north and Gwadar in the south. 'From CPEC's entry point, Gwadar, to its exit point, in Gilgit-Baltistan, the state's response to local dissent and alienation has been an overbearing security presence'.[7]

Most of the financing under CPEC consists of loans, not investment. This could worsen Pakistan's debt problem, which has already assumed crisis proportions. This will certainly add to the current account deficit, and place pressure on the Pakistani rupee once the repayment starts. Most of the projects are in the infrastructure and power sectors which do not generate foreign exchange needed for repayment.

'During Prime Minister Imran Khan's visit to China, on October 8, 2019, no particular mention was made on the halting pace of the China-Pakistan Economic Corridor (CPEC)'.[8] The CPEC may not be a panacea for Pakistan's problems. Other countries have done better, despite Pakistan's much longer exposure to that country. 'Bangladesh's exports to China have been recorded at $ 3.3 billion in July 2019, as compared to Pakistan's that stand at $ 1.9 billion'.[9]

The CPEC will affect 'Gilgit-Baltistan' more than 'Azad' Jammu and Kashmir. The main artery of CPEC runs through this territory. It also has more hydro-power potential. The impact could be more beneficial, in case it gets fair remuneration, though this is unlikely under the present dispensation. Whether or not it benefits, it will have to bear the damage in terms of water inundation and population displacement. This will also bring in an influx of outsiders to the province.

5 August 2019 and Pakistan's Reaction

Pakistan never accepted India's argument of autonomy for J&K as sufficient. As such, it need not have been concerned about the abolition of Article 370 announced in the Indian Parliament on 5 August 2019. It chose however to give a shrill response. Pakistan's protests lacked credibility as it did not provide constitutional protection for preserving demography or property rights in either 'Azad Jammu and Kashmir' or 'Gilgit-Baltistan'. Prime Minister Imran Khan convened a meeting of the National Security Council. 'AJK' Prime Minister Raja Farooq Haider made speeches in the 'AJK Assembly', which was also addressed by Prime Minister Imran Khan. The issue did not achieve much traction internationally despite Pakistani and Chinese attempts to rake it up.

This was a 'good crisis' for Raja Farooq Haider. He belongs to the Muslim Conference, and was aligned with PML-N. He lost his political patron when Nawaz Sharif was forced out of power before the end of his term. The change in government in Islamabad eventually produces a change in Muzaffarabad. However, Pakistani rulers have been cautious in upsetting the status quo in 'Azad' Jammu and Kashmir whenever tensions mount with India. Thus, Raja Farooq Haider got a reprieve. For POK politicians, increase in profile of the 'Kashmir cause' transforms the territory into a front-line state. This may cause hardship for the people, but the leadership thrives.

Imran Khan also benefited from the artificial 'crisis' Pakistan trumped up, though for him the situation carries risks as well. A few months before India announced the re-organization of Jammu and Kashmir, Pakistan had received a bail-out from the IMF. But this came with 'conditionalities' on fiscal discipline and better efforts at resource mobilization. This was bound to generate socio-economic tensions and political fall-out for the regime. Unmindful of these pressing issues, Imran Khan embarked on his agenda of 'Ehtesaab' or accountability. The opposition saw in this, an attempt at political vendetta. The increase in tension with India also carries risk for Pakistani rulers. Ayub Khan was weakened by the 1965 war, and the 1971 defeat forced the military junta out of power. A civilian politician is much weaker to face the consequences. Therefore, the tensions have to be moderated.

The crisis gave an opportunity to both Pakistan's Prime Minister and his 'AJK' counterpart, for grandstanding. Raja Farooq Haider made an impassioned speech in the 'AJK' Assembly on 14 August 2019. But he did not forget his domestic agenda. He made an appeal to Prime Minister Imran Khan to attempt political reconciliation with the opposition. Maryam Sharif was arrested barely a week earlier on 8 August on charges of corruption. The arrest was made on the orders of the National Accountability Bureau when she was visiting her father, former Prime Minister Nawaz Sharif, in jail.[10]

Raja Farooq Haider made a speech in the 'AJK' Assembly on 8 August[11] after his return from Islamabad, where he had gone to attend a meeting of the

National Security Council. While making a reference to alleged repression on the Indian side of the LOC, he also mentioned difficulties like "**constitutional problem, 'Azad Gilgit-Baltistan'**" on the Pakistani side of the Line of Control (LOC). This was a public admission of an unequal arrangement imposed on 'AJK' by Pakistan through the 'interim constitution', as well as separation of the Northern Areas from it. He said that after India's recent decision to abolish Articles 370 and 35-A, there was no agreement left between the two countries, except the Indus Water Treaty. The statement had no logic as Articles 370 and 35-A were part of Indian Constitution, which had nothing to do with any bilateral agreement. He said that now there is no LOC, and we are back to the Ceasefire Line. The comment that the Indus Water Treaty was still valid reflects pragmatic concern in preserving a treaty where India generously agreed to give 80 per cent of water to the lower riparian.

In his speech of 8 August, Raja Farooq also called for extending 'AJK' laws to Jammu and Kashmir. This was an interesting comment from the Prime Minister, who cannot extend 'AJK' laws to Northern Areas, now called 'Gilgit-Baltistan'. He gave a sombre assessment of Pakistan's international and domestic contexts. During his visit to Islamabad, he had called on Foreign Minister Qureshi. According to Raja Farooq Haider, Pakistan was disappointed with the reactions of an Arab country with which it had very close relations in the past, that the changes in J&K were India's internal affair. He said that only Muslim countries who supported Pakistan were Turkey, Malaysia and, to some extent, Iran. He also conveyed a gloomy assessment of the domestic situation, where the session of the Pakistan National Assembly was followed by the arrest of Maryam Nawaz Sharif. Raja Farooq said that as a result, all the attention was diverted from the 'Kashmir cause' to domestic discord in Pakistan.

Raja Farooq Haider also made a pointed reference to the Northern Areas in his speeches on 14 August 2019.[12] He said that Gilgit and Skardu used to send two representatives to the Kashmir Assembly during the Maharaja's period. While he motioned towards 'President' of 'AJK', Sardar Masood Khan, the point would not have been lost on Prime Minister Imran Khan who was present. Raja Farooq also said that the people of Jammu and Kashmir had maintained their 'Kashmiri identity' despite [oppression by] rulers from the time of Akbar to Vajpayee and Modi. He emphasized Kashmir's diversity, and stressed unity in diversity. 'AJK' has 98.5 per cent Muslims now—this percentage is higher than that of Pakistan, which has 98 per cent Muslim population. His attachment to diversity in Jammu and Kashmir is interesting considering its absence in 'AJK'.

Prime Minister Imran Khan, in his speech on 14 August in the 'AJK Assembly',[13] did not respond to the pointed reference by Raja Farooq to the representation of Gilgit and Skardu in the Kashmir Assembly. He was dismissive of the advice by his host on following a policy of national reconciliation. He does not have to—on the 'Kashmir' issue, no Pakistani politician can afford to be seen as deviating from the politically 'correct' line in public discourse. PM Imran Khan's speech was a repeat of his performance earlier in the Pakistan National Assembly where he blamed India and took upon himself the task of projecting the 'Kashmir cause' abroad. He told the 'AJK' Assembly that he would act as its ambassador.

Six months later, another set of speeches were delivered in the 'AJK Assembly' by Raja Farooq and Prime Minister Imran Khan on the occasion of Kashmir Solidarity Day on 5 February 2020. This time, Raja Farooq[14] cautioned PM Imran Khan against accepting US mediation on Kashmir. He also suggested that Pakistan should seriously study the consequences of India's collapse so that it does not find itself unprepared, as the West was when the Soviet Union disintegrated. He repeated his advice that PM Imran Khan should rise above partisan politics. PM Imran Khan[15] had added to his litany of charges against India by referring to the Citizenship Amendment Bill, which has no link with the 'Kashmir issue'. He made a pointed attack on Prime Minister Modi. He rejected Raja Farooq's advice about national reconciliation. He said that the process of accountability was part of democratic politics, and cited approvingly President Xi Ping's actions who has jailed 450 ministers.

Two things stand out from the public response of the 'AJK Prime Minister' and Prime Minister Imran Khan. The 'Kashmir cause' is embedded in Pakistan's domestic politics. Second, neither of them mentioned developments within 'Azad Jammu and Kashmir'. 'Azad' Jammu and Kashmir Prime Minister made a reference to the separation of the Northern Areas. PM Imran Khan did not respond.

While Pakistan went around creating a hullabaloo on the abolition of Article 370, it kept very quiet about the 'Gilgit-Baltistan Order of 2018', which abolished the list of 61 items on which the elected Assembly could legislate. The Order with some minor changes was upheld by the Pakistan Supreme Court in January 2019. The Pakistan government recently went back to the original 'G-B Order of 2018' against which the people elected the Assembly and the Supreme Appellate Court of the territory had vehemently protested.

Pakistan is protesting against the division of Jammu and Kashmir State between two Union Territories. Actually, 'Azad' Jammu and Kashmir, and 'Gilgit-Baltistan' have been organized and run as units tightly controlled by the Federal Ministry of Kashmir Affairs and Northern Areas since their inception. Their situation is worse. While people of Union Territories in India can vote even for seats in the National Parliament, the people of these two territories cannot do so. If this is due to their status as territories awaiting a Plebiscite that raises a more serious question—about changes brought about by Pakistan in those two territories, including ceding a part of them to China without waiting for a Plebiscite. The democratic deficit in the two entities cannot be justified in terms of any UN resolution, and goes against the spirit of the UN Charter.

Budget

Gilgit-Baltistan had a budget outlay of Pakistan Rs. 62.9577 billion for the fiscal year 2019-20. An amount of Rs. 37.71 billion or 60 per cent of the total outlay was allocated for non-development budget and Rs. 17.40 billion or 40 per cent for development projects.[16] The education and health sectors received only Rs. 1.26 billion and 587 million rupees, respectively.[17] This represented a paltry 2 per cent for education and 0.93 per cent for health out of the total budget outlay. For a territory which ranks amongst the lowest in terms of the Human Development Index (HDI) in Pakistan or Pakistan-controlled areas, this perpetuates the problem of under-development.

'Azad Jammu and Kashmir' on the other hand had a budget outlay of Pakistani Rs. 121.56 billion for FY 2019-20, which included Rs. 97 billion for non-development budget and Rs. 24.560 billion for development purposes. This included Rs. 25 billion from income tax and other taxes, while 54 billion rupees were allotted as Federal grant and over 18 billion rupees as state resources.[18] Out of the annual development budget, 40 per cent accounted for the communication sector, which seems unusually high for any country or region, unless, this reflects road building or communication network for the military in a forward area. The budget reflects lower priority for social sectors like education (11 %) and health (3 %).[19]

COVID

'Gilgit-Baltistan's strategic location has also made it most exposed to China's latest export. It has the highest incidence of COVID cases amongst Pakistan's provinces or Pakistan-controlled territories. The territory with a population of 1.25 million had 501 confirmed cases as on 15 May 2020. 'AJK' had 105 confirmed cases against a population of 4.05 million. The total number of cases in Pakistan with a population of 212.2 million was 37,218. *In per capita terms, the incidence of Covid in G-B was 15 times higher than the 'AJK' and more than twice as high as Pakistan's average.* The territory is the main artery of CPEC.[20] As we have seen above, Gilgit-Baltistan budget for FY 2019-20 allocated less than 1 per cent of budget resources to the health sector.

While the region continues to struggle with its problems of under-development, Pakistan's establishment continues to strengthen its control over this strategic region. The latest in this series is the Pakistan Supreme Court's judgement extending the Election Act 2017 to Gilgit-Baltistan. This further exposes Pakistan's dubious claim that it treats the area as a distinct legal entity awaiting Plebiscite. Pakistan's laws and constitution have been extended to the territory as a result of executive action. Judicial intervention by Pakistan's Supreme Court has only reinforced the trend. Under the notification issued by President Alvi of Pakistan, the Gilgit-Baltistan Order of 2018 has been amended to provide an interim government in G-B pending elections. This resurrects the controversial Order, which had been struck down by the Gilgit Supreme Appellate Court last year.

The Pakistan government not only selectively quotes UN resolutions; it is also selective in applying judgements of its own Supreme Court. The SC judgement of 1999 calling for judicially enforceable fundamental rights and a representative government is yet to be implemented. The Supreme Court in turn is complicit in quashing the order of the Supreme Appellate Court of Gilgit-Baltistan, which had challenged Islamabad's authority by rejecting Gilgit-Baltistan Order of 2018. Would grant of 'provincial status' to G-B help better protect the interests of the people of the territory? The enthusiasm for such a status is decidedly muted in case of 'Azad' Jammu and Kashmir.

NOTES

1. 'Conflict Dynamics in Gilgit-Baltistan' written by Izhar Hunzai, the CEO of the Aga Khan Rural Support Program operating in Gilgit-Baltistan, as quoted in '*The Permanent Liminality of Pakistan's Northern Areas The Case of Gilgit-Baltistan*' by Hamna Tariq, Page 4, Trinity College Digital Repository.
2. Feyyaz, "Geopolitics, Statehood, Violence, and Space compression in Gilgit-Baltistan," p. 38, as quoted in '*The Permanent Liminality of Pakistan's Northern Areas The Case of Gilgit-Baltistan*' by Hamna Tariq, Page 4, Trinity College Digital Repository, page 22, Trinity College Digital Repository.
3. George Stöber, "Religious Identities Provoked: The Gilgit 'Textbook Controversy' and its Conflictual Context,", as cited in '*The Permanent Liminality of Pakistan's Northern Areas The Case of Gilgit-Baltistan*' by Hamna Tariq, Page 23, Trinity College Digital Repository.

4. Aziz Ali Dad, "Boundaries and Identities: The Case of Gilgit-Baltistan," Crossroads Asia Working Paper Series, no. 34 (2016): 24 as cited in '*The Permanent Liminality of Pakistan's Northern Areas The Case of Gilgit-Baltistan*' by Hamna Tariq, Page 23, Trinity College Digital Repository.
5. Hunzai, Izhar, *Conflict Dynamics in Gilgit-Baltistan*, US Institute of Peace, 2013. www.jstor.org/stable/resrep12204. Accessed 16 May 2020.
6. *Daily Times*, 'CPEC opportunities and risks' by Naveed Aman Khan, January 4, 2020.
7. Ibid.
8. *Tribune*, 'CPEC and the wages of mismanagement' by Durdana Najam, October 16, 2019. Accessed on 16.5.2020.
9. Ibid.
10. *BBC*, Maryam Nawaz Sharif, opposition politician arrested in Pakistan, 8 August 2019.
11. www.samaa.tv., You Tube, 8 August, 2019.
12. *Public TV*, You Tube, 14 August, 2019.
13. *ARY News*, You Tube, Prime Minister Imran Khan's speech in 'AJK Assembly', 14 August 2019.
14. *92 News HD*, You Tube, Prime Minister Raja Farooq Haider's speech in 'AJK Assembly' on 5.2.2020.
15. *92 News HD*, You Tube, Prime Minister Imran Khan's speech in 'AJK Assembly' on 5.2.2020.
16. *The Nation*, Meraj Alam, June 21, 2019.
17. *Radio Pakistan*, GB Govt. presented an annual budget of Rs. 62.95 billion for 2019-20, June 20,2019.
18. AJK tax free budget with total outlay of Rs. 121 billion announced in Muzaffarabad, Radio Pakistan, www.radio.pk, accessed on 15 May 2020.
19. *The Nation*, 'AJK unveils record Rs. 1.21 trillion budget for 2019-20' by Altaf Hameed Rao.
20. Covid.gov.pk

9

Pakistan's Nuclear Brinkmanship: Continued Reliance on Nuclear Weapons

Dr. Shalini Chawla

Nuclear deterrence plays a crucial role in India-Pakistan relations, which continues to stay troubled with escalating tensions between the two nations. India-Pakistan hostility is distinct and the conflict between the two countries has been at four levels: *Conventional, Sub-conventional, Nuclear* and (now) *Cyberwarfare & Propaganda.* Nuclear weapons remain integral to Pakistan's overall strategic positioning against India. While New Delhi's nuclear objectives have been primarily political for deterrence, on the other hand, Islamabad acquired nuclear weapons for *war prevention* and to conduct the policy of sub-conventional warfare through terrorism without fear of Indian military retaliation. This explicitly explains Pakistan's nuclear positioning which relies on a *first use doctrine* projecting a low nuclear threshold and an element of uncertainty.

There have been significant developments in the last few years that have added stress in strained India-Pakistan relations. The nuclear dimension has been highlighted extensively by Pakistan. Prime Minister Imran Khan has repeatedly stressed on the threat of a nuclear war after India's punitive airstrikes in Balakot and much more after the revocation of Article 370. Emphasising the nuclear factor by Pakistan does display its immaturity and desperation to attract global attention towards Kashmir. The abrogation of Article 370 by India did leave Pakistan surprised and the state has been reacting furiously on various fronts displaying its anxiety to deal with Jammu and Kashmir's new status. Pakistan has launched a propaganda/narrative war, and is making aggressive efforts to fallaciously project India as a state run by "Nazi ideology" under Prime Minister Modi, highlighting Kashmir at every possible national and international forum.

Prime Minister Imran Khan in his unrelenting tweets and addresses has repeatedly highlighted various aspects of the nuclear threat; for example, both India and Pakistan possess nuclear weapons and thus, any crisis in the region is alarming; Pakistan has nuclear weapons and thus, the probability of a nuclear war is high; India's nuclear weapons are a threat to global and regional security, etc.

In the past, Pakistan has used the nuclear card spasmodically and this stems from its basic insecurity as a state and its failure to develop its strengths. Islamabad has long tried to balance its domestic vulnerabilities with nuclear weapons that it treats as the ultimate guarantor of its survivability and security. Its nuclear history and thinking explicitly explains its nuclear behaviour and brinkmanship that we see today.

Why Nuclear Weapons?

Pakistan's nuclear objectives explain its nuclear doctrine and posturing that we see today. Islamabad wants nuclear weapons for deterrence and, more importantly, war prevention. The nuclear weapons are projected as the *ultimate guarantee* for Pakistan's security and survivability. Pakistan's nuclear aims can be summed up in three points:

1. *To neutralise India's superior conventional military capability*: India's conventional military superiority and Pakistan's desire to neutralise India's superiority has largely shaped Pakistan's overall defence build-up. Acquiring nuclear capability, according to it, was essential to compensate for the conventional imbalance, which it felt, was responsible for its loss in the 1947, 1965 and 1971 wars (Pakistan Prime Minister Zulfiqar Ali Bhutto started the nuclear weapon programme after the 1971 war).
2. *To continue strategy of sub-conventional war through terrorism against India*: Pakistan has tried to project its nuclear assets as an instrument of blackmailing. The acquisition of the nuclear capability (in 1987) enhanced Pakistan's capability to wage and escalate the covert war in Kashmir. The policymakers in Pakistan seem to be convinced that they will be able to carry on, or rather accelerate, their activities in Kashmir under the broader threat of using nuclear weapons, if required, and this would constrain India's strategic moves.
3. *Desire to be visualised as the leader of the Islamic world*: Pakistan's nuclear weapons (and strategy) are also motivated by its deep desire to emerge as a formidable country of the Muslim world and to be visualised as the

leader of the Islamic world. It perceived nuclear weapons capability as a "currency of power" which would enhance its strategic image in the international community in general and Muslim countries in particular. In this pursuit, it did seek financial help from the Muslim countries for nuclear weapon acquisition (in the 1970s and 1980s) and (later) illegally transferred nuclear technology to Iran, Libya and North Korea.

Pakistan's Nuclear Doctrine

In the pre-nuclear test period, Pakistan's doctrine was that of ambiguity. Although, Pakistan even today does not have an officially announced doctrine, statements made by responsible policymakers in Pakistan have clearly outlined the basic elements in its nuclear doctrine. There is an unofficial code adopted by the Pakistani leadership, based on *Indo-centricity, credible minimum deterrence, strategic restraint* and *first use.* Interestingly and rather ironically, the code asserts the principles of a peaceful programme revolving more around maintaining a balance against the Indian force build-up, but it includes making a first strike in response to not only a conventional attack by India but also a posed threat from India.

Minimum Nuclear Deterrence

This is one of the basic tenets of Pakistan's nuclear doctrine. The concept of credible minimum deterrence is not based specifically on the numbers but it is the weapon arsenal including the nuclear weapons, delivery systems, command and control and the doctrine and strategy, based on the perceived threat perception from India. Credible minimum deterrent force intends to build a minimum force capable of inflicting nuclear destruction on India. Prime Minister Nawaz Sharif very distinctly talked about it in May 1999 when he highlighted the key elements of Pakistan's nuclear policy at the National Defence College: "Nuclear restraint, stabilisation and minimum credible deterrence constitute the basic elements of Pakistan's nuclear policy."[1]

The reasons for Pakistan's (initial) adoption of credible minimum deterrence are obvious. Pakistan desires a financially viable nuclear arsenal as the whole logic of going nuclear was Pakistan's inability to cope with India's conventional military build-up, primarily due to the financial constraints. The term "minimum" begs definition and can be interpreted differently by the states. Pakistan's minimum deterrence appears to be based on the capability to inflict unacceptable damage or assured destruction. Pakistan asserted minimum deterrence but has a fast-growing arsenal and reportedly possesses approximately 160 warheads.[2]

First Use Doctrine

Pakistan has long held the belief that being the weaker state it can compensate for weakness by taking a bold initiative, preferably with strategic surprise, to attack Indian military capability and thus reduce the adverse margin of capabilities. This was the military strategy it practised in wars it waged against India, including the last one in Kargil in 1999, and, more importantly, the war through terrorism across the border for around six decades now. Seen in the context of this strategic mindset, it is not surprising that it has adopted a nuclear doctrine of "First Use". In fact, it has often claimed that it would/could use nuclear weapons at the very beginning of the war with India if the Indian military even crossed the international border.

Rejecting India's proposal for a joint no-first-use pledge in the aftermath of the nuclear tests, Pakistan took the stand that it would be the first to use the nuclear weapons to counter India's conventional capability. Lt. Gen. Sardar Lodhi (retd.) has justified Pakistan's dismissal of India's offer:

> "India's offer of a treaty to be signed by the two countries, agreeing not to be the first to use nuclear weapons against each other is one-sided and would benefit India only, as it has a superior conventional force. It may be more apt for both countries to sign a mutual test ban treaty to start with, followed by a no-war pact."[3]

Pakistan's argument has been that, in the likelihood of a conventional attack, or in a situation when India has breached the defence line causing a major setback to the defence and security arsenal of Pakistan, then, due to the fear of being defeated in a conventional war against India, Pakistan will resort to the first use option. Pakistan will go for nuclear weapons first even if the attack from the Indian side is with conventional weapons. Thus, a first use policy according to the Pakistani leadership provided credible security guarantees to their national sovereignty.

The same logic for first use was used by NATO during the Cold War when it suggested that it would be the first to use nuclear weapons in a conflict, as they perceived that a hostile Soviet Union had an overwhelming advantage in conventional forces. Following the collapse of the Soviet Union, NATO has tried to play down the role of nuclear weapons but it maintains the doctrine that gives them the leverage to use nuclear weapons first in case of a conventional attack.

The scenarios in which Pakistan would opt for nuclear weapons have been spelled out by the Pakistani elites in the past (on different occasions) and cultivated the posture of irrational rationality to try and enhance the effect of this posture. Lt. Gen. Khalid Kidwai, head of the Strategic Planning Division in Pakistan's Nuclear Command and Control system, in 2002, in an interview to Italian journalists, claimed that nuclear weapons would be used only "if the very existence of Pakistan as a state is at stake." But he went on to state that Pakistan would definitely use nuclear weapons in case the deterrence fails and:

1. If India attacks Pakistan and conquers a large part of its territory (space threshold);
2. If India destroys a large part either of Pakistan's land or air forces (military threshold);
3. If India proceeds to the economic strangling of Pakistan (economic strangling);
4. If India pushes Pakistan into political destabilisation or creates large-scale internal subversion in Pakistan (domestic destabilisation).[4]

The last two elements based on economic strangulation and domestic destabilisation cannot be seen in isolation and it would not be incorrect to say that these vaguely draw vast parameters that can potentially include various steps taken by the Indian government in the wake of acute tension or conventional confrontation.

The effort from the Pakistani leadership has been to convey a message to India that any reaction from India against Pakistan could possibly form a ground for the use of nuclear weapons. The need for Pakistan to maintain this position of first use is further exacerbated with India's assertion that the possibility of a conventional war is not ruled out even with the two states possessing nuclear weapons. This has been proved more than once, during the Kargil war, and again with India's retaliation—Uri surgical strikes and in the 2019 Balakot airstrikes.

Possibility of Pre-emption

Pakistan's obsessive reliance on the doctrine of first use policy seems to be emerging from two factors. First, Pakistan wants to keep an option open for "pre-emptive nuclear strikes" against India and it is convinced that its pre-emptive strikes would lead to the destruction of India's retaliatory capabilities and/or restrict Indian political decision-making. Secondly, Pakistan has failed to consider the consequences of Indian retaliation. The Pakistani leadership seems to assume that India would not opt for nuclear weapons against it even after getting hit.

Assumptions related to India's strategic culture could be one of the strong factors shaping Pakistani assumption which had seem to be intensified with India's non-reactive approach (with conventional means) towards the Pakistan-sponsored terrorist attacks (till recently!).

India in its nuclear strategy and doctrine has adopted "restraint" as a responsible and politically mature nation-state. But the Indian restraint cannot be read by Pakistan as an unending and open-ended policy of India. New Delhi shall resort to retaliation to a Pakistani nuclear strike given the situation and the consequences for Pakistan would be fatal.

Weapon of Last Resort

Most of the Pakistani writings pre-1998 pointed towards build-up of the nuclear capability against the Indian conventional forces and thus, implied its first use. But there was a projection of a shift in the Pakistani thinking regarding the use of nuclear weapons and adoption of a relatively moderate stand by claiming nuclear weapons as the "weapon of last resort".

Abdul Sattar (former Pakistan Foreign Minister), Agha Shahi and Zulfiqar Ali Khan jointly authored an article in *The News* on October 5, 1999, which stated:[5]

> "Although the precise contingencies in which Pakistan may use nuclear weapons have not been articulated or even defined by the government, the assumption has been that if the enemy launches a war and undertakes a piercing attack to occupy large territories or communications junctions, the *weapon of last resort* would have to be invoked."

President Pervez Musharraf, in May 2002, said that if it came to war between the nuclear-armed rivals, he would "respond with full might."

In April 2002, in an interview published in the German magazine, *Der Spiegel,* Musharraf said:

> "If the pressure on Pakistan becomes too great, then as a last resort, the [use of] atom bomb is also possible."[6]

Musharraf's statement of last resort was made in 2002 and in the same period in his address to Army Corps in Karachi, he said that war with India was averted due to his repeated warnings for using "unconventional" means (interpreted most erroneously as nuclear weapons) in case of India breaching the red line. This no doubt (also) implied use of large number of guerrilla/jihadi fighters rather than nuclear weapons. Otherwise, there is contradiction in Pakistan's stance where, on one side it claims to use its nuclear weapons as a last resort, and on the other is convinced that the threat of nuclear weapons was successful in deterring Indian military posture.

Nuclear Policy Based on Restraint and Responsibility

In the mid-2000s, Pakistan's endeavour was to project itself as a *responsible* nuclear power. The need to do so was exacerbated with India and the USA signing the nuclear deal. Pakistan has been keen for a similar nuclear agreement with the USA and thus, projection of a responsible nuclear posture became inevitable. In 2006, Lt. Gen. Khalid Kidwai, in his address to the Naval Postgraduate School, Monterey, said that Pakistan had dealt with formidable challenges by developing a nuclear policy based on "restraint and responsibility" with four salient features:

> "(1) deterrence of all forms of external aggression; (2) ability to deter a counter-strike against strategic assets; (3) stabilization of strategic deterrence in South Asia; and (4) conventional and strategic deterrence methods."

Gen. Khalid Kidwai talks about "deterrence to all forms of external aggression", which should include both conventional and nuclear aggression. This is in line with the statements made by Pakistani policymakers in the past. Deterring India's conventional posture remains the prime objective of Pakistan's nuclear weapons. Kidwai talks about building the ability to deter a counter-strike against strategic assets. Pakistan has expanded its arsenal and the delivery systems substantively in order to threaten a disarming strike to wipe out, or at least drastically reduce, India's retaliatory capability [deter counter-strike].

Full Spectrum Deterrence

India's stance on the probability of a conventional war under the nuclear overhang challenged Islamabad's conviction about New Delhi's consistent restrain and hesitation in responding militarily to a Pakistan-sponsored act of terror.

Pakistan did make an effort to adopt a posture of a "restrained and responsible nuclear power" in 2006-2007. This posture was necessary from Pakistan's point of view as the leadership was trying to convey the message to the West and the international community that its nuclear arsenal is safe and not threatened by a potential jihadi takeover. Pakistan did see a remarkable rise in terrorist attacks and suicide bombings after 2007 with the creation of the Tehrik-i-Taliban Pakistan (TTP) which was prominent by its anti-state agenda.

On April 19, 2011, Pakistan tested its short-range surface-to-surface multi-tube ballistic missile Hatf-9 (NASR). The official press release by NASR said:

> "[The NASR Weapon System] has been developed to add deterrence value to Pakistan's Strategic Weapons Development programme at shorter ranges. NASR, with a range of 60 km, carries nuclear warheads of appropriate yield with high accuracy, [and] shoot and scoot attributes. This quick response system addresses the need to deter evolving threats."[7]

NASR provides Pakistan with short-range missile capability in addition to the long-range ballistic missiles and cruise missiles. Also, according to Pakistani military officials, Hatf-9 belongs to the category of tactical nuclear weapons (TNW) and is a low-yield battlefield deterrent, capable of inflicting damage on armed brigades and divisions.[8] According to Pakistan, Hatf-9 is its counter to India's *Cold Start Doctrine*, which envisions limited conventional response from the Indian side in response to sub-conventional attacks on India originating from Pakistani territory.

Pakistan claimed it is developing a sea-based nuclear force to be able to match India's nuclear triad. The Naval Strategic Force command was announced in 2012. In January 2017, Pakistan conducted the first test of its SLCM, the Babur-3, from a submarine. It is estimated that Babur-3 has a range of 450 km and will be carried on Pakistan's diesel-powered Agosta 90B submarine.

Pakistan is seemingly proud of the full spectrum deterrence and it conveniently claims to have developed the nuclear capability to be launched from all the three platforms—land, air and sea. Full Spectrum Deterrence for Pakistan also implies full spectrum of scenarios, since Pakistan maintains a projection of a low nuclear threshold and also an element of uncertainty. The nuclear posture seems to rely on the *threat of use of nuclear weapons* to deal with a wide range of crises vis-à-vis India.

Conclusion

Pakistan's nuclear posture does reflect some distinct contradictions. It talks about being a restrained and responsible nuclear power but at the same time relies on a *first use* doctrine and boasts about the *TNWs* and *Full Spectrum Deterrence*. It continues to assert that it does not want to start a war with India, highlights the disastrous consequences of a nuclear war but repeatedly flags the threat of nuclear conflict, creating war hysteria in the region. It would not be incorrect to state that Pakistan has very *rationally adopted the posture of irrationality*.

Pakistan's nuclear posturing did suffer a blow to some extent with India's airstrikes in Balakot on February 26, 2019, in retaliation to the terror attack in Pulwama claimed by the Jaish-e-Mohammed (JeM) on February 14, 2019. But, it seems that Pakistan's reliance on nuclear weapons to serve its strategic objectives has not been altered. Its reliance on nuclear deterrence has intensified with constantly growing asymmetries between India and Pakistan over the last two decades. At this point of time, Pakistan's repeated flagging of nuclear threat can be attributed to mainly two factors:

1. Firstly, Pakistan has spent an enormous amount of national resources in the build-up of the nuclear arsenal on the pretext that nuclear weapons are the ultimate weapons for a state's survival and security. Pakistan has always prioritised its defence expenditure even though it has been at the cost of the socio-economic development of the country. The leadership at this point wants to justify the enormous nuclear build-up to its own population and assure them that nuclear weapons will ultimately guard Pakistan's fortune.
2. Secondly, Imran Khan wants to remind India and the international community about the presence of nuclear weapons in the region and the dangers emanating from a potential nuclear war. Pakistan is certainly trying hard to get international attention on Kashmir by flagging the nuclear threat.

Disclaimer: Some sections of the paper have been published in Shalini Chawla, "Pakistan's Nuclear Positioning", Defence and Diplomacy, vol. 9, No... 2, Special Issue: Nuclear Dynamics, January-March 2020, pp 1-12.

NOTES

1. "Remarks of the Prime Minister of Pakistan, Nawaz Sharif, on Nuclear Policies and the CTBT," National Defence College, Islamabad, May 20, 1999.
2. Hans M. Kristensen and Matt Korda, "Status of World Nuclear Forces," *Federation of American Scientists*, April 2020, https://fas.org/issues/nuclear-weapons/status-world-nuclear-forces/. Accessed on May 10, 2020.
3. Lt. Gen. F.S. Lodhi, "Pakistan's Nuclear Doctrine," *Defence Journal*, at, http://www.defencejournal.com/apr99/pak-nuclear-doctrine.htm. Accessed on May 10, 2011.
4. As cited in Paolo Cotta-Ramusino and Maurizio Martellini, *Nuclear Safety, Nuclear Stability and Nuclear Strategy in Pakistan*, Landau Network–Centro Volta Report, January, 2002.
5. Agha Shahi, Zulfiqar Khan and Abdul Sattar, "Securing Nuclear Peace", *The News*, October 5, 1999.
6. Cited in H.S. Rao, "Pak May Use Nukes in the Event of War: Musharraf," rediff.com,April 6, 2002, at http://www.rediff.com/news/2002/apr/06pak2htm
7. Rodney W. Jones, "Pakistan's Answer to Cold Start?", *The Friday Times*,vol. XXIII, no. 13 (May 13-19, 2011), at http://www.thefridaytimes.com/13052011/page7.shtml. Accessed on November 12, 2011.
8. "Pakistan successfully test-fires nuclear capable Hatf-9," *The Express Tribune*, April 20, 2011.

10

Pakistan's Defence Production: Developing Indigenous Capability

Dr. Shalini Chawla

In July 2019, Chief of Army Staff, Pakistan, General Javed Bajwa, at a two-day seminar on "Defence Production: Security through Self-Reliance" said, "There is a need to amplify indigenization through fully integrated Public and Private Organisations in Defence production for meaningful progression in defence of the country."[1]

Pakistan's defence modernisation has been at an accelerated pace in the last two decades owing to its growing strategic relationship with China and its phased alliance with the USA post 2001. Chinese assistance came in the form of supply of military equipment (starting in the mid-1960s), nuclear weapons (technology and weapons) and a robust cooperation in Pakistan's indigenous defence build-up. Some of the significant achievements for Pakistan in defence production include production of battle tanks (Al-Khalid, Al-Zarrar), co-production of the Karakoram K-8 and assembly and co-production of the JF-17s. The need to develop the indigenous defence capability was felt within Pakistan after the US sanctions were imposed in 1965 and then in the 1990s which led to complete suspension of delivery of US equipment (and spare parts). Apart from gaining self-reliance, Pakistan aims to use its defence production capabilities to export defence equipment to the Muslim nations in order to boost export earnings and, more importantly, build-up alliances and create its position as a leader of the Islamic world.

Background

Pakistan "inherited insecurity" at the time of its creation and the Pakistani leadership felt that it had received an unfair share in the defence resources at the time of partition. Pakistan's desire to be self-sufficient was described well in former Army Chief Abdul Waheed's statement, "It is a time-tested fact that no country can maintain her armed forces on borrowed weapons. To be self-confident in the community of nations, Pakistan must become self-sufficient in defence production."[2]

Pakistan's early efforts towards indigenous defence production can be traced to the tenure of first Prime Minister of Pakistan Liaquat Ali Khan, who issued a directive to establish an ordnance factory to manufacture .303-inch calibre rifles and its ammunition in Rawalpindi. After his assassination, the second Prime Minister of Pakistan, Khawaja Nazimuddin, proceeded with the plans and in 1951, the foundation stone of four industries at Wah cantonment was laid and four workshops were opened. Presently, Pakistan has 14 large factories and subsidiaries fulfilling the defence needs of its armed forces.

Eventually, building the industrial complex set-up at Wah was started and by 1954, a few other facilities were completed. The production of various stores such as 25 Pdr and 40 mm anti-aircraft guns ammunition, 2-inch and 3-inch mortar shells, etc., was started. In the early 1960s, the explosives factory—which included the manufacture of nitric acid, sulphuric acid recycling plants for recovery of waste acids and plants for production of intermediates such as acetone, ether and plant for production of propellants and explosives—was set up with foreign assistance.[3] However, the decades of the 1950s and 1960s did not witness much growth of defence production facilities and the nation's defence needs were met mostly by the USA. The suspension of US military assistance after 1965 did intensify the desire in Pakistan to move towards self-reliance. President Zulfikar Ali Bhutto encouraged indigenous defence production owing to mainly four factors:

1. Pakistan's experience in 1965 and 1971 clearly proved that dependence on external sources for defence equipment restricted its war fighting capability.
2. Bhutto wanted to control the Bonapartist tendencies in the Pakistan Army.
3. He believed that defence production would have a spillover impact on the overall economic growth.
4. Bhutto visualised Pakistan's dominant role in the Islamic world and he believed that defence production would enable Pakistan to successfully play the role of the *praetorian guard of the Islamic bloc.*[4]

A *Defence Production Division* in the Ministry of Defence was created in 1972. The 1980s under General Zia and the 1990s saw a wide expansion of defence production activities and a large number of varied projects were undertaken in this period.

Defence Production in Pakistan

Starting with an establishment at Wah in cooperation with British Royal Ordnance, a number of defence production facilities were developed in Pakistan. Today, there are over 20 public sector units and over 100 private sector units engaged in the production of defence-related products. While it will not be feasible for this paper to go into the details of all the public sector units, the major public sector units that have expanded significantly and contributed towards self-reliance of the defence industry are discussed for an understanding of Pakistan's defence production.

Pakistan Ordnance Factories

Pakistan Ordnance Factories (POF), Wah, responsible for conventional weapons production, comprises 14 factories. POF is the oldest and the largest complex of defence production units in the country. Progressively set up after 1950 on the model of the Indian Ordnance Factories, they meet almost all the total ordnance needs of the Pakistani armed forces. The POF complex is spread over a radius of 100 km and employs more than 40,000 personnel. This complex has helped to establish and develop a number of sister defence production facilities.

The 14 factories in the complex of POF are as listed below:[5]

1. Weapons Factory
2. Machine Gun Factory
3. Small Arms Ammunition Factory
4. Tank and Anti-Tank Ammunition Factory
5. Medium Artillery Ammunition Factory
6. Heavy Artillery Ammunition Factory
7. Brass Mill
8. Steel Foundry
9. Tungsten Carbide Factory
10. Tungsten Alloy Factory
11. Explosives Factory
12. Propellants Factory
13. Filling Factory
14. Clothing Factory for Uniforms.

POF produces around 112 major items and millions of components for supply to the Pakistani Army, Navy and Air Force. Major productions of the POF include: automatic rifles, anti-tank ammunition, bombs, aircraft ammunition, anti-aircraft ammunition and tank ammunition.[6] Initially, POF products were mostly of British origin produced under licence. There has been a significant amount of investment in the POF and reports suggest that all inputs required for the products starting from raw materials to new technologies are available at the POF.[7]

The POF has always been seen to engage in joint ventures, starting with the Royal Ordnance Factories, UK, in 1951, and set up the first plant for the production of .303 ammunition and corresponding weapons.[8] US Small Arms production facilities for 7.62 calibre ammunition to NATO standards were set up with Germany. This was followed by various other joint ventures with China and Czechoslovakia. Starting in the mid-1950s, the increasing procurement of Chinese products did allow POF products to follow both NATO and other international standards.[9]

The POF became the beneficiary of Pakistan's strategic relationship with China, long alliance with the USA and Pakistan's consistent approach of expanding its options for defence requirements in the West (France, Germany, and Britain). The POF utilised its surplus capacity to cater to local requirements and expand its export base. For example, during the corona virus crisis POF has been producing facemasks and hand sanitizers. Reports suggest that POF has been producing close to 25,000 facemasks and 10,000 litres of hand sanitizers on a daily basis.[10]

POF exports have expanded over the years and the importing nations include Bahrain, Bangladesh, Cambodia, Canada, Denmark, Germany, Hong Kong, Switzerland, Singapore, Sri Lanka, the UAE, Indonesia, Jordan, Kuwait, Malaysia, Myanmar, Saudi Arabia, the UK and the USA. Pakistan defence industry indigenous build-up was aimed to expand Pakistan's footprint in the Muslim world and it is interesting to note that the majority of nations importing from the POF are Muslim nations.

Heavy Industries Taxila (HIT)

Heavy Industries Taxila (HIT), located near Taxila, was set up with the help of China. Until the mid-1960s, Pakistan was receiving imported tanks, initially from the USA (the M-47 and M-48 Patton class in the 1950s and 1960s) and then from the Chinese (the T-59, which was produced in China from the Soviet

T-54 design, built under licence).[11] In 1971, a Heavy Rebuild Factory Project (P-711) was conceived with Chinese assistance and technology to rebuild T-59 tanks. As the fleet of T-59 tanks manufactured by China grew, Pakistan felt the need for a facility to rebuild and modernise the tanks.[12] The facility is spread over 48 acres of land and is capable of rebuilding tanks and power packs as well as manufacturing individual optical and electrical components. When production started in 1981, the HRF had the capacity to rebuild 100 tanks and 250 engines every year and by October 1990, that capacity had been able to service 1,000 tanks and 2,000 engines.[13] Eventually, the Heavy Rebuilt Factory (HRF) at Taxila was renamed *Heavy Industries Taxila*.

HIT, which employs over 7,000 workers, and is devoted to land combat systems, witnessed a rapid growth in the 1980s when it started to produce the T-69 MBT (Main Battle Tank) with Chinese help. Some of the important products of HIT include: *Tank Al-Khalid*, which is an outcome of decade-long Sino-Pakistan efforts; *Tank Al-Zarrar*, which is again a product of Chinese assistance, came into being to keep the fleet of T-59 and T-69 tanks technologically and operationally compatible with modern tanks; *APC Talha*, which is an indigenously designed and manufactured all-terrain, amphibious infantry support vehicle.[14]

Apart from these, Pakistan has developed additional variants of the M113 series APC for the Pakistan Army. A six-wheeled road version *APCSaad* has been developed; Infantry *Fighting Vehicle Al-Hamza* has been developed with a Chinese-made one-man turret and 25 mm cannon; and *ARV-W653* have been manufactured at the HIT, the licence for which was obtained from China. The variations and upgraded versions of the products have continued in the facility to cater to the evolving needs of the Pakistan army. For example, in 2016, the Cavalier Group unveiled its new 8x8 armoured vehicle in the category of Mine Resistant Ambush Protected (MRAP), the HAMZA 8x8 at IDEAS, the International Defence Exhibition in Karachi.[15]

Pakistan Aeronautical Complex (PAC)

Pakistan Aeronautical Complex at Karma, north of Islamabad, was established in 1973. This facility is the nucleus of the aeronautical industry in Pakistan and is dedicated to overhaul and repair Chinese and French aircraft in the Pakistan Air Force inventory. It also undertakes the manufacture of light aircraft and assembly of ground-based radars. PAC consists of the following factories:

The *Mirage Rebuild Factory* (MRF) undertakes a variety of aircraft and engine overhauls. For the last four decades, the MRF became a benchmark of MRO for

Western systems technology through overhauling of the Mirage aircraft.[16] The facility is responsible for structure repair of Western platforms and weapons systems of the Pakistan Air Force. Recovery of the Saab aircraft, which the PAF acquired from Sweden, was done at the MRF.[17]

Overhauling and structure repair of a variety of other jet engines, apart from the Mirages, is carried out at the MRF. These include F-16, C-130, Karakoram-89, T-37, SAAB aircraft.[18]

The Aircraft Rebuild Factory *is the premier Maintenance Repair and Overhaul facility and has undertaken the task of overhauling Chinese origin fighter, trainer and light passenger aircraft: F-6, FT-5, K-8, Y-12, F-7, F-7P and JF-17.*[19]

The Aircraft Manufacturing Factory (AMF) was established in 1975 with the objective of assembling Mushshak (MFI-17) light aircraft/basic trainer with knockdown kits received from foreign sources. It is the only aircraft manufacturing concern in Pakistan, and since 1981, it has been engaged in the manufacture of the light, robust, basic trainer-cum-surveillance aircraft Mushshak, the super Mushshak, a variant with a more powerful engine, cockpit air-conditioning, electric instruments and several other improvements.[20]

Pakistan has focused on Air Force modernisation in the last two decades. Critical capabilities of the AMF include:[21]

- Manufacture of the K-8 in the 1980s
- Manufacture of Unmanned Aerial Vehicle, FALCO in 2008
- Co-production and sub-assemblies of structural parts of the JF-17.

China and Pakistan entered into deals for the co-development of a fourth-generation fighter aircraft, the JF-17 (earlier called the FC-1). China delivered two Joint Fighter (JF-17) Thunder advanced jets to the Pakistan Air Force in March 2007 for flight tests and evaluation. The JF-17 is designated to be a low-cost combat aircraft to meet the tactical and strategic requirements of the Pakistan Air Force with reduced reliance by Pakistan on imports. The JF-17 is co-developed by Pakistan and China and is being built by China's Chengdu Aircraft Industry Corporation (CAC) and Pakistan Aeronautical Complex (PAC). There have been reports that the design was developed by the MiG complex in Russia and transferred to China after the Russian Air Force cancelled procurements. The JF-17 is fitted with RD-93 engine and the initial batch of JF-17s delivered to Pakistan was fitted with the Chinese radar KLJ-7 Multi-role Pulse-Doppler.

In 2007, the Pakistan Air Chief announced that Pakistan had increased its initial target of buying 150 JF-17s to 250 aircraft.[22] This represented Pakistan's confidence in the aircraft and a quantum jump in the Pakistan aircraft industry. Pakistan has received JF-17 Block I and II, and Block III is awaited. China has reportedly overhauled JF-17 Block I. It is interesting to note that Pakistan still lacks the capability of overhauling its growing fleet of JF-17 fighter jets.[23] The PAF fleet currently has 85 JF-17 Block I and II, operationally deployed.[24] Regarding the production of the aircraft, PAC holds the exclusive rights of 58 per cent of JF-17 airframe co-production work.[25]

Kamra Avionics Production Factory was established in 1983 as a small radar maintenance centre. The facility deals with a wide range of activities in the field of aviation electronics. It undertakes the overhauling of Air Defence ground radars and life cycle maintenance of avionics systems of the existing fleet of the PAF.[26]

Heavy Mechanical Complex Ltd. (HMC)

Heavy Mechanical Complex Ltd. (HMC), located in Taxila, is not officially part of the defence production establishment since it is a major heavy engineering subsidiary of the State Engineering Corporation (SEC), controlled by the Ministry of Industries and Production, Government of Pakistan. This was established in 1979 with Chinese assistance and is the largest undertaking of this type in Pakistan.[27] But the Heavy Forge Factory at this complex is significantly important for Pakistan's defence production requirements. HMC is capable of undertaking the designing, engineering and manufacturing of industrial plants and machinery. It manufactures equipment for a large variety of areas including hydroelectric power plants, thermal power plants, oil and gas processing plants, steel structure, railway equipment, etc.[28]

Institute of Optronics

Institute of Optronics was established to assemble/manufacture the night vision devices for the armed forces in 1985 at Rawalpindi. The Institute has established production and testing facilities based on Image Intensifier Tubes to meet a series of military specifications and needs for night vision devices. Night Vision Devices are playing an increasingly important role in command and control, surveillance, accuracy of firepower, etc.[29]

Margalla Electronics (ME)

Based in Islamabad, Margalla Electronics was established in 1984 as a self-reliance project under the defence Production Division to support the Defence Services in the field of electronics.

Air Weapons Complex

The Air Weapons Complex (AWC) located in Wah/Kamra is the leading organisation in Pakistan in the field of Air Delivered Weapons/Systems. The organisation is dedicated to developing and producing different varieties of air and ground weapons, including extended range weapons, target penetration bombs and Infrared Search and Track Systems.[30]

Naval Dockyard

While the Pakistan Navy has received varied attention over time, overall it was accorded low priority in the country till a couple of decades ago. The Navy's share is believed to be around 10 per cent of the defence budget of Pakistan. Pakistan Naval Dockyard is the main facility for naval weapon systems production and maintenance. It was established in 1952 and undertakes repair works, modernisation and refit of Pakistan Navy ships, submarines and craft. The Dockyard provides technical assistance and repairs a wide variety of equipment.

The PN Dockyard has been taking extensive indigenous construction projects like the production of missile boats, mines counter-measure vessels (MCVM) and AGOSTA 90-B submarines.[31]

In 1971, Naval Dockyard began indigenous construction activities with support craft (1,000 tons floating dock). Over a period of time, the dockyard has produced various auxiliary and naval vessels. These include, Midget Submarines Demagnetizer Ship and 200=ton Missiles Craft Mine Countermeasure Vessels. The most prestigious production of the Dockyard is the assembly under licence of the French submarine AGOSTA 90-B, which is a state-of-the-art submarine with the latest sensors and combat systems. The facility did gain technical expertise as it was engaged in the construction of the Agosta 90-B submarine with French assistance. The Pakistan Navy received its first submarine from France. The second submarine was constructed at the PN Dockyard and handed over to the Navy in 2003 and the third submarine was undocked in 2006.[32]

Karachi Shipyard & Engineering Works (KSEW)

Karachi Shipyard & Engineering Works (KSEW) is working as an autonomous commercial organisation under the Ministry of Defence Production. It was established in the mid-1950s and was incorporated as a public limited company in 1957. KSEW was set up to boost the naval manufacturing industry and fulfil Pakistan's indigenous ship building, ship repairing and heavy engineering requirements. It is one of the few public sector units that has achieved significant capability and is a profit-generating entity of the Ministry of Defence Production.[33] The naval production facility undertakes shipbuilding, ship repairs, submarine and warship construction, and other engineering tasks such as construction of infrastructure of power plants.[34] In 2006, the Pakistan Navy ordered four F-22P type frigates from China. It was agreed that the fourth F-22P will be manufactured in Pakistan at a Karachi shipyard to fulfil a pledge to transfer Chinese shipbuilding technology that was part of the April 2005 agreement to build the frigates. In order to undertake the construction of the F-22, KSEW underwent massive upgradation in 2008-09.[35]

The fourth F-22P PNS ASLAT was inducted in the PN in September 2013. PNS ASLAT is the first frigate of the Navy, which has been indigenously built at KSEW. The production was done in collaboration with the China Shipbuilding and Trading Company.[36] The latest achievement of the KSEW has been development of the first indigenously-designed Fast Attack Craft (Missile)—or, FAC (M)-4—along with the Maritime Technologies Complex.[37]

In 2018, the Pakistan Navy commissioned PNS Moawin—a 17,000-ton fleet tanker—the largest warship ever constructed at the Karachi Shipyard and Engineering Works in collaboration with Savunma Teknolojileri Mühendislik (STM) of Turkey.[38]

National Development Complex (NDC)

The foundation of the National Development Complex (Integrated Defence Systems) Fatehjung, was laid in 1993 with the object of developing an infrastructure for indigenous development and production of modern weapon systems. The NDC, in fact, consists of a cluster of research, development, and manufacturing units under the aegis of the Pakistan Atomic Energy Commission (PAEC). The units were consolidated for the indigenous development and manufacture of modern weapon systems for Pakistan.[39] The Complex manufactures a large variety of products, which include missile systems, launchers, specialised aerial weapons like Area Denial Bomb PSD-1 and Fuel-Air Explosive Bomb FAE-1 and defence electronics.[40]

In the late 1980s, Pakistan signed an agreement with China for the purchase of M-11 (estimated range 300 km) and possibly M-9 ballistic missiles. China, in turn, facilitated the agreement by building a turnkey facility in Pakistan where such missiles could be produced.[41] In 1994, US Intelligence agencies detected the construction of such a facility in Fatehjung, 40 km west of Islamabad. The configuration and design of the Fatehjung plant matched the M-11 missile facility in Hubei province in China. Technicians and engineers from China Precision Machinery Import/Export Corporation were sighted at the plant.[42] The facility was completed in 1997-98 and is believed to produce the Hatf-III/Ghaznavi (M-11) and Hatf-IV/Shaheen-I (possibly M-9) solid fuelled ballistic missiles. Some reports suggest the sourcing of the missile parts from the cities of Lahore, Karachi and Gujranwala and finally their assembly at Fatehjung plant. It is believed that the facility now manufactures the Chinese M-11 and M-9 ballistic missiles.[43] While complete details of the capabilities of the facility are not in the public domain, reports suggest that NDC has the potential to cater to important defence requirements including:[44]

- Missile systems
- Launchers
- Area Denial Bombs PSD-1
- Fuel Air Explosive Bombs FAE-1
- Defence-Electronics
- Military Fuses.

National Radio Telecommunication Corporation (NRTC)

National Radio Telecommunication Corporation was established with Japanese collaboration (Nippon Electric Company) and has been producing high-quality telecommunications equipment for the defence services, Pakistan Telecommunication Corporation Ltd. (PTCL) and other organisations since 1965-66.[45]

Some of the critical production of the NRTC includes Communication Security Solutions, Backbone Communication Solutions (Microwave Line-of-Sight Systems), Software Defined Radio Systems and Integrated Land Mobile Radio Systems.[46]

Pakistan Machine Tool Factory (Pvt) Ltd. (PMTF) is a precision engineering goods manufacturing facility, established in technical collaboration with Oerlikon-Buhrle & Co. of Switzerland and commenced production in 1971. PMTF with a work force of approximately 1,900 personnel is engaged in the production of machine tools, automotive transmission and axle components, gears for locomotives, pressure die cast parts and other products. Facilities in the factory include designing, machining, forging, heat treatment, assembly, die casting, etc.[47]

Research and Development Establishments

The main research and development organisations include:

- Defence Science and Technology Organisation (DESTO)
- Armament Research & Development Establishment (ARDE)
- Military Vehicles Research and Development Establishment (MVRDE)
- Naval Research and Development Authority (NRDE).

Conclusion

Pakistan's indigenous defence production has expanded significantly in the last four decades. The small arms and light weapons industry has been developed significantly fulfilling the requirements of not only Pakistan's military but also of more than 30 nations, which are presently importing weapons from Pakistan. POF follows both the NATO/USA standards and Chinese standards, specifications and calibres in their production. This provides Pakistan's defence industry a wider market for its products.

The initial focus was restricted to small arms and light weapons, primarily to ensure supply during war against India and also to reduce dependence on foreign supplies. Eventually, Pakistan defence production has progressed towards producing not only major land equipment like the Al-Khalid and Al Zarrar but also, fourth generation aircraft, JF-17s and frigates.

Some of the key factors that need to be understood regarding Pakistan's defence production are:

1. Majority of the defence production of units were established to cater to servicing Chinese equipment and to assemble/co-manufacture and produce Chinese equipment (under technology transfer agreements). For example, the co-production of JF-17 aircraft and production of F-22 frigates for the Navy. Chinese assistance in defence production has been critical. Pakistan has also been a recipient of Russian technology through direct defence acquisitions and indirectly in its defence production through China; for example, the JF-17 engine RD-93 is a Russian one.
2. Indigenous defence capability build-up has given Pakistan some degree of self-reliance and it no more feels threatened of losing the supply of American weapon systems.
3. Initially concentrating on building small arms/light weapons production capabilities and export capacity in order to:
   (a) Ensure sufficient arms/ammunition for prolonged war against India,

(b) Enable sufficient small arms supplies to jihadi organisations without having to depend on outside supplies (as was the case in the Afghanistan War in the 1980s).
(c) Expand export to offset costs of production of these weapons by increasing the economies of scale.

4. Focus of defence production in the last two decades has been the Air Force and the Navy. Post the Kargil war, there has been a change in Pakistani thinking which is inclined towards prioritising build-up of the Air Force and aerial maritime strike capabilities of the Navy. India's punitive air strikes at Balakot post the Pulwama terror attack and then the PAF's (supposedly) demonstrative air strikes in the Poonch-Rajauri-Naushera sector in Jammu and Kashmir have certainly reinforced Pakistan's commitment in the Air Force build-up for future wars.
5. Pakistan defence industry has been increasingly catering to the requirements of the smaller Muslim nations. From the very beginning, it pursued the objective of building its image as a leader of the Islamic world. Pakistan has made aggressive efforts to expand its defence export base, which has strengthened its strategic partnerships. For example, it has supplied *Mushshak* to multiple countries, including Saudi Arabia and Oman. It has been gearing up to export J-17s to four countries including Malaysia, Myanmar and Nigeria. Turkey plans to buy MFI-17 Super Mushshak aircraft from Pakistan. Defence production is assisting Pakistan to build and strengthen its alliances (particularly in the Muslim world).
6. Pakistan's defence exports have also targeted the market of India's (existing) defence products like Nigeria, Bangladesh and Myanmar.

Although Pakistan has been projecting itself as a major defence manufacturer. Yet, as far as major defence equipment is concerned, Pakistan defence industry has yet to come up with an indigenous design. Most of the major weapon systems which are reportedly manufactured by the Pakistan defence industry are restricted to overhaul/repair, assembly of the major components and licensed manufacture of some of the weapons. Research and development in Pakistan defence industry still needs to grow in order to get to the final steps in indigenous defence production, which implies the "design and development of the weapon systems" followed by the "design and development of the components." Pakistan's ongoing economic stress should logically be a constraint to defence production and expansion, but given the power dynamics in Pakistan where the military dominates defence decision making, it is likely to come up with solutions to continue defence production.

Disclaimer: Some parts of the article are from the author's book, Shalini Chawla, *Pakistan's Military and Its Strategy* (New Delhi: Knowledge World, 2009).

NOTES

1. "COAS General Bajwa unveils way forward for Pakistan's self-reliance in defence industry", *Times of Islamabad,* July 19, 2019, https://timesofislamabad.com/19-Jul-2019/coas-general-bajwa-unveils-way-forward-for-pakistan-s-self-reliance-in-defence-industry. Accessed on April 1, 2020.
2. Message by Gen. Abdul Waheed for the seminar on "Self-Reliance in Defence" (Rawalpindi: MoD, January 16-17, 1993), p. 11, as cited by Ayesha Siddiqua-Agha, *Pakistan's Arms Procurement and Military Build-up, 1979-99, In Search of a Policy* (New York: Palgrave, 2001), p. 109.
3. Abdul Qadeer, "POF—Through The Decades," *Defence Journal,* vol. xix, no. 9-10, 1993, as cited in *Strategic Digest,* April 1994, pp. 564-67.
4. Aabha Dixit, "Defence Production in Pakistan," *Asian Strategic Review 1991-92* (New Delhi: Institute for Defence Studies and Analyses, 1992), p. 287.
5. "Wah Cantonment Pakistan Ordnance Factories (POF)," https://fas.org/nuke/guide/pakistan/facility/wah.htm. Accessed on March 20, 2020.
6. Ibid.
7. Ibid.
8. GlobalSecurity.org, "Weapons of Mass Destruction, Wah Cantonment," http://www.globalsecurity.org/wmd/world/pakistan/wah.htm. Accessed on March 30, 2020.
9. "Golden Jubilee of Pakistan Ordnance Factories (POF) Wah," at http://www.pakpost.gov.pk/philately/stamps2001/pof.html
10. "Pakistan Ordnance Factories manufactures face masks, hand sanitizers," *Arab News,* March 26, 2020, https://www.arabnews.pk/node/1647331/pakistan. Accessed on April 20, 2020.
11. John Kaniyalil, "Defence Production in Pakistan," *Strategic Analysis,* May 1993, pp. 229-47.
12. "FAS, Weapons of Mass Destruction, Taxila," https://fas.org/nuke/guide/pakistan/facility/taxila.htm. Accessed on January 1, 2020.
13. Mushahid Hussain, "Pakistan's heavy armour; Upgradation/modernisation programme," *Defence Journal,* October 1990, p. 7, as cited by Aabha Dixitt, p. 293.
14. *Jane's Armour and Artillery 2005-2006,* p. 359.
15. https://defence.pk/pdf/threads/please-welcome-hamza-apc-6-x-6.523534/
16. "Pakistan Aeronautical Complex Kamra," https://www.pac.org.pk/mrf. Accessed on May 3, 2020.
17. Ibid.
18. Ibid.
19. "Pakistan Aeronautical Complex Kamra, ARF MRO," https://www.pac.org.pk/arf-mro. Accessed on May 1, 2020.
20. *Janes's All the World's Aircraft 2005-2006,* p. 357.
21. For details see, "Pakistan Aeronautical Complex Kamra, AMF Capabilities," https://www.pac.org.pk/amf-capability. Accessed on April 2, 2020.

22. "Interview, Air Chief Marshal, Tanvir Mahmood Ahmed, Pakistan's Chief of Air Staff," *Jane's Defence Weekly*, April 4, 2007, p. 34.
23. Franz-Stefan Gady, "China Overhauls Pakistan Air Force JF-17 Fighter Jet," *The Diplomat*, May 22, 2019, https://thediplomat.com/2019/05/china-overhauls-pakistan-air-force-jf-17-fighter-jet/. Accessed on June 1, 2019.
24. *The Military Balance 2019 IISS* (London: Oxford University Press, 2019), p. 299.
25. "Pakistan Aeronautical Complex Kamra, JF 1-7 Thunder Aircraft," https://www.pac.org.pk/Jf-17. Accessed on May 1, 2020.
26. "Pakistan Aeronautical Complex Kamra," https://www.pac.org.pk/apf. Accessed on March 30, 2020.
27. "FAS, Taxila," http://www.fas.org/nuke/guide/pakistan,facility/taxila.htm. Accessed on March 20, 2020.
28. Ibid.
29. Institute of Optronics, August 23, 2019, https://www.epicos.com/company/13872/institute-optronics-iop. Accessed on January 12, 2020.
30. "FAS Weapons of Mass Destruction, Kamra Air Weapons Complex," https://fas.org/nuke/guide/pakistan/facility/kamra.htm. Accessed on April 2, 2020.
31. GlobalSecurity.org, "PN Dockyard (Karachi)," Pakistan Naval Dockyard, globalsecurity.org. Accessed on April 1, 2020.
32. Ibid.
33. "Pakistan Navy launches indigenously-designed FAC(M)-4 at Karachi Shipyard event", *The News*, November 27, 2019, defencenews.in. Accessed on April 1, 2020.
34. "Karachi Ship Yard and Engineering Works Ltd" at, http://www.depo.org.pk/index.php?a=profile&id=13
35. Karachi Shipyard & Engineering Works Limited (KSEW), GlobalSecurity.org, https://www.globalsecurity.org/military/world/pakistan/ksew.htm. Accessed on April 13, 2020.
36. Navy gets fourth F-22 Frigate", *The Nation*, September 4, 2013, at http://www.nation.com.pk/karachi/04-Sep-2013/navy-gets-fourth-f-22-frigate. Accessed on March 13, 2020.
37. "Pakistan Navy launches indigenously-designed FAC(M)-4 at Karachi Shipyard event," *The News*, November 27, 2019, defencenews.in. Accessed on April 1, 2020.
38. "17,000 ton fleet tanker commissioned at PN Dockyard," *Dawn*, October 17, 2018. Accessed on April 1, 2020.
39. *Missile Facilities: National Defence Complex (NDC)*, at, http://www.nti.org/e_research/profiles/Pakistan/Missile/3294_3327.html. Accessed August 2008.
40. "FAS Weapons of Mass Destruction, Fatehjung," National Development Complex, http://www.fas.org/nuke/guide/pakistan/facility/fatehjung.htm. Accessed on April 2, 2020.
41. Ibid.
42. Ibid.
43. Ibid.
44. "FAS Weapons of Mass Destruction, Fatehjung," National Development Complex, https://fas.org/nuke/guide/pakistan/facility/fatehjung.htm. Accessed on April 12, 2020.
45. National Radio and Telecommunication Corporation, http://www.nrtc.com.pk/index_1.htm. Accessed on January 10, 2009.
46. National Radio and Telecommunication Corporation, https://www.nrtc.com.pk/about.html. Accessed on April 15, 2020.
47. Pakistan Machine Tool Factory (Pvt) Ltd., http://www.pmtfl.com/profile.htm. Accessed on April 10, 2020.

11

Cyber Profile and Operations of Pakistan

Dr. Gulshan Rai

I. CYBER PROFILE

The global transformation taking place in the world is characterized by the convergence of digital, physical and biological technologies in such a way that are changing both the world around us and the ideas too, influencing industrial and economic prosperity, socio-development and concept of national security. The changes are historic in nature in terms of size, speed, scope and complexities. Technologies like Artificial Intelligence, Machine Learning, Big Data, Cloud Computing, Genetic Engineering, and neurosciences are influencing and altering the way nations produce, consume, communicate, move and interact with other countries in the world. This ubiquitous and virtual nature of technologies, while bringing economic prosperity and faster socio-economic development is also resulting in cyber crimes, disruptions to the digital and critical information infrastructure and raising issues of a geo-political nature. Nations are adopting, building digital infrastructure and expanding the reach of the Internet, framing public policies and legal frameworks and application of technologies to bring development in their societies in the form of industry 4.0. Nations are also exploiting these technologies to gain advantage in geopolitical issues.

Digital Landscapes in Pakistan

The digital landscape of Pakistan, during the last 10 years, has registered a significant surge. New technologies are quickly getting integrated into strategies in the country both for development in domestic and international relations and the utilization and exploitation of cyberspace which has become a useful and important tool.

The world economic forum in its "The Global Information Technology Report 2018" has ranked Pakistan (in terms of overall score) at 107th position among 144 countries. The index reflects the technological readiness of the country.

Readiness Index of Pakistan 2018

	Item	*Rank*
1.	Overall score	107
2.	Enabling environment	109
3.	Human capital	109
4.	Innovation capabilities	89
5.	Adaption of Information and Communication Technology's (ICT)	127
6.	Infrastructure	93

Source: The Global Information Technology Report of World Economic Forum 2018.

Essential Headline Digital Data of Pakistan (2020)

Total Population	*Mobile Phone Connections*	*Internet Users*	*Active Social Media Users*
218.7 Million	164.9 Million	76.38 Million	37 Million
Urbanization	*vs Population*	*Penetration*	*Penetration*
37%	75%	35%	17%

1. 14th rank in the World Growth Rate 17%.
2. Facebook, WhatsApp, Instagram, Twitter, Google, Snap Chat, LinkedIn, and Wikipedia, the most popular.
3. Penetration of Social Media 17%, Growth 7%.
4. Access to Social Media on Mobiles 98%.

Digitalization in the financial sector, especially during the last five years, has resulted in little growth in financial inclusion in Pakistan. Seventy eight of the population does not have access to financial services. The penetration of financial services is low in the extreme northern and western parts of the country. Population with credit cards is largely in Lahore, Islamabad, and Karachi. The poor financial inclusion reflects weak delivery of citizen-centric services and social development.

Financial Inclusion (January 2020)

	Item	*Percentage*
1.	Population with accounts in financial institutions	18
2.	Population with credit cards	1
3.	Population with mobile money accounts	6.9
4.	Population of women having credit cards	0.7
5.	Population of men having credit cards	1.2

E-commerce

The e-commerce market in Pakistan in 2019 was around US$ 2 billion registering a growth of 73 per cent over the previous year. Fashion, electronics and media sectors accounted for more than 70 per cent of the e-commerce market followed by food and beverages, furniture, travel and consumer items. About 44 million people made online purchases in 2019; (about 8 per cent of the total market). Chinese companies like Alibaba and Ant Financials have made significant investments in setting up E-commerce platforms in Pakistan. Alibaba has set up a platform like "daraz.pk" and Ant Financials has invested in microfinance banking with telecom service provider, Telenor.

E-commerce Status (January 2020)

	Item	*Amount/Percentage*
1.	Total e-commerce	US$ 2 B
2.	People on line	21%
3.	Men making online transactions	12% of total online
4.	Women making online transactions	3.4 % of total online
5.	Number of people making digitally enabled payments	30.60 million
6.	Total value of digital payment	US$ 9.8 B
7.	Growth rate in 2019	18%
8.	Spent on digital advertisement of which 50% through social media	US$ 860 M
9.	Average growth on digital spend	13%

II. CYBER SECURITY PROFILE OF PAKISTAN

Nature of Threats

The cyber security and cyber threat scenario of Pakistan is constantly evolving and becoming complex, just like elsewhere in the world. The country is facing multifaceted cyber threats and cyber breaches. The range and variety of cyber incidents extend from normal web site defacement, ransom ware, denial of services, ATM frauds, card skimming, malware injunction, phishing (of all nature), spyware, BOTs, DNS poisoning, stealing of information/data and crypto mining, etc. The complex cyber incidents of the nature of Advanced Persistent Threats (APTs) are very common in Pakistan. Such incidents are several thousand every day and are on the rise. Symantec, an erstwhile US security company, reported that more than hundred thousand cyber incidents were observed and monitored in Pakistan. Pakistan ranks eighth among countries having the worst cyber security. The country is today a hotbed for BOTs-cum-Trojans, web shells.

Security companies in the world estimate that there are around 300,000 BOTs-cum-Trojans installed in the cyber infrastructure in Pakistan. The malicious SPAM generation in Pakistan is estimated to be around 1.9 per cent of total malicious SPAM generated worldwide. Pakistan had a malware encounter rate of 18.94 per cent in 2018. The malicious threat observed in Pakistan has been well above the world average. The top 10 malwares and potentially unwanted software in Pakistan raged between 6.8 per cent and 30.1 per cent in 2019 (Microsoft Intelligence Report 2019). Around 30 to 35 per cent of communication bandwidth is lost in Pakistan because of traffic originating from malware, BOTs and Trojans. Techniques like Spear Phishing, malware injunction, Zero Day exploits and vulnerabilities in the software and embedded systems are generally used for exploitation of computer networks, computer systems and other devices/ equipment including those deployed as part of perimeter security.

Key Parameters relating to Cyber Security, 2019

(in per cent)

Country	*Rank*	*Score (Cyber Security)*	*(Malware Infected Mobile)*	*Financial Malware Attack*	*Computer infected with Malware*	*Attack of Cryptomining*	*Best Prepared to prevent Cyber Attacks*
Pakistan	8	40.33	28.13	0.8	9.96	2.41	0.407

Source: Year 2020; Global Security Index (ITU).

Cyber Adversaries

There are many anonymous groups supported by numerous terrorist organizations in the country that install such BOTs for launching cyber attacks while keeping themselves hidden. The campaign relating to Hacktivism, cyber bullying, creation and circulation of fake news within and outside Pakistan are run using such BOT networks and web shells. The anonymous groups are well-connected and supported. Such groups have trained cadres that are hired by others for running campaigns and spamming within and outside the country. The Federal Investigation Agency (FIA) estimates that there are more 3,000 fake Twitter handlers in Pakistan exploiting BOT net in the country. Exploiting the virtual and anonymous nature of cyber technology, the fake twitter handles are also opened in different countries. The anonymous groups in Pakistan cause serious cyber security concerns and weaken the cyber infrastructure in the country.

Crypto Mining

Crypto currency is virtual money used anonymously to buy and sell goods and services both online and in the physical world. Pakistan had on an average monthly crypto currency mining rate of about 1.47 per cent. Countries like Japan, Ireland and China have crypto currency rate of about 0.02 per cent.

Distribution of Attacks (2019)

Fake Accounts	*Account Hijacking/ Identity Thefts*	*Malware Distri- bution*	*Deface- ment*	*Targeted Attacks*	*Ransom ware*	*Malicious Script Injunctions*	*Denial of Services*	*Malicious Spam*
2.2	14.7	34.3	2.2	10.7	12.2	3.6	1.7	1.8

Recent Important Cyber Incidents

There are several significant cyber incidents that occurred in the Government, corporate, private and public organizations in Pakistan. The trend reveals a huge increase in hacked and breached data from sources that are increasingly accessed and used by citizens and organizations within and from outside Pakistan. The websites of almost all ministries and departments of the Federal and Provincial governments have been hacked. The important ones are Ministries of: Railways, Transportation, Defence, Interior, Water, Power, Information, Environment, Food Security, etc. Careem, a ride-hailing App, was hit by cyber attack which resulted in compromising information of 14 million user's data of riders from multiple countries including Pakistan. Similarly, cyber attacks on almost all banks have surfaced and are occurring periodically in the country. The FIA has reported that all Pakistani banks (around 22 in number) were hacked by cyber attackers in 2018 resulting in a loss of data like email ids, account numbers, details of ATM cards, phone numbers and other customer identities. Hackers installed skimmer devices in ATM machines to hack card details. The entire dump of data stolen during the cyber attack was posted on the Dark Web. The data was later used to withdraw money in cash from ATMs and undertake transactions on the Net. The techniques of Spear Phishing water hole and malware injunction (APT Vectors) were used in all these cases. Similarly, there have been significant cyber attacks on critical infrastructure, particularly power and water grids and defence networks and installations. A hacker group of a Middle East country bordering Pakistan hacked telecommunication services of Pakistan which lasted for a couple of days resulting in discontinuation of service.

Operation Shaheen

The operation targeted government and military organizations in Pakistan. Members and operations of the Pakistan Air Force were targeted with Spear phishing messages that phished a large number of documents and files relating to the military and Government of Pakistan.

In 2019, the Pakistan Navy faced targeted APT attacks, where vital information was stolen from secure military networks and misleading documents planted.

Operation on the Foreign Office

The hackers from a country friendly to Pakistan have been reported to be regularly targeting entities and foreign offices of Pakistan. The vulnerabilities in the Cyber Infrastructure are exploited. The specific incidents where the attacks continued for a considerable period related to the time of consideration and debate on important resolutions in the UN Security Council. The purpose of spying through the cyber tool was to ascertain the diplomatic as well as related military strategy of Pakistan on such issues.

The cyber security companies have consensus, in general, that the cyber infrastructure in Pakistan has poor resilience and is vulnerable to cyber attacks. The complex and large number of cyber incidences raises concern about Pakistan cyber security capability, particularly when it comes to its nuclear weapons and installations.

China Belt and Road Initiative to Drive Cyber Attack Activities

The Belt and Road Initiative (BRI) is an ambitious multi-tier and multi-year project across Asia, Europe, Middle East and Africa to develop land (Silk Road economic belt) and maritime (maritime Silk Road) trade networks that will project China's influence globally. It is expected that BRI will also be a driver of cyber threat activity in Pakistan. It would catalyse the emergence of several new groups of perpetrators, both state and non-state, within and outside Pakistan which may use their capabilities to exploit the vulnerabilities in the cyber infrastructure of Pakistan thereby endangering their security and data. It must be noted that BRI would control much of the critical Information Infrastructure of Pakistan—including financial systems, power grids and defence installations. The probe of their vulnerabilities by foreign states, non-state actors and criminals would not only be dangerous to the integrity of Pakistan but to the security of its neighbouring countries also.

Cyber Crimes

The FIA, which coordinates investigation of cyber crime cases in the country, had reported that there was a rise in cyber crimes in 2018 by about 25 per cent over the previous year. The agency conducted 2,295 inquiries, registered 255 cases and made 209 arrests in 2018. The important cyber crime cases registered in Pakistan largely fell into one of nine categories, namely

(i) email hacking
(ii) password hacking
(iii) hacking of online banking transactions
(iv) data diddling
(v) cyber stalking
(vi) cyber bullying harassment and blackmailing of women
(vii) ATM frauds
(viii) hacktivism
(ix) cyber jihad

The infrastructure for investigations of these cases is poor. FIA has set up 15 cyber forensic labs in the country; however, the labs are not fully functional due to non-availability of skilled personnel.

Cyber Jihad

Incidents relating to cyber jihad have doubled during the last three years. Several groups and persons having strong affiliations with Islam and with specific agenda have been observed to be engaged in cyber jihad in Pakistan. These groups have used cyberspace as a tool for spreading ideology with the specific aim to change the ideas of others and set their minds in 'desirable' directions. These groups and individuals are fully supported by state agencies. The tailor-made nlog and Web links are posted on social media platforms to target and exploit the minds of the extremely religiously educated classes not only in Pakistan but in the rest of the world. Such religiously educated classes are easy to mould in any direction. Terrorist organizations use them for vested interests to carry out cyber jihad against states like India, whom they consider as an enemy state. In fact, this has also become a rising threat for Pakistan too.

Hacktivism

Hacktivism or activism in Pakistan is also on the rise. There are many perpetrators or groups of perpetrators that are defacing, stealing or misusing personal data of citizens, (illegitimately sourced from Government) for the purpose of political extremism, ethnic association, terrorism, and employment. Both state and non-state actors are involved in hacktivism in Pakistan.

Gaps in the Cyber Security Architecture and Policies

Pakistan has a long way to go in enhancing the resilience and security of cyber infrastructure and implementation of robust technology architecture, cyber security strategy and legislation. There are a number of impending factors halting the overall cyber security posture in the country. This includes a level of awareness and knowledge regarding malicious activities happening in the country and in cyber space, lack of cyber readiness and proportion of national spending in the area of cyber security. There is a dire need to consider the concerns relating to Pakistan cyber operations which are impacting domestically. In general, the technical architecture of telecom networks and configuration of ICT systems particularly of large projects are flat and weak. E-government services, financial sector and capital markets particularly require attention with respect to enhancing resilience and security posture. The security architecture provides many technical possibilities by which hackers may breach the perimeter security and intrude into networks and systems. The criminal justice legal framework to address cyber security and cyber crime cases is ill equipped. This is one of the countries in South East Asia which is not having its own national CERT. The existing Computer Emergency Response Team, known as PAKCERT, a private entity, lacks in facilities and capabilities needed for such security organizations.

Key Federal Government Legislations and Policies Relating to Telecommunications and IT

1.	Pakistan Telecom (Reorganization) Act, 1996
2.	Electronic Transactions Ordinance, 2002
3.	Electronic Crime Act, 2015
4.	Prevention of Electronic Crime Act, 2016
5.	National Digital Policy, 2018
6.	Telecom Policy, 2015
7.	Broadband Policy, 2004
8.	Mobile Cellular Phone Policy, 2004
9.	IT Policy and Action Plan, 2000

Cyber Security Structure in Pakistan

National Centre for Cyber Security (NCCS)

A joint initiative of the Higher Education Commission (HEC) and Planning Commission was set up in 2018. The centre consists of R&D labs in different specialized areas of cyber security. Its mandate is to build a cyber security ecosystem in Pakistan.

National Response Centre for Cyber Crimes (NR3C)

NR3C set up in 2007 under FIA deals with technology-related crimes in Pakistan. The centre has built up expertise in investigation of cyber frauds and cyber crime cases. It has 15 centres in different parts of the country. They have facilities of digital forensic vulnerability and penetration testing and monitoring of social media.

Pakistan Computer Emergency Response Team (Pak CERT)

Pak CERT is a private entity providing emergency response in the area of cyber security in Pakistan. It also offers other associated functions like digital forensic malware reverse engineering and testing of software and related products and services.

Organizational Structure of Information Technology and Telecommunication Sector

The Ministry of Telecommunication and Information Technology (MOTIT), Pakistan, is concerned with the subject and all aspects of Information Technology and Telecommunications in the country. The other key organizations concerned with Information and Communication Technologies are:

1. *National Assembly subcommittee on IT and Telecommunications*
2. *Pakistan Telecommunications Authority (PTA):* The PTA is telecom sector regulator responsible for all policies relating to establishment, operation and maintenance of telecommunication. It includes auction of frequency spectrum and advising the Government on matters related to telecommunication.
3. *National Telecommunication Corporation (NTC):* NTC provides ICT-related services to the Federal Government, Armed Forces, Defence projects, Provincial governments and Government institutions.
4. *Pakistan Software Board (PSEB):* An apex body mandated to promote the IT industry in the domestic and international market. PSEB facilitates the IT industry through a series of projects and programs in infrastructure development, human resources, strategy, research and promotion of newer technologies.
5. *National IT Boards (NTB):* NTB is an autonomous organization, which offers Information Technology support to Federal ministries and their organizations and divisions. It has been recently restructured to address the implementing of E-governance applications.

6. *Special Communications Organization (SCO):* SCO develops, operates and maintains telecom infrastructure services in Pak Occupied Kashmir.
7. *Telecom Foundation:* A trust engaged to pursue the welfare activities of employees of the public sector organizations in the ICT sector in Pakistan. It also sets up industrial ventures and commercial projects in ICT.
8. *Universal Service Fund (USF):* USF promotes the development of telecommunication services in un-served and under-served areas and skill development within the country. The fund consists of contributions by telecom operators.
9. *Virtual University of Pakistan:* A public sector organization (non-profit) undertaking and promoting skill development in the area of ICT, particularly newer technologies. It offers undergraduate and post-graduate courses through the distance learning mode.
10. *Ignite National Technology Fund:* It supports R&D projects in the area of technology development within industry and the academia. It also supports start-up units and sets up national incubation centres and programs relating to skill creation. The fund is headed by the Minister of IT and Telecom. Representatives of the telecom industry, ISPs and academia are members of the governance structure of the fund.

III. CYBER OPERATION ACTIVITIES AND ACTORS

Nature of Operations

Pakistan has been proactive in exploiting cyber technologies and undertaking cyber operations for almost 15 years now. They have quickly integrated new technologies to diplomatic and military strategies. It is generally felt that Pakistan has invested more resources in developing its cyber operations than on investments in enhancing resilience of its cyber infrastructure. Credible evidence indicates that its cyber operations activities were initially more of the nature of cyber harassment, mainly limited to website defacement and posting/inserting a page with harmful content. Such cyber operations were typically of low intensity, unsophisticated and caused little damage. Website operators and administrators were the major economic victims of such cyber operations. However, over a period, particularly since 2008, the cyber operations activities of Pakistan started implanting web shells. The use of APT techniques has been observed since 2012.

Targeting Profile

Based on cyber operations and attack frequency, persistence and compromises, it is assessed that the targeting profile of Pakistan has three directions:

1. Military, diplomatic and governmental bodies, in particular ministries of Defence and Foreign Affairs (and their bodies and offices irrespective of their location) in Pakistan's or abroad with focus on India, Bangladesh and Afghanistan.
2. Economic, media and business entities.
3. Domestic targeting possibly as part of surveillance.

Evidence has also emerged where cyber operations activities have been extended to some other countries in the Middle East, Southeast Asia, BIMSTEC and SAARC regions. International cyber security firms have observed that Pakistan hacktivists, cyber jihadis and hackers were the first in South Asian countries to exploit cyberspace for their vested and geopolitical operations.

Operative Patterns of Cyber Operations

There are many reports published by international cyber security companies describing the mode of cyber operations in Pakistan. Primarily, six modes are involved, namely:

(i) Framing international perception by posting fake news websites and blogs;
(ii) Influencing local population in countries including Pakistan. This involves psychological operations and morphing established sources and spread of fake information;
(iii) Religious propaganda and cyber terrorism;
(iv) Intelligence gathering and cultivating sources;
(v) Intrusion in websites and data bases by installing web shells and remote access tools (RATs) thereby creating BOT nets and controlling cyber systems;
(vi) Focus on collecting information of cyber defence of other countries.

Techniques Used in Cyber Operations

Taking over Administrator Rights

Cyber operations have been and are carried out by using a variety of tools and techniques, for example:

(i) Deploying and using proxy servers,
(ii) Key loggers,
(iii) Social engineering,
(iv) Spear phishing mails and decoys,

(v) Water holes,

(vi) Hosting of websites and blogs on the social media platform to act as pivots.

Spear Phishing is an important technique of sending an e-mail that appears to come from a trusted source. In all the cyber operations of Pakistan, specific tools are used to scan versions of software installed/used in the software of perimeter security devices, operating systems, web servers and other systems and sub systems, and port scan to ascertain vulnerabilities in the systems, website structure, application software and communication networks. The vulnerabilities are thereafter exploited. APTs are used to send spear phishing mails to get access to victims network and computer/mobile devices, infect them with spyware and key loggers, web shell malwares and ultimately control administration rights of the infrastructure. In the entire process, multiple types and at times dedicated and customize malware are used. Most of the domains are registered on weekdays. New domains are regularly registered

Advanced Persistent Threat Vector (APTs)

APTs are used to create fake news websites and blogs on social media platforms. The fake blogs/news websites could be fake log in pages or websites encouraging people to download specific infected files which may be Word or Excel files. The links of such fake news websites/blogs are also sent via emails or posted on social media platforms and messenger Apps like WhatsApp. The links lure targeted officials to click which results in downloading of malware in the systems and devices. The malicious links/malwares are connected to different intermediate computer systems hosted at different locations which finally connect to command and control computer systems, called C&C servers. The entire process of connecting the victim system and networks to C&C servers are opaque and hidden. The locations of the intermediate systems and their domains are changed on a regular basis, sometimes daily, weekly, etc (depending on the targeted victim).

Recently, Mythic Leopards APT Vector, named APT 36, indigenously coded in Pakistan has been linked to that country. The modus operandi of the said vector was to spy in a similar way. Spear Phishing emails were used to install malicious Excel files. It focused its resources on hacking Indian government entities to gain intelligence and steal information.

Targeting military personnel and diplomatic officials

Spear phishing mails, water hole methods, web links posted on blogs and social media platforms using APT techniques are deployed to steal the identities of diplomatic officials and military personnel. Malicious documents are spoofed on the Microsoft Office and Excel platforms by using Visual Basic/Python and other software. Such documents infected with malware are sent as attachments to emails. The captions of the attachments are made attractive and catchy such as "military doctrine"; "military strategy"; "contingency plan", etc. The morphed mails and attachments are thereafter sent to targeted officials and military personnel as if such emails had been sent/originated from known reliable sources. The control and administration of their end devices are taken over remotely by the Pakistani perpetrators.

Chats using fake Facebook persona

Pakistani APTs, using fake Facebook personas with fake females' photos, to start a conversation with their targets on Facebook Messenger and similar platforms and push them to download a video call application infected with stealth malware. A well-trained female cadre is deployed. The malicious application enabled Pakistani perpetrators to steal gigabytes of data relating to government communications, pictures of official documents, GPS coordinates and other personal details such as ATM card numbers, PIN details, and phone directories, etc. Security companies around the world have discovered a set of custom-built tools, namely, Stealth Mango and Tangelo, that were conducting surveillance on video applications and devices based on "Android" and "IoS" mobile platforms. The tools were detected to be deployed within Pakistan, India, Iraq, Iran, Afghanistan and the UAE. These tools were observed to be operated by military actors of Pakistan.

Nature of Malware, APTs Vector and Technological Sophistication

Cyber security experts who studied the malware and APTs used by threat actors of Pakistan felt that they did not use complex technology and generally were not sophisticated. They are sourced from hackers' forums or open source projects and those that are freely available on the Internet. Some of the malware and APT vectors used by Pakistani actors are:

> Bitterburg, Dark Comet RAT; Python/Peppy; GRAVITY RAT; Sink Series, ScaVenger, Snivel, Bundoor, Luminosity Link RAT; MSIL/Crimson; njRAT, APT 36, etc.

There is reliable evidence that Pakistani actors have, since 2016, been building malware and APT vectors. Such indigenous malwares, however, are observed to be relatively unsophisticated and built from codes copied from particularly

Chinese APTs and also those built by threat actors like the Lazarus group of North Korea. APT 36 is the first APT vector where indigenization is significant. The Pakistani threat actors, however, have gained expertise to capitalize on publicly available cyber tools and also combine relatively simple malware with spear phishing decoying and watering hole attacks. The threat actors, using such techniques and tools have so far managed to steal a significant volume of information from their targets.

Actors Involved in Cyber Operations in Pakistan

Numerous actors are involved in cyber operations in Pakistan. They may be primarily divided into two groups, namely non-state actors and state actors.

Non-state Actors

There are more than 20 non-state actor groups in Pakistan. They are:

> APT36, GORGOAN group, REMCO, NANOCORD, Shadow008, Pakistan Cyber Army (PCA), Pakistan Haxors Crew, Pakistan Pirates, Pakistan Cyber Attackers, Romantic, Viru Shacker, Intruders, Gujjar, Dr@cul@, Alone Injector, Z Company, Virkid, MaDleTs, Team Pak Cyber Experts, etc.

The majority of non-state actors are hacktivists and so-called patriotic hackers. Many of the non-state actors are front-end and fully supported by terrorist organizations of Pakistan. These non-state actors generally participate in website defacement, fake social media handlers and low-level intrusion in computer devices, networks and databases. Many of them publicly claim their operations. Most of the non-state actors are largely concentrated in bigger towns in Pakistan. Some such actors are also located in different parts of the world. Some of them are affiliated with state actors and well-connected with some other non-state actors, so called anonymous groups operating elsewhere in the world. The technology competence of non-state actors is relatively low but has been significantly strengthened in recent years. There is evidence that non-state actors have started deploying some APT techniques too.

State Actors

The state actors of Pakistan fall into two groups; namely, those operated by and within various units of the defence forces (called military actors and include Army, Air Force and Navy) and by Inter-Services Intelligence (ISI), the military intelligence agency of Pakistan. The two groups work under the overall guidance and supervision of Inter-Services Cyber Command. The DG (M), ISI coordinates the entire cyber operations. They are well-connected and also with a large number of non-state actors. In fact, a number of tasks and operations are undertaken by the state actors jointly and in collaboration with non-state actors (who act as fronts, so as to have deniability). In addition, the Air Force and Navy also have their independent cyber operation cells.

The two command level units, namely, "Intelligence Group" and "Technology Group", control cyber operations. These units are supported by cells at brigade level, most of which are located in Garrison Headquarters, Rawalpindi and Lahore and at the borders with India. Some of these brigade units focus their operation on India, while others undertake activities on other south Asian and SAARC countries like Bangladesh, Afghanistan, Myanmar, etc. The units have specified tasks and are adequately equipped with cyber tools. Pakistan has established camouflage cyber cells in the Middle East that coordinate the procurement of cyber tools for military actors.

The Inter Services Public Relations Group (ISPR), stationed at Joint Services Headquarters, formulates much of the media policy of Pakistan's military, counter negative propaganda, fake news and other type of jihadi propaganda. It also garners national support for the armed forces. The Social Media Cell (SMOC) at ISPR plans the social media policy and operations for the armed forces of Pakistan in active collaboration with the ISI.

The ISPR liaises closely with non-state actors and jihadi groups in Pakistan and other non-state actors elsewhere in the world. The ISPR and the command-level units have designated social media officers. They have gained expertise and operate through a cadre of professionally trained males and females. The latter are used effectively for honey-trapping. SMOC operate fake lottery operations, largely for funding some of the operations. The state actors commonly use APT techniques and vectors for their operations.

Resources with State Actors

These actors, for the last five years, are continuously evolving their malware tool kits and maintain a consistent supply of exploits, including some zero-day exploits. The volume and timing of their operations which include shifting of their intermediate domain hosting computer systems indicate their significant size and resources available and invested by these actors. The phishing of the sheer volume of data, its processing and further exploitation suggest the capability of the state actors and networks of Pakistan.

National Defence University

The National Defence University and Institute of Strategic Studies Research and Analysis, under the Ministry of Defence, work closely with defence forces and ISI. These institutions overtly undertake and fund strategic studies, both in Pakistan and abroad, keeping the interest of the armed forces and ISI. These institutions have a number of experts in different areas of cyber technology from Pakistan and overseas. The skill sets are varied and are being strengthened.

International cooperation

Pakistan has active engagements on cyber issues with international bodies and institutions. Targeting, Victimlogy, operator pattern and technical artefacts of malwares and APT vectors used by Pakistan state actors strongly indicate a nexus between APT state actors of China and North Korea (Lazarous group). The nexus between these countries is evident in the number of cyber operations carried out by Pakistani state actors in India and South East Asian countries.

Pakistan has earmarked significant resources to train their cyber professionals in universities abroad. It also supports post-graduate level programs in cyber technology for their citizens in leading universities abroad.

Conclusion

Pakistan is following an offensive postured cyber policy. Such a policy is dangerous, counterproductive and undermines norms of behaviour in cyber space. Pakistan needs to realize that its policy of offensive cyber operations to deter countries near them is dangerous in cyber space. New thought processes being debated and perused worldwide are in the direction of authorizing pre-emptive offensive operations to respond to cyber operations like that of Pakistan. Strategies and policies of a nation must start from an accurate understanding of the domain, its resources and capabilities and not from imagined and borrowed from other ad hoc and random sources and countries. Pakistan needs to consider more prudent and restrained approach to its cyber operations. It is essential for Pakistan to invest its resources in implementing fast and secure digitalization in the country which will go a long way towards socio-economic development and delivering citizen-centric services. Any adverse cyber operations will be counter-productive as it will attract retaliation, which will be detrimental to the growth of the economy of Pakistan. Also with the emergence of Internet of Things and Artificial Intelligence, Machine learning and BIG DATA where everyday objects from thermostat to home security devices can be controlled online, the risk of well-funded actors hacking into networks of such devices would be disastrous.

APPENDIX A

CYBER PROFILE OF PAKISTAN

Information Technology

The industry relating to digital and information technology has fast expanded in Pakistan. This industry has been regarded as a successful sector economically even during the financial crisis in the country. The first "Information Technology (IT) Policy and Implementation Strategy" announced in 2000, laid the foundation of Information Communication Technologies (ICT) sector. The "Telecom Policy" announced in December 2015 led to rapid expansion of telecom infrastructure across the country. Like many developing countries, Pakistan also created a "Universal Service Fund" (USF) which helped in Internet and mobile penetration in the interior areas of the country. Later, in 2018, Pakistan announced its comprehensive "National Digital Policy". The policy aims to enhance productivity in the public sector, socio-development, improve standards of IT infrastructure and use it as a management tool for adoption of ICT in the country. It provides an integrated approach for the promotion and development of ICT as a sector and also as an enabler and includes national capacity building, export-led growth and global positioning of Pakistan in the area of ICT. The Government has implemented several programs and schemes, which included 100 per cent foreign equity and 100 per cent repatriation of profit, 15 years tax holiday (expired in 2019), tax holiday for venture capital, accelerated depreciation rate and other incentives. Several international ICT companies from the USA, Spain, Germany, Norway, Malaysia and China have established their offices or operate through local distributors.

Size of the ICT industry and exports

The Information Technology sector in Pakistan has witnessed significant growth during the last five years. This sector has contributed about 1 per cent to the GDP of Pakistan and is estimated to be US$ 5 billion. It doubled in the past four years and the government expects it to grow in the next 2-3 years, to US$ 7 billion. The IT and ITES exports were estimated to be around US$ 3.2 billion in 2019. This also included the amount which the country's freelancers earned by providing their services and also from those companies that do not bring their revenues to Pakistan. There are more than 5,000 IT firms/companies/units developing and providing IT products, solutions and services in Pakistan. The IT units and companies developing and exporting services are largely concentrated in Karachi, Lahore and Islamabad. More than 2,000 IT companies are exporting products and services to around 50 countries. However, the Middle East, a few European countries and the USA are major export destinations.

Like many developing countries, Pakistan has developed IT parks and several incubation centres in Islamabad, Lahore, Karachi and Quetta. The infrastructure and resources at the parks and incubation centres are being regularly enhanced under funding from the Federal Government. There is, in general, growth in setting up start-up units in the technology sector. As per available information, more than 25 start-up units are reported to be working in the area of ICT, mainly located in Karachi and Lahore. These start-ups are small and engaged in low-level development of technologies, customization and interfacing of imported IT products in the local environment, developing Urdu language interface, etc. There is no Unicorn start-up in Pakistan. There are about five start-ups developing cyber security products and services like vulnerability assessment, penetration testing and low level of digital forensic products.

Software development

The software development activity in Pakistan is growing rapidly. IT companies are mainly engaged in developing software for use in different types of businesses, consumer applications and services. The increasing size of Android smart phones, tablets and iPads has given a boost to development of the mobile applications and APPs development industry in Pakistan. Locally-made low-cost software packages, both in English and Urdu, are developed and made available for implementation in schools, small-sized hospitals, hotels and domestic stores. Large software applications systems like Enterprise Resource Planning (ERP) and such other applications for manufacturing and service industries like textiles, pharmaceuticals, food and beverages and power plants are imported and customized. On an average, 22 per cent of the software development activities are accounted towards enterprise software and professional software services account for about 14 per cent.

Data centres

There are about 21 recognized data centres including 'clouds' in the country confirming to tier-2 and tier-3 standards. Such data and cloud centres have been set up by both domestic and foreign companies. There are about four cloud data centres in Islamabad, 11 in Karachi and 6 in Lahore. The important and large ones are set up by Pakistan Telecommunication Limited (PTCL), National Telecommunication Corporation (NTC), Wateen (UAE), Rapid Computers, etc.

Standards and testing infrastructure

About 175 ICT companies in Pakistan hold international certification like ISO 27001, ISO 20001 and CMM level. There are 4-5 ICT companies which hold CMM i certification. The industries associations aided by the Pakistan Government are encouraging and helping the ICT units to obtain international certification. The current infrastructure to test the ICT products with respect to quality and cyber security is weak and far from any reasonable standard.

E-Governance and ICT adaption

Pakistan, over the years, has been pursuing the concept of the E-governance and E-commerce. Several comprehensive computerization programs and schemes have been implemented in the key areas of core economy sectors and offices of the ministries of the Federal and Provincial governments. These include Law and Order, Railways, Other Transportation, Finance, District Administration and Citizen Services. There is, however, a significant digital divide in the ICT adaption in the Federal Government vis-a-vis the provinces.

The financial sector, particularly banks, have deployed sophisticated and fairly advanced ICT solutions (typically core banking applications). Most of such advanced level solutions are generally imported from the USA and Western countries, but have been customized to meet local requirements. Urdu language interface has also been added in certain modules in many software systems. The stock exchanges and capital markets have been upgraded into computer-based trading systems. These are connected to investment companies, treasury departments, etc. National Data Base and Registration Authority (NADRA) has implemented a massive comprehensive computerized registration system for issue of important documents such as national identity cards, passports, immigration and those relating to permanent residence of Pakistani citizens. The implementation of computerization, however, is improving and progressively covering more and more sectors. The large private and public sector companies have computerized their process to a significant extent.

Telecommunication in Pakistan

The telecommunication infrastructure has significantly improved in Pakistan, particularly after the announcement of the regulation of the telecom sector in 2001. Currently the revenue of this sector is around US$ 3.6 billion. In 2018, an amount of around US$ 580 million was contributed by the sector as tax to the government. Significant investments have been made both, by foreign companies, particularly Norwegian and Chinese, and domestic companies (aided by the Government) in the fixed line and mobile networks. Fibre cable systems have been laid and are being extended throughout the country to aid the expansion in the reach of the network. Pakistan had set up the Pakistan Telecommunication Company Limited (PTCL) in 1994. However, the real impetus was seen after another government company, namely, Ufone (Pakistan Mobile Company Limited) was set up. PTCL has signed an MOU with China Telecom (Global) to lay fibre optic network in the underserved areas in Pakistan

Pakistan follows a policy of open licence. Fixed Line Telecom licences are given initially for a period of 20 years which is reviewed after every five years. The mobile communication operations are licensed initially for 15 years which may be extended. In general, 100 per cent foreign equity is permitted in all sectors of the economy including telecommunications. As per reports, FDI in the telecom sector is currently around US$ 2.6 billion. An amount of about US$ 4.6 billion has been invested by domestic companies. The FDI has been made mainly by Chinese companies. The others include those from Malaysia, Norway, the United Arab Emirates and Egypt. Foreign companies like Intelsat, Nokia, ZTE, Huawei, Ericsson, Siemens, and Alcatel have also made significant investments in telecom operations in Pakistan.

The Pakistan telecommunication infrastructure includes: microwave radio relay, coaxial cable, fibre optical cable, cellular and satellite networks. Telecommunication infrastructure and, more so, mobile is primarily concentrated in the western, central and south central parts in the country. Pakistan is connected to the rest of the world through nine undersea submarine cable systems (SEA-ME-WE-3, SEA-ME-WE-4, SEA-ME-WE-5, I-ME-WE, AAE, TW-1, SRG, PEACE and Africa-1). The telecommunication infrastructure is also proposed to be connected to the BRI infrastructure under implementation by China. The undersea cable provides links to Asia, Middle East, Africa, and Europe. International Gateway Exchanges are operating at Karachi (2 nos.) and one at Islamabad. The satellite connectivity has been working through Intelsat satellite stations (Atlantic Ocean and Indian Ocean).

The Emirates Telecommunication Corporation has a significant stake in the government telecom company, PTCL. The domestic fibre cable backbone has been set up by PTCL and private sector companies like Wateem, Mobilink and MultiNet. Interconnection of telecom infrastructure is compulsory for the telecom service providers. Like many other developing countries, Pakistan telecom service providers also have Universal Service Fund (USF) obligations.

Mobile communications

Mobile sector is the most active among the telecommunications and has grown rapidly over the last five years with a growth rate of about 6.5 per cent (2019). There are 164.9 million mobile connections (as of January 2020) covering about 76 per cent population in the country. Forty-five per cent of the mobile connections (76 million) are in the 4G broadband category. The country is served by four large mobile network operators, namely, Jazz, Telenor Pakistan, Ufone and Zong. Among these four, Jazz is the largest with 59 million subscribers followed by Telenor (46 m), Ufone (23.1 m) and Zong (15.6 m). The country is also serviced by a number of mobile virtual network operators. The Chinese telecom companies dominate the sector. Heavy investments are being made in the infrastructure like mobile towers and connecting the same with fibre. The mobile communications currently operate in 2G, 3G and 4G modes. There is, however, a fast expansion and transition to 4G connectivity in the LTE (VoLTE) mode across the country. The download speed generally ranges between 4 and 6 Mbits in the 4G mode of communication.

5G services

All the four big mobile operators have conducted field trials (in Karachi and Lahore) for commencing 5G mobile operations, particularly 4.5G LTE A. A task force has been set up to finalize the modalities and auction of spectrum. It is, however; generally felt that it may take more than a year to commence 4.5G mobile communications. The operations in the 5G mode may be delayed till 2025.

Internet Service Providers (ISPs)

There are around fifty (50) Internet service providers in the country. However, only eight (8) ISPs have a countrywide presence. The Internet traffic of Pakistan is currently around 80 Terabits. The Internet deploys IPV4 protocol.

Internet exchange

Pakistan Internet exchange (PIE), operated by PTCL, facilitates exchange and routing of Internet traffic between ISPs, within and out of the country. The Internet exchange, apart from routing, provides a means to monitor and possibly block incoming and outgoing traffic and conduct Internet surveillance. The entire incoming and outgoing traffic is monitored which includes email, keyword search and also stored data for a specified period. ISPs are required to retain traffic data for a minimum of 90 days and also collect real-time data and record information on the directions of the Federal Investigation Agency and Pakistan Telecommunication Authority.

Internet surveillance and national URLs filtering and blocking system

Internet surveillance and censorship is regulated by the Pakistan Telecommunication Authority (PTA) and Federal Investigation Agency (FIA) under the directions of the Government, the Supreme Court and the Ministry of Information and Telecommunication (MOIT). PTA, in 2019, blocked nine (9) lakh URLs (Unique Resource Locator). Most of the blocked URLs were carrying and providing content against the sentiments of the State and the armed forces of Pakistan. Social media sites like YouTube and Face book were censored and blocked for a long duration till the two social media giants launched local versions of the website.

ISPs in Pakistan have installed systems for filtering and blocking of URLs. Such systems primarily have been installed along the lines of "Golden Shield" or "Great Firewall of China". The filtering equipment has, in general, a capacity to block and filter 50 million URLs. The web content of the nature of blasphemous, pornography, and against the Armed forces are, in general, filtered. All the Torrent sites are banned in the country. This software-based system based on DNS (Domain Name System) tampering techniques are commonly used to filter and block URLs. On an average, more than 10 million URLs are monitored daily by the ISPs.

EXTERNAL

12

India–Pakistan Relations Following Imran Khan's Assumption of Office

Amb. Satish Chandra

India-Pakistan relations have been rocky and mired in suspicion since inception. They have traversed periods of dialogue, more often than not sterile, and those of minimal interaction, interspersed on occasion by wars. Since Imran Khan's assumption of office as Prime Minister in August 2018, India-Pakistan relations have, perhaps, been at their lowest ebb leaving aside periods of actual military conflict. They are currently marked by the absence of any substantive dialogue, operation of the respective high commissions at Cd'A level, a stymied SAARC process with the summit scheduled to have been held in Islamabad in 2016 on hold, mudslinging at the UN and other multilateral fora, suspension of bilateral trade, sharp diminution in people-to-people and communication links, an escalation in ceasefire violations, and Pakistan's constant support to terrorist activities directed against India. Moreover, while even at the worst of times in the past, a certain level of civility and courtesy had been maintained betwixt the leadership of the two countries, this is now no longer the case. Pakistani leaders like Imran Khan and Foreign Minister Qureshi have crossed all limits of decency when referring to their Indian counterparts. The latter, for instance, following his boycott of his Indian counterpart's address to the UN General Assembly in September 2019, told reporters that it was not possible for him to sit with the "murderer of Kashmiris".[1] Pakistan's petty churlishness towards Indian leaders reached a new high in September 2019 with its denial of over-flight clearance for the special aircraft taking President Kovind to Iceland and Prime Minister Modi to the USA.

The current phase of the downward slide in India-Pakistan relations predates

Imran Khan's assumption of office and may be traced back to when Nawaz Sharif was Prime Minister. This downslide may be mainly attributed to Pakistan's persistence with the use of terror against India despite Prime Minister Modi's endeavours to normalise ties. The most significant of these initiatives may be listed as his invitation to Nawaz Sharif for his swearing-in ceremony in May 2014, their meeting in Ufa, on the sidelines of the SCO summit, on 10 July 2015, which paved the way for the NSAs' meetings on terrorism, and his surprise visit to Raiwind on 25 December 2015 to felicitate Nawaz Sharif on the occasion of the latter's grand-daughter's wedding. These moves were responded to with acts of cross-border terrorism and violence against India. Indeed, in conformity with its standard operating procedure of subverting every Indian initiative aimed at promoting detente, Pakistan, soon after the meeting between the two Prime Ministers in Ufa, undertook a vicious terror attack in Gurdaspur district on 27 July resulting in around 20 casualties. Similarly, soon after Prime Minister Modi's Raiwind visit, a terror attack was conducted by Pakistan on the Pathankot airbase on 2 January 2016, and was followed up by an attack on the Uri army camp on 18 September 2016, which resulted in the deaths of 18 soldiers and left another 30 injured. It is such actions that led India to respond with its surgical strikes of 28 September 2016 and to stymie the convening of the 19th SAARC summit, which was scheduled to be hosted by Pakistan in November 2016.

The fact that Pakistan had been upping the ante in its use of terror against India well before Imran Khan's assumption of office as Prime Minister is apparent from the dramatic increase in ceasefire violations and infiltration bids in Jammu and Kashmir in the 2016-2017 period. As per the South Asian Terrorism Portal, Pakistani ceasefire violations rose from 449 in 2016 to 971 in 2017, and infiltration bids rose from 222 in 2015 to 419 in 2017.

It is also significant that on 24 July 2018, Pakistan, under the aegis of the caretaker government, released 20 postage stamps glorifying terrorism in Jammu and Kashmir.

Some in India had high expectations of improved ties with Pakistan following Imran Khan's election victory as he had visited India often, had many Indian friends, had a liberal education at Oxford, had in the past spoken out against Pakistan's military, and in his victory speech in July 2018 had called for good relations with India asserting that if the latter took one step forward for improving ties, Pakistan would take two steps.[2] These hopes were misplaced, as Pakistan's policies towards India are set by its military and not by its civilian government. Moreover, Imran Khan himself has never been soft on India even in his cricketing avatar when he openly confessed that he saw cricketing encounters with India as a jihad. Throughout his election campaign he denigrated India and, as pointed out by Christophe Jaffrelot, "Khan's nationalism also makes him deeply hostile towards India".[3] Indeed, even in his victory speech, the discerning would have noted that Imran Khan did not refrain from alleging that the Kashmiris had been suffering for the last thirty years, that Kashmir is the "core" issue and that the two countries need to come to the table to "fix" the problem.[4] Finally, being so deeply beholden to the Army for his having come to power, Imran Khan cannot possibly take any step without their concurrence on issues so important as relations with India, and it is, therefore, impossible for him to make moves directed at improving ties with the latter.

India-Pakistan relations got off to a bad start, ab initio, when the only Indian dignitary invited by Imran Khan for his swearing-in ceremony was former cricketer Navjot Singh Sidhu, a serving minister in the Congress government in Punjab. Apart from Sidhu, two other important persons were invited from India, notably Sunil Gavaskar, and Oxford buddy Vikram Mehta. While the former did not attend, the latter who is currently head of Brookings India did.

Sidhu was warmly feted at the swearing-in ceremony, and was hugged by General Bajwa, the Pakistan Army Chief. The latter, in total disregard of protocol, told Sidhu that Pakistan proposed to facilitate the visit of Sikh pilgrims from India to the Kartarpur Sahib Gurdwara by opening a corridor to it from the Indian border. This move was no more than a response to a decades-old Indian request and, as such, should have been conveyed to India through normal diplomatic channels rather than to Sidhu who, along with Pakistan, milked it for all it was worth for cheap political capital.

Notwithstanding the foregoing, Prime Minister Modi and the External Affairs Minister, Sushma Swaraj, sent congratulatory letters to their counterparts on their assuming office, calling for meaningful and constructive engagement for the benefit of the people of the entire region. These letters elicited a favourable response, which talked of bringing a positive change, mutual desire for peace, and Pakistan's readiness to discuss terrorism. In these circumstances, Pakistan's suggestion for a meeting between the Foreign Ministers on the sidelines of the United Nations General Assembly (UNGA) meetings in New York was readily accepted by India. However, soon thereafter, Pakistan-based terrorist entities brutally killed three police personnel in Jammu and Kashmir. India's strong protests to Pakistan and call for remedial action by it were met with outright denial. Under such circumstances, India called off the proposed meeting between the Foreign Ministers of India and Pakistan in New York.[5] Clearly, the reversal of the Indian decision on 21 September 2018, within 24 hours of having taken it, marked recognition of the fact that any dialogue with the Imran Khan government was meaningless, as it had no intention of curbing the export of terror to India. Pakistan's determination to continue using terror as an instrument of foreign policy against India, and the latter's recognition that any call for dialogue by the former was merely a ploy to maintain the fiction of normalcy, inevitably, led to the continued deterioration in bilateral relations not only through the remainder of 2018 but also through 2019 and into 2020.

The downturn in India-Pakistan ties was on open display at the UNGA in 2018 with the foreign ministers of the two countries making trenchant statements against the other country. The Indian External Affairs Minister slammed Pakistan for spawning terrorism and exporting the same to India and detailed how the latter's repeated attempts since 2014 to reach out to the former for dialogue had been rebuffed repeatedly with brutal terrorist actions. The Pakistan Foreign Minister, on his part, lambasted India for turning down dialogue on "flimsy grounds", for committing serious human rights violations in Kashmir, and for repeatedly violating the ceasefire line. He went on to call for a just settlement of the Kashmir issue based on UN Security Council resolutions and the will of the Kashmiri people. Such acrimonious exchanges at international fora were repeated and were symptomatic of the deep-rooted malaise in India-Pakistan relations.

The heightened Pakistani rhetoric against India extended to the highest levels in its government with Imran Khan taking the offensive in December 2018 and repeatedly contending that the minorities were being mistreated in India.

If the first few months of the Imran Khan regime in 2018 were bad for India-Pakistan relations, 2019 was a disaster. On 29 January 2019, Shah Mahmood Qureshi, the Pakistan Foreign Minister, in an unprecedented act of wanton interference in India's internal affairs, telephoned Hurriyat Conference chairman and separatist leader Mirwaiz Umar Farooq, and discussed with him Pakistan's efforts to internationalise the Kashmir issue. India reacted sharply to this with its Foreign Secretary summoning the Pakistan High Commissioner the next day and conveying to him its condemnation of this action in the strongest terms. According to a Ministry of External Affairs press release issued on 30 January 2019,

> "The Foreign Secretary conveyed that this deplorable act has violated all norms for the conduct of international relations even by Pakistan's own standards. The Pakistan Foreign Minister's actions are tantamount to direct

> interference in the internal affairs of its neighbour. Foreign Secretary underscored that by this action Pakistan has confirmed yet again that it officially abets and encourages individuals associated with terrorism and anti-India activities. It has exposed to the entire international community, Pakistan's duplicity in professing its desire for normal relations with India on the one hand, while openly inciting anti-India activities on the other."[6]

In early February 2019, in a routine meeting with the media, the Ministry of External Affairs spokesman made it clear that there was no question of talks with Pakistan as it continued to be involved with terrorist activities directed against India. In this context, he specifically referred to Pakistan's failure to take action against the perpetrators of the Mumbai and Pathankot terror attacks, its permitting the use of its territory by terrorist outfits, and the fact that its ministers share the platform with international terrorists as, for instance, was the case of the Religious Affairs Minister who shared a platform with Hafiz Saeed on 30 September 2018 with both making vitriolic anti-Indian speeches.

The Pulwama terrorist attack in February 2019 and the amendment of Article 370 in August along with the chain of events that they set in motion were, without doubt, the most important developments to aggravate the downturn in bilateral ties. In the following paragraphs, these will be examined along with Pakistan's sponsorship of terrorism against India inclusive of its ceasefire violations, Indus Waters Treaty-related issues, the evolution of the Kulbhushan Jadhav case, as well as the diminution in people-to-people, commercial, and communication links, all of which had a negative impact on bilateral ties. Perhaps, the main positive development was the opening of the Kartarpur corridor but here again the goodwill that Pakistan could have gained was to a large extent negated by the latter making it a money making enterprise and using it to further stoke Sikh separatism. The continued annual exchange on 1 January of the lists of each other's nuclear installations in 2019 and 2020 in accordance with a long-standing bilateral agreement between the two countries, the meetings of the Locust Warning organisations of the two countries at Munabao and Khokrapar in mid-2019 to exchange information on locust swarms afflicting the region, the participation of the two countries in a joint anti-terror drill in Russia under the aegis of the SCO, and the continued functioning of the Indus Waters Commission, can, of course, be assessed positively.

Kartarpur Corridor

The visits by Indians and Pakistanis to religious shrines in the other country is governed by a bilateral protocol signed in 1974 between two countries. The existing agreement between the two countries under this protocol envisages the visits of three Hindu and four Sikh pilgrimages every year to 15 shrines in Pakistan, and five Pakistani pilgrimages to seven shrines in India.[7] Under the agreement, pilgrims can travel only in groups on the basis of visitors' visas. The Kartarpur Sahib Gurdwara is not covered under the existing agreement though India had since long been pleading for its inclusion.[8]

The importance of the Kartarpur Sahib Gurdwara arises from the fact that Guru Nanak Dev lived there for about 18 years prior to his demise in 1539. The gurdwara is located in Pakistan about 120 km northeast of Lahore on the banks of the Ravi and barely around 4 km from the Dera Baba Nanak shrine in Gurdaspur district of India.

Taking into account the longstanding pleas from the Sikh community, Prime Minister Vajpayee, during his visit to Pakistan in February 1999, proposed that a corridor be built connecting the Kartarpur Sahib Gurdwara in Pakistan to the Dera Baba Nanak shrine in India to enable Indian pilgrims to visit the former and return the same day. This proposal was reiterated by India from time to time but elicited no response from Pakistan. It was only during Imran Khan's swearing-in ceremony on 18 August as cited above that General Bajwa, out of the blue, and without any query in the matter told Sidhu that Pakistan was ready to open the Kartarpur corridor on the occasion of Guru Nanak's 550th birth anniversary. Pakistan, however, did not deem it fit for weeks on end to convey this directly to the Government of India. It was the latter, acting on a request in the matter by the Punjab Government, which took up the matter with Pakistan to build the said corridor with suitable facilities on its side of the border for the visits of Indian pilgrims while undertaking to do the same from the Dera Baba Nanak shrine to the international border.

With Pakistan agreeing to the said request, a foundation stone-laying ceremony was held at Dera Baba Nanak on 26 November 2018 followed by a foundation laying ceremony at Kartarpur Sahib on 28 November. While on the Indian side, the foundation stone was laid by the Vice President and the ceremony was attended by many dignitaries including the Governor and the Chief Minister of Punjab, Captain Amarinder Singh, on the Pakistan side the ground-breaking ceremony was led by Prime Minister Imran Khan in the presence of several dignitaries. Pakistan had invited Sushma Swaraj, Captain Amarinder Singh and Sidhu for this ceremony. While Sidhu attended, neither Sushma Swaraj nor Captain Amarinder Singh did so. India was represented by Hardeep Puri, Minister for Housing and Development and Harsimrat Kaur Badal, Minister for Food Processing Industries. Capt. Amarinder Singh bluntly stated that he was unwilling to visit Pakistan on account of its continued use of terror against India. Always suspicious about Pakistan's move to open the Kartarpur corridor he rightly feared that it would use the same to promote its Khalistan agenda. Indeed, the timing of the offer for opening the corridor on the occasion of the 550th birth anniversary of Guru Nanak in November 2019 fits in well with Pakistan's efforts to promote separatism in Punjab as it falls on the eve of "Referendum 2020" being propagated by the NGO "Sikhs for Justice" (SFJ) which has long been campaigning for the creation of Khalistan. Pakistan, by facilitating the visits of Indian pilgrims to Kartarpur, not only hopes to win brownie points with the Sikh community in India but also to use the visits of hundreds of Sikhs to Kartarpur to incite them to take to separatism as indeed it has done all along during similar visits to other Sikh shrines.

After tortuous negotiations extending for well over six months in the midst of the heinous Pulwama terrorist attack, the Balakot air strike and the anger generated in Pakistan following the amendment of Article 370, India and Pakistan finally signed the Kartarpur Sahib Corridor Agreement on 24 October 2019. The main features of the agreement are:

- Visa free travel along the corridor by Indian pilgrims of all faiths and Persons of Indian Origin (PIOs);
- Pilgrims need to carry only a valid passport but PIOs will also need to carry their OCI card;
- The corridor will be open from dawn to dusk. Pilgrims travelling in the morning will have to return the same day;
- The corridor will be operational throughout the year, except on notified days, to be informed in advance;
- Pilgrims will have a choice to visit as individuals or in groups, and also to travel on foot;
- India will send the list of pilgrims to Pakistan 10 days ahead of the travel date. Confirmation will be sent to pilgrims four days before the travel date;
- Sufficient provision for 'langar' and distribution of 'prasad' will be made by Pakistan;
- Pakistan will levy a service charge of US$ 20 per pilgrim per visit.

India had argued long and hard against the levy of the aforesaid service charge but in the end capitulated in order not to jeopardise the agreement on the eve of the 550th birth anniversary of Guru Nanak. Clearly, Pakistan has not undertaken this exercise out of any genuine goodwill and hopes to milk it, both to promote separatism in Punjab and to reap commercial benefits.

While India lost out on the issue of the service charge, it was able to prevail on Pakistan to allow use of the corridor to all Indian citizens, not just Sikhs, as well as PIOs, to do so from dawn to dusk and not merely from 8 AM to 5 PM and to do so only on the basis of passports and OCI cards, where necessary, and not any additional documentation like Pakistani permits and Indian security clearance certificates. Furthermore, while Pakistan had, initially, insisted that the pilgrims come in groups of not less than 15, India was able to get it to agree that the pilgrims could use the corridor individually or in groups and could do so even on foot. Finally, while Pakistan, initially, made known that it would only permit 500 pilgrims per day, India made it clear that provision must be made for accommodating 5,000 pilgrims on a daily basis and on special occasions the number could swell to 10,000.

India was not remiss in expeditiously developing the required infrastructure for receiving the pilgrims and facilitating their smooth movement through the corridor. This, inter alia, includes a 4.2-km four-lane highway connecting Dera Baba Nanak from the Amritsar–Gurdaspur Highway, a state-of-the-art air-conditioned passenger terminal building akin to an airport with over 50 immigration counters to cater to about 5,000 pilgrims a day, and a robust security infrastructure complete with CCTV surveillance and public address systems.

Prime Minister Modi inaugurated the Dera Baba Nanak integrated checkpost and flagged off the first jatha of over 500 pilgrims on the corridor on 9 November 2019. The jatha inter alia included former Prime Minister Manmohan Singh, Akal Takht Jathedar Harpreet Singh, Punjab Chief Minister Captain Amarinder Singh, former Chief Minister Parkash Singh Badal, Sukhbir Singh Badal, Harsimrat Kaur Badal, Navjot Singh Sidhu and indeed all the 117 MLAs and MPs from Punjab including ministers.[9] Speaking after the event, while at the Dera Baba Nanak shrine, the Prime Minister thanked his Pakistani counterpart for understanding India's sentiments on the Kartarpur corridor.

Later, Prime Minister Imran Khan inaugurated the Kartarpur corridor and met members of the Indian pilgrim party. Pakistan's nefarious agenda did not take long to reveal itself as the pilgrims were greeted with the video of a song that featured slain Khalistani separatists, including the infamous Jarnail Singh

Bindranwale, prompting Chief Minister Amarinder Singh to once again assert that he had warned of this "since day one...Pakistan has a hidden agenda here."

Imran Khan, in his speech, used the occasion to play up to the Sikh community as well as to castigate the Indian government. On the former, he made out that as soon as he learnt from Sidhu of the desire of the Sikh community for the corridor, he decided to open it up and that the move to do so is indicative of the high regard that Pakistan has for the Sikhs and for communal harmony. This flies in the face of the admission by Sidhu that he was informed of this decision by the Pakistan Chief of Army Staff on his own at Imran Khan's swearing-in ceremony.[10] The fact that the opening of the Kartarpur corridor was the brainchild of General Bajwa was corroborated by Sheikh Rashid, the Pakistan Railway Minister, who further added that this was designed to hurt India.[11] Moreover, Foreign Minister Qureshi's oft-quoted assertion that Pakistan's move on the Kartarpur corridor constituted a "googly" reflects that the exercise was motivated not by any sense of empathy for the Sikh community but by opportunism and political considerations.

But, over and above the Sikh dimension of Imran Khan's speech, the latter was marked by its strident anti-Modi content and by an almost hysterical diatribe on the Kashmir issue. Both were avoidable and the inauguration of the Kartarpur corridor was certainly not the occasion on which to have dwelt on them so aggressively. On the former, tapping into the criticism against Modi by the Indian opposition about his alleged divisive agenda, Imran Khan parroted the homily that great leaders unite and not divide and went on to state that a "leader does not spread hatred and seek votes on the basis of religion."[12] Such an impolitic approach by Imran Khan inevitably militates against the possibility of any sort of an equation being developed between the prime ministers of the two countries.

As regards the Kashmir issue, while Imran Khan argued, as many Pakistani leaders have in the past, that its resolution was a sine qua non for good India-Pakistan relations, both he and his Foreign Minister went ballistic and used language rarely heard even at the worst of times. Imran Khan asserted, "What we are witnessing in Kashmir today is not a territorial issue anymore. It has escalated to a humanitarian crisis. Unfortunately, things have gotten even worse for the people of Kashmir who are treated like animals deprived of their basic human rights and besieged by the presence of 9 lakh soldiers." In a similar vein, Foreign Minister Qureshi, noting that Modi having thanked Imran Khan for opening the corridor, should also give the latter a chance to thank him by "lifting the curfew in Kashmir, ending the use of pellet guns, ending the violations of human rights, and by ending the communication blackout."[13]

Pulwama Terrorist Attack and Balakot Riposte

The Pulwama suicide terror attack, on the afternoon of February 14, 2019, set in motion a chain of events that accentuated the downturn in India-Pakistan ties in evidence since Imran Khan's assumption of office.

The attack was directed at a convoy carrying over 2,500 CRPF jawans from Jammu to Srinagar. It entailed the ramming of an explosives-laden SUV into one of the buses carrying the jawans on National Highway 44 near Avantipora town. The Jaish-e-Mohammed (JeM) immediately claimed responsibility for the attack, which was executed by a twenty-year-old Kashmiri school dropout who was one of its members. Forty CRPF jawans were killed and scores injured in what was the deadliest terror attack in Kashmir for decades.

Soon after the attack, Prime Minister Modi tweeted that "a befitting reply will be given to the perpetrators of the heinous attack and their patrons". The Foreign Secretary summoned the Pakistan High Commissioner and lodged a very strong demarche with him demanding that Pakistan take **"immediate and verifiable action"** against the JeM and that it immediately stop any groups or individuals associated with terrorism operating from its territories. India, additionally, recalled its High Commissioner in Pakistan for consultations, withdrew the accord of MFN treatment to Pakistan, imposed a 200 per cent duty on all imports from Pakistan, and announced that it would undertake the maximal utilisation of the Indus Waters in accordance with the Indus Waters Treaty. None of these measures imposed much immediate pain on Pakistan and were largely symbolic in nature. This is all the more so since annual Pakistani exports to India were only about half a billion US dollars and the action on the maximal utilisation of the Indus Waters Treaty was already underway and will take time to implement.

Though the JeM claimed responsibility for the attack, the Pakistan Foreign Ministry immediately denied the country's linkage to it. Imran Khan chose to respond only on 19th February—five days after the event—in a televised interview. In a departure from past practice, apart from the belated response, he had not a word of condemnation for the heinous attack or of sympathy for the bereaved families. Instead, apart from a flat denial of any Pakistani role in the attack, he warned that any Indian adventurism would invite assured retaliation.

Within two weeks of the Pulwama terror attack, the IAF, on 26 February, undertook a highly successful airstrike against a major JeM training camp located near Balakot in the Khyber Pakhtunkhwa province of Pakistan without taking any losses or facing any resistance from the Pakistan Air Force (PAF). It was the first time since 1971 that the IAF had acted against targets in Pakistan and like the surgical strikes of 2016 was a demonstration of India's capacity and will to react to Pakistan's use of terror against it far more aggressively than in the past. The rationale and nature of this strike was explained in the following terms in a statement issued by the Foreign Secretary on 26 February:

> "India has been repeatedly urging Pakistan to take action against the JeM to prevent jihadis from being trained and armed inside Pakistan. Pakistan has taken no concrete actions to dismantle the infrastructure of terrorism on its soil.
>
> "Credible intelligence was received that JeM was attempting another suicide terror attack in various parts of the country, and that fidayeen jihadis were being trained for this purpose. In the face of imminent danger, a pre-emptive strike became absolutely necessary.
>
> "In an Intelligence-led operation in the early hours of today, India struck the biggest training camp of JeM in Balakot. In this operation, a very large number of JeM terrorists, trainers, senior commanders and groups of jihadis who were being trained for fidayeen action were eliminated. This facility at Balakot was headed by Maulana Yousuf Azhar (alias Ustad Ghouri), the brother-in-law of Masood Azhar, Chief of JeM.
>
> "The Government of India is firmly and resolutely committed to taking all necessary measures to fight the menace of terrorism. Hence, this non-military pre-emptive action was specifically targeted at the JeM camp. The selection of the target was also conditioned by our desire to avoid civilian casualties. The facility is located in thick forest on a hilltop far away from any civilian presence."[14]

While the "non military" nature of the action was well taken, as no military sites were targeted, its "pre-emptive" nature, while true in a medium term sense, was open to question and the general perception was that the strikes were a retaliation for the Pulwama terror attack. This perception did not, however, invite any opprobrium either at home or abroad barring the OIC's condemnation of the Balakot airstrike and its call for restraint on both sides. This must, however, be weighed against the fact that the OIC received Sushma Swaraj as its guest of honour at the OIC Foreign Ministers' Meeting at Abu Dhabi on 1-2 March 2019 despite Pakistan's feverish endeavours to get the invitation cancelled.

Pakistan reacted to the Indian airstrike at Balakot with an effort to launch air attacks against military sites in Jammu and Kashmir the following day. The IAF was prepared and successfully thwarted the PAF, which had to retreat and dump its ammunition in Jammu and Kashmir. There was, however, a dog fight in which Pakistan lost a F16 aircraft and India lost a MiG 21 Bison with its pilot ejecting and being captured by Pakistan. This confrontation further enhanced tensions and the armed forces of the two countries were on high alert to cater for any contingency. However, neither side apparently wished to push matters further and with the release on March 1, 2019, of the pilot captured by Pakistan, tensions gradually eased though relations remained embittered. It is reasonable to assume that the USA played a key role behind the scenes role to pressure Pakistan to release the Indian pilot so essential for a de-escalation of tensions.

International reactions to the Pulwama attack and the Indian riposte were largely favourable to India. Pakistan was seen as the sponsor of terror and the Balakot air strike was perceived as justified. While, following the Pulwama attack, there was an outpouring of sympathy for India with scores of countries coming out in its support, after the Balakot airstrike most countries called on both India and Pakistan to exercise restraint. Countries like France and Australia called on Pakistan to curb the operations of terrorist groups in its territory with the former going so far as to acknowledge India's "legitimacy to ensure security".[15] The USA was, however, the most supportive of India with its National Security Advisor, John Bolton, telling his Indian counterpart, "We support India's right to self-defence", and Secretary of State Mike Pompeo declaring on twitter, "We stand with #India as it confronts terrorism. Pakistan must not provide safe haven for terrorists to threaten international security."[16]

The Indian and Pakistani narratives relating to many of the developments pertaining to Balakot were strikingly different. Thus while India claimed a highly successful Balakot attack in which many terrorists were killed and the camp damaged, Pakistan made out that the attacks missed the target and that there were no casualties. Similarly, on the aerial engagement, while admitting the loss of one MIG aircraft, India held that Pakistan had used F16s, of which one was shot down, the latter projected that no F16's had been used, none had been shot down and that it had shot down not one but two Indian aircraft. It made little difference that India cited the remains of an AMRAAM missile on its soil as proof of the use of F16s, which alone could have fired it. The fact of the use of F16s, notwithstanding Pakistan's assertions to the contrary and US silence, is also evident from a reprimand delivered to the Pakistan Air Chief by the then US Under Secretary of State for Arms Control and International Security Affairs in a letter in August 2019 regarding the movement of F16s in the following terms: "While we understand from you that these aircraft movements were done in support of national defence objectives, the US Government considers the relocation of aircraft to non-US government authorised bases concerning and inconsistent with the F-16 Letter of Offer and Acceptance."[17] Nevertheless, the thought remains that India's perception management was below par and Pakistan did much better in promoting its projections.

Fallout of amendment of Article 370 on India-Pakistan relations

The amendment of Article 370 on August 5, 2019, making the laws passed by the Indian Parliament applicable to the Indian State of Jammu and Kashmir, its bifurcation into two Union Territories, notably those of Jammu and Kashmir and of Ladakh, and the imposition of a clampdown in the area for security reasons, raised Pakistan's visceral antipathy towards India to fever pitch. This was reflected in the following retaliatory actions, which had been approved in an Imran Khan chaired National Security Council Meeting held on 7 August 2019.[18]

1. Protest against India's revocation of the special status of Jammu and Kashmir.
2. Downgradation of diplomatic relations with India by sending back the Indian High Commissioner and by not permitting the Pakistan High Commissioner-designate to India from taking up his assignment.
3. Suspension of bilateral trade.
4. Closure of Pakistani airspace to India for one month from 6 August to 5 September on all days except Sunday from 2.45 to 11 AM.
5. Observance of the upcoming Independence Day on 14 August in solidarity with Kashmiris and 15 August as a black day.
6. Taking up the matter in the UN including the UN Security Council.
7. Activation of all diplomatic channels to highlight human rights violations in the Valley.

It may be pointed out that Pakistan's anger at the amendment of Article 370 by India is unjustified and hypocritical. Unjustified, because Jammu and Kashmir is an integral part of India. The legality of its accession to India is beyond challenge since its ruler had duly signed an Instrument of Accession in favour of India as required under the prevailing dispensation and as was done by all the princely states acceding to India. The accession was also sanctified through expression of popular will as represented by a democratically elected State Constituent Assembly which, in 1954, ratified the State's accession to India and the innumerable elections subsequently held therein. Accordingly, India is well within its rights to deal with the State in accordance with its own constitutional processes. Hypocritical, because Pakistan has systematically been changing the status quo in the part of Kashmir illegally occupied by it through force of arms. As early as 1949 itself,

Pakistan had bifurcated the part of Kashmir seized by it into two, the so-called Azad Jammu and Kashmir with an area of about 11,639 sq km, and the Northern Areas comprising Gilgit and Baltistan with an area of about 72,495 sq km. Both are directly controlled by Islamabad with the former having a few trappings of democratic institutions minus the substance. The framework of administrative arrangements for these two areas has been modified repeatedly over the years. Additionally, change in the population mix in the region by settlement of Punjabis and Pathans therein, the ceding of 5,180 sq km from this area to China under the 1963 Sino-Pakistan Boundary Agreement, and the construction of the China Pakistan Economic Corridor through the area which legally belongs to India, constitutes a material alteration of the status quo which is not in Pakistan's competence.

The raison d'être for Pakistan's discomfiture with the amendment of Article 370 and the reorganisation of Jammu and Kashmir is that it degrades the opportunities available to it to fuel the forces of disaffection in the State. Article 370 had not only bred separatism and kept alive the pernicious two-nation theory but also prevented the mainstreaming of Jammu and Kashmir into the Indian polity. Accordingly, the amendment of Article 370 and bringing Jammu and Kashmir directly under the Union Government will make Pakistani machinations in the area far more difficult than was the case earlier.

Clearly the main thrust of Pakistan's retaliatory action was to embark on a no-holds barred diplomatic blitzkrieg against India based on untruths and fuelled by hatred. Pakistan's diplomatic jihad designed to internationalise the Kashmir issue and malign India comes naturally to it as it has done so repeatedly in the past. On this occasion, however, Pakistan went into overdrive and adopted a multi-pronged strategy entailing the lambasting of India in the media as well as at all possible fora through its leaders and supporters, the organisation of demonstrations against India, some of which, like in London, turned violent, the effort to pass a resolution on the issue against India at the UN Human Rights Council (UNHRC), the endeavour to persuade the UN Security Council (UNSC) to take up the issue, and the activation of the Organisation of Islamic Cooperation (OIC) in the matter. In order to sustain these moves Pakistan set up a Kashmir cell in the Foreign Ministry as well as in its embassies.[19]

In a foretaste of the nature of its diplomatic campaign against India, Imran Khan on 6 August, while addressing the National Assembly on the amendment of Article 370, asserted that India had never been interested in talks, that India's action was part of the government's racist ideology of putting Hindus above all and repressing other groups, that the move was in violation of Indian and international laws, that India would crack down even harder in the State and may initiate ethnic cleansing, and that there may be another Pulwama which could escalate into an India-Pakistan conflict. Imran Khan concluded by asserting that he would inform the Western world of "what the Indian government is doing in Kashmir and what it is doing to Muslims and minorities in India goes against everything the Western world believes in."[20]

In a similar vein, Imran Khan in an article of 30 August 2019 in the *New York Times* titled "Imran Khan: The World Can't Ignore Kashmir. We Are All in Danger" made out that Modi had spurned all his efforts for dialogue, that Modi "gained global notoriety for the 2002 pogrom against local Muslims", that his first term was marked by lynchings of Muslims, Christians and Dalits, that the amendment of Article 370 is "illegal under the Constitution of India, ... is a violation of the United Nations Security Council resolutions on Kashmir and the Shimla Agreement..." and that following the clampdown by India in Kashmir, "thousands have been arrested and thrown into prisons across India. A blood bath is feared in Kashmir when the curfew is lifted. Already, Kashmiris coming out in defiance of the curfew are being shot and killed." If the world did not intervene, the situation could escalate into a military conflict between India and Pakistan, both of which were nuclear armed countries.

The speeches made by Modi and Imran Khan in that order at the UNGA on 27 September were a study in contrast. While the former spoke of issues of development, climate change, multilateralism, technology, etc., and refrained from even a mention of Pakistan or Kashmir, nearly half of the latter's speech was a rant on the lines of his *New York Times* article about the Modi Government and the alleged atrocities being perpetrated by it in Kashmir. The only additional new twists in this speech were that India's actions in Jammu and Kashmir would lead to the radicalisation of India's Muslim population and that this was the time "the UN must insist on Kashmir's right to self determination!"

In pursuit of its efforts to pass a resolution against India in the UNHRC, the Pakistan Foreign Minister followed up his letter of 4 August 2019 to the High Commissioner of Human Rights and telephonic conversation of 8 August 2019 with another letter later in the month highlighting "in detail the context and consequences of India's illegal and unilateral actions of 5 August 2019."[21] The letter inter alia underscored that "India's actions constitute flagrant violations of the UN Charter, relevant Security Council resolutions, international law and India's own solemn commitments" and that the international community must "call upon India to rescind its unilateral actions, lift the curfew and other draconian measures, and restore fundamental rights of the Kashmiri people."[22] The stage for Pakistan's move was well prepared as the previous High Commissioner for Human Rights, a Jordanian diplomat, close to Pakistan, had in 2018 brought out a highly biased and critical report on India's actions in Kashmir. The current High Commissioner had in July 2019 brought out an update thereon which was similarly critical of India.

On 10 September 2019, the Pakistan Foreign Minister addressed the UNHRC in an effort to push it to act against India and in so doing, resorted to all manner of falsehoods crossing even all limits of decency. He, for instance, accused the Indian government of committing genocide, of converting Kashmir into "the world's largest prison" and of being "murderous, misogynistic, and xenophobic".[23]

In a deft response, the Indian position was ably presented by Vijay Thakur Singh, Secretary in the Ministry of External Affairs. She dwelt on India's ethos and the strength of its democratic institutions which ensured the human rights of everyone in the country, and pointed out that the measures taken in respect of Jammu and Kashmir were within the framework of India's Constitution and designed to ensure that the progressive measures being enacted in the rest of the country were also applicable to it. She also underlined that all these actions were an internal issue for India and it would brook no interference. While admitting that some restrictions had been imposed, these were being eased and were temporary and preventive measures to ensure safety from cross-border terrorism. In a pungent but dignified criticism of Pakistan she asserted, "We should call out those who are misusing this platform for malicious political agendas under the garb of human rights. Those who are attempting this speak on the human rights of minorities in other countries are trampling upon them at will in their own country. They cry victim when they actually are the perpetrators.... One delegation has given a running commentary with offensive rhetoric of false allegations and concocted charges against my country. The world is aware that this fabricated narrative comes from the epicentre of global terrorism, where ring leaders were sheltered for years. This nation conducts cross-border terrorism as a form of 'alternate diplomacy'."[24]

Eventually, Pakistan did not succeed in having a resolution passed against India at the September session of the UNHRC as it could not muster the 16 votes out of the 47 members needed to have the same admitted, much less the 24 votes required to actually pass it. The reason for Pakistan's failure lies not only in the fact that it has much less heft than India but also because there is a subliminal appreciation that it is responsible for much of the problem. This is not to say that India did not spend much precious diplomatic capital in explaining its case on Kashmir to the international community and on ensuring that the vast majority of countries did not align with Pakistan.

The activation of the UNSC on the Kashmir issue has always been on Pakistan's agenda and the amendment of Article 370 provided it with the opportunity to press its case. Accordingly, from August 1, 2019, till 12 December 2019, it wrote as many as seven letters to the UNSC and the Secretary General inter alia expressing Pakistan's "serious concerns over India's illegal and unilateral actions in IOJ&K and the resultant human rights and humanitarian situation as well as India's belligerent rhetoric and steps on the ground posing serious risks to peace and security", and calling on the UNSC to play a "proactive" role.[25]

Pakistan's efforts on this score also did not yield its desired results. While it was able to get two closed-door informal meetings of the UNSC on the issue, solely due to China's staunch support, notably in August 2019 and January 2020, these were infructuous. Far from being critical of India, they did not even come out with a statement as all the other members of the UNSC felt that this was a bilateral issue and one in which UN intervention would be inappropriate.

Activation of the OIC in Pakistan's favour expectedly posed no problems, as, since 1990, it has always been supportive of the latter on the Kashmir issue. It has also long had a Special Representative on Kashmir and advocates self-determination in Kashmir. At its fourteenth Islamic Summit (May-June 2019) in Saudi Arabia, the OIC reiterated its position on Kashmir, emphasising the role of the UN resolutions in settling the issue.[26] However, it is notable that the then Indian External Affairs Minister, Sushma Swaraj, was the guest of honour at the Islamic Foreign Ministers Conference in Abu Dhabi earlier on 1 March 2019. Her presence at the conference so angered Pakistan that its Foreign Minister boycotted the meeting. Nevertheless, the conference did pass its customary anti-Indian resolutions. Moreover, the OIC Ministerial Contact Group passed a very strong resolution on India's actions in Jammu and Kashmir in its meeting held in September 2019 on the margins of the UNGA. However, post 5 August 2019, no such resolution has been passed by the OIC Foreign Ministers.

While Pakistan enjoys considerable clout in the Islamic world, India's strong bilateral relationships with important players like Saudi Arabia, the UAE, etc., make it difficult for the former to count on all-out support, barring the usual proforma anti-India resolutions on issues like Kashmir. In this context, it would not be out of place to mention that the UAE for instance "has signalled support for India's decision to revoke Article 370, claiming that the legislative move could improve the prevailing social and security situation in J&K."[27] Pakistan does, of course, have some all-weather friends in the Islamic world, most notably Turkey and Malaysia, which have adopted a blatantly anti-Indian stance in the recent developments pertaining to Kashmir. Finally, it would be prudent for India not to discount the Islamic factor in its stand-off on the Kashmir issue as it has an highly emotive appeal and Pakistan is milking it for all it is worth. Furthermore, it has been skilful in leveraging its strong linkages with Malaysia and Turkey to ensure that Saudi Arabia does not tilt too much towards India. This was in evidence when it leveraged its impending participation in the Kuala Lumpur Islamic Summit spearheaded by Turkey and Malaysia—a thinly disguised effort at creating an alternative to the Saudi-led OIC—to get Saudi Arabia to agree to the convening of an OIC Conference in early 2020 specifically dedicated to the Kashmir issue.

It would be evident from the foregoing that Pakistan was unable to sway the international community against India in regard to the various actions taken by it relating to Jammu and Kashmir through 2019. Countries generally regarded these moves as internal to India and that differences between the latter and Pakistan relating to Jammu and Kashmir were best resolved bilaterally. However, this does not mean that countries were not concerned with developments in the State and, should the curtailment of civil liberties be prolonged by a few more months, opinions could change. This is all the more so as popular perceptions of India's moves in Jammu and Kashmir, particularly in the Western world, have gone against it. This has no doubt been coloured to some extent by opinions expressed by the Indian opposition and the liberal media but also points to the Government's glaring lack of any effort at meaningful perception management.

Pakistan's Sponsorship of Terrorism against India

Pakistan's sponsorship of terrorism against India both in Jammu and Kashmir and in the Punjab has clearly escalated since Imran Khan's assumption of office.

The South Asia Terrorism Portal citing official statistics indicates that Pakistani ceasefire violations—resorted to in order to facilitate the infiltration of terrorists—showed a dramatic increase from 449 in 2016 to 971 in 2017 and to 2,140 in 2018. In 2019, as per a reply by the Defence Minister to a question in the Rajya Sabha, these increased further by over 50 per cent to 3,479.[28] The intensity of such violations has rendered null and void the India-Pakistan ceasefire agreement of 2003.

Indeed, on nearly all violence-related parameters, as compiled by the South Asia Terrorism Portal, the security situation in Jammu and Kashmir reveals deteriorating trends. Thus, incidents of killings in 2018 increased to 205 from levels of a year earlier of 163, terrorism-related incidents in 2018 rose to 614 from 342 in 2017, and stone-pelting incidents in 2018 rose to 330 from 264 in 2017. In 2019, up to 17 February, J&K recorded 74 fatalities as against 34 for the corresponding period in the previous year. The total fatalities in 2018 were 451 as against 358 in 2017.

Pakistan's long-standing moves to stoke the fires of Sikh separatism increased sharply from 2018 onwards. After a 11-year gap, Khalistani terrorists launched a major attack killing three and injuring 20 on 8 November 2018 in Amritsar district. Two members of the Khalistani Liberation Force (KLF) were arrested and confessed that the grenade had been provided by the Pakistan-based KLF chief and that three others based abroad were also involved. This attack had been preceded by another grenade attack in Jullundur district on 14 September 2018 with the involvement of the Jammu and Kashmir based Ansar Ghazawat-ul-Hind. This lends credence to the theory that Pakistan is trying to create a nexus between Islamic and Sikh terrorist outfits. The growing extent of Sikh terrorism is borne out by the statement of the Minister of State for Home Affairs on January 2, 2019, in the *Rajya Sabha* that during the preceding two years in Punjab a total of 18 Khalistani terrorist modules were neutralized resulting in the arrest of 95 Khalistani operatives. Evidence has also come to light of Pakistan using GPS-fitted drones to drop arms and drugs across the border in Punjab to promote separatism.[29]

Pakistan has also funded and backed the obscure US-based Sikhs for Justice (SFJ) group which in August 2018 launched the "Khalistan Referendum 2020" campaign in London. The 'referendum' purportedly aims to determine the wishes of the Sikh community settled across the globe on the issue of Punjab's 'liberation' from India by 2020, and then pursue a referendum through the intervention of the United Nations. It is no surprise, therefore, that the moment India formally indicated its decision on going ahead with Kartarpur corridor in November 2018, Pakistan gave permission to the SFJ to open its office in Lahore and the latter a few days thereafter declared, 'the Kartarpur corridor is a bridge to Khalistan'.[30] This proves the point that Pakistan's decision to open the Kartarpur corridor was driven not by goodwill but by its separatist agenda directed against India.

Financial Action Task Force (FATF)

The FATF is a 39-member inter-governmental body established in 1989 to combat money laundering, terrorist financing and other related threats to the integrity of the international financial system. Pakistan has long been under its scrutiny and was on its grey list from 2008 to 2010, from 2012 to 2015, and from June 2018 to date. In June 2018, it had agreed to complete a 27-point action plan by September 2019 which would have enabled it to get off the grey list. However, notwithstanding Pakistan's feverish lobbying to get off the grey list, the steadfast support of China, Malaysia and Turkey, and moves like the recent arrest of Hafiz Saeed, the FATF plenary in Paris from 16 to 21 February 2020 decided to continue to keep Pakistan on the grey list as it found that 13 of the 27 points of the action plan still remained to be addressed. The FATF has urged Pakistan to complete the pending actions by June 2020. Failure to do so could lead to it being placed on the black list.

The happenings in the FATF are evidence of the fact that while Pakistan has not succeeded in getting off the grey list, India, on its part, has failed to have it placed on the black list which, on the merits of the case, should have happened. All that India can take satisfaction from is that it has succeeded in keeping the FATF's spotlight squarely on Pakistan's close linkages with terrorist outfits and support to terrorist financing.

Indus Waters Treaty Related Issues

The Indus Waters Treaty, concluded in 1960, is heavily weighted in Pakistan's favour as it was allocated 80 per cent of the flows of the Indus waters whereas India, though having 40 per cent of the catchment area, was allocated only 20 per cent and, additionally, was required to pay the former 62 million pounds sterling for construction of replacement canal works.

As per the Treaty, while India was given exclusive rights over the use of the waters of the three eastern rivers, it was accorded very limited rights on the use of the western rivers and that too with many onerous limitations. Pakistan has fully exploited the Treaty to stymie Indian projects on the western rivers. Accordingly, the Treaty has failed to contribute to improved ties between the two countries as originally hoped by India.

The Baglihar and Kishenganga projects are but two of several Indian projects which have been delayed for years due to Pakistan's objections. The former was, at Pakistan's insistence, taken to a neutral expert in 2005 and the latter to a court of arbitration in 2010. In both cases, the projects were cleared albeit at considerable cost and much loss of time.

Indeed, on the Kishenganga project, Pakistan is insisting on it being referred again to a court of arbitration on technical design issues which are more appropriately addressed by a neutral expert as stipulated in the Treaty. It had also asked for arbitration on the Ratle project. India reacted on October 4, 2016, by requesting the World Bank to appoint a neutral expert for this purpose. The latter initiated both the processes—appointment of a neutral expert and constituting a court of arbitration—simultaneously on November 10, 2016. Following India's demarches in the matter, the World Bank on December 12, 2016, announced a pause in both the processes initiated by it and called on both parties to explore "alternative ways to resolve their disagreements". It further convened meetings of the concerned secretaries of the two countries under its aegis for this purpose in August and September 2017 which were infructuous. Meanwhile, India has proceeded ahead with these projects and, in fact, Prime Minister Modi inaugurated the Kishenganga project in May 2018. Later, in September 2018, the Pakistan Foreign Minister personally complained to the World Bank President that the undertaking of the Kishenganga and Ratle projects by India was in violation of the Indus Waters Treaty and that arbitration proceedings as requested by Pakistan in respect of them should be initiated.

Following the Uri terror attack in September 2016, the Modi government, as a means of penalising Pakistan, decided to maximise its use of the Indus waters within the framework of the Indus Waters Treaty. Accordingly, in order to ensure full utilisation of all the waters of the eastern rivers, it decided in December 2018 to fast track three projects, namely the Shahpur Kandi dam on the Ravi, the Sutlej-Beas link canal, and the Ujh dam on the Ujh river, a tributary of the Ravi. Additionally, several projects on the Chenab are already under construction such as Pakal Dul and Lower Kalnai with many others in the pipeline like Sawalkot and Bursar. With Jammu and Kashmir now a Union Territory, it is to be hoped that these projects will be executed much more speedily.

The Indus Waters Commission mechanisms functioned relatively smoothly in the last couple of years notwithstanding strained India-Pakistan ties. Two meetings of the Commission took place in 2018 and the next one is scheduled for 2020. Under the aegis of the Commission, a three-member Pakistan delegation inspected the projects being undertaken by India on the Chenab in January 2019, some of which had been objected to by Pakistan in the meetings of the Commission.

Rising India-Pakistan tensions, in the immediate aftermath of the amendment to Article 370, led India on 21 August 2019 to indicate that it had refused to renew a 1989 agreement, under which it was, as a goodwill gesture, supplying hydrological data to Pakistan free of cost over and above the requirements of the Indus Waters Treaty.[31]

Kulbhushan Jadhav Case

The Kulbhushan Jadhav case continued to poison India-Pakistan relations throughout Imran Khan's premiership. It may be recalled that the Pakistani authorities alleged that they had arrested Kulbhushan Jadhav, a long retired Indian naval officer, on March 3, 2016, in Balochistan for spying. The fact, however, is that he had been involved in business in Iran for several years and was kidnapped from there by terrorist elements and handed over to Pakistan which chose to project him as an Indian spy involved in the promotion of terrorism in Balochistan. The exercise was essentially a ploy to substantiate Pakistan's long-standing and ill-founded charges of India's involvement in terrorism in Balochistan as a counter to India's charges of Pakistan's use of terrorism against it which have acquired traction globally.

India was informed of Kulbhushan Jadhav's arrest only on 25 March 2016 and its repeated efforts at securing consular access to him as mandated under the Vienna Convention met with no success. Indeed, Jadhav was tried without India's knowledge and sentenced to death in Pakistan by a military court in April 2017. On learning of this, India raised the matter with the International Court of Justice (ICJ) in May 2017 which shortly thereafter issued a binding order requiring Pakistan to stay Jadhav's execution pending its final judgement. Following detailed and impassioned presentations from India and Pakistan, the last of which took place in February 2019, the ICJ issued its final ruling on 17 July 2019 in a near-unanimous 15 to 1 judgement with the sole dissent being voiced by the Pakistani judge on the panel. While the judgement did not accept India's appeal for Jadhav's release, it unequivocally ruled that Pakistan was in violation of its obligations under the Vienna Convention on account of its delay in notifying India of his arrest and in failing to provide him with consular access. It went on to not only call for the according of consular access to him but also demanded the suspension of his execution and a review of the entire process of his trial and conviction.

The ICJ's judgement was a clear slap in the face of Pakistan and within a few days thereafter it made an offer to India for consular access to Jadhav. However, the consular access scheduled to take place on 2 August 2019 did not materialise as it was hemmed in with conditions like the presence of Pakistani authorities which would have impeded its very purpose. Eventually consular access was finally provided on 2 September 2019.

Hyderabad Fund Case

Following hard on the heels of the ICJ verdict which went largely in India's favour in the Kulbhushan Jadhav case, the UK High Court in its rulings of October and December 2019 dealt a crushing blow to Pakistan's longstanding claim on the one million pounds sterling plus one guinea deposited with its High Commissioner in London in 1948 by the Nizam of Hyderabad's Finance Minister.

The background to the said transfer is that the Nizam's government had been colluding with Pakistan for Hyderabad's secession from India and had gone so far as to secure arms from it. Following Hyderabad's accession to India in 1948, the Nizam asserted that the money had been transferred to the Pakistan High Commissioner without his permission. Accordingly, in 1954, he moved the UK court for release of the aforesaid funds which had been deposited in the London account of the Pakistan High Commissioner. However, Pakistan stymied any forward movement in the matter as it invoked sovereign immunity and the matter remained in limbo till 2013. In the interim, the Nizam and India reached an understanding on how the said monies were to be shared between his grandsons and the Indian government.

In an effort to seize these funds, which currently amount to pound sterling 35 million, Pakistan in 2013 sued the Nat West Bank which was the custodian of these monies and which was keeping them till their rightful owner was legally established. In so doing, Pakistan had to waive the sovereign immunity invoked by it earlier and the matter went to the UK High Court which dismissed its claims to these funds. In the process, the Court rejected several Pakistani arguments propounded in its support. The Court, for instance, rejected the contention that India was timed out on its claim, as it was Pakistan that had blocked proceedings. Secondly, it rejected the contention that the Indian action in Hyderabad was "illegal" and not in accordance with the provisions of the India Independence Act as the UK had accepted this move and, further, since the heirs to the Nizam and India had reached agreement in the matter. Finally, while accepting that Pakistan had indeed supplied arms to Hyderabad, it held that there was no evidence that the funds deposited in the Nat West Bank by the Pakistan High Commissioner were used for the purchase of these arms or were even a gift to Pakistan and as such these funds could not be considered as belonging to Pakistan. In these circumstances, the Court not only dismissed Pakistan's claims but also opined that the Nizam was the rightful beneficiary and in the context of his agreement with India, the latter along with his two grandsons, Prince Mukarram Jah, the titular eighth Nizam of Hyderabad, and his younger brother, Muffakham Jah, were legally entitled to these funds. The Court left it to the princes and India to divide the money among themselves. To add insult to injury, it also required Pakistan to meet 65 per cent of the legal costs incurred by India and by the two grandsons of the Nizam. The amounts payable by Pakistan on this account are pound sterling 2,802,192.22 to India, pound sterling 1,835,445.83 to Prince Muffakham Jah, and pound sterling 795,064.63. to the eighth Nizam of Hyderabad, Prince Mukarram Jah.[32]

People-to-People, Commercial, and Communication Links

Commercial Links

India-Pakistan trade in 2019 plummeted to almost zero, a far cry from 1948-49 when India accounted for 56 per cent of Pakistan's exports and 32 per cent of its imports, and was effectively its largest trading partner till 1955-56. It is of course true that as relations kept going downhill so did bilateral trade.

The year 2019 will go down as annus horribilis in India-Pakistan trade as, immediately after the Pulwama terror attack, India withdrew the MFN treatment that it had unilaterally accorded to it since the 1990s and imposed 200 per cent duty on all imports on Pakistan. Additionally, in April 2019, it stopped all cross-LoC trade. Following India's amendment of Article 370, Pakistan banned all trade with India.

The impact of these actions has been telling with Pakistan's exports to India in March 2019 falling to $ 2.84 million from the previous year's level of $ 34.61 million and in June 2019 descending to $ 1.2 million from $ 41.79 million. Truck traffic from Pakistan to India in April-November 2019 fell to 348 trucks from 4,381 trucks in the earlier year during the same period and from India to Pakistan it was 113 trucks in April-November 2019 as compared to 223 trucks for the same period in 2018.[33]

Communication Links

Communication links between India and Pakistan today have been squeezed to virtually zero with no bus, train, sea, or air services being operated for travel by either to the other country barring the Srinagar-Muzzafarabad and the Poonch-Rawalkot bus services. Accordingly, direct travel from one country to the other country is either through third party commercial aircraft or on foot through the Attari-Wagah check post or through the Kashmir bus services referred to above.

Direct air travel between India and Pakistan was earlier being undertaken by PIA on the Mumbai-Karachi and Delhi-Lahore sectors. The former was shut down in 2017 due to lack of traffic and the latter has since also been terminated following the Balakot airstrikes when Pakistan shut its airspace. Use of Pakistani airspace has been severely restricted for use of aircraft from India. Indeed, use of Pakistani airspace was not even permitted for President Kovind's visit to Iceland in September 2019 and Prime Minister Modi's visit to the USA in September 2019 and Saudi Arabia in October 2019.

Soon after the amendment of Article 370, Pakistan, on 9 August 2019, cancelled the Samjhauta Express through the Attari-Wagah checkpost and the Thar Express operating through the Khokrapar-Munabao checkpost.[34]

On 10 August, Pakistan suspended the bus services to India on the Lahore-Delhi, Lahore-Amritsar, and Nankana Sahib-Amritsar routes.[35] On 19 August, it suspended the weekly Poonch-Rawalkot bus service only to revive it the following week.

Soon after the amendment to Article 370, Pakistan stopped all mail service between the two countries. This was undertaken unilaterally and without any prior notice in violation of the International Postal Union norms. In November, the Pakistan media reported that the mail service between the two countries was being resumed but parcel service would remain suspended. There was, however, no official announcement to this effect.[36]

Jinnah House

Pakistan, under Imran Khan, also chose to once again rake up the long-standing controversy on Jinnah House. As may be recalled, Jinnah had, in 1936, built a plush residence on a huge two-and-a-half acre plot located in Mumbai's Malabar Hill area. With India's partition in 1947 and the departure of Jinnah and his sister, Fatima Jinnah, to whom he had willed the property in 1939, to Pakistan, Jinnah House was declared as evacuee property in 1949 and till 1981 was rented by India to the British High Commission.[37]

Through the next few years, the Pakistan government made several efforts to get India's permission to lease Jinnah House to it for running a consulate from Mumbai. These efforts secured no traction and the property continued to remain under India's control and for some time was being used by the Indian Council for Cultural Relations. Subsequently, it was made known in early December

2018 that the property was being transferred to the Ministry of External Affairs for developing it on the pattern of Hyderabad House.[38]

Reacting sharply to this development, the Pakistan Foreign Office spokesperson boldly, in flagrant disregard for the truth, asserted that Pakistan had a claim to Jinnah House and did "not accept that anyone tries to take custody of it. They (Indians) have already accepted that it belongs to Pakistan. We have record of it."[39]

Conclusion

The India-Pakistan relationship, which during Imran Khan's premiership, is arguably at its lowest ebb, is unlikely to see any amelioration in 2020 and, indeed, in the foreseeable future. This is due to a variety of factors, most notably Pakistan's anti-India DNA, the fact that a few important players, instead of imposing costs on Pakistan for its use of terror against India, have ended up actually supporting it for one reason or the other, and the Modi government's unwillingness to play out the charade of business as usual with Pakistan as done by earlier governments even whilst being subjected to terrorist attacks by it.

Clearly, the single-most important factor in the downtick in India-Pakistan ties must be attributed to Pakistan's inimical mindset towards India which finds expression in all manner of activities designed to undermine the latter including, inter alia, through the export of terror and promotion of separatism. Kashmir is merely an excuse for the troubled relationship. Even if it were resolved, Pakistan would find other bones to pick with India. As Christine Fair puts it in her very perceptive book titled *Fighting to the End: The Pakistan Army's Way of War*, "Pakistan's revisionism persists in regard to its efforts not only to undermine the territorial status quo in Kashmir but also to undermine India's position in the region and beyond." She further contends that for the Pakistan Army "resisting India's rise is a necessary condition for the survival of Islamic Pakistan" and even civilian institutions share this thought process.

Another important but often overlooked factor in the downturn in India-Pakistan ties has been the fact that a few, but important, players far from curbing the latter in its use of terror against the former have actually encouraged it by providing it with financial, military diplomatic assistance. China is guilty on all counts. This is, to an extent, understandable as it is a self-professed all-weather ally of Pakistan and has systematically sought to stem India's rise. But even the USA, which boasts of being India's strategic ally, while curbing its own direct financial assistance to Pakistan, has with a wink and a nod allowed billions of dollars of economic assistance being channelled to it through the international financial institutions. It is, therefore, no surprise that the UK, which played a seminal role in Pakistan's creation, continues to play the wet nurse to it to this day turning a blind eye to its many inimical moves against India, and insidiously acting against the latter. Similarly, countries like Saudi Arabia and the UAE have provided billions of dollars to Pakistan to shore up its precarious finances. The OIC and, in particular, countries like Turkey and Malaysia, have unabashedly been in Pakistan's camp and against India on the issue of Jammu and Kashmir. Buoyed with such support, Pakistan sees no pressing reason with giving up on its anti-Indian policies as it gets by in the international community with barely a rap on its knuckles.

Finally, some could also attribute the downtick in India-Pakistan ties to the refusal of the Modi government to play to Pakistan's tune of business as usual as done by his predecessors even as the latter persisted with its anti-India agenda. The Modi government's approach that talks and terror do not go together and its determination to penalise Pakistan for its terrorist attacks through the surgical and Balakot strikes inevitably contributed to the downtick in ties but as a self-respecting government, it cannot be faulted for these moves. Indeed, one could argue that the Modi government has not done enough to impose costs on Pakistan for its relentless export of terror against India. It can and should, for instance, relentlessly play on Pakistan's fault lines and develop a suite of policies, including diplomatic, political and economic measures, which would compel the latter to abandon its use of terror against India.[40]

NOTES

1. "FM Qureshi boycotts Indian counterparts speech at UN in protest against Kashmir oppression", 26 September 2019, *Dawn* https://www.dawn.com/news/1507495/fm-qureshi-boycotts-indian-counterparts-speech-at-un-in-protest-against-kashmir-oppression
2. "Imran Khan's Speech in Full", *Al Jazeera,* 26 July 2018, https://www.aljazeera.com/news/2018/07/imran-khan-speech-full-180726124850706.html
3. "Imran Khan, the Army's Choice" Christophe Jaffrelot, *The Nation,* Sept. 4, 2018.
4. "Imran Khan's Speech in Full", *Al Jazeera,* 26 July 2018, https://www.aljazeera.com/news/2018/07/imran-khan-speech-full-180726124850706.html
5. Bilateral Brief: India-Pakistan Relations, 7 February 2020, https://mea.gov.in/Portal/ForeignRelation/Bilateral_Brief_POK_feb_2020.pdf
6. Press release titled "High Commissioner of Pakistan summoned in connection with the telephone conversation initiated by the Foreign Minister of Pakistan with Mirwaiz Umar Farooq from the All Parties Hurriyat Conference", https://www.mea.gov.in/press-releases.htm?dtl/30962/High+Commissioner+of+Pakistan+summoned+in+connection+with+the+telephone+conversation+initiated+by+the+Foreign+Minister+of+Pakistan+with+ Mirwaiz + Umar+Farooq+from+the+All+Parties+Hurriyat+Conference

7. Bilateral Brief: India-Pakistan Relations, 7 February 2020, https://mea.gov.in/Portal/ForeignRelation/Bilateral_Brief_POK_feb_2020.pdf
8. http://164.100.24.220/loksabhaquestions/annex/14/AU3214.pdf
9. "First batch of Indian pilgrims enters Pakistan through Kartarpur Corridor" 9 November 2019. *The Economic Times* https://economictimes.indiatimes.com/news/politics-and-nation/first-batch-of-indian-pilgrims-enters-pakistan-through-kartarpur-corridor/articleshow/71982479.cms?from=mdr
10. "Visit to Pak was not 'political', hugged Gen Bajwa in 'emotional' moment: Navjot Singh Sidhu", 21 August 2018, *The Economic Times* https://economictimes.indiatimes.com/news/politics-and-nation/visit-to-pak-was-not-political-navjot-singh-sidhu/articleshow/65487171.cms?from=mdr
11. Pak minister claims opening of Kartarpur corridor was Army chief's brainchild to hurt India", 1 December 2019, *Times of India,* https://timesofindia.indiatimes.com/world/pakistan/pak-minister-claims-opening-of-kartarpur-corridor-was-army-chiefs-brain-child-to-hurt-india/articleshow/72311152.cms
12. "Lift all Restrictions in Kashmir: Pak PM Imran tells India at Kartarpur Inauguration Ceremony" datelined 9 Nov. 2019, https://timesofindia.indiatimes.com/world/pakistan/lift-all-restrictions-in-kashmir-pak-pm-imran-tells-india-at-kartarpur-inauguration-ceremony/articleshow/71985317.cms
13. Ibid.
14. Statement by Foreign Secretary on 26 February 2019 on the strike on JeM training camp at Balakot, https://www.mea.gov.in/Speeches-Statements.htm?dtl/31089/Statement+by+ Foreign +Secretary+on+26+February+2019+on+the+Strike+on+JeM+training+camp+at+Balakot
15. European Union, China, France ask India-Pakistan to exercise restraint after IAF airstrikes, https://www.indiatoday.in/india/story/india-airstrike-pakistan-jaish-e-mohammed-world-reaction-1465511-2019-02-26
16. https://carnegieendowment.org/2019/03/14/smoldering-volcano-pakistan-and-terrorism-after-balakot-pub-78593SHL
17. "US pulls up Pakistan for misusing F-16 fighter jets against India after Balakot airstrikes, says report". BusinessTodayfile:///C:/Users/HP/Documents/US%20pulls%20up%20Pakistan %20for%20misusing%20F16%20fighter%20jets%20against%20India%20 after%20 Balakot%20airstrikes,%20says%20report.html
18. "Pakistan reacts to Article 370 abrogation by downgrading diplomatic ties with India, suspending bilateral trade, partially shutting airspace", *First Post,* 8 August 2019.
19. "Pakistan plans Kashmir cell, desk at embassies", *New Indian Express,* 17 August 2019. https://www.newindianexpress.com/world/2019/aug/17/pakistan-plans-kashmir-cell-desk-at-embassies-2020320.html
20. "Article 370 revocation: Imran Khan warns of another Pulwama". *Economic Times,* August 6 2019, https://economictimes.indiatimes.com/news/politics-and-nation/article-370-revocation-imran-khan-warns-of-another-pulwama/articleshow/70556045.cms?utm_ source =contentofinterest&utm_medium=text&utm_campaign=cppst
21. http://mofa.gov.pk/foreign-minister-writes-to-un-high-commissioner-for-human-rights-2/
22. Ibid.
23. Pakistan Foreign Minister Shah Mehmood Qureshi's full speech on Kashmir at UNHRC: Lies, falsification and distortion, https://zeenews.india.com/world/pakistan-foreign-minister-shah-mehmood-qureshis-full-speech-on-kashmir-at-unhrc-lies-falsification-and-distortion-2233519.html
24 "Full text of India's statement at UNHRC: Revoking Jammu and Kashmir's special status is

country's sovereign decision, says MEA Secy" First Post 11 Sept 2019

25. Text of Foreign Minister's letter to President of Security Council and UN Secretary General Pakistan Foreign Ministry website file:///C:/Users/HP/Documents/Text%20of%20Foreign%20Minister% E2% 80%99s%20letter%20to%20President%20of%20Security%20Council%20and%20UN%20Secretary%20General%20%E2%80%93%20Ministry%20of%20Foreign%20Affairs.html
26. "OIC and its views on Kashmir: India's Achilles heel in the Islamic world?" by Ketan Mehta, https://www.orfonline.org/expert-speak/oic-views-kashmir-india-achilles-heel-islamic-world-56584/
27. "OIC and its views on Kashmir: India's Achilles heel in the Islamic world?" by Ketan Mehta, https://www.orfonline.org/expert-speak/oic-views-kashmir-india-achilles-heel-islamic-world-56584/
28. Pakistan involved in over 3,000 ceasefire violations along J&K border in 2019: Rajnath Singh, *India Today*, New Delhi, February 10, 2020, https://www.indiatoday.in/india/story/pakistan-involved-over-ceasefire-violations-along-jammu-kashmir-border-2019-defence-minister-rajnath-singh-1645144-2020-02-10
29. "GPS-fitted drones from Pakistan dropped arms into Indian territory: Punjab Police" *Livemint* 25 Sept. 2019, https://www.livemint.com/news/india/gps-fitted-drones-from-pakistan-drop-weapons-into-indian-territory-1569424734523.html
30. South Asia Terrorism Portal https://www.satp.org/terrorism-assessment/india-punjab
31. "India stops sharing hydrological data with Pakistan". *Times of India,* 22 Aug. 2019, http://timesofindia.indiatimes.com/articleshow/70779099.cms?utm_source= contentofinterest&utm_medium=text&utm_campaign=cppst
32. "Nizam of Hyderabad funds: UK High Court orders Pakistan to pay millions in legal costs" *India Today,* Dec. 19, 2019, https://www.indiatoday.in/business/story/nizam-of-hyderabad-funds-uk-high-court-orders-pakistan-to-pay-millions-in-legal-costs-1629880-2019-12-19
33. "India-Pak trade: already low volumes collapsed in 2019". *Indian Express,* 20 January 2020.
34. "Pakistan suspends final rail link to India over Kashmir dispute." Reuters, 9 August 2019, https://www.reuters.com/article/us-india-kashmir-pakistan-rail-idUSKCN1UZ0XV
35. "Pakistan suspends India-Pakistan bus services on 3 routes". *India Today,* 10 August 2019, https://www.indiatoday.in/india/story/pakistan-suspends-india-pakistan-bus-services-3-routes-1579586-2019-08-10
36. "Pakistan resumes postal mail service with India: Pak media". 19 November 2019, *The Economic Times,* https://economictimes.indiatimes.com/news/politics-and-nation/pakistan-resumes-postal-mail-service-with-india-pak-media/articleshow/72123407.cms?from=mdr
37. Story of Jinnah House where partition of India was discussed, https://www.indiatoday.in/india/story/jinnah-house-malabar-hill-mumbai-968908-2017-04-01
38. Mumbai's Jinnah House to be MEA property, to host top-level meets, banquets, *Hindustan Times,* 19 December 2018, https://www.hindustantimes.com/india-news/external-affairs-ministry-getting-jinnah-house-in-mumbai-transferred-in-its-name-sushma-swaraj/story-5l5PVWVie2HfkdBiM2Re2L.html
39. Jinnah House in Mumbai belongs to Pakistan, says Foreign Office, *Economic Times,* 18 December 2018, https://economictimes.indiatimes.com/news/politics-and-nation/jinnah-house-in-mumbai-belongs-to-pakistan-says-foreign office/articleshow/67180055.cms?utm_source=contentofinterest&utm_medium=text&utm_campaign=cppst
40. "India's Relations with its SAARC Neighbours". Monograph, July 2019 by Satish Chandra, Vivekananda International Foundation.

13

Some Reflections on the India–Pakistan Binary and De-Securitisation

T.C.A. Raghavan

"Pakistan has made a horrible mess of itself, almost as if, because it wants to be the antithesis of India, it must embrace failure if India is a success. So it sinks into hell, rises into chaos, and many Indians gloat over its agony as the wages of sin. It is easy to hate Pakistan, even easier now to sneer at it, but loathing cannot form policy, any more than an unrequited love can. Sadly though, policy on Pakistan is often made either by the raptors or by the rapt.

The raptors—the hawks of Lutyens Delhi—are fearful pests, rising on hot air to great heights, where they go around in circles and shriek. But ask what India should do, and the hawk on Pakistan turns out to be not the hawk of falconry, but the hawk-and-spit, expectoration passed off as policy, or of the hawk-and-sell, the devious flogging of the shoddy and the squalid. Cursed with both a north and a south block, it is dense and costive, so nothing goes in and nothing comes out. If the hawk has its reasons, reason cannot understand them.

—**Satyabrata Pal** *(d. 2019), former Indian High Commissioner to Pakistan (2006-09) (S Pak, Engaging Pakistan, India Quarterly, Volume 65, No. 4 (2009), pp. 361-371.)*

The Engagement Disengagement Binary

The India-Pakistan binary of "Engagement-Disengagement" would sum up a major stream of the diplomatic history of the subcontinent in the past quarter century. In this period, India has had six prime ministers, five different governments and seven general elections. Virtually every part of the political spectrum of the country has, at some point of time in this period, either formed the government or been in it as part of a coalition or a supporter.

In the same period in Pakistan, there have been 10 prime ministers and five general elections. In between 1999-2008, there was a near decade-long period of military rule. Again, as in the case of India, over this quarter century, virtually the entire political spectrum of Pakistan has been associated with government, in one form or the other.

The "engagement-disengagement" binary has very evidently a structural basis.

It is also a fact that the engagement-disengagement binary has intensified in both directions over time. The greater the intensity of engagement, equally significant and fraught has been the disengagement that followed. The Lahore Bus Initiative was followed by Kargil, the Agra summit followed by the attack on our Parliament, the CBM/structured dialogue process of 2004-2008 was severely undermined with the Mumbai terrorist attack of November 2008 and the Pathankot attack in January 2016 followed the Prime Minister's visit to Lahore a few days earlier. There could be other instances also.

It is also interesting that a new initiative with reference to engagement, or for that matter, disengagement, has not been a consequence of political change in terms of a new government reversing the policies of its predecessor. Engagement, disengagement and engagement again has characterized policies of the same government. The NDA under Prime Minister Vajpayee from 1998 to 2004 went from engagement to disengagement to engagement to disengagement and ended its tenure at a high note of engagement. This diplomacy encapsulated a tumultuous history through the Lahore bus initiative, Kargil, the hijacking of IC 814, the Agra Summit, the attack on our Parliament, Operation Parakaram and the Islamabad Summit. The UPA I disengaged following the Mumbai serial blasts of July 2006 but reversed that course by instituting the Joint Anti-Terrorism Mechanism. Such examples can be cited up to now, for example, the opening of the Kartarpur corridor in the midst of a high period of India-Pakistan tension.

There are different takeaways from this narrative chronology and the conclusion drawn or the principle extracted varies depending on points of view held. To some, the problem lies in embarking upon a process of engagement in the first place even at a cost of compromising on core principles—thus the enormity of Kargil and the hijacking of IC 814 were put aside and General Musharraf invited to Agra; after the attack on Parliament and Operation Parakaram a hand of friendship was again extended; the thread of engagement was picked up post the Mumbai attack of November 2008, etc. (Incidentally in Pakistan, there are similar views: these boil down to the question of how to accord primacy to Kashmir in any India-Pakistan engagement.)

In this view, given the history of India-Pakistan engagement, it is a form of lunacy to persist with or embark upon engagement knowing that disengagement following a breakdown is inevitable. This conclusion is also derived from what is believed to be the very nature or constitution of Pakistan—an analysis similar to that of A.J.P. Taylor, for example, with regard to Germany through most of the 20th century. Epigrams, some well known, he crafted seemingly have a resonance in the India-Pakistan context too: "Every German frontier is artificial, therefore impermanent; that is the permanence of German geography", or, "The German character was determined by their geopolitical position", etc. A critique of engagement with Pakistan is thus also often based on similar analysis with reference to "essentialist" features of Pakistan.

Another critique of engagement is the consistency argument. This is that political initiatives are inconsistent with government's prevailing narrative—thus the initiative that culminated in PM Vajpayee's historic visit to Lahore in January 2004 was inconsistent with the policy adopted after the attack on our Parliament in 2001; the opening of the Kartarpur corridor was inconsistent with the stated fundamentals guiding policy then of isolating Pakistan, talks and terror cannot coexist, etc. Such critiques of political initiatives to overcome an India-Pakistan paralysis have a long history. Shyama Prasad Mukherjee and K. C. Neogy resigned from the Union Cabinet in April 1950 following the Nehru-Liaqat Pact on minorities in Bengal; Atal Bihari Vajpayee led a protest against the Simla Agreement; and there are many other examples. In each case, there was a robust counter critique. The strongest defence of the Nehru-Liaqat Pact in the weeks immediately after its conclusion came from the then Deputy Prime Minister, Sardar Vallabhai Patel, and this defence was made first not in Delhi but rather in Calcutta—Shyama Prasad Mukherjee's city and the site where the Pact was most discussed and debated. Vajpayee was to himself critique his criticism of the Simla Agreement and he mounted his defence of the pact in Islamabad when he travelled there as Foreign Minister of India's first non-Congress government in 1978.

Whatever may be the disagreements between the respective protagonists in the Engagement-Disengagement binary, there is generally a consensus on the reason why processes of engagement have ended. These reasons are obvious and self-evident. Political initiatives ended repeatedly on the anvil of political and institutional instability in Pakistan or more specifically when civil-military tensions in Pakistan moved up a few notches. Thus, the Lahore Bus Initiative that led to the famous Lahore Declaration and MOU was undermined by Pakistani military adventurism in Kargil reflecting the fact that the interface between PM Nawaz Sharif and Gen. Parvez Musharaff had become unworkable. Those critical of political initiatives and engagement could very well argue that this was predictable and therefore a high profile initiative was an unnecessary risk. Indeed, there were many who made precisely this point even as the initiative rolled out and later felt vindicated as the scale of the intrusion in Kargil became clear.

This point, regardless of the vehemence and passion that 'bad faith' inevitably generates, however, misses the specific context in which the Lahore Bus Initiative was taken. This was a post May 1998 decision with both India and Pakistan now declared nuclear weapon states. Secondly, in the period immediately preceding and unrelated to the nuclear issue, something unusual appeared to be happening in Pakistan: The Prime Minister seemed, after a very long period, actually to be in charge, having replaced an incumbent Chief of Army Staff, Chief Justice and President. These two factors explain much of Indian diplomacy of the time and an objective post mortem will have to take that into account.

We encounter similar situations nearer our own time. In 2014—around the time the new NDA government was sworn in—Pakistan was again at an interesting juncture. Recently-elected Prime Minister Nawaz Sharif had appointed a trusted follower as President and the long-serving army Chief and Chief Justice had finally retired. This provides the context to situate the initiatives to engage with Pakistan and to persist with that engagement for the next two years. This was despite the fact that Pakistan's lack of internal coherence was to reassert itself strongly through this period and in its wake followed the ingress of the army. This undermined whatever steps were taken by India but the point remains of an overall context in which political initiatives of the kind that were taken made eminent sense.

The Regional Context

However tempting it may be to do so, it is important to resist seeing India-Pakistan relations on a standalone basis. The relationship has always been part of a wider context of regional and international forces. These sometimes nuance bilateral relations and sometimes affect them deeply—but their influence cannot be underestimated.

The year 1979 is significant in India–Pakistan history and a great deal that happened subsequently is traced back to it. The execution of Zulfikar Ali Bhutto, the consolidation of power by General Zia-ul-Haq and his drift to Islamism are important milestones of this period in Pakistan. In India, the first non-Congress government since 1947 ended and in the elections that followed the Congress came back. Each of these internal factors did weigh on bilateral relations but it was the regional and international context that was the more significant determinant. The revolution in Iran, the Soviet invasion of Afghanistan, the cementing of a US-China concert all meant that the politics and conflicts of the Cold War would also play a major role in sub-continental politics and India-Pakistan relations. Another year of tectonic shifts was 1989 with the Soviet withdrawal from Afghanistan, the coming down of the Berlin Wall and the end of the Cold War in Europe. It is not a coincidence that the present insurgency in Jammu and Kashmir dates back to that time with all its attendant ramifications for India-Pakistan relations. 9/11, the global financial crisis, the political assertion of China alongside the crystallization of a Pak-China nexus over the past decade are international factors that have moulded India-Pakistan relations over the past two decades. Regionally, the situation in Afghanistan, greater proximity between India and the Gulf states, the emergence of a robust Russia-China interface, all have similarly impacted bilateral relations. This is not to deny the role of strictly bilateral developments such as a terrorist attack in triggering a crisis. The point however is to keep the larger context of policy formulation constantly in view.

Desecuritization as a Policy Approach

Is it feasible to envisage an India-Pakistan relationship that is desecuritized, if not wholly at least partially or significantly? Unless realism is abandoned to a great degree, the difficulties in this are self-evident. Some aspects of the India-Pakistan relationship resemble other chronically or excessively securitized neighbourhood situations—North and South Korea or Israel and some of its Arab neighbours. There are differences of course—principally that is neither of these two cases are dramatic crests and troughs as visible as in the India-Pakistan case. This is evidently because there is a latent potential for desecuritization although this potential exists alongside numerous pitfalls and dangers. Together—the potential and the dangers—also explain the crests and troughs that have marked India-Pakistan relations over the decades.

In the period after the Pathankot airbase terrorist attack (January 2016), India-Pakistan relations moved into a new phase. The process of how this happened is well known and need not be recapitulated in detail. The principal milestones of the process follow from the major terrorist attacks on Indian security forces in Uri (September 2016) and Pulwama (February 2019). The feature that emerged thereafter was that kinetic responses would acquire a strategic dimension in terms of signalling both to Pakistan and to domestic public opinion the postures of the Government of India with regard to the threat of terrorist attacks from Pakistan.

Even in so highly securitized a relationship over the past 70 years, this phase has been unusual in terms of both its intensity and duration. At the same time, despite this period of high tension and poor atmospherics, a significant bilateral measure in the form of the opening of the Kartarpur Saheb corridor (November 2019) was put in place. A step that would have been difficult to take in the best of times was taken at the near worst of times. Another point of importance merits mention. Significant breakthroughs of this kind in the past are associated with periods of upswings in bilateral relations—the Kokraphar-Munabao Rail Link in 2006 or the Srinagar-Muzaffarabad Bus Service in 2005 for instance; both took place at a time when India- Pakistan relations were looking better than they had for decades, perhaps ever, and constructive engagement was at a high. The fact that a long-standing demand—considered and not found possible to implement many times earlier—of the Sikh community would be agreed to and implemented by both governments at a time of very high tension when their relations were minimal is thus both unusual and significant.

The primacy to kinetic operations in overall policy towards Pakistan and the opening of the Kartarpur corridor sum up in fact all the perplexities of neighbourhood policy.

It is too early to envisage what a post-corona world would be like and the extent to which traditional geopolitics would be impacted by the fallout of the pandemic. That there will be change is certain. Just as terrorism was imprinted on the geopolitical agenda post 9/11, we can expect the pandemic to leave some kind of impression also. What that will be cannot be said with precision but we can guess its broad contours in general terms. What we can say with some measure of certainty is that we are now moving into a realm where non-traditional security has moved up some notches in terms of mental space occupied and therefore in settling governmental and global priorities. This is not to postulate a retreat of traditional geopolitics but only that non-traditional security issues will now play a somewhat more enlarged role than hitherto in global and regional politics.

How would this change impact India-Pakistan relations and would it impart to them a trajectory of de-securitization? It is hazardous to make predictions about any aspect of this particular relationship. Nevertheless even at this early stage, the tea leaves can be read. It is surely no coincidence that the moribund SAARC suddenly received a leg up with the outset of the pandemic in South

Asia. This reassertion of its intrinsic narrative value suggests in fact the more general trend—the insertion of the realm of non-traditional security into that of geopolitics. The fact also is that the course of the Covid pandemic so far has shown up severe deficiencies and shortcomings in both India and Pakistan not just of health infrastructure but also fundamental governance issues.

Public health issues are in fact an unexplored terrain in the India-Pakistan interface. As compared to other areas in the non-traditional security domain, they have a certain advantage in that they are relatively distanced or insulated from spillover effects of traditional geopolitical divides. In brief, health issues do not appear to have the political ramifications associated with issues of water security or scarcity, glacial melt, environmental pollution, etc., which have generally come in the way of India and Pakistan developing a workable agenda on non-traditional security.

So light has been placed on existing global priorities and infirmities. How sustained and how intense the consequential shift will be is more difficult to say. It certainly will not mean that traditional geopolitics will disappear—that does not happen in the real world.

No matter what the contours of the post-Covid world are, it will still remain a security-dominated world. But some moving up in the priority list of non-traditional security issues, including public health, can be expected. Not surprisingly, the onset of the pandemic in South Asia saw the assertion of the narrative value of SAARC and that through cooperation in the health sector.

How will this reordering impact, if at all, on historically so heavily securitized a relationship such as India-Pakistan? Over the past seven decades there have been three principal attempts to desecuritize the India-Pakistan agenda. This has been attempted through introducing elements from the non-traditional security domain principally as a means of reducing the intensity of existing differences. Two of these were failures; one was, relatively speaking, a greater success. The success story was in the division of the Indus system of rivers through a treaty that pragmatically ring fenced river waters sharing from all the other contestations of India-Pakistan geopolitics including Jammu and Kashmir. This ring fencing could not however be enlarged or deepened largely as a result of the political turn Pakistan took post 1965 and especially after 1989.

The two failures were in the field of energy—represented by the Iran-Pakistan-India (IPI) gas pipeline—and economics: the prolonged suboptimal levels of trade ending finally in a lock jam in 2019 which will require great skill of political initiative to undo. The reasons for the failures are obvious enough: the IPI gas pipeline proved to be a bridge too far because of the difficulties in combining India-Pakistan issues with the geopolitics of Iran. The trade initiative was also full of promise but faced the problem that the two economies are basically competitive rather than complementary and the difference in size meant that balance of trade issues acquired greater prominence than would have been otherwise.

Other domains of non-traditional security—climate change, glacial melt, water availability, environmental pollution—have developed only a limited traction in the India-Pakistan context largely because these spill over into the domain of traditional geopolitics and security issues. This means a burden too heavy for the science involved to bear on its own.

Why should the Covid-19 pandemic then suggest the possibilities of desecuritized elements being introduced in the India-Pakistan agenda? Principally, because it is classically 'non traditional', not having a direct relationship with shifts in the traditional arenas of the India-Pakistan polemic which allows a certain potential and protection similar to that of a largely forgotten area of India-Pakistan cooperation—Locusts. Cooperation in this sector has been low key, largely unnoticed but significantly continuous and uninterrupted.

From early this year, the Food and Agriculture Organization has been warning of a humanitarian crisis on account of locusts across East Africa and the Horn of Africa reaching through West Asia to south Pakistan and north-west India. Locusts attack crops and therefore directly impact food security of the affected area. Press reports have been quoting government officials in Sindh in Pakistan as this being the worst infestation in three decades and World Bank officials talk of a possible twin crisis—a combined Covid-19 and locust outbreak. If the epicentre for the latter appears to be East Africa, the impact will be felt as far east as South Asia. Some weeks before the full impact of the corona virus was visible, Pakistan had in fact declared a "national emergency" to deal with the locust threat. In India, the border areas of Gujarat and Rajasthan may also face an onslaught later in the year.

What is interesting, however, is the below-the-radar cooperation and exchange of information that traditionally takes place between border districts in India and Pakistan to combat this menace. Through the worst of the India-Pakistan crisis in the past two decades and even earlier, locust officers have met frequently and regularly, akin to the meetings of the Indus Waters Commission ring fenced from the larger politics of India-Pakistan issues. The FAO plays a facilitator's role in this and provides a convenient multilateral umbrella as a cover for this exercise to have continued year in and out through the multiple crises and clashes between the two countries. A seldom cited source for continuous India-Pakistan dialogue that leapfrogs the disengagement engagement binary is a section in the FAO website that will reveal to the interested researcher the minutes of all India-Pakistan meetings on combating locusts, regularly held over the decades.

In brief, what the locust example shows is that in certain areas of non-traditional security, insulated from other contested arenas, sustained cooperation is possible. In the desert that otherwise characterizes India-Pakistan diplomacy, this means a very high mark. Of course, locusts and the corona virus are different. The former is not restricted by national boundaries while the latter is and can be with restrictions on physical movement of people. Nevertheless, both inhabit the domain of non-traditional security and if there is one lesson from this pandemic which will be learnt globally is that this domain is too vital to be left alone. A de-securitisation agenda, no matter how ambitious, will always have its well-defined parameters and limits given the levels of mistrust between India and Pakistan and the weight of the unresolved issues that divide them. Yet to consciously embark on to this terrain seems inescapably in our national interest. To do so would however require some amount of reorientation of our own mindsets and this is where the observations of the late Shri Satyabrata Pal cited at the beginning of this essay merit recall.

14

Kashmir: The 5 August 2019 Decisions and their Progressive Impact

Lt. Gen. Syed Ata Hasnain (Retd)

Since 1989, J&K has continued to reel under the effects of a proxy hybrid war launched from across the border/LoC by Pakistan in a quest towards what it perceived as an unfinished agenda of the Partition of India in 1947. It was also an attempt at retribution for the loss of East Pakistan (now Bangladesh) in 1971. Considering the economic and military asymmetry between Pakistan and India, a direct approach towards war fighting to wrest the territories of J&K was always considered a difficult proposition, except perhaps in 1965 when Pakistan launched a general war in the hope that a militarily weakened India (as a result of the Sino-Indian border war of 1962) could be defeated. The strategy employed by Pakistan has followed a pattern of testing our will by causing internal strife using a mix of foreign and local terrorists, increasing the alienation of the people of J&K against India and creating sufficient triggers to project the feasibility of a war between two nuclear-armed neighbours with a hope of some international mediation. India stuck steadfastly to a counter-strategy of neutralizing the terrorists, drastically reducing their strength through a combination of continuous military operations and engagement with the people by the Indian Army to wean them away from external influence through a hearts-and-minds campaign. It mixed this with operations at the Line of Control (LoC) to neutralize attempts at infiltration and encroachment on the territory of J&K while maintaining a tolerant stance towards the separatists respecting their rights as part of India. Having frequently and cyclically reduced the footprint of sponsored terrorism, a political initiative towards cementing better integration of the people was always expected. However, that political initiative proved largely elusive. Separatism continued to survive while democratic principles that India ceaselessly followed were exploited by the adversaries.

Articles 370 and 35A were two constitutional provisions of a temporary nature to give J&K a special status within the Indian Constitution, taken as a temporary measure until J&K's final status was finally decided. Their inclusion was the subject of many a debate. While they assuaged the feelings of the people with a sense of exclusivity, they also kept alive the idea of J&K becoming either independent or seceding to Pakistan; and notion of disputed status, which as per Indian perception had been overtaken by the history of Pakistan's attempts to wrest it by force. These provisions were concessions amounting to limited autonomy. The best time to have removed them through legislation was 1972 after the signing of the Shimla Agreement in the wake of India's path-breaking military victory and the burial of the 'Two-Nation' theory with the creation of Bangladesh. The concessions continued to give scope to the exploitation of the 'azadi' (independence) sentiment prevalent in Kashmir and instigated by Pakistan from 1989 to 2019.

In 1994, while under intense international diplomatic pressure brought about by a US-Pak campaign, some deft handling by India's political community neutralized Pakistan's vile propaganda. On 22 February 1994, India's Parliament passed a joint resolution with full political consensus, outlining clearly that all territories under the erstwhile Maharaja of Kashmir before the signing of the Instrument of Accession to India on 26 October 1947 belonged to India and that it would aspire to regain all those territories. An abrogation of the special constitutional provisions for special status at that stage may have pegged India's claims more handsomely but those were tentative times in terms of India's strategic confidence to face the world and make its claim known in more aggressive terms. This was the second opportunity lost. With rare political consensus and two tall leaders such as Prime Minister Narasimha Rao and prominent member of the Opposition Atal Bihari Vajpayee coming together, abrogation of the constitutional provisions may have been carried out without a flutter. Twenty-five years later that moment came back but without political consensus constraining the government to take extraordinary measures to maintain order and balance, something perceived necessary given the history of strife in J&K and the Pakistani propensity to propel anti-India sentiments through artful play of the ideological card.

The Decisions of 5 August 2019

The decisions of 5 August 2019 were taken with an element of calculated risk that faced the potential of mayhem, complete breakdown of public order and warnings of Kashmir's complete capitulation to separatists. Such warnings had been issued even by mainstream political leaders of J&K. The main decisions included the abrogation of Articles 370 and 35A, thus bringing the state of J&K within the ambit of the Indian Constitution without any special status. It also meant the end to the powers of the J&K State Assembly to frame rules for the citizenship of the state. The administrative decisions split the state into two Union Territories (UTs). The first was Ladakh as a UT without a legislature and a Lt-Governor with executive powers. The second was the UT of J&K with a provision for a bicameral legislature, a Lt-Governor as its head and a Chief Minister as its Chief Executive. The Government of India promptly published two maps showing J&K with PoK within its boundaries and Ladakh with the territories of Gilgit-Baltistan (GB) and Aksai Chin. The decision to keep J&K together as a single UT was by far one of the best decisions taken on 5 August 2020.

Lesser-informed opinion perceived the end of the so-called J&K problem and a triumphal attitude appeared to exist post the decisions. However, it was clear that conflict would persist since Pakistan still possessed the means to pursue its strategy towards the pursuance of proxy war. Subdued violence would mark the change in the environment and the politics of J&K would never be the same again. What most observers may be unaware of is the fact that the preparation on the security front for eventual abrogation of the two Articles began almost two years before the event. Perhaps Uri 2016 and, finally, Pulwama 2019 were the two important waypoints which confirmed the need for such 'conflict transformation'.

The Run-up to the Decisions

Indian policy had earlier remained focused upon going only the kinetic way targeting the terrorists and remaining soft on the separatists, the over-ground workers (OGWs), the anti-national media, many government servants, the banking system which supported financial conduits for siphoning money, corruption, support to the terror networks and also bankrolling of the street agitations. In short, an entire eco-system had functioned and remained untouched. This was taken for granted even as the Indian Army and the police forces battled the terrorists. It was a terror-based 'Proxy War Ecosystem', the nexus of politics, media, and shady third sector organizations. It also included NGOs, lawyers, academics, intellectuals and bankers. It is this ecosystem that came under the focus of the security apparatus from 2017 onwards for the first time. Its neutralization was only partially achieved in the short time since 2017 because it is deeply embedded with multiple networks. The proverbial 'All of Government' approach to counter a hybrid proxy war just about started to come into its own in 2017. Even after 5 August 2019, the campaign to fight the ecosystem and bring the required 'All of Government' approach will take time to embed into the Indian strategic culture for it to become an abiding strategy. Both aspects are crucial to defeating the proxy war and creating a fully integrated J&K.

The Impact

To get a meaningful idea of the impact of the decisions of 5 August 2019, almost a year later there is a need to examine the effect in the international and diplomatic dimensions, external and internal security situation on the LoC, governance, and the attitude of the people who are rightly considered the centre of gravity of such a hybrid war. Transformational decisions by themselves cannot become game changers; they also need solid and rational backing against the counter forces that inevitably follow in an attempt to reverse the trends.

International domain: On the international plane, the impact was positive across the international community except for China and some Islamic nations. Two attempts to raise the J&K issue at the UNSC by China were more transactional in nature to tick the box in support of Pakistan. Prime Minister Narendra Modi scored high with the Middle Eastern nations, Saudi Arabia, Bahrain and the UAE. Even the Organization of Islamic Cooperation (OIC) did not have anything negative to say and the broad consensus appeared to term the 5 August 2019 decisions as an internal matter of India. However, realizing that there could be no permanence in such support should Pakistan's diplomatic outreach outweigh India's efforts, Indian diplomatic efforts have continued. Efforts to take the diplomatic corps of New Delhi and selected members of a European Union delegation to Srinagar on guided tours, interaction with the people and security briefings did not make the desired impact because the international media was insufficiently convinced about the post-decision handling of the situation. As the seat of government of J&K moved from Srinagar to Jammu in November 2019, the national focus shifted as did international attention. A series of events such as the Citizenship Amendment Act (CAA) and the Covid-19 pandemic helped keep the focus away until early April 2020 when Pakistan's first efforts at infiltration commenced, post an intense winter. In a way, this interlude did work positively for India. Time was gained to loosen the firm grip over liberties and partially open the Internet which appeared to becoming the sticky issue on freedom of speech. Subsequently the Covid-19 lockdown has assisted in preventing a resurgence of networks and the media has remained low-key too.

Internationally, the period after November 2019 should have been used by

India to build upon its early diplomatic gains through informal and formal outreaches. Not much has been done to reach out to international think tanks and the international media to explain the Indian narrative. Pakistan has focused on issues well outside the ambit of the Shimla Agreement of 1972; it has also unofficially expressed the opinion that the provisions of the Shimla Agreement no longer apply with the change in the constitutional status of J&K. Its narrative is harping upon the UN resolutions calling for plebiscite, self-determination issues and alleged human rights violations. These need effective countering with the Indian narrative. India continues to only justify the abrogation of the constitutional provisions without explaining its narrative about the Instrument of Accession of 26 October 1947 which clearly and legally ceded J&K to India. There has been little attention to highlight how the UN resolutions have been rendered void by Pakistan's attempts to forcibly wrest J&K in 1965, 1971, 1989 onwards and in 1999. The Shimla Agreement 1972 too is almost unknown in international circles outside academic circles. Its emphasis on bilateralism and no mediation, as the means to resolving J&K, accepted and agreed by Pakistan is not well known either. The Indian narrative needs better packaging and far more comprehensive understanding by our missions abroad although efforts towards that are ongoing.

Internal security: In the field of internal security, care was taken to tighten loose ends which could trigger disturbances instigated by separatists. A fear existed that the response of the state's mainstream polity could also be unpredictable. Threats to internal security are all based upon public perception, internal politics and instigation from Pakistan. Peace prevailed and the protest industry of Kashmir sponsored by Pakistan, directed by the separatist leaders and led in the streets by increasingly younger men and some women could not get going; it needed leadership, along with network activation since nothing is on auto mode. This same eco-system related to internal security had taken several years to create and extended down to the tehsil and even block levels. It included the universities, faculties of schools and colleges, media owners and prominent journalists, bank officials and hundreds of non-descript, low-profile people working as OGWs. Efforts by security forces and agencies to neutralize the OGWs always seemed to come to naught. Thoughtfully, from 2017, this system had been targeted by the government from Delhi and later directly under Governor's Rule. It is too complex to be undone in a hurry and will need several years of professional effort to take it down but the proactive action to isolate the leadership and prevent network activation paid dividends.

What has been achieved progressively since 5 August 2019 is that the separatists have been isolated and their hold over the system weakened. With clandestine financial networks dented money is not finding its way into hands of instigators; preventive detentions have reduced the nuisance potential on the streets. The government has displayed a level of confidence by withdrawing 10,000 armed policemen from Kashmir.

Among the elements of the broad strategy that the establishment followed to prevent resurgence of instability due to renewed efforts of Pakistan expected to commence in early summer 2020, has been a strong convergence of focus on counter infiltration and Intelligence-based operations in the hinterland. With terrorist numbers down in the hinterland and limited recruitment, this strategy suited the intent of preventing a surge in numbers and in leadership. With India's attention on the Covid-19 pandemic, the first reported major infiltration attempt took place in early April 2020 with more following thereafter. These were successfully interdicted at the LoC or in the proximity of the reception areas. By mid-August 2020, approximately 150 terrorists had been neutralized, with 45 alone in the month of June 2020. The rapid success achieved has been due to a few factors. Intelligence flow has been of a higher order and coordination by terrorists has been limited due to the control on mobile communication. In addition, the Covid-19 lockdown has restricted terrorist flexibility and mobility with forced stay at safe houses for longer durations. The attempt to activate North Kashmir has not succeeded and no counter-strategy has been resorted to by the terrorists. In previous years, terrorists retained the capability to attempt wresting the initiative by targeting off-duty policemen, soldiers and their families. This inability in 2020 can be ascribed to the absence of leadership. High-profile leaders such as Riyaz Naikoo have been eliminated creating a major void in terror capability.

Shift of the infiltration focus by Pakistan towards Jammu-Kathua and the Poonch-Rajouri sector has been expected due to failure to penetrate the Kashmir grid. Attempts to revive terrorism in the south of the Pir Panjal have not succeeded so far and unlikely due to strong resentment among the population.

The separatists have also been rendered ineffective due to their isolation, inability to meet and coordinate, and the neutralization of financial networks run by OGWs. It has forced even S.A.S. Geelani to virtually retire after resignation from the All Party Hurriyat Conference (APHC). However, the APHC may yet be marginally effective in its nuisance value although there is no confirmation about its current status.

Failure to trigger instability may lead Pakistan to resort to spectacular acts such as the Pulwama IED attack to emphasise the message that the movement has not ended and yet retains capability. This threat exists mainly from IEDs because that is one domain where a determined terror module may sneak past all security and create havoc of very serious proportions; recalling Pulwama 2019 and the attack on the J&K Assembly in 2001. A high—profile act by one of the proxy terror groups could be planned and executed. In view of the situation on the northern borders with China, such an act will present India with a dilemma on response due to the prevailing border tensions. It calls for effective Intelligence collection and rapid dissemination at all times. High-profile actions could also include an Uri-type action by infiltration with shallow objectives near the LoC.

There are people's movements spreading across the world and there is much talk of a third coming of the Colour Revolutions that have progressively characterised the domain of street protests from the end of the Cold War. The Arab Spring was the second coming in 2011 but Bolivia, Lebanon, Iraq, Indonesia and Hong Kong have all been in turbulence in recent months with attempts at transformational political regime change. With violence in Kashmir under control and most domains of the eco-system being effectively targeted, the possibility of instigated street protests in Kashmir akin to a Colour Revolution appears remote. However, predictability in Kashmir remains mostly low and the emergence of a diffused leadership is always live.

The Connection with the Chinese Coercive Attempts in Ladakh

While on security, it is also essential to take stock of the likely effect of the situation which has developed along the northern borders with China since May 2020 and the impending possibility of a new international balance of power post the Covid-19 pandemic. India has been proactive in its external psychological operations to the extent that there have been frequent references by political leaders on the need for reintegrating PoK and GB, the territories of J&K under occupation of Pakistan. There have been muted references to Aksai Chin (under Chinese occupation) too. Based on reports from the Indian Meteorological Department (IMD), India's official television channel Doordarshan and All India Radio have commenced weather bulletins for GB and PoK. Indian social media accounts increasingly carry a public desire to see the integration of all these areas with J&K. The cumulative effect of the 5 August 2019 decisions and the progressive psychological pressure placed by India probably has both Pakistan and China worried about the future of the China Pakistan Economic Corridor (CPEC) which passes through this area. Among the reasons being ascribed to

China's sudden provocation in Ladakh has been the increasing Indian pro-activeness on re-integration of GB and PoK with J&K. This may not be entirely true but may be counted as one of the inputs that indicated India's growing strategic confidence with which China has been uncomfortable. In fact, India's progressive handling of the post 5 August 2019 situation in J&K and Ladakh with renewed confidence and the inability of Pakistan to find options to retrieve the situation may have partially contributed towards instigating the Chinese action. Ladakh offers the best ground for a limited Sino-Pak collusion to pressure India militarily at a time when the pandemic has also affected the Indian economy. Pakistan is also reported to have moved approximately 20,000 troops to GB as a sympathetic gesture of support for China. Chinese coercion may last the campaigning season of 2020 with Pakistan making increasing efforts to retrieve lost control over the situation in J&K. This is the reason why there must be no dilution in efforts to prevent resurgence of instability in J&K and all options must be war-gamed for a potential 'big act' by Pakistan-sponsored elements in J&K.

Governance

With administrative reorganization leading to Union Territory (UT) status for J&K, it is expected that development through better governance will become an important driver for future narratives. More direct oversight on various projects will hopefully curb corrupt practices and ensure delivery of authorised funds to the right quarters. The large outlay of central assistance to J&K must continue and the impact of better governance through balanced allocations must be palpable across the UT. This by itself will make a major difference in perception and communicate India's strong desire to see prosperity in J&K.

To really qualify for a landmark decision, the constitutional and administrative changes must deliver quality governance and that too in a very short time. Some things will be needed early enough and no one is rooting for restoring of the electoral process in that time frame. The confusion in the minds of the public must be addressed by a direct outreach; call it a hearts-and-minds approach but that terminology unfortunately draws cynicism from many who do not understand the larger strategic gains from such action. The return of Kashmiri Pandits must be discussed with their leadership and ways of ensuring this even in the environment of existing mistrust must be sought. The right environment will need to be created for their security with a mechanism to restore unsold but occupied properties.

One of the areas that can make a major impact is a revamp of the bureaucracy. J&K needs a fresh, honest, motivated, committed, and efficient bureaucracy and the Centre must aid in this by progressively posting well-experienced administrators to take over a part of the responsibilities of administration.

The Government of India has been prudent in its approach to issues concerning demography. It's only eight months later and after considerable deliberation, that the rules for domicile status have been framed. Any Indian citizen can apply provided he or she meets the criteria. Applicants should have resided in J&K for 15 years, or studied in the state for seven years and appeared in either the Class 10 or the Class 12 examination there. Children of Central Government officers (Army, paramilitary forces, IAS, IPS), and employees of public sector undertakings and banks, central universities, etc., who have served in Jammu & Kashmir for 10 years will also be eligible to apply for gazetted and non-gazetted government jobs. These included those who work outside the state. Many laws not repealed by the 5 August 2019 decision have since been repealed by the government. Although initially received with negative sentiment, it is to be seen how many will actually apply under the new rules. Politically, these new rules will be resisted once political activity resumes.

There will be clamour for more resources for Jammu as against Kashmir due to perceived inequity in allocations over years. The Lt-Governor's administration must strongly desist from falling victim and must use discretion to ensure a fair distribution of resources. Jammu perceives that it has suffered in the entire exercise of restructuring of the administration by remaining clubbed with Kashmir. Yet, the Government's decision not to divide Jammu from Kashmir was correct because there is such intrinsic linkage between the two segments of J&K that eventual solutions to separatism could never be found if Kashmir had been separated as an administrative entity. It is Jammu that will provide many solutions to resolve the problem of separatism in J&K. This aspect must be recognized by the leadership and work on greater affinity between the two sides of the Pir Panjal must begin in earnest.

Although by August 2020 a year has passed and the J&K government may not have enough on the governance plate to showcase complete normalcy due to the ongoing security operations, there is no harm in now identifying a few domains of governance where delivery will make a larger impact; education and youth opportunities are some of them. The initial period of stabilisation, plus the shift of the capital to Jammu for winter and then the pandemic have taken their toll of time. However, time may be running out because effective governance is one of the main issues that will ensure better bonding of the people with the rest of India.

Political Activity

It is important to restore political activity in J&K to involve the people and the political parties in order to finally emerge from the events of this period. There is a perception that Panchayati Raj will step in to take the place of mainstream political activity, with more direct empowerment of the people. This remains only a hope because getting such activity off the ground is a difficult proposition. A level of rapprochement with mainstream political parties or the creation of alternatives is a must but both have their constraints. A period bereft of political activity may emerge akin to 1990-96 but without separatist politics being allowed to rule the roost. This is a domain where greater credibility will need to be garnered for better international endorsement. Electoral activity in the true sense appears some distance away. Therefore, an elected government taking charge anytime in the future is unlikely. That is all the more reason for the Central Government to ensure better supervision and delivery of better governance in an early timeframe.

The Hearts-and-Minds Game

The one aspect that security managers in India need to be concerned about is the alienation and angst evident in the population in Kashmir. There are some false narratives that all Kashmiris have welcomed the new constitutional provisions and the administrative arrangement. While many assume (and it is not entirely wrong) that there is a silent groundswell of support for India, it is the element that is alienated that rules the roost. In this regard, it may be advisable to extend the Indian Army's military civic action (MCA) project, Operation Sadbhavana, to a much higher level of engagement of the public at the strategic level. The MCA project is an essential part of any counter-insurgency campaign and has achieved some impact. Involvement of the entire government machinery in a typical counter-hybrid proxy war campaign, with an 'all of government' approach may be the answer; the concept will need much larger thinking through. The Central Government's decision to send some prominent ministers to informally interact with the common people was an outstanding decision which has not been followed up by more, due to the Covid-19 pandemic. A one-off effort may not achieve much. Persistent effort of this kind with prominent Indian personalities who are effective communicators would be the way forward and adapted progressively as per the lessons that emerge.

Information and Influence Operations: Enhancing Effectiveness of Communication Strategy

This remains India's critical weakness and needs a transformational approach to overcome the disadvantage it suffers for insufficiency of focus towards it. Once a momentous decision has been taken, a clear strategy needs to be evolved. One of the elements of that strategy is the necessity for communication. In this case, it is the message to the people of J&K that they are an inseparable part of India. Every means to communicate that message must be adopted. It needs a structured approach and J&K can be the first of the domains where a special composite organization with legislative backing must undertake the outreach. It cannot be the responsibility of different organizations such as the Army, Intelligence agencies or civil bureaucracy, all doing their own. It needs expertise, structure, academic back-up, funding and a strategy vetted at the highest level. The idea should be to secure the population from false propaganda and fake news and inculcate in subsequent generations of Kashmiris a love for India, through powerful counter narratives. Civilian information warriors under the supervision of the Army, police and Intelligence agencies must be the executors of this strategy.

Conclusion

Having faced proxy war for 30 years, there is no doubt that India will yet continue to suffer the same for some time. The realization of the mistakes of the past, of having only addressed the military aspects of hybrid war, is dawning on the Indian strategic community. The targeting of the terror eco-system in J&K has paid initial dividends but there is much more to be done. The post 5 August 2019 situation has been challenging but from the security angle the nation has succeeded in maintaining stability. The pandemic has been the biggest attention diverter that has worked against the integration process and yet also assisted it in some ways. The integration process will be a long haul which will suffer setbacks due to Pakistani intransigence. A lot will depend upon what the Kashmiris view as favourable to them in the new emerging India and how conversations are made with them. Finally, there is a need for a strategy to integrate J&K, an upfront strategy that must be secured against any political manoeuvring. The intent must be clear; J&K must be better integrated with India through the political, social, economic and psychological domains. The salutation 'Jai Hind' must sound as music to the ears of all the people of J&K to make the decisions of 5 August 2019 a final success.

15

The Paradox of Asymmetry: China–Pakistan Relations

Sushant Sareen

The hyperbole used to describe the China-Pakistan relationship contains a paradox of asymmetry that underlines their bilateral relations. China's economic, political, diplomatic and military clout and capabilities far outstrips anything that Pakistan brings to the table. On virtually every aspect in the bilateral relationship, China is the giver and Pakistan is the taker. In the last few years, Pakistan's dependence on China for not just military and strategic support but also for keeping it financially afloat has increased tremendously.[1] And yet, the paradox is that in this asymmetrical relationship, the stronger party is often seen to be leaning over backwards to accommodate the weaker party. The Chinese do occasionally express their displeasure with some things the Pakistanis do.[2] They also often balk when their own interests conflict with the demands that Pakistan makes of them.[3] But in the aggregate, the relationship not only continues to endure but is in fact getting stronger despite the occasional strains and undue expectations that either side has from the other. Walking out of the relationship is not even an option for either country because both seem to be gaining from it—Pakistan gets the diplomatic, economic and military support it seeks, and China gets its 'Israel' in the region, one of its only 'genuine' friends in the world.[4]

On the face of it, the unequal relationship that exists between China and Pakistan seems to be loaded in favour of the latter. After all, China has been pouring in billions of dollars to not just prop up Pakistan's failing economy but also fund expensive infrastructure in that country. Militarily, Pakistan is China's largest market for armaments. Diplomatically, China stands as a bulwark behind Pakistan and pulls its chestnuts out of the fire on issues ranging from terrorism to NSG membership. Strategically, there is almost complete convergence between the two countries on their bete noire—India. For Pakistan, China's animus towards India is a huge strategic asset for counter-balancing India. Therefore, it makes a lot of sense for Pakistan to cultivate China and derive all the benefits and heft that this relationship brings with it.

But if China is so deeply invested in Pakistan, it isn't out of strategic or economic altruism. Dig a little deeper and it is clear that China isn't giving a free lunch to Pakistan and finds enough strategic benefit and economic returns to justify its engagement with Islamabad. In both tangible and intangible forms, the returns China gets for its investment justifies its doubling its relationship with Pakistan. For every loan given to Pakistan for budgetary or balance-of-payments support, China charges a fairly decent interest rate. The concessional loans forwarded to Pakistan for various projects, including the China-Pakistan Economic Corridor (CPEC), are balanced by the hefty rates of returns that are expected to accrue to Chinese companies handling these projects. As already mentioned, Pakistan is the biggest export market for the Chinese defence industry, accounting for over 40 per cent of defence exports in 2018.[5] Between 2014 and 2019, nearly 73 per cent of Pakistan's defence imports came from China.[6] In terms of trade, China is Pakistan's largest trading partner and enjoys a massive trade surplus.[7] While Pakistan's exports to China were around $ 1.6 billion in 2018, the imports were nearly $ 16 billion. The data from China puts Chinese exports at over $ 18 billion and imports at just over $ 1 billion. Add to all this, the strategic value of the relationship that accrues to China—Gwadar port, cat's paw against India, a springboard for Chinese presence in the western Indian Ocean and Middle East—and it is clear that China is getting what it wants out of the relationship.

The kind of influence that China wields in Pakistan is quite like that of the USA in the latter half of the last century. To appease and accommodate the Chinese, the Pakistanis are ready to go to any length. The easiest way to push through any project is to attach a Chinese label to it. Once a Chinese entity is roped in, all objections and obstacles to any project magically disappear. Pakistan has even launched military operations on the nudging of the Chinese. The Lal Masjid operation in 2007 was prompted by Chinese pressure after Islamists attacked a Chinese massage parlour in Islamabad. Even the Zarb-e-Azb operation in North Waziristan was partly aimed at showing to the Chinese that Pakistan was cracking down on Uyghur terrorists based in the erstwhile Tribal Agency.[8] Corruption scandals, when involving the Chinese, shut down suddenly. One glaring example of this came recently when the Imran Khan government set up an inquiry commission to probe the Independent Power Producers (IPPs).[9] The Commission's report was quite scathing. But the report was given a burial because it included the goldplating done on some of the Chinese power projects set up under CPEC. This was done after the Chinese protested and pressured the Pakistan government to back off and in return promised to resolve the issues related to these power projects.[10] Another scandal involving the Multan Metro Bus project also died a quiet death.

At the political level, the silence of the Pakistan government on the genocide of Uyghur Muslims in China and the sinification of Islam that is being rammed through by the Chinese Communist Party is quite deafening. For a country that prances around the world as the 'Fortress of Islam' and the sole nuclear weapons Islamic State (the pun is entirely intended because given the treatment meted out to religious minorities, Pakistan is more of an Islamic State than an Islamic Republic), the Pakistanis have been remarkably silent on the mistreatment of Muslims in China. This is despite the fact that Pakistan is often in the vanguard of raising the so-called Muslim causes—Palestine, Rohingyas, Kashmir, Islamophobia and what have you —around the world. Forget about raising the issue globally or even with the Chinese, the Pakistanis have gone out of the way to issue certificates of good behaviour to Beijing. This was done through the instrumentality of a delegation of Pakistani mullahs who travelled to Xinjiang and came back with glowing reports of how good the Uyghurs have it in China. Pakistan's Prime Minister, Imran Khan, has on multiple occasions pleaded complete ignorance when questioned about the mistreatment of Muslims in China. But it is not just the callous disregard of Chinese Muslims but also the total disregard of the human trafficking of Pakistani citizens that shows how far Pakistan is ready to stoop to appease the Chinese. The scandal of how Pakistani girls were duped into marriage with Chinese men and then sexually exploited was also buried and all the accused Chinese let off by the Pakistani judicial system.

But probably the single-most egregious example of the clout of the Chinese in Pakistan is the setting up of the CPEC Authority and the draft new law, which pretty much makes the CPEC Authority a parallel government and virtually makes the chairman of the Authority the Deputy Prime Minister of the country.[11] At one level, if passed, this law will give a constitutional role to the Pakistan Army and directly insert it in the governance structure of the country. Ever since the CPEC project was initiated, the Pakistan army has been trying hard to get a seat on the table for deciding and executing projects. The Nawaz Sharif government resisted this encroachment attempt, but Imran Khan gave in, first by setting up the CPEC Authority, and now by proposing this law which will transform the CPEC Authority into virtually a sovereign entity nominally under the control of the Prime Minister. What is important is not just how much the Pakistan Army was pushing for the Authority, but even more that both the CPEC Authority and the new law have been demanded by the Chinese because of the slack pace in the execution of the CPEC projects.[12]

The steps being taken by Pakistan to reinvigorate and re-energise CPEC and the strenuous efforts being made to convince the Chinese that Pakistan is committed to CPEC are entirely understandable for two reasons. The first is that Pakistan just cannot afford to rub China the wrong way on CPEC because that could jeopardise the larger strategic relationship which is so critical for Pakistan. Having lost the patronage of the USA, Pakistan now looks to China to provide it the strategic lift and heft to confront India. There is no way that Pakistan can do anything that could mark the beginning of cracks in their relationship with China, because once these cracks appear, they only widen. The second reason is that, economically, CPEC is the only game in town for Pakistan. There is hardly any other country which is investing serious money in Pakistan to fund infrastructure and generate economic activity. CPEC is therefore a lifeline that is keeping Pakistan afloat. There are of course concerns that this lifeline could very well become a noose around Pakistan's neck in the future. But the way Pakistan operates, the future is always at a discount, something to be negotiated when the time comes. In any case, in the Pakistani thinking, there will be no future if it is unable to traverse through the clear and present crisis it faces, especially economically.

In a way, for now, CPEC is a good fit for both China and Pakistan. Both countries think it will get them what they want. The Pakistanis believe that the more the Chinese are invested in Pakistan, the less the chances of their losing interest in Islamabad in the future. In fact, the Pakistanis feel confident that China has really no choice but to give in to most, if not all, of Pakistan's demands especially in the economic sphere. This is the reason senior Pakistani officials and politicians have said that China be told clearly that it must bailout Pakistan if it wants to keep its investments secure. A ruling party senator, Nauman Wazir Khattak, has said, "If the Chinese want a return on their investments/loans, they need to invest/loan more money to Pakistan. And if China is not ready to revise the terms of the China-Pakistan Economic Corridor, it must be prepared to wait for decades for returns". According to another report, Pakistan's finance ministry has let it be known that "Islamabad considers that CPEC could only run in a smooth manner if Islamabad successfully avoids bailout package from the IMF so China will have to come forward to allocate special provisions for keeping Pakistan's economy afloat..."[13] Yet another report quotes a Pakistan government economist as saying that "Beijing cannot afford to bankrupt Pakistan, in part because of the country's importance as a counterweight to India...for China, repayment of the debt burden will be secondary to maintaining a good political and economic relationship with Pakistan".[14] Finally, there is the clownish former interior minister, Rehman Malik, who has proposed that Pakistan should sell half its foreign loans to China on the condition that these will be repaid in easy instalments preferably without interest and with a moratorium of 5 years.[15]

The Chinese on the other hand believe that the more they invest in Pakistan, the closer they pull Pakistan into their sphere of influence and achieve their strategic objectives.[16] According to a report published in 2017, the Chinese had prepared very grand plans about how the CPEC would unfold and transform Pakistan. The 'long-term plan', the details of which haven't yet been made public, would for all practical purposes convert Pakistan into a satellite state.[17] Apart from radically changing Pakistan's agriculture, and culture, the plan envisaged visa-free travel for the Chinese, basically making Pakistan a playground for them. Later, there was a proposal wherein the Yuan would be legal tender in Gwadar. While the Pakistanis downplayed the long-term plan and claimed that it had not yet been finalised, they balked over the making of Yuan legal tender. The important point is that the Chinese plans of virtually taking over Pakistan were part of their larger strategic designs in the region, in which Pakistan would be their pivot. Therefore, while at one level each country has significant interests attached to the other, at another level each side's interests don't quite correspond with the other's interests.

Not surprisingly then, there have been a few blips in the bilateral relationship over the last couple of years, especially after the 2018 elections in which the military establishment engineered the ouster of Nawaz Sharif and his party and 'selected' Imran Khan for the post of Prime Minister. The Chinese had invested quite heavily in the Sharif brothers who had gone whole hog to operationalise the CPEC. Before the elections, the Chinese had heaped encomiums on Shahbaz Sharif and credited him with what they called 'Punjab Speed' of ushering in development and progress.[18] This was a great compliment because it compared with what the Chinese often refer to as 'Shenzhen speed' to denote the rapidity with which projects were executed and completed. But after regime change in

Islamabad, the Chinese very nimbly dumped the Sharifs, and seamlessly switched their preference to the new Prime Minister, Imran Khan, calling him China's 'best friend'.[19] The Chinese premier, Li Keqiang, congratulated Imran Khan and said in his message: "I appreciate your positive remarks of firmly developing China-Pakistan relations. I look forward to establishing good working relations and personal friendship with you".[20]

Although in his first speech after winning the elections, Imran Khan reaffirmed that his government would seek to strengthen relations with China and will work towards the success of CPEC, he had been quite lukewarm to CPEC when he was in the opposition.[21] In 2014, during his infamous dharna that forced the Chinese president to postpone his visit, Imran Khan derided CPEC and denied that the Chinese were going to invest $ 35 billion claiming that the Nawaz Sharif government was going to take loans on high interest rates,[22] and added for good measure that Pakistan's future generations would have to repay these loans.[23] Even on the eve of the 2018 elections, he had been insisting on reviewing the CPEC projects. The PTI election manifesto, while calling CPEC "Pakistan's golden opportunity" also stated that "Pakistan is not fully benefiting from CPEC-related investments due to insufficient transfer of knowledge and capabilities, lesser partnerships with local businesses and our high dependence on imports of goods and services from China".[24]

Within days of the new government taking office in 2018, the de facto commerce minister, Razak Dawood, indicated in an interview to the *Financial Times* that the Pakistan government was going to review all CPEC projects and was even considering putting them all on hold for a year. Although the interview was denied by Dawood, it did the damage and really spooked the Chinese.[25] The fact that the Chinese foreign minister was visiting Islamabad at the same time as the interview was published caused a lot of embarrassment to both the 'Iron Brothers'. One of the reasons for Wang Yi's visit was to gauge where the new Imran Khan government stood on CPEC, and the Dawood interview forced the Pakistanis to fall over themselves to placate the Chinese.[26] Foreign Minister Shah Mehmood Qureshi assured his Chinese counterpart that Pakistan would give top priority to CPEC projects and that the change in government in Islamabad would not have any impact on the 'all weather friendship' between the two countries.[27] Similar assurances were held out by the army chief, Qamar Bajwa. For his part, Wang Yi told Prime Minister Imran Khan that the Chinese wished to work with the new government to enhance the strategic partnership between the two countries.[28] The Chinese tried to brush aside the FT report by calling it "ill intentioned" and "based on distorted and misquoted information", adding that it reflected what it called "total ignorance and neglect of the CPEC or China-Pakistan traditional partnership".[29]

But what Dawood had said to FT was not an off-the-cuff remark. Long before he joined the government, he had expressed serious reservations over the way the CPEC projects were edging out and marginalising Pakistani businesses.[30] After his FT interview, it was revealed that there was a big tussle between Pakistan's business lobbies from Lahore and Karachi over how much access the Chinese should be given to the Pakistani market. CPEC had become a big point of contention between the Lahore business lobby which was entering into new ventures with Chinese companies, and the Karachi lobby which was losing out to the Chinese economic onslaught in Pakistan's market.[31] With the ascension of Imran Khan, the Karachi lobby gained the influence it had lacked under the Pakistan Muslim League-Nawaz (PML-N) dispensation, and it was using its proximity to power in Islamabad to level the playing field, or at least get some part of the action.

The Chinese were quick to understand the game and they quickly co-opted the naysayers by farming out fat deals to them. For instance, Dawood's company got to participate in the Mohmand Dam project. Other Karachi-based business houses also got a chance to cut deals with the Chinese. At the same time, the Chinese announced that they would add social sector and regional development schemes to the CPEC projects portfolio.[32] This was in part aimed at reaching out to Imran Khan who was not quite enamoured of the infrastructure-based focus of CPEC and wanted that the project had to support the agricultural sector, create employment opportunities and attract foreign investment from other countries.[33] This was one reason why the Chinese declared that the CPEC would be broadened to include other countries to invest in the projects. Of course, when the Pakistanis tried to rope in the Saudis to become part of CPEC, the Chinese objected and told the Pakistanis that they weren't willing to countenance any third country becoming part of the strategic scheme under CPEC and that the Saudis were only welcome to the extent of investing money in specific projects and not being inserted as a partner in CPEC.

To further sweeten the deal for Pakistan, the Chinese announced that the focus of CPEC would shift from being supply driven to being demand driven.[34] In other words, CPEC would henceforth be more aligned to Pakistan's own priorities and demands. The Chinese concluded phase two of the Free Trade Agreement with Pakistan in which they gave some more concessions to Islamabad.

Assurances were also given to increase imports from Pakistan. In fact, Chinese officials promised to double their imports. This was music to Pakistani ears until someone did the math and realised that this would mean just an additional $ 1 billion in exports and would hardly address the huge imbalance in trade between the two countries. But perhaps the most significant assurance that the Chinese gave to the Pakistanis was on the issue of debt because there had been people warning that Pakistan could be caught in an unsustainable situation when the time came to pay back the money being sunk into CPEC projects.[35]

The entire BRI project had the taint of debt-trap diplomacy attached to it with the examples of Sri Lanka and some Central Asian states that were unable to service their astronomical debts to China and were forced to cede land and give long-term leases on ports and other infrastructure developed by the Chinese. The US Secretary of State, Mike Pompeo, had already warned that the USA would block any IMF assistance to Pakistan to prevent that money being used to pay off Chinese debts.[36] Shortly after this warning, Wang Yi had visited Islamabad and said that "CPEC has not inflicted a debt burden on Pakistan...when these projects are completed and enter into operation, they will unleash huge economic benefits...creating considerable returns for Pakistan's economy".[37] On more than one occasion, the Chinese ambassador to Islamabad held out the same assurance and announced that "if Pakistan was in need, China would never ask Pakistan to repay its loans in time".[38] In a statement, the Chinese embassy also said that not only will China "never force Pakistan to pay back the debts" but also that "Chinese loans have no strings attached".[39]

There is of course a bit of contradiction in some of these assurances. For a long time, the Chinese and the Pakistanis have been insisting that CPEC is an investment and no loans are being given. The debt is mostly being given by China to its companies and not to Pakistan. The Chinese companies would be able to service the debt from the user charges and tariffs that have been contracted with Pakistani authorities. This means that the only debt that the Chinese government can restructure and postpone is that given by it for balance-of-payments or budgetary support. Interestingly, so far there has been no announcement of any adjustments being made on the repayments through user charges and tariffs on investments made under the CPEC umbrella. What also raised eyebrows in Pakistan was the fact that even as Chinese activity under CPEC was gathering pace and the Chinese were claiming that they had invested nearly $ 20 billion, the Pakistani balance sheets did not reflect this investment. Pakistan's imports skyrocketed but foreign direct investment (which is what CPEC was being touted as) remained anaemic, hovering around $ 1-2 billion. As noted by a Pakistani analyst, "the outflows on debt servicing will go from the Pakistani [banking] channel, but the inflows are not being routed through it".[40]

Clearly, the Chinese aren't giving a free lunch to the Pakistanis. By all accounts, the repayment obligations to Chinese investors will force Pakistan further into hock to its 'all-weather friend'. The Americans have for long been warning Pakistan to reconsider its involvement in CPEC. The former US State Department point-person for South and Central Asia, Alice Wells, cautioned Pakistan that there was no transparency in CPEC projects and that Pakistan's debt burden was rising on account of Chinese financing of expensive loans.[41] She had earlier pointed out that the CPEC projects were extremely expensive and gave the example of the thermal power projects under CPEC that cost $ 1.5 million per megawatt while the cost of similar non-CPEC projects were set up at half this cost.[42] Although both Pakistan and China protested vehemently and dismissed Wells' remarks, the fact is that Pakistanis are realising that as the CPEC power projects get plugged into Pakistan's electricity grid and the repayments start, Pakistan will sink deeper into insolvency. According to one estimate, just the capacity payments alone to the power producers will rise to PKR 1.5 trillion by the end of 2021, a large part of which will be due to the Chinese power producers.[43] This is an unsustainable proposition. Pakistan is therefore trying desperately to renegotiate these contracts. According to a report, Pakistan is trying to get the Chinese to relax the payment obligations for the CPEC power projects.[44] This includes seeking a reduction in the interest rate by around 2.5 per cent, and extension in the repayment period from 10 to 20 years. This is despite the fact that since 2018 Pakistan has been falling back in making payments for projects that have already come online forcing some of the Chinese companies to reconsider their investments in CPEC projects.[45] What is interesting is that fact that when these projects were negotiated, the Chinese had insisted and Pakistan had agreed to not only allow Chinese power producers the first charge on the tariffs collected, but also set up a revolving fund to ensure timely repayments.

Apart from the Chinese not having so far agreed on cutting slack for the beleaguered Pakistanis on the issue of repayments, they have also forced the Pakistanis to give them huge tax breaks on their projects and operations. Recently, after some resistance, Pakistani lawmakers were forced to concede a 40-year tax holiday for Gwadar port and its free zone.[46] Earlier, the government had refused to share the Gwadar port contract with the lawmakers because it was a confidential document.[47] To put this simply, the Chinese aren't really giving their Iron Brother a free lunch; they might be making it seem like a free or even a very cheap lunch, but no such thing is happening. Quite to the contrary, the Chinese are ensuring that they continue to extract a reasonable return on their investment. It is for this reason that a top Pakistani bureaucrat publicly stated that "the long-term plan of China Pakistan Economic Corridor (CPEC) 'stunting', as it did not result into a 'mutually constitutive' development alliance between the two sides".[48] According to this bureaucrat who has remained involved in CPEC right from its inception, "corporations on both sides joined hands with the help of some political elites and a handful of bureaucrats, channelizing their investments into such ventures where the short-term benefits were personalized and long-term risks were socialized".

While China hasn't as yet eased the terms of repayment on the commercial projects, they have been quite forthcoming in doling out billions of dollars to prop up the Pakistan economy. In a sense, if the former is reflective of China's commitment to its business interests, the latter is an emphatic statement of China's commitment to its strategic partnership with Pakistan. China cannot let the CPEC, which has been classified as a flagship project of BRI, fail. But even less can it allow Pakistan to fail. After 2018, there was a palpable cooling off of China's zeal in completing the CPEC projects and ushering in phase-II of the grand scheme, which included SEZs and other infrastructure projects. Since 2019, both China and Pakistan have smelt the coffee and moved forward to reiterate their commitment to CPEC. They have not only been taking up CPEC, but also taken the next steps for phase-II of the project. Projects that had been held up because of price considerations or financial reasons have once again been kick-started.[49]

Notable among these is the ML-1 railway line. Pakistan had earlier balked at the $ 8.2 billion cost that this project would entail. But now it seems the issue of financing has been sorted out, although the details haven't been made public. A few hydel power projects have also been given the green light, including the Diamer Bhasha dam. This mega project is likely to cost over $ 14 billion. Earlier, there were reports that China had made certain demands that made the Pakistanis balk. According to reports, China was virtually demanding sovereignty on the project that is to come up in the Gilgit-Baltistan region of Pakistan-occupied Kashmir. But now, it seems things have been ironed out, though once again the details aren't known.

The situation post the COVID-19 pandemic has also brought China and Pakistan closer. Pakistan clearly has no other benefactor like China which brings not just economic assistance but also strategic heft to the table. For China, Pakistan is one of its few friends. At a time when a huge pushback is developing against Chinese attempts to impose their hegemony, Pakistan remains a steadfast ally of Beijing. The relationship will only deepen going forward because neither can afford to walk away. There will be the occasional hiccups but nothing so serious as to drive a wedge between the countries. For the foreseeable future, the bonding between the 'Iron Brothers' will remain as strong as steel, and nothing will be allowed to rust this all-weather relationship.

NOTES

1. Sushant Sareen, "China and Pakistan's 'Iron Brotherhood': The Economic Dimension and their implications on US hegemony", ORF Occasional Paper, New Delhi, February 7, 2019.
2. Geo News, "Aaj Shahzaib Khanzada Kay Sath", Karachi, September 5, 2017.
3. Umair Jamal, "Why did China Pull Support for Pakistan at the Finanacial Action Task Force", *The Diplomat,* Tokyo, February 26, 2018.
4. Mohan Malik, "China factor in India-Pakistan Conflict", US Army War College, *Parameters,* Vol. 33, Issue 1, 2003.
5. Ambaj Sahu, "Analysing the trends in China-Pakistan arms transfer", ORF Young Voices, New Delhi, June 14, 2019.
6. "Pakistan ranks 11th in arms imports", *The News International,* Karachi, March 10, 2020.
7. SBP Annual Report, "Exports and Imports by Selected Countries/Territories", State Bank of Pakistan, October 28, 2019.
8. Sushant Sareen, "ZARB-e-AZB an evaluation of Pakistan Army Anti-Taliban Operations in North Wazirstan", Vivekananda International Foundation, February 12, 2015.
9. *ARY News,* "IPP Report: National Kitty faced Rs 4 tr loss due to irregularities in the power sector", April 22, 2020.
10. "CPEC energy projects", *Business Recorder,* Karachi, June 16, 2020.
11. "Govt proposes more power to CPEC authority", *The Express Tribune,* Karachi, June 14, 2020.
12. Azam Khan, "CPEC Project delayed: CPEC authority set up at China's request", *BBC Urdu.com,* Islamabad, July 20,2020.
13. Mehatab Haider, "Keeping economy, CPEC intact: Pakistan seeks friends to avoid IMF bailout", *The News International,* Karachi, March 28, 2018.
14. Go Yamda and Stefania Palma, "Is China's belt and road working? A progress report from eight countries", *Nikkei Asian Review,* Tokyo, March 28, 2018.
15. "Rehman Malik pens secrets to resurrect crippling economy in a letter to PM", *The Express Tribune,* Karachi, October 21, 2018.
16. Maria Abi Habib, "China's 'Belt and Road' Plan in Pakistan takes a Military Turn", *The New York Times,* New York, December 19, 2018.
17. Khurram Hussain, "CPEC master plan revealed", *Dawn,* Islamabad, June 21, 2017.
18. Huzaifa Rehman, "China discards 'Shenzen speed' for Punjab speed', *The News International,* Karachi, July 26, 2016.
19. "China says Imran is best friend", *The News International,* Karachi, July 28, 2018.
20. "Chinese PM congratulates Imran", *The News International,* Karachi, August 18, 2018.

21. "Chairman Imran Khan's speech after results of election 2018", Pakistan Tehreek-e-Insaf.
22. "Talks apart, I won't leave Islamabad until PM resigns: Imran", *The News International*, September 6, 2014.
23. "For the record: Imran says his directives come from masses, not army", *The Express Tribune*, Karachi, September 6, 2014.
24. Pakistan Tehreek-e-Insaf Manifesto, PMO Office.
25. Jamil Anderlini, Henry Sender and Farhan Bokhari, "Pakistan rethinks its role in Xi's Belt and Road Plan, *Financial Times*, September 9, 2018.
26. Syeda Mamoona Rubab, "Terms and Conditions: Is the PTI renegotiating CPEC", *The Friday Times*, Lahore, September 13, 2018.
27. Baqir Sajjad Syed, "CPEC top priority, Qureshi assures Chinese minister", *Dawn*, Islamabad, September 10, 2018.
28. Muhammad Saleh Zafar, "China wishes to work with new govt in Pakistan", *The News International*, Karachi, September 10, 2018.
29. Baqir Sajjad Syed, "Islamabad, Beijing reaffirm commitment to CPEC", *Dawn*, Islamabad, September 11, 2018.
30. Nasir Jamal, "Descon head wants level playing field under CPEC", *Dawn*, Islamabad, January 8, 2018.
31. Tom Hussain, "In Pakistan, Chinese money grapples with Karachi- Lahore divide", *South China Morning Post*, Hong Kong, September 16, 2018.
32. Khaleeq Kiani, "Pakistan, China agrees to broaden CPEC base", *Dawn*, Islamabad, September 10, 2018.
33. Syed Irfan Raza, "CPEC focus must be on job creation, agriculture: Imran", *Dawn*, Islamabad, October 9, 2018.
34. Khalid Mustafa, "China to make CPEC demand-driven programme", *The News International*, Karachi, September 29, 2018.
35. Syed Hasan Javed, "CPEC could develop into Pakistan's debt trap", *The Express Tribune*, Karachi, December 11, 2017.
36. CNBC Transcript, "US Secretary Mike Pompeo speaks with CNBC's Michelle Caruso-Cabera", July 30, 2018.
37. "China not saddling Pakistan with debt: Chinese FM", *The Express Tribune*, Karachi, September 8, 2018.
38. "Projects being carried out under CPEC free of corruption: envoy", *Dawn*, Islamabad, November 23, 2019.
39. Statement of the Spokesperson from the Chinese embassy in Pakistan, Embassy of People's Republic of China in Islamic Republic of Pakistan, May 21, 2020.
40. Khurram Husain, "Mystery of CPEC Payments", *Dawn*, Islamabad, June 21, 2017.
41. Baqir Sajjad Syed, "Blacklisted firms got CPEC project contracts, says Wells", *Dawn*, Islamabad, January 22, 2020.
42. "A Conversation with Ambassador Alice Wells on the China-Pakistan Economic Corridor", Wilson Centre, Washington DC, November 21, 2019.
43. Salman Siddiqui, "Capacity payments projected at Rs1.5tr, *The Express Tribune*, Karachi, June 27, 2020.
44. Khaleeq Kiani, "Pakistan urges China to soften terms for power deals", *Dawn*, Islamabad, April 16, 2020.
45. Israr Khan, "Circular debt and late-payments: Chinese investors may withdraw from the Pak power sector", *The News International*, June 21, 2018.

46. Shahbaz Rana, "Gwadar agreement: Senate body backs 40-year tax break", *The Express Tribune,* Karachi, June 24, 2020.
47. Mubarak Zeb Khan, "Gwadar port contract is confidential', federal secretary informs Senate Panel", *Dawn,* June 19, 2020.
48. Mehtab Haider, "CPEC long-term plan stunting for Pakistan-senior official", *The News International,* March 11, 2020.
49. Faseeh Mangi, "Belt and Road Re-emerges in Pakistan with flurry of China deals", *Bloomberg,* New York, July 16, 2020.

16

Pakistan–Saudi Arabia–Iran Triangle: How it Affects India's Interests

Lt. Gen. Syed Ata Hasnain (Retd)

Ever since the partition of India in 1947, Pakistan has lived with abiding animosity towards India. While the Jammu & Kashmir (J&K) issue has been one of the sticky subjects between the two nations. Pakistan's general attitude flows from a historical ideological baggage termed the 'Two Nation Theory' and an attempt to equate itself geopolitically with India. Geographically a part of the Indian subcontinent, it has preferred to pursue linkage more with West Asia due to the Islamic connect, perceiving a potentially diluted identity within South Asia due to the presence of pluralistic India. Instead of exploiting the cultural and ethnic bonds that exist with India it chose very early to veer towards religious linkages to extract what it perceives as strategic advantage for itself, and against India. These linkages took it closer to West Asia, the Gulf nations in particular, and Saudi Arabia the most. With Iran it enjoyed a good relationship due to the commonality of linkages with the USA as part of the Cold War pacts. Post 1979 and the Iranian Revolution, this relationship hasn't soured but has remained transactional. With Iran remaining culturally and in sectarian terms removed from the Gulf countries, its relationship with Pakistan is challenged by the binary partisanship of geopolitics of the Islamic world and the Gulf region.

There can be no doubt that Pakistan is geo-strategically blessed (some call it cursed). Among the factors that give it this advantage is the access it provides from Central Asia, Afghanistan and China, to the Indian Ocean with both India in the east and Iran in the west unable to play their roles due to geopolitical compulsions. It also borders Afghanistan and thus has deep stakes in what it calls 'strategic depth' obtained by Afghanistan's land mass but equally by the religious, cultural and ethnic links it hopes to exploit to advantage. Pakistan also considers itself an aspirant for the leadership of the Islamic world, at least an equal to many others such as Saudi Arabia, Iran and Turkey in the west, and Indonesia and Malaysia in the east. This ambition also partially stems from the intent of bringing the weight of 57 Islamic nations, which form the Organisation of Islamic Cooperation (OIC), against India.

Pakistan identified both Saudi Arabia and Iran as two core Islamic nations whose geostrategic location and geopolitical strength at various times could work to its advantage. An evaluation of the Pakistan-Saudi-Iran triangle makes an interesting study in Islamic geopolitics especially in these challenging times which are witnessing rapid and unpredictable change in the world order based upon emerging dynamics and a new balance of power. This analysis examines Pakistan's individual linkages with the two Islamic nations and delves into the larger geopolitical game of Islamic and international politics and the effect this potentially bears on India's interests.

It may be appropriate and interesting to commence this with the context of current times. There is a crisis in Pakistan-Saudi relations today (August 2020). Paradoxically, the crisis has arisen because of the special relationship that has existed between the two nations for a long time leading to all kinds of mutual expectations. Pakistan expected a committed and energetic Saudi backing to its efforts to rally the Islamic world against India in the wake of the Indian decision on 5 August 2019 to fully integrate J&K by abrogating all special provisions for J&K which existed in the Indian Constitution. Commonly referred to as Articles 370 and 35A these were a kind of lifeline Pakistan exploited to promote separatism and anti-India sentiment with the intent of J&K's eventual secession. That is because the provisions gave exclusivity to J&K which in many ways assisted in the maintenance of separatist thinking which Pakistan fed upon for its agenda against India.

Given exponential improvement in Indo-Saudi ties since 2014, Saudi Arabia has been reluctant to treat India-Pakistan relations with a binary approach. The Indian decision on J&K proved to be an occasion when the Saudis exercised prudence instead of any blind support for Pakistan based upon Islamic ties. It chose to term India's decision as an internal affair and refused to convene an OIC meeting to discuss the issue, much to the chagrin of Pakistan. Saudi Arabia's change of stance has been based upon realist pragmatism nudged by the US-Israel combine to view the future potential conflicts in West Asia where Iran is the common nemesis. Saudi Arabia is aware of India's proximity to the US-Israel combine and also views India as an important customer for energy besides the non-partisan Indian expatriate community which makes up a large part of its working population. Pakistan's obsessive pursuit of its J&K agenda which was threatening to get relegated led it to first agree to join Turkey, Iran and Malaysia in attending an Islamic summit at Kuala Lumpur outside the aegis of the Saudi-controlled OIC in December 2019. The summit with an agenda to discuss increasing international Islamophobia was an obvious attempt to dilute the Saudi hold over the international Islamic fraternity. Behind it was the crafty hand of Turkey's Recep Taiyap Erdogan who seeks restoration of a leadership role for his country; almost akin to a recall of Ottoman times. Iran being Saudi Arabia's sectarian nemesis was on board and Malaysia sought its own primacy perceiving its economic strength as a passport to a greater role within the Islamic fraternity. Pakistan had no reason to attend this other than to raise the issue of J&K. However, under deep obligation to the Saudis for the financial bailout packages of 2018, Prime Minister Imran Khan had little option than to withdraw from the Kuala Lumpur summit under prodding from Saudi Arabia. As a face saver, Pakistan's Foreign Minister, Shah Mehmood Qureshi, announced that the Saudis had accepted the holding of an OIC Foreign Ministers' meet at Islamabad in April 2020; the Saudis had no such intent and April 2020 passed with the Covid-19 pandemic at its height. On the first anniversary of the Indian decision to abrogate Articles 370 and 35A and reorganize the J&K administrative set up, Pakistan was under internal pressure for the relative lack of any meaningful action on J&K which was progressively leading to better Indian integration of the territory.

Earlier, in late 2018, with the Pakistan economy in shambles and a severe balance-of-payments crisis looming, it was Saudi Arabia that had provided Pakistan two economic packages. First was a loan-cum-aid of 3 billion US$ and the second a 3.2 billion US$ energy credit. These helped Pakistan stay afloat until the IMF agreed to provide a 6 billion US$ loan after much US scrutiny. Although deeply indebted to the Saudis, Pakistan's leadership lost its balance when, in the wake of the anniversary of the abrogation of the special status of J&K, Foreign Minister Shah Mehmood Qureshi bitterly complained of the Saudi lack of sensitivity over J&K. He also threatened to recommend to Prime Minister Imran Khan to convene a meeting of Islamic countries that are ready to stand with Pakistan on the issue of J&K.

With Pakistan's options severely curtailed after 5 August 2019 and little traction in its international campaign, Qureshi's uncharacteristic complaint took many by surprise. There were unconfirmed reports of Pakistan being forced to return the Saudi loans with commensurate borrowing from China. However, the importance of the Saudi-Pak relationship may have been underestimated. Pakistan made ardent efforts to neuter Qureshi's insensitive comment especially in the light of an article by Dr. Ali Awwad Asseri, a former Saudi Ambassador to Pakistan, in the *Arab News*. Dr. Asseri, largely known for his promotion of the Saudi-Pak relationship, expressed surprise at Qureshi's obstinacy. The Army Chief, General Qamar Bajwa, rushed to Riyadh along with the ISI Chief Lt. Gen. Faiz Hameed but was denied an audience with Prince Mohammad bin Salman further confirming that the Pak-Saudi relationship was under threat.

There is a perception that Imran Khan appears to feel that time is running out and that if no international traction on J&K is achieved it may turn into a fait accompli and hence the attempt to pressure Saudi Arabia. However, for a better understanding of the strength of the Pak-Saudi relationship in the currency of time, a look at the background is necessary. Pakistan and Saudi Arabia's interests have been in congruence with each other for many years. Some of them can be identified as:

- Saudi Arabia, as the custodian of the most significant Islamic shrines, draws not only the government but the people's passionate and obsessive attention in Pakistan. The basic Islamic ideology is common, being Sunni, although Pakistan's 'Sunnism' was actually of a different shade until Zia-ul-Haq commenced giving it a Saudi-oriented obscurantist colour in the Eighties.
- Saudi Arabia considers Pakistan's large Muslim population base suitable for the propagation of its obscurantist Wahabi form of Sunni Islam. A less educated populace, with poverty and a feudal society, is tailor made for this.
- In particular, after the Iranian Revolution of 1979, Saudi fears of a potential surge in Shia Islam's efforts to dominate the Islamic world led it to cultivate Pakistan as a geostrategic balancer since it shares Iran's eastern boundary.
- In 1977, Zia-ul-Haq conceived Pakistan's strategy of retribution against India. Among other things, it included nuclearisation of Pakistan to remove asymmetry and befriending of a rich Arab state to bankroll Pakistan's military modernization. Saudi Arabia was the best bet given its overflowing coffers of petro dollars and growing clout in the Islamic world.
- The year 1979 was significant from the Saudi-Pak point of view. The Soviet invasion of Afghanistan and the Iranian Revolution brought

Pakistan to prominence in the eyes of the USA and the Saudis. Besides attempting to balance the aspirations of Iran's Shia surge, Pakistan was the natural choice to counter the Soviets in Afghanistan by use of sub-conventional warfare. For nine years (1980-89), transnational Islamic jihadis bankrolled and armed by the USA and the Saudis fought the Soviet Army. The effort was led, coordinated and virtually masterminded by Pakistan's Intelligence agency, ISI. In the course of that effort, almost three million refugees poured into Pakistan's western border tracts where they were housed, fed and converted to the Saudi ideology of Islam; the Taliban was created here. Its links with Pakistan and Saudi Arabia have always remained intact.

- A protocol was signed between Pakistan and Saudi Arabia on 14 December 1982 following the latter's request for military manpower assistance. Even earlier, through the 1970s and then the 1980s, up to 15,000 Pakistani troops were stationed in Saudi Arabia to provide it security. This included personal protection of the royal family leading to closer bonds of friendship. Pakistan also provided troops for the security of the holy shrines in the run-up to Gulf War 1. The domain of security continued to steer the relationship when Saudi Arabia became the only country taken into confidence before the conduct of the retaliatory nuclear tests by Pakistan in 1998 at Chagai Hills. In its wake, the Saudis largely bailed out Pakistan from the effects of the sanctions imposed by the USA and other powers.
- A nuclear-armed Pakistan has been considered by Saudi Arabia as a foil against Iran's nuclear ambitions; a sort of support in waiting should a contingency arise.
- Nearly 2.6 million Pakistani expatriates work in Saudi Arabia repatriating 4.5 billion US$ to Pakistan every year, which substantially contributes to the meagre Pakistan economy.
- Besides the 6.2 billion US$ loans, aid and credits in 2018, another important development was the conclusion of the largest-ever Saudi investment deals worth $ 20 billion in Pakistan, including an oil refinery in Gwadar worth $ 10 billion and the remaining investments in a petrochemical complex, mining and renewable energy sectors. This is less known and much less publicized.

An issue that rocked the boat of Saudi-Pak relations to some extent was Pakistan's refusal to send its army to fight Iran-supported Shia Houthi rebels in

Yemen in 2015 when Saudi Arabia decided to set up a coalition of Islamic nations. The Pakistani reason was the ongoing internal instability and the border-related issues with India and its legislature endorsed the decision. Yet Saudi Arabia appointed former Pakistan Army Chief, General Raheel Sharif, as the Commander of the Islamic Military Counter-Terrorism Coalition.

From the foregoing, it can be clearly ascertained that the Saudi-Pak relationship in the political, economic and military domains has been transformational in nature. The USA too has strategically backed Pakistan's Saudi link which has been in full convergence with US interests. Israel which has over the last few years developed a healthy working relationship with Saudi Arabia also has an informal relationship with Pakistan which the latter does not wish to officially admit due to sensitivity in the Islamic world connected with the Palestinian cause. The Pakistani denial of any such relationship partially helps shore up Pakistan's leadership claims in the Islamic fraternity. With the recent decision of the Saudi-backed UAE to establish relations with Israel, Pakistan has been adamant that it will not follow suit. This issue is not yet a major point of difference between the Saudis and Pakistan but is a pointer that Pakistan is in greater sync with Iran and with Turkey's recent emerging anti-Israel bias.

Former Pakistan Ambassador to the USA, Hussain Haqqani, who is on the wrong side of the Pakistani establishment, in a recent article in the Indian online news magazine *The Print* says, "Believers in Pakistan's inevitable strategic salience expect that after Afghanistan, the USA will also withdraw gradually from the Middle East. In their imagination, Pakistan would then be China's link to the Middle East, making it Beijing's go-to satrap in tapping Middle East oil and securing Gulf shipping lanes. The hope is that Pakistan can then fulfil its old dreams of exercising paramountcy over Afghanistan, resolving disputes with India (including Kashmir) on its terms, and finding its rightful place as the Muslim world's natural leader and sole nuclear weapons power". He alludes to a Pakistani propensity to draw closer to a potentially emerging equation involving China-Iran-Turkey. With China's rising power and ambitions and Turkey apparently seeking a restoration to Ottoman status, Pakistan perceives strategic advantage in this. However, the idea of ditching Saudi Arabia to align closer with this dispensation must not be immediately imagined. Former Ambassador to Pakistan Ali Awadh Asseri's recent article in the *Arab News* dated 23 August 2020, likely a sponsored one, bears the important title 'Saudi Arabia and Pakistan: A Partnership too Important to Fail'. It is appreciative of the relationship but gives unsubtle warnings to the Pakistan leadership. He goes on to state, "If Foreign Minister Qureshi's veiled reference is towards another Kuala Lumpur-style gathering, then it is a dangerous proposition that could be least expected from a brotherly country". He further elaborates, "Let us not allow baseless rhetoric to jeopardize a time-tested relationship or create a rift within the Ummah". Both statements reveal the importance of the Pak-Saudi relationship which may not take a negative turn as easily as perceived by some observers.

In the emerging dynamics, the possibility of a closer Iran-Pak relationship has often been referred to. Iran appears to be emerging as the preferred strategic partner for China for a couple of reasons. First, the strained relationship with the USA suitably fits the age-old strategic belief, 'an enemy's enemy is a friend'. Second, Iran is Russia's preferred partner too and has played a role in ensuring a strong Russian presence in West Asia through the joint campaign in Syria and against the ISIS in both Iraq and Syria. Third, guaranteed energy supply is assured for China. The same can be achieved with Saudi Arabia too but would remain suspect due to US pressure. China has probably presumed that the Saudis would anyway sell their oil to China even without a strategic partnership, until pressured by the USA, for which China would have the continuing Iranian alternative. Fourth, the Pakistan-Iran-Turkey land-based continuum gives the advantage of the Russia-China access to the Indian Ocean, Persian Gulf and the Mediterranean.

Does Pakistan have a historical relationship with Iran that can assure it a greater balance in its strategic interests; more than what exists with Saudi Arabia? This is an important issue that needs analysis.

Pakistan and Iran share strong historical, religious, cultural, and linguistic bonds. The relationship has witnessed its ups and downs, but despite all that, the two countries have maintained a smooth path. Pakistan's ties with Iran are historically much deeper than with any Arab nation. A strong Persian influence permeated the Islamic culture of undivided northern India, something which Pakistan inherited. Its national anthem is largely in Persian. Pakistan is a majority Sunni state and Iran overwhelmingly Shia; the former has a sizeable Shia minority that could be as high as around 20 per cent of the population. Prominent Pakistanis such as the country's founder, Muhammad Ali Jinnah, and its first president, Iskander Mirza, were Shia Muslims. Unlike Saudi Arabia's obscurantist Sunni Wahabi ideology, Pakistan's original Sunni ideology is much more tolerant, something that facilitated ties with Iran. Iran was not only the first nation to recognize Pakistan but its ruler, the Shah, was also the first head of state to visit it, and both countries allied themselves with the USA against the Soviet Union. Although bilateral relations became more complicated after the 1979 Iranian Revolution, the two continued to cooperate in Afghanistan where both supported the 'mujahideen' during the anti-Soviet war. In many recent instances of Saudi-Iran differences, Pakistan has traversed a neutral path and many times even opted to support Iran. Pakistan opposed Saudi-backed plans to attack the Syrian government in 2013 and criticized US airstrikes against the Assad regime in 2018. In 2015, Pakistan's parliament voted not to send Pakistani troops to fight in the Saudi-led war in Yemen. Pakistan supported the 15 July 2015 Joint Comprehensive Plan of Action (JCPOA) to put an end to sanctions on Iran; the Saudis opposed it completely. When tensions between Riyadh and Teheran escalated, following Saudi Arabia's execution of a Shia cleric in 2016, Pakistani officials conducted shuttle diplomacy to mediate between the two; although not too many gave much credence to Pakistani mediation. The two nations have their run of border problems with rebels from either side targeting security forces but these have never reached serious proportions. Thus even though the relationship has been most cordial, it has at best been transactional unlike the transformational proportions assumed by the Saudi-Pak relationship.

In May 2016, the visit of Prime Minister Narendra Modi to Teheran resulted in the signing of an India-Iran-Afghanistan Trilateral that promised the development of Chahbahar port, the construction of the Chahbahar-Zahedan railway line and linkage to the Afghan border. This would have enabled Indian capability to access Afghanistan and the Central Asian Republics, something denied to India by Pakistan for many years. Pakistan was never happy about this arrangement but did not let it hurt its relationship with Iran. That entire agreement has fallen through because of US sanctions re-imposed after the virtual abrogation of JCPOA in 2018, giving Pakistan great satisfaction. However, it is on Jammu & Kashmir (J&K) that Iran has been more than forthcoming towards Pakistan. Earlier a little reticent in going the full way to condemn Indian handling, after 5 August 2019 it was one of the few nations which went public in its criticism of India. J&K now appears in the Iranian supreme leader's speeches.

Imran Khan has long advocated closer ties with Teheran. His party, PTI, supported the 2015 JCPOA, opposed deploying Pakistani troops in Yemen, and also opposed the appointment of General Raheel Sharif to head the Islamic counter-terrorism coalition because it could affect Pakistan's relations with Iran.

With a reset in the international order and an emerging change in the balance of power, a cleavage in Pakistan-Saudi relations definitely holds India in greater stead. Saudi Arabia and the UAE along with other Arab Gulf nations have all been supportive of India and the same is likely to continue although China too is attempting to make economic and strategic inroads in the Gulf. The Turkey-

Iran link has been far from friendly with India and sees greater advantage in linkages with China and thereby Pakistan. Russia is the swing nation in this emerging balance-of-power equation. India must therefore endeavour to continue to retain and build upon its relationship with Russia. However, in the post Covid-19 period, uncertainties remain and the dynamics are yet emerging. There is no guarantee of a complete Saudi and Gulf nations' swing in favour of India although the Indian Government's ardent efforts at building relationships with these nations since 2014 is likely to spell a distinct advantage. India's promised civilizational relationship with Iran has been the subject of much Iranian scorn. India cannot afford binary choices here and must retain its relationship with Iran. The US Presidential election holds the key to this. A victory of the Democrats may lead to an eventual restoration of JCPOA, giving India a window to return to doing business with Iran; Chahbahar and the Zahedan rail link being the two major projects. However, with Saudi Arabia and other Gulf nations much more favourably disposed towards India, pursuing this line too may prove to be a challenge for India.

17

Pakistan–Turkey–Malaysia and the OIC

Dr. Yatharth Kachiar

Introduction

Pakistan is losing allies at an increasingly fast rate. The rift between Islamabad and Riyadh is wider than before. In August 2020, Pakistan's Foreign Minister, Shah Mahmood Qureshi, accused the Organisation of Islamic Cooperation (OIC) of failing to convene a Foreign Ministers meeting on the Kashmir issue. He threatened to call a separate meeting of Islamic countries in case the OIC did not heed its demands. Such threats have further irked Saudi Arabia—the current Chair of the OIC—who viewed it as a direct challenge to its leadership of the Islamic world. Saudi Arabia's traditional primacy in the Islamic world is frequently challenged by the non-Arab Muslim countries led by Turkey, Malaysia and often supported by Iran and Pakistan. In December 2019, Pakistan backed the Kuala Lumpur Summit, also known as the Perdana Dialogue, hosted by Malaysia. Islamabad did not attend the summit due to Saudi pressure who viewed it as a direct challenge by non-Arab Muslim countries to the Saudi-dominated OIC.

In recent years, apart from Pakistan's all-weather friend, China, the only two countries that have been unflinchingly providing diplomatic support to Pakistan at the global level are Turkey and Malaysia. Both the countries have played a crucial role in keeping Pakistan out of the blacklist of the Financial Action Task Force (FATF). Also, the leaders of Turkey and Malaysia have backed Pakistan's position on Kashmir at various fora, including the UN General Assembly (UNGA), after India decided to revoke Article 370. In a bid to show his support to Pakistan on Kashmir, President Erdogan equated the issue of Kashmir with the Battle of Gallipoli, which was fought between the Allied Powers and Ottoman

Empire during World War I. In February 2020, while addressing Pakistan's Parliament, President Erdogan said, "there is no difference between Gallipoli and Kashmir.... Turkey will continue to raise its voice against the oppression."[1] Similarly, during his UNGA speech, former Malaysian Prime Minister Mahathir Mohamad alleged that India has "invaded and occupied" Jammu and Kashmir.[2] On another occasion, President Erdogan had retorted, "We will continue to stand by Pakistan in the future, as we did in the past...the brotherhood law in Islam requires sharing agitations and being involved in them besides supporting the fellow believers. Short-term interests, daily reckonings cannot hinder our everlasting and eternal brotherhood."[3]

Against this backdrop, the following chapter will attempt to analyse the reasons behind Pakistan's growing bonhomie with Turkey and Malaysia. It argues that apart from the need to diversify and increase their economic and defence cooperation, what binds these three countries together is their Islamic identity, their close association with the ideology of Muslim Brotherhood, and their desire to showcase leadership within the Muslim community. However, in their bid to emerge as the new voice of the Muslim community throughout the world, Turkey, Malaysia and Pakistan are in danger of crossing the red lines of Saudi Arabia. Saudi Arabia considers itself as the leader of the Muslim world, not only because of its geopolitical clout but also because of the presence of Islam's two holiest places—Mecca and Medina.

Challenging Saudi Arabia

The Kuala Lumpur Summit, hosted by Malaysia in December 2019, brought the rift within the Islamic world out in the open. Traditionally, the Saudi Arabia-led OIC is known as the collective voice of the Muslim world. Formed in 1969, with a total membership of 57 states, the OIC aims to protect and safeguard the interests of Muslims all over the world. By hosting a summit of Muslim countries outside the purview of OIC, Malaysia challenged the traditional primacy of the OIC and thereby Saudi Arabia in the Islamic world. One of the major objectives of the summit was to revive the 'golden period' of Islamic civilisation traditionally dated from the eighth to the fourteenth centuries when the Muslim community led the world in science, commerce, and culture.[4] The summit was originally planned by the former Malaysian Prime Minister, Mahathir Mohamad, to discuss the major issues concerning the Muslim world after consulting with other like-minded states such as Pakistan and Turkey during the trilateral meeting in September 2019 in New York on the sidelines of the UNGA session.

As the reports suggest, Pakistan Prime Minister Imran Khan strongly backed the Malaysia-led initiative and declared his participation in the event. The Kuala Lumpur summit provided a new platform to Pakistan to create an anti-India front and discuss issues such as Kashmir.[5] After being snubbed by the OIC as well as the Gulf countries such as Saudi Arabia and the UAE on the Kashmir issue, Pakistan sought to utilise this new platform to rally the Muslim world on Kashmir. It is important to note that Pakistan's Prime Minister had criticised the OIC for its failure in forming a cohesive front in favour of Islamabad on the Kashmir issue. During his visit to Malaysia in February 2020, PM Imran Khan targeted the OIC and lamented the lack of unity within the Islamic world. He said, "We have no voice and there is a total division amongst (us). We cannot even come together as a whole on the OIC summit meeting on Kashmir."[6]

The Kuala Lumpur summit was attended by 450 delegates from several Islamic countries including Iran, Qatar, and Turkey who have been continuously challenging the supremacy of Saudi Arabia in the Islamic world. Interestingly, the summit was also attended by members of the militant Palestinian Islamist movement *Hamas,* an offshoot of the Muslim Brotherhood and designated as a terrorist organisation by the USA.[7] The Political Bureau member of *Hamas*, who attended the Kuala Lumpur event included Mousa Abu Marzook and his colleagues, Khalil Al-Hayya, Izzt Al-Rashiq and Husam Badran, along with other officials such as Sami Abu Zohri, Osama Hamdan and Jamal Isaa.[8] Saudi Arabia and its allies in the Gulf region snubbed the summit. Interestingly, after showing initial enthusiasm for the summit, Pakistan reneged its participation in the summit following PM Imran Khan being summoned to Saudi Arabia in December 2019, just before the summit. As the reports suggest, Riyadh showed its displeasure over Pakistan's proposed participation in the Malaysia-led initiative that was perceived as an attempt to create another platform for the Islamic countries that could threaten the existence of the OIC.[9] The summit was also criticised by the OIC secretary-general, Yousef al-Othaimeen, who is a Saudi national, as an attempt to weaken Islam and Muslims by holding "summits and meetings outside the framework of the OIC, especially at this time when the world is witnessing multiple conflicts".[10]

Recently, the Pakistan Foreign Minister threatened to call a meeting of Islamic countries if the OIC failed to raise the Kashmir issue in a manner favourable to Islamabad. He also praised Turkey and Malaysia for their support on the Kashmir issue. Such a strong criticism of Saudi leadership and a threat to create a rival bloc did not go well with Riyadh. Consequently, Saudi Arabia demanded that

Pakistan should repay the USD 1 billion debt four months ahead of its repayment period. Pakistan managed to repay the required debt after borrowing it from China on a short-term notice. Saudi Arabia has always played the role of a traditional donor country to ease out Pakistan's economic woes during the time of crisis. In one such attempt, in 2018, Saudi Arabia had announced a USD 6.2 billion package, which included a USD 3.2-billion Saudi oil facility. Reports suggest that the package given by Saudi Arabia had the provision of renewal for two more years. The deal signed between Pakistan and Saudi Arabia for provision of USD 3.2 billion worth of oil on deferred payment expired two months ago, and Riyadh has not moved ahead on Islamabad's request to extend the facility. Pakistan Army Chief General Qamar Javed Bajwa's visit to Saudi Arabia to mend the diplomatic rift did not yield any positive result as Crown Prince Mohammed bin Salman refused to meet him.

Identity, Ideology and Leadership of the Islamic World

The primary force that binds Pakistan, Turkey and Malaysia is the pre-eminence of Islamic issues in the foreign policy of these countries. By invoking religion and giving excessive importance to the issues concerning the Muslim community worldwide, these countries aim at forging a space for themselves in the Islamic world and strengthening their support base at home. Since his rise to power, Imran Khan has projected himself as the protector of Islam and the Muslim community. In 2019, during his UNGA speech, while defending the rights of Muslim women to wear the hijab, he said, "A woman can take off her clothes in [some] countries, but she cannot put on more clothes."[11] The Pakistani Prime Minister also spoke at length on the rise of "Islamophobia" and how a few people in the Western countries have contributed to its upsurge by writing anti-Islamic literature such as "The Satanic Verses".[12] At the same time, he warned the European countries not to marginalise the Muslim communities as it only led to radicalisation. He also stated that "there is no such thing as radical Islam, but only one Islam and that is the Islam we follow of Prophet Muhammad".[13]

Similarly, Turkey, under President Erdogan, relinquished its secular Kemalist legacy and began pursuing a pan-Islamist foreign policy. In his various speeches, President Erdogan has boasted about Turkey's Ottoman heritage and its credentials to lead the Islamic world. The pan-Islamist approach in Turkey's foreign policy became evident during the Arab uprisings in countries like Syria, Libya, and Egypt. Turkey's constant support to the Muslim Brotherhood globally and its backing of Sunni jihadi proxies in the case of Syria and Libya has led to its isolation in the wider West Asian region. However, the full vigour of Turkey's pan-Islamist ambitions is apparent in its approach to the Israeli-Palestine conflict. It is important to note that before the Justice and Development Party's (AKP) ascension to power in Turkey, Ankara and Tel Aviv shared a strategic partnership that enabled them to have close cooperation on issues of defence and security. Nevertheless, the two countries strained ties after the *Mavi Marmara* incident in 2010 in which Israeli military killed 10 Turkish activists on a ship en route to Gaza to deliver humanitarian aid and breach the blockade imposed by Israel. Since then, bashing Israel for its policies in the West Bank and Gaza became a routine task for President Erdogan. In 2017, the Turkish President called the US decision to recognise Jerusalem as the capital of Israel as the "redlines for Muslims".[14] Similarly, after the Israeli parliament decided to adopt a law that defined the country as the nation-state of Jewish people, President Erdogan stated that "this measure has shown without leaving the slightest room for doubt that Israel is the world's most Zionist, fascist and racist state."[15]

The foreign policy approach adopted by Malaysian Prime Minister Mahathir Mohammad is no different from the leaders of Pakistan and Turkey. The centrality of Islamic issues in the rhetoric adopted by PM Mahathir was visible during the Kuala Lumpur summit in 2019. He stressed the need for a unified voice among the Muslim majority states. PM Mahathir said, "Fratricidal wars, civil wars, failed governments and many other catastrophes continue to confront many Muslim countries and Islam without any serious effort being made to end or reduce them or to rehabilitate the religion."[16] While speaking on foreign affairs, PM Mahathir has often invoked religion and threats to Muslims worldwide to strengthen his support base at home and in other friendly countries. After describing the US killing of Iranian military commander Qassem Soleimani as an act of immorality, Malaysian PM said, "Muslim countries should unite to protect themselves against external threats."[17] Again, during an interview in 2018, PM Mahathir stoked a major controversy for his anti-Semitic comments. He said, "If you are going to be truthful, the problem in the Middle East began with the creation of Israel. That is the truth. But I cannot say that."[18] Further, PM Mahathir also "challenged historical accounts that six million Jews were killed in the Holocaust, arguing that the figure was four million."[19] On a question regarding his book '*The Malay Dilemma*' in which he described Jews as "hook-nosed", he said, "they are hook-nosed. Many people called the Malays fat-nosed. We did not object, we did not go to war for that."[20]

Apart from the Islamic identity, what binds these countries together is their close association with the ideology propounded by the Muslim Brotherhood.

Originated in Egypt in 1928 as an Islamist movement against the prevailing Western ideas of secularism and excessive materialism, the Muslim Brotherhood stressed on the need to return to original puritanical Islam. Over the years, "its scholars had derived the principles of democratic governance from Islamic norms, calling for a national constitution, parties, free elections, responsible government, and rights of citizens."[21] Apart from founding various branches in the Arab world, the broad ideology of the Muslim Brotherhood also influenced political movements in countries such as Pakistan, Turkey, and Malaysia. As an analyst observes, "the same ideology has undergone important shifts over the years, adapting itself to the different political environments of specific national settings".[22] It is important to note that Saudi Arabia, the UAE, and Egypt have declared the Muslim Brotherhood as a terrorist organisation.

For instance, in Pakistan, the Jamat-i-Islami's chief ideologue, Abul-ala-Maududi, was strongly influenced by the ideas of the founder of the Muslim Brotherhood, Hasan-al-Banna. Before 1947, Maududi firmly believed in the universalism of Islam and thereby opposed the idea of nationalism, which he viewed as inconsistent with the concept of the *Ummah*.[23] Since its inception, the Pakistani state, which was founded as the homeland for Muslims of the Indian subcontinent, carries within itself an inherent conflict regarding its identity. As an analyst argues, for Pakistan's founding father, Muhammad Ali Jinnah, Muslims of the subcontinent constituted a single nation and thereby he "sought accordingly to establish a largely secular framework in which they could achieve political independence. Islamists led by Maududi and *Jamat-i-Islami*, by contrast, emphasised the idea that Islam should constitute the ideology of Pakistan state, arguing for a constitution that would privilege Sharia law."[24]

After its establishment, during the 1950s and 1960s, Pakistan became the epicentre of pan-Islamist activities. In this regard, Hussain Haqqani writes, "Leaders of the Arab Muslim Brotherhood, including Said Ramadan, travelled to Pakistan for conferences proclaiming the unity of the Muslim *Ummah*".[25] This linkage has remained intact even in recent times. In 2011, the leaders of the *Jamat-i-Islami* (JI) met the members of the Egyptian Muslim Brotherhood in Cairo and resolved to promote true Islam and work towards the betterment of the Muslim community all over the world. After the win of Muslim Brotherhood member, Mohammad Morsi, in the Egyptian presidential elections in 2012, a local division of JI in Karachi held a special ceremony to celebrate Morsi's success. As reports suggest, during the event, a JI leader said, "Congratulations to *Ikhwane Muslameen* (Egyptian Brotherhood) on their glorious success. The sacrifices of the martyrs, Imam Hasan al Banna, Syed Qutb and thousands of activists, have borne fruit in the shape of the revolution in Egypt. God willing, an Islamic revolution is Pakistan's destiny too."[26]

Similarly, President Erdogan's linkages with the Muslim Brotherhood movement goes back to the 1970s when he was beginning his political career under the leadership of Necmettin Erbakan, the father of political Islam in Turkey. When Necmettin Erbakan died in 2011, his funeral was attended by the leading figures in the Muslim Brotherhood and global Islamist movements such as Hamas leader, Khaled Meshaal, the Muslim Brotherhood's former spiritual guide, Mohamed Mahdi Akef and Qazi Hussain Ahmed, Amir of the Pakistani Jammat-e-Islami (JI).[27] At his funeral, Tunisian Islamist leader Rashid al-Ghannouchi said, "In the Arab world in my generation, when people talked about the Islamic movement, they talked about Erbakan...it is comparable to the way they talked about Hassan al-Banna and Sayyid Qutb."[28] Carrying the baton forward, President Erdogan has become the prime supporter of the Muslim Brotherhood movement across the globe. The relationship between Turkey's ruling AKP and the Muslim Brotherhood strengthened with the beginning of the Arab Spring. After the Egyptian military delivered a severe blow to the Muslim Brotherhood-led government of Mohamed Morsi, the members associated with the movement found sanctuary in Turkey. As an analyst noted, "Brotherhood branches from all over the Arab world have set up shop in Istanbul and receive political and financial support from Ankara; Brotherhood members freely conduct business and run television stations from Turkey".[29]

In Malaysia, the resurgence of two stalwarts of political Islam, Mahathir Mohammad and Anwar Ibrahim, during the 2018 Parliamentary elections, stunned watchers of Malaysian politics. The duo formed the Pakatan Harapan (Alliance of Hope) coalition to oust the previous ruling coalition government of Barisan Nasional (BN) led by Najib Razak in the 2018 elections, which ruled Malaysia for 60 years from 1957 to 2008. With his strong linkages to the Muslim Brotherhood, Anwar Ibrahim, the former Deputy Prime Minister in the previous regime of Mahathir Mohammad (1981-2003), was seen as the politician who brought Islamisation into Malaysian politics. He was the founding leader of Malaysia's Islamic youth movement, Angkatan Belia Islam Malaysia (ABIM).[30] However, in 1998 he fell out with Mahathir Mohammad due to policy differences on the economy and was later jailed on charges of sodomy. The vacuum left by Anwar Ibrahim's absence in Malaysian politics benefitted the country's oldest and largest opposition party, the pan-Malaysian party (PAS), which also draws inspiration from Egypt's Muslim Brotherhood. As an analyst noted, when Anwar was jailed, "many Malay voters found PAS to be a natural draw for them."[31]

However, unlike Anwar Ibrahim's inclusive and liberal Islamist approach to politics, PAS supports the establishment of an Islamic state in Malaysia. According to reports, the Muslim Brotherhood considers PAS as a model of a successful Islamic party that has the potential of winning elections and ruling. The strong linkage between PAS and the Muslim Brotherhood came to the forefront during an event in London in 2005 when PAS president, Hadi Awang, was invited to speak alongside renowned Muslim Brotherhood scholar, Sheikh Yusuf al-Qaradawi, one of the Brotherhood's most controversial and prominent clerics. As an analyst observes "the fact that Hadi Awang was put on the same stage as Yusuf Qaradawi shows the level of respect that the Muslim Brotherhood gives to him."[32]

As explained earlier, the Muslim identity and the prevalence of a common affinity towards the ideology of the Muslim Brotherhood in Pakistan, Turkey, and Malaysia has acted as a catalyst for mutual cooperation in the diplomatic, socio-economic, and military realms. In the last five years, Pakistan-Turkey trade volume has increased from USD 600 million to USD 800 million. The two countries decided to discuss a free trade agreement in 2020 to boost the bilateral trade volume up to USD 5 billion. Pakistan and Turkey have strong cooperation in areas such as the energy sector, education and Diaspora, culture and tourism development and facilitation, halal accreditation and conformity assessment, and trade facilitation.[33]

More importantly, the military dimension of the Pakistan-Turkey relationship further strengthens the ties between the two countries. According to reports, in 2018, Pakistan acquired "30 Turkish-made T-129 attack helicopters at the cost of USD 1.5 billion and the Pakistan Navy commissioned a 17,000-tonne fleet tanker built in collaboration with a Turkish defence company in the southern Pakistani port city of Karachi".[34] Besides, Pakistan also purchased four MILGEM corvettes from Turkey in 2019.[35]

Since assuming office in 2018, PM Imran Khan has made two official visits to Malaysia in two years. During his 2019 visit, Pakistan and Malaysia signed five MOUs in several areas including telecommunications, information technology, and power generation, while also strengthening collaboration in sectors like agriculture, banking, and energy. During PM Imran Khan's visit, Malaysia showed interest in acquiring JF-17 Thunder jets from Pakistan.[36] In his second visit to Malaysia in 2020, PM Imran Khan and Malaysian PM

Mahathir reiterated the 2007 Malaysia-Pakistan closer economic partnership agreement (MPCEPA) and inked the Treaty of Extradition to enhance better cooperation in areas of security and transnational crime. On this occasion, PM Mahathir said, "As two peace-loving Islamic nations, both of us agreed to increase the collaborative efforts between our two countries, to uphold the true values of Islam while strengthening the solidarity of the Muslim *Ummah*".[37]

In May 2019, Pakistan, Turkey and Malaysia held their first ministerial-level trilateral meeting that was attended by their respective foreign ministers. The meeting was held on the sidelines of the 14th OIC summit in Jeddah. After the meeting, Turkish Foreign Minister Çavuþoðlu emphasised that "as major democracies and economies of the Islamic World, we would further our cooperation and would make better use of our combined potential."[38] Regarding the same meeting, Pakistani Foreign Minister Shah Mehmood Qureshi said, "This important trilateral initiative will go a long way in fostering unity, cooperation and development across the Muslim world."[39] Further, during PM Mahathir's visit to Ankara in July 2019, the leaders of Turkey and Malaysia once again reiterated the necessity of creating "solidarity between Turkey, Malaysia and Pakistan for the unity of the Islamic world".[40] President Mahathir stressed that "Cooperation between Malaysia and Turkey will help relieve the Muslim *Ummah* from being subjugated by others."[41] In response to the camaraderie shown by the Turkish and Malaysian leaders, Pakistani Foreign Minister welcomed the "emphasis on Malaysia, Turkey and Pakistan working together to initiate a Muslim renaissance and unite the Muslim world".[42] The leaders of the three countries met during the sidelines of the UNGA meeting in September 2019 and discussed ways to enhance cooperation in various areas.[43] During the meeting, it was decided that the trio would jointly start an English-language channel specifically dedicated to confronting the rising Islamophobia in the world. Further elaborating on this initiative, PM Imran Khan said "the channel will correct the misperceptions which bring people together against Muslims and would contextualise the issue of blasphemy. Series and films will be produced on Muslim history to educate and inform our own people and the world. Muslims will be given a dedicated media presence in the proposed channel."[44]

Conclusion

The troika of Pakistan, Turkey, and Malaysia are aspiring to dethrone Saudi Arabia from its position as the established leader of the Islamic world. To an extent, the three countries together, and especially if they further collaborate with other like-minded countries like Iran and Qatar, will be able to pose a serious threat to Saudi leadership of the Muslim world. Partially, the churning of these new regional alliances in the Islamic world became possible due to Saudi Arabia's narrow approach and vision towards many issues such as fighting an unending war in Yemen, the boycott of Qatar, alleged involvement in the murder of Jamal Khashoggi, and Crown Prince Mohammad-bin-Salman's authoritarian approach to consolidate power by arresting and detaining the members of the royal family. In addition to these self-serving goals of Saudi Arabia, the renunciation of the Palestinian cause by the Kingdom and strengthening relations with Israel might cast a shadow of doubt in the Arab streets regarding Saudi Arabia's credibility to lead the Islamic *Ummah*. In 2020, after President Trump revealed his 'Middle East peace plan', a blueprint to resolve the Israeli-Palestinian conflict, "the Saudi foreign ministry expressed appreciation for Trump's efforts and support for direct peace negotiations under Washington's auspices."[45] However, the 57-member OIC rejected the plan and issued a joint statement where it called "on all member states not to engage with this plan or to cooperate with the US Administration in implementing it in any form".[46]

With Riyadh taking a hands-off approach on issues such as Palestine; Turkey, Pakistan, and Malaysia have tried to fill the vacuum by being most vocal on issues central to the Islamic world. Further, Saudi Arabia's and the Gulf countries' soft stance towards India on the Kashmir issue and its efforts to include India into the ambit of the OIC indicates the potential division of the Islamic world into two rival blocs. Saudi Arabia's soft stance towards Kashmir is motivated by Riyadh's plan to diversify its oil-based economy. In this respect, India has emerged as an important partner for the Gulf countries with its growing economy and huge market.

In order to succeed, the nascent trilateral coordination between Pakistan, Turkey and Malaysia will require more substance other than their ideological commitment to Islamism and their desire to lead the Islamic world. The lack of economic and military strength will pose a major challenge for the triumvirate to lead the Islamic world and fulfil its aspirations. As mentioned earlier, Pakistan reneged its participation in the Kuala Lumpur Summit in December 2019 under Saudi pressure. Recently as well, the premature repayment of the Saudi loan after borrowing it from China and expiry of the oil facility indicates tough times ahead for Saudi-Pakistan ties. Pakistan has built its financial reserves by taking loans from other countries. The expiration of the Saudi oil facility and returning the loan to Riyadh will drain the already depleted reserves of the Central Bank. The heavy dependence of Pakistan's economy on the support provided by the

Gulf countries and Saudi Arabia and the presence of a huge work force there will always triumph over any other strategic calculation. The vulnerability of Pakistan's foreign policy to outside pressure due to its own economic needs will make any alliance joined by the country that is contrary to Saudi interests, suspect.

NOTES

1. Turkish Prez Recep Tayyip Erdogan compares Kashmir with Gallipoli, *Economic Times*, 16 February 2020, Retrieved from https://economictimes.indiatimes.com/news/defence/turkish-prez-recep-tayyip-erdogan-compares-kashmir-with-gallipoli/articleshow/74144656.cms?from =mdr
2. Malaysia's Mahathir stands by Kashmir comments despite palm oil boycott by India traders, Reuters, 22 October 2020, Retrieved from https://www.reuters.com/article/us-india-malaysia-trade/malaysias-mahathir-stands-by-kashmir-comments-despite-palm-oil-boycott-by-india-traders-idUSKBN1X11BB
3. After Erdogan Supports Pakistan on Kashmir, India Asks Turkey Not to Interfere, *The Wire*, 15 February 2020, Retrieved from https://thewire.in/diplomacy/erdogan-pakistan-kashmir-india
4. At Malaysia's KL Summit, the Muslim world's most pressing concerns got no mention, *South China Morning Post*, 24 December 2019, Retrieved from https://www.scmp.com/week-asia/opinion/article/3043413/malaysias-kl-summit-muslim-worlds-most-pressing-concerns-got-no
5. PM's visit to Saudi Arabia aims to assuage Riyadh's reservations, *Dawn*, 13 December 2019, Retrieved from https://www.dawn.com/news/1521991
6. Imran Khan attacks OIC for failing to speak in single voice on Kashmir, *The Economic Times*, 5 February 2020. Retrieved from https://economictimes.indiatimes.com/news/international/world-news/imran-khan-attacks-oic-for-failing-to-speak-in-single-voice-on-kashmir/articleshow/73969446.cms?from=mdr
7. Is the Muslim Brotherhood a Terrorist Group? *The New York Times*, 30 April 2019. Retrieved from https://www.nytimes.com/2019/04/30/world/middleeast/is-the-muslim-brotherhood-terrorist.html
8. Adnan Abu Amer, How Malaysia is becoming Hamas' gateway to Asia, *Al Monitor*, 20 December 2019. Retrieved from https://www.al-monitor.com/pulse/originals/2019/12/kuala-lumpur-summit-hamas-diplomatic-ties.html
9. Saudi Arabia, Pakistan snub Malaysia's Muslim summit, Reuters, 18 December 2019. Retrieved from https://www.reuters.com/article/us-malaysia-muslimalliance/saudi-arabia-pakistan-snub-malaysias-muslim-summit-idUSKBN1YM0G3
10. OIC criticises Malaysia's Muslim summit, *Business Standard*, 19 December 2019. Retrieved from https://www.business-standard.com/article/pti-stories/oic-criticises-malaysia-s-muslim-summit-119121900050_1.html
11. Full Transcript of Prime Minister Imran Khan's speech at the UNGA, *Business Recorder*, 27 September 2019, Retrieved from https://www.brecorder.com/2019/09/27/524851/full-transcript-of-prime-minister-imran-khans-speech-at-the-unga/
12. Taking on 'Islamophobia', Imran Khan ignoring China's Muslim oppression, *Business Standard*, 4 October 2019, Retrieved from https://www.business-standard.com/article/international/taking-on-islamophobia-imran-khan-ignoring-china-s-muslim-oppression-119100400169_1.html

13. Ibid.
14. Erdogan: Jerusalem status a red line for Muslims, *Al Jazeera*, 5 December 2017, Retrieved from https://www.aljazeera.com/news/2017/12/erdogan-jerusalem-status-red-line-muslims-171205070449352.html
15. Turkey-Israel war of words as Erdogan slams 'nation-state' law, *Al Jazeera*, 25 July 201. Retrieved from https://www.aljazeera.com/news/2018/07/turkey-israel-war-words-erdogan-slams-nation-state-law-180724185332890.html
16. Mahathir Mohamad: Muslim world 'in a state of crisis', *Al Jazeera*, 19 December 2019. Retrieved from https://www.aljazeera.com/news/2019/12/mohamad-mahathir-muslim-world-state-crisis-191219091837516.html
17. Muslims should unite after Iran commander's killing, Malaysian PM says, *CNBC*, 7 January 2020. Retrieved from https://www.cnbc.com/2020/01/07/muslims-should-unite-after-iran-commanders-killing-malaysian-pm-says.html
18. Back to old habits, Malaysia's Mahathir calls Jews 'hook-nosed', *Reuters*, 2 October 2018. Retrieved from https://in.reuters.com/article/malaysia-politics-mahathir-jews/back-to-old-habits-malaysias-mahathir-calls-jews-hook-nosed-idINKCN1MC13L
19. Ibid.
20. Ibid.
21. Diplomatic challenges from the Muslim world, *Livemint*, 25 March 2020. Retrieved from https://www.livemint.com/news/india/diplomatic-challenges-from-the-muslim-world-11585154238694.html
22. Peter Mandaville (2016), Islam and International Relations in the Middle East: From Umma to Nation-state, in *International Relations of the Middle East*, Louis Fawcett (ed.), Oxford University Press: Oxford, p. 183.
23. Ibid, p. 183.
24. Ibid, p. 183.
25. Hussaid Haqqani, Islamism and the Pakistani State, Hudson Institute, 9 August 2013. Retrieved from https://www.hudson.org/research/9952-islamism-and-the-pakistani-state
26. Drawing parallels between Jamaat-e-Islami and Muslim Brotherhood, *The Express Tribune*, 18 July 2012. Retrieved from https://tribune.com.pk/story/409788/drawing-parallels-between-jamaat-e-islami-and-muslim-brotherhood/
27. Global Muslim Brotherhood Leadership Gathers At Erbakan Funeral, *The Global Muslim Brotherhood Daily Watch*, 20 March 2011. Retrieved from https://www.globalmbwatch.com/2011/03/20/global-muslim-brotherhood-leadership-gathers-at-erbakan-funeral/
28. Svante E. Cornell, Erbakan, Kýsakürek, and the Mainstreaming of Extremism in Turkey, Hudson Institute, 4 June 2018. Retrieved from https://www.hudson.org/research/14375-erbakan-k-sak-rek-and-the-mainstreaming-of-extremism-in-turkey
29. Lorenzo Vidino, Erdogan's long arm in Europe, *Foreign Policy*, 7 May 2019. Retrieved from https://foreignpolicy.com/2019/05/07/erdogans-long-arm-in-europe-germany-netherlands-milli-gorus-muslim-brotherhood-turkey-akp/
30. Anwar Ibrahim: The Malaysian leader that never was, *BBC News*, 4 March 2020. Retrieved from https://www.bbc.com/news/world-asia-16440290
31. The rising force in Malaysia's opposition, *Al Jazeera*, 10 February 2013. Retrieved from https://www.aljazeera.com/indepth/features/2013/02/201321092433869462.html
32. Ibid.
33. Strong will to take Turkish-Pakistani trade, economic ties to new heights, *Daily Sabah*, 14 February 2020, Retrieved from https://www.dailysabah.com/economy/2020/02/14/strong-will-to-take-turkish-pakistani-trade-economic-ties-to-new-heights

34. Turkey-Pakistan defence industry deals peak in last two years, *Middle East Monitor*, 26 February 2020. Retrieved from https://www.middleeastmonitor.com/20200226-turkey-pakistan-defence-industry-deals-peak-in-last-two-years/
35. Ibid.
36. Hannan R. Hussain, Looking East: The Evolution of Pakistan-Malaysia Economic Ties, *The Diplomat*, 25 March 2019. Retrieved from https://thediplomat.com/2019/03/looking-east-the-evolution-of-pakistan-malaysia-economic-ties/
37. Malaysia and Pakistan leaders reaffirm close ties, *Arab News*, 5 February 2020. Retrieved from https://www.arabnews.com/node/1623136/world
38. Participation of Foreign Minister Çavuþoðlu in the OIC Meetings, 29-31 May 2019, Ministry of Foreign Affairs, Turkey. Retrieved from http://www.mfa.gov.tr/sayin-bakanimizin-ondorduncu-iit-zirvesine-katilimi.en.mfa
39. Pakistan lauds Muslim renaissance trilateral initiative, *Andalou Agency*, 26 July 2019. Retrieved from https://www.aa.com.tr/en/asia-pacific/pakistan-lauds-muslim-renaissance-trilateral-initiative/1542600
40. Ibid.
41. Ibid.
42. Shah Mahmood Qureshi, *Twitter*, 26 July 2019. Retrieved from https://twitter.com/SMQureshiPTI/status/1154819488438730752?ref_src=twsrc%5Etfw%7Ctwcamp%5Etweetembed%7Ctwterm%5E1154819488438730752&ref_url=https%3A%2F%2Fwww.aa.com.tr%2Fen%2Fasia-pacific%2Fpakistan-lauds-muslim-renaissance-trilateral-initiative%2F1542600
43. Pakistan, Turkey, Malaysia discuss ways to enhance cooperation, *Radio Pakistan*, 25 September 2019. Retrieved from https://www.radio.gov.pk/25-09-2019/pakistan-turkey-malaysia-discuss-ways-to-enhance-cooperation
44. Pakistan Turkey and Malaysia launch an unprecedented initiative in trilateral summit, PM Khan announced, *Times of Islamabad*, 26 September 2019. Retrieved from https://timesofislamabad.com/26-Sep-2019/pakistan-turkey-and-malaysia-launch-an-unprecedented-initiative-in-trilateral-summit-pm-khan-announced
45. Organisation of Islamic Cooperation rejects Trump peace plan, Al Jazeera, 3 February 2020, Retrieved from https://www.aljazeera.com/news/2020/02/oic-hold-emergency-meeting-trump-middle-east-plan-200203064919675.html
46. Ibid

18

Pakistan–Russia: Reluctant Partners?

Dr. Yatharth Kachiar

Introduction

During the Cold War period, the relations between Pakistan and Soviet Russia were sluggish as both countries were operating on two different sides of the strategic spectrum. In the era of bipolarity, when the international system was divided into two rival blocs, Pakistan chose to be a close ally of the USA. During the same period, Indian foreign policy was more tilted towards the Soviet Union. Without fighting a direct war against each other, Pakistan and Russia were involved in supporting armed and diplomatic activities against each other that had disastrous ramifications not only for their relations but also for the stability and security of South Asia. For instance, Soviet Russia's pro-India stance at the global level on many issues such as Kashmir had irked Pakistan throughout the Cold War period. In 1971, India and Russia signed the 'The Indo-Soviet Treaty of Friendship' that assisted the Indian leadership in taking necessary action against the Pakistani atrocities in what was then East Pakistan. It eventually led to the partition of Pakistan and the formation of a new nation-state, Bangladesh. Similarly, Pakistan's role in the defeat of the Soviet army in Afghanistan eventually contributed to the disintegration of the Soviet Union. During the 1979-89 war in Afghanistan, Pakistan became the pivot of the US' strategy of defeating the Soviet Union. Backed by the USA and Saudi funding, Pakistan during this period became the core supplier and training ground for jihadis, as well as the conduit for weapon supplies to them.

The relations between the two countries improved gradually with the end of the Cold War. They picked up the pace more recently, especially after the USA first announced the reduction of its troops from Afghanistan in 2012, followed by a timetable for full withdrawal in 2014. Although the US Administration retracted its earlier decision of a complete drawdown of American forces by 2014, it indicated the inevitability of the departure of the US troops from Afghanistan. At the same time, Russia, under President Putin, is demonstrating an enormous willingness to expand its influence in its near and extended neighbourhood. In Afghanistan, Russia is aiming to reassert its position because of the country's critical geostrategic location at the border of the Central Asian region. Russia's concerns relate to the growing instability, terrorism, and drug trafficking in Afghanistan, which has the potential to spill into the neighbouring Central Asian countries and ultimately into Russia. At the same time, the growing presence of the Islamic State Khorasan Province (ISKP) in Afghanistan is an uncomfortable reality for Moscow. The presence of ISKP in Afghanistan threatens Moscow's strategic interests on three fronts: first, the radical Sunni ideology of ISKP can lure Russian citizens into travelling to Afghanistan as foreign fighters; second, the North Caucasian militant groups could ally with ISKP which can prove disastrous for Russian security; and finally, the violent extremism of ISKP could spillover to Central Asian states which in turn threatens the Russian interests in the region.[1] In this context, Pakistan becomes a crucial country within Russian strategic imagination due to its strategic location and influence within Afghanistan. At the same time, Russian overtures come as timely help for Pakistan as it was already struggling with the deterioration of relations with the USA under the Trump Presidency. Further, another critical factor that has pushed Russia towards normalizing and strengthening ties with Pakistan is India's increasingly close ties with the USA.

Evolving Ties in the post-Cold War Era

The geopolitical setting shifted with the end of the Cold War; however, it did not bring any immediate positive development in Pakistan-Russia relations. For a long time, even after the end of the Cold War, the relations between the two remained dormant. One of the reasons behind this low-key phase was Moscow's cordial ties with India. However, as India began moving closer to the USA in the new geostrategic configuration, Russia also started exploring its relations with Pakistan. In the last decade, Pakistan and Russia have taken significant initiatives to strengthen their ties. President Musharaff's visit to Moscow in 2003, the first-ever by a Pakistani leader in 33 years, broke the ice between the two countries. During his visit, the two countries established joint working groups on issues of counter-terrorism, strategic stability, and economic and cultural cooperation.[2] In April 2007, the relations between the two countries exhibited signs of improvement as the Russian Prime Minister Mikhail E. Fradkov arrived in Islamabad on a three-day official visit. The visit was aimed at boosting and diversifying bilateral cooperation.[3]

In 2010, Russia made a drastic shift in its South Asia policy by holding a quadripartite summit with Afghanistan, Pakistan, and Tajikistan in Sochi. The major thrust of the summit was on the evolving situation in Afghanistan. It was an indication of a change in Russia's approach towards Pakistan. The policymakers in Moscow started reviewing their traditional approach of perceiving Pakistan as part of the 'regional problem' and a hindrance in advancing Russia's interests in playing a more significant role in the region.[4] This Russian shift in its policy approach towards Pakistan was rooted in the US decision of curtailing its presence in Afghanistan by 2014. The possibility of the withdrawal of American security cover from Afghanistan enhanced Russian qualms about the spillover of Islamic fundamentalism and terrorism from Afghanistan to Central Asia, and further into southern Russia. It brought a realization within policy circles in Moscow that involving Pakistan would be critical to resolving any crisis emanating from Afghanistan. Therefore, to gain more advantage inside Afghanistan in the post-2014 scenario, Russia began intensifying its relations with Pakistan.[5]

In 2011, for the first time, Russia publicly endorsed Pakistan's bid to get full membership in the Shanghai Cooperation Organisation (SCO).[6] Pakistan joined SCO as a full member along with India in 2017.[7] In 2012, a new chapter was opened in Pakistan-Russia relations with the visit of Army Chief General Ashfaq Parvez Kayani to Moscow. Marked as a "historic trip", General Kayani's visit to Moscow was the first-ever visit by a military chief from Pakistan to Russia.[8] It also indicated a marked transformation in Russia's policy as it overcame its initial hesitancy in developing full-fledged ties with Pakistan. As the deadline for the US military drawdown from Afghanistan neared, Russia began cultivating deeper relations with Pakistan.

Political Cooperation

After their turbulent relations over the years, the shared interests between Pakistan and Russia brought the two countries together. On the sidelines of the 73rd UN General Assembly session in 2018, Foreign Minister Shah Mahmood Qureshi and his Russian counterpart, Sergey Viktorovich Lavrov, stressed the "need to translate the gradually increasing multi-dimensional partnership between the two countries into a multi-faceted strategic partnership".[9] As mentioned earlier, the primary reason behind this growing bonhomie was their mutual understanding of the developing situation in Afghanistan. With significant security and economic stakes in the Central Asian region, it becomes imperative for Russia to ensure that terrorism from Afghanistan did not spill over into its periphery. In 2019, during China's Belt and Road Forum, President Putin suggested integration between Russia's Eurasian Economic Union (EEU) and the Belt and Road Initiative (BRI).

Similarly, Afghanistan's stability is critical for neighbouring Pakistan to ensure a secure environment for the long-term durability of the China-Pakistan Economic Corridor (CPEC). In this regard, Russia and Pakistan share a similar understanding of what constitutes a threat in Afghanistan and how to bring peace to the country. Both the countries consider the terrorist group, Islamic State Khorasan Province (ISKP), a much more significant threat than the Taliban in Afghanistan. To curtail this threat from ISKP, Russia and Pakistan have supported the Taliban through diplomatic and military means in Afghanistan.[10] The strategy of supporting the Taliban and not the Afghan army to fight the counter-terrorism battle against the ISKP shows the overlapping interests of both the countries in Afghanistan which includes curtailing the American influence by encouraging a counter-front to the US-led democratic structure in the country.

In this context, the Afghan peace process served as an important motivator behind the increased Pakistan-Russia bonhomie. The Taliban, since its inception, has received military, financial and logistic support from the Pakistani state. It is in Pakistan's interest that the Taliban regains power in Kabul, as it would help it to advance its strategic goals in the region. Therefore, Pakistan has always supported the idea of engaging the Taliban diplomatically.[11] In the last few years, this stance of the Pakistani state has received widespread recognition from the countries such as the USA, Iran, China, and Central Asian nations. Russia also took no time in endorsing the standpoint of Pakistan in favour of political talks with the Taliban. As an analyst argues, "The beginning of the US-Taliban peace talks in October 2018 was a diplomatic victory for both Russia and Pakistan."[12] Further, to assert its influence as a significant player at the global stage and to reinforce its position in Afghan politics, Russia established the Moscow format of negotiations with the Taliban. Unlike the US-Taliban negotiations, the Moscow format involved various stakeholders such as regional powers, Afghan opposition leaders, and the Taliban.

Apart from cooperating on Afghanistan, in July 2019, Pakistan and Russia held the fourth round of bilateral political consultations in Moscow. According to reports, the two sides "identified areas for further cooperation in political, economic, trade, investment, defence, energy, agriculture, education, culture and tourism."[13] The two sides also decided to increase parliamentary exchanges to boost the bilateral cooperation and deepen the understanding of each other's views. Given these positive developments and diverse areas of cooperation between both the countries, Russia's reaffirmation of its traditional position on the Kashmir dispute signalled a significant limitation of the growing Pakistan-Russia relations. After India's decision of abrogating Article 370 in Kashmir, Russia gave a lukewarm response to Pakistan and stated its consistent position that "tensions need to be de-escalated and the Kashmir issue must be resolved through bilateral talks".[14]

Pakistan-Russia Defence Cooperation

The defence cooperation between the two countries is still at a nascent stage considering the recently established bonhomie. In 2014, the Kremlin decided to lift its long-standing arms embargo on Pakistan as both the countries began negotiating the sale of Mi-35M attack helicopters.[15] As an analyst argued, Russia anticipated that the Mi-35M could act as a "replacement for the US-made AH-1 Cobra attack helicopters that Islamabad has relied upon for years, primarily to aid in its counter-insurgency operations against militant Islamists located along its border with Afghanistan."[16]

In 2014, Pakistan and Russia signed a landmark defence cooperation agreement. The agreement paved the way for information exchange on "politico-military issues; cooperation for promoting international security; intensification of counter-terrorism and arms control activities; strengthening collaboration in various military fields, including education, medicine, history, topography, hydrography and culture; and sharing experiences in peacekeeping operations."[17] In June 2016, the two countries concluded the Mi-35M deal worth USD 153 million during the then Chief of Army Staff (COAS) General Raheel Sharif's visit to Russia. The Pakistan Army Aviation Corps (PAAC) received four Mi-35M helicopters from Moscow in 2017.[18]

The military cooperation between the two countries was further cemented with the beginning of the joint military exercise. In 2016, the first annual military drill dubbed 'Friendship Exercise' was held at Cherat in Khyber Pakhtunkhwa involving 200 military personnel from Pakistan and Russia. The second iteration of the military exercise took place in Russia's North Caucasus Republic of Karachayevo-Cherkessia.[19] In October 2019, the two countries completed the fourth round of annual military exercise in the southern Russian city of Krasnodar.[20] Also, in 2018, at the inaugural meeting of the Russia-Pakistan Joint Military Consultative Committee (JMCC), the two countries signed an agreement to train Pakistani troops at Russian military institutes.[21] During the visit of Vice Admiral Kaleem Shaukat to Russia in 2018, the two countries signed an MoU to strengthen cooperation in the maritime domain.[22] In December 2018, the marine forces of the two countries held naval drills in the North Arabian Sea to promote the capacity of joint operations between the two navies.[23] The naval and military exercises conducted by the two countries indicates the shifting regional alliances as well as Russia's desire to play a more significant role in the South Asian region. For Pakistan, deepening of ties with Russia is crucial to diversify its options in case of further worsening of relations with the USA, and to safeguard itself from excessively relying on the USA or China.

Economic Engagement

The volume of trade between Pakistan and Russia has improved marginally from USD 442 million in 2017 to USD 532 million in 2018. According to the Russian trade representative, "The bilateral trade volume between both the countries is far less than its potential."[24] To deepen their engagement in the economic field, Pakistan and Russia took some proactive steps. In 2015, the two countries agreed to conjointly build the 1,100-kilometre Karachi-Lahore gas pipeline, also known as the North-South gas pipeline, for the transportation of Re-gasified Liquefied Natural Gas (RLNG) from Karachi to Lahore. The project aimed at catering to the lack of capacity in the existing gas infrastructure of Pakistan to transport an additional large volume of gas supplies from the southern to the northern regions of the country. The project worth USD 2 billion with a capacity to carry 1.2 bcf/d (billion cubic feet per day) of gas, was initially supposed to be completed by 2017.[25] However, the company, RT Global Resources, nominated by the Russian government for the project was a subsidiary of ROSTEC, another Russian company facing US sanctions. The Pakistan government had asked Russia to provide a sanction-free consortium. In January 2020, Pakistan approved the consortium of Russian companies, LLC Eurasian Pipeline and Federal State Unitary Enterprise (FSUE) for the project. According to reports, the two countries signed the protocol for the completion of the project in January 2020, and the commercial agreement is likely to be signed between Pakistan's Inter-State Gas Limited and Russian Joint Venture later in the year.[26]

In another positive development, Pakistan and Russia inked an agreement to end a 39-year old Soviet-era trade dispute in November 2019. Under the newly-signed deal, Pakistan will "return USD 93.5 million to Russia within 90 days of the signing of the agreement and clear pending exporters' claims amounting to USD 23.8 million as per the settlement agreements reached in

2016-17."[27] The trade dispute dates back to the Soviet era when the erstwhile USSR imported textiles and other materials from Pakistan. To facilitate the ease of payments, it was settled that the Economic Affairs Division would disburse the payment through the State Bank of Pakistan in the two accounts opened by Soviet Russia in the National Bank of Pakistan (NBP). However, according to reports, "after the disintegration of the Soviet Union, some exports payments were left unpaid, and the trade dispute got prolonged."[28] After repeated failed attempts to resolve the issue, efforts to sign the deal were initiated by the previous Pakistan Muslim League-Nawaz government and the incumbent regime of Prime Minister Imran Khan has decided to execute it. The settlement of the trade dispute will open up new economic opportunities for Pakistan and Russia especially in the energy sector and Pakistan Steel Mills. Russia had conveyed its willingness to invest USD 14 billion in Pakistan's energy sector. However, this investment could not be made earlier since Russian law does not allow the state to invest in countries with which it has trade disputes.

Further, in December 2019, a 64-member Russian delegation headed by Russian Minister of Industry and Trade Denis Manturov visited Pakistan. During the four-day official visit of the Russian delegation, Moscow and Islamabad inked their "largest-ever cooperation deal, worth billions of dollars, to expand trade and business. It includes huge investments in energy, rail and steel industries."[29] Under the recently-signed agreements, Russia agreed to provide financial assistance worth USD 1 billion for the rehabilitation and upgrading of the Pakistan Steel Mills (PSM) project.[30] Previously, in February 2019, Russia had promised an investment of USD 14 billion in Pakistan's energy sector. It included USD 10 billion in an offshore gas pipeline project, USD 2.5 billion for the North-South pipeline project, and the remainder on building underground storages in Pakistan.[31]

To initiate the USD 10 billion offshore pipeline project, Pakistan's Inter State Gas Systems (ISGS) and Russia's Gazprom signed an inter-corporate agreement to conduct a feasibility study in February 2019 to supply natural gas from the Middle East to Pakistan and other parts of South Asia. The deal will allow Russia to export 500 million to 1 billion cubic feet per day of gas to meet the growing energy demands in Pakistan due to the rapid development of the China-Pakistan Economic Corridor. Gazprom would conduct a feasibility study at its own cost with no financial implications for Pakistan. The project is also aimed at bringing Pakistan on the world map as the transit country for offshore gas pipelines.[32] Further, according to reports, "a Russian company has developed a project to convert the Muzaffargarh thermal power station to coal and establish a 600-megawatt coal-fired power plant at Jamshoro. Also, Moscow will help to construct a railway track from Quetta to Taftan."[33]

Conclusion

The fluid dynamics of international politics is difficult to fathom. President Trump's decision for a hasty withdrawal from Afghanistan provided a unique opportunity for Pakistan and Russia to forge a closer alliance with each other. Russian security interests in Afghanistan led it to form a transactional relationship with the Taliban. The reports suggest that at least since 2015, Russia has been sharing Intelligence information about ISKP movements in Afghanistan with the Taliban. There have also been alleged accusations that Russians have provided the Taliban with arms and bounties to kill the American and coalition forces in Afghanistan.[34] Both Russia and Pakistan consider the Taliban a key stakeholder in Afghanistan's future. The mutual alignment of interest between the two countries in Afghanistan continued throughout various highs and lows of the US-Taliban talks that eventually culminated in a 'withdrawal deal' on February 29, 2020.

At present, the real strategic thrust behind Pakistan-Russia relations lies in their collaboration in Afghanistan. At the military and economic levels, the relation between Pakistan and Russia is still at a very nascent stage, especially when compared to India's closer ties with Russia. At present, Russia has sold only four Mi-35M attack helicopters and a few Mi-171Es of the civilian variant to Pakistan. It is a minuscule transfer of military equipment, especially when compared with the magnitude of the Indo-Russian arms trade. Nevertheless, the political symbolism behind this low arms trade cannot be brushed aside. In any case, there is a considerable possibility of the widening of military cooperation between Pakistan and Russia. Pakistan has already shown interest in buying Pantsir surface-to-air missile systems and T-90 tanks from Russia and is optimistic of boosting the defence trade as it involves mutual benefits for both sides.[35] After losing some of its share of the arms market in India to the USA and Israel, Pakistan seems an attractive and untapped market for the Russian arms industry. Russia's share of the supply of conventional weapons to India has decreased from a high of 70 per cent in 2010-14 to 58 per cent in 2014-18.[36] Despite this, one of the significant limitations that might hamper the strengthening of Pakistan-Russia relations is the ailing economy of Pakistan that makes it challenging to invest in the purchase of highly advanced military equipment. At the same time, the US sanctions against the Russian companies will also affect Russia's ability to offer timely delivery of commercial projects and any other financial aid to Pakistan.

Until now, Russia has pursued a careful approach in enhancing its ties with Pakistan because of its bid to maintain a balance between India and Pakistan. India, a time-tested strategic partner with its enormous economic market, is crucial for Russia. However, the dynamic nature of international politics indicates that the onus of keeping the Russians away from Pakistan lies on India which it can easily do by taking some proactive steps in improving the economic partnership and strengthening the strategic understanding with Russia.

NOTES

1. Sajjan M. Gohel & Allison Bailey (2020), "This Time Russia is in Afghanistan to Win", *Foreign Policy*, 1 July 2020. URL: https://foreignpolicy.com/2020/07/01/russia-afghanistan-united-states-bountygate/
2. Helena Rytövuori-Apunen (2016), *The Regional Security Puzzle around Afghanistan: Bordering Practices in Central Asia and Beyond*, Barbara Budrich, Toronto, p. 199.
3. Russian PM arrives, *Dawn*, 12 April 2007. Retrieved from https://www.dawn.com/news/241984/russian-pm-arrives
4. Vladimir Radyuhin, Changing face of Russia-Pakistan ties, *The Hindu*, 9 September 2010. Retrieved from https://www.thehindu.com/opinion/lead/Changing-face-of-Russia-Pakistan-ties/article15907578.ece
5. Sadhavi Chauhan, Russia-Pak relations: Beyond Putin's cancelled trip to Islamabad, ORF, 3 October 2012. Retrieved from https://www.orfonline.org/research/russia-pak-relations-beyond-putins-cancelled-trip-to-islamabad/
6. Russia endorses full SCO membership for Pakistan, *Dawn*, 7 November 2011. Retrieved from https://www.dawn.com/news/671932
7. 'It is a historic day': Pakistan becomes full member of SCO at Astana summit, *Dawn*, 9 June 2017. Retrieved from https://www.dawn.com/news/1338471
8. Shift in policy?: Army chief to make 'historic' Moscow trip, *The Express Tribune*, 3 September 2012. Retrieved from https://tribune.com.pk/story/430434/shift-in-policy-army-chief-to-make-historic-moscow-trip/
9. FM Qureshi, Russian counterpart discuss boosting ties in various sectors, *The Express Tribune*, 29 September 2018. Retrieved from https://tribune.com.pk/story/1813925/1-fm-qureshi-russian-counterpart-discuss-boosting-ties-various-sectors/
10. Kashif Hussain, Russia-Pakistan Relations with Afghanistan: Broadening Strategic Convergence. *South Asian Voices*, 18 October 2019. Retrieved from https://southasianvoices.org/russia-pakistan-relations-and-afghanistan-broadening-strategic-convergence/
11. Samuel Ramani, What's Driving Russia-Pakistan Cooperation on Afghanistan?, *The Diplomat*, 9 May 2017. Retrieved from https://thediplomat.com/2017/05/whats-driving-russia-pakistan-cooperation-on-afghanistan/
12. Ibid.
13. Pakistan, Russia hold 4th round of bilateral political consultation, *The Express Tribune*, 5 July 2019. Retrieved from https://tribune.com.pk/story/2006543/1-pakistan-russia-hold-4th-round-bilateral-political-consultation/

14. Kashmir brings Pakistan-Russia relations into focus, *Asia Times*, 20 August 2019. Retrieved from https://asiatimes.com/2019/08/kashmir-brings-pakistan-russia-relations-into-focus/
15. Zachary Keck, Russia Ends Arms Embargo Against Pakistan, *The Diplomat*, 4 June 2014. Retrieved from https://thediplomat.com/2014/06/russia-ends-arms-embargo-against-pakistan/
16. Ibid.
17. Baqir Sajjad Syed, Pakistan, Russia sign landmark defence cooperation agreement, *Dawn*, 21 November 2014. Retrieved from https://www.dawn.com/news/1145875
18. Franz-Stefan Gady, Pakistan Begins Receiving Advanced Attack Helicopters From Russia, *The Diplomat*, 12 April 2018. Retrieved from https://thediplomat.com/2018/04/pakistan-begins-receiving-advanced-attack-helicopters-from-russia/
19. Franz-Stefan Gady, Pakistan, Russia to Hold Joint Military Exercise, *The Diplomat*, 17 October 2018. Retrieved from https://thediplomat.com/2018/10/pakistan-russia-to-hold-joint-military-exercise/
20. Pakistan-Russia Druzhba 2019 military exercise concludes in Krasnodar, *The News*, 11 October 2019, Retrieved from https://www.thenews.com.pk/latest/539773-pakistan-russia-druzhba-2019-military-exercise-concludes-in-krasnodar
21. Franz-Stefan Gady, Pakistan, Russia to Hold Joint Military Exercise, *The Diplomat*, 17 October 2018. Retrieved from https://thediplomat.com/2018/10/pakistan-russia-to-hold-joint-military-exercise/
22. Vinay Kaura, Russia signs naval cooperation deal with Pakistan: Recent warmth in Moscow-Islamabad ties may worry New Delhi, *Firstpost*, 3 August 2018. Retrieved from https://www.firstpost.com/world/russia-warming-up-to-pakistan-is-the-elephant-in-the-room-in-moscow-new-delhi-ties-india-must-safeguard-long-standing-relations-4888711.html
23. Pakistan, Russian navies hold joint drills in Arabian Sea, *The Express Tribune*, 1 December 2018. Retrieved from https://tribune.com.pk/story/1858222/1-pakistan-russian-navy-hold-joint-drills-arabian-sea/
24. 'Pakistan, Russia trade lower than potential', *The Tribune*, 10 October 2019. Retrieved from https://tribune.com.pk/story/2076114/2-boosting-ties-pakistan-russia-trade-lower-potential/
25. North–South Gas Pipeline Project (NSGP), ISGS. Retrieved from https://isgs.com.pk/projects/nsgp/
26. Pakistan approves structure for $2b North-South Gas Pipeline, *The Nation*, 22 January 2020. Retrieved from https://nation.com.pk/22-Jan-2020/pakistan-approves-structure-for-dollar-2b-north-south-gas-pipeline
27. Pakistan settles Soviet-era trade dispute with Russia, *The Tribune*, 7 November 2019. Retrieved from https://tribune.com.pk/story/2095099/2-pakistan-settles-decades-old-trade-dispute-russia/
28. Ibid.
29. Russia looks to invest in Pakistan in a big way, Ministry of Economic Development, Russian Federation, 9 December 2019. Retrieved from http://www.ved.gov.ru/eng/general/news/19/26239.html
30. Ibid.
31. Boost for cash-strapped Pakistan as Russia plans to invest $14 billion in energy sector, *The Financial Express*, 7 February 2019. Retrieved from https://www.financialexpress.com/economy/boost-for-cash-strapped-pakistan-as-russia-plans-to-invest-14-billion-in-energy-sector/1480194/
32. Pakistan signs offshore pipeline agreement with Gazprom, Reuters, 7 February 2019. Retrieved from https://www.reuters.com/article/pakistan-russia-gazprom/pakistan-signs-offshore-pipeline-agreement-with-gazprom-idUSL5N2022ZB

33. Pakistan, Russia ties in a big boom, *The Nation*, 9 December 2019. Retrieved from https://nation.com.pk/09-Dec-2019/pakistan-russia-ties-in-a-big-boom
34. Charlie Savage, Mujib Mashal et. al. Suspicions of Russian Bounties Were Bolstered by Data on Financial Transfers", *The New York Times*, 30 June 2020, URL: https://www.nytimes.com/2020/06/30/us/politics/russian-bounties-afghanistan-intelligence.html
35. Krzysztof Iwanek, Russia's Looming Arms Sale to Pakistan Sets Up a Dangerous Game, *The Diplomat*, 16 May 2019. Retrieved from https://thediplomat.com/2019/05/russias-looming-arms-sale-to-pakistan-sets-up-a-dangerous-game/
36. Nivedita Kapoor, Russia-Pakistan relations and its impact on India, ORF, 3 July 2019. Retrieved from https://www.orfonline.org/expert-speak/russia-pakistan-relations-impact-india-52715/

19

Pakistan and the Afghan Peace Process

Gautam Mukhopadhaya

Introduction

After over 50 years of violent political competition, Soviet military intervention, internationally supported armed insurgency outsourced to Pakistan, civil war amongst the Mujahideen, repressive Taliban rule, Pakistani machinations and tutelage, the US-led war on terror in Afghanistan, renewed Taliban insurgency and military offensives, and daily acts of cross-border terrorism that now include newer actors, in the midst of 18 years of relative peace, freedoms and democracy that has seen a new generation of Afghans come of age, all Afghans are tired of violence and terrorism and desperate for peace. Past efforts to embark on direct and indirect peace and reconciliation efforts by the Afghan government and the international community have not succeeded in the face of Taliban intransigence, Pakistani obstructionism, and failures on the part of the international community and the Afghan government.

Although motivated by its own narrow interests, the US-led direct talks facilitated by Pakistan leading to the US-Taliban Agreement in Doha on February 29, 2020, have therefore generated hopes against hope that in the absence of any alternative to a continued military stalemate, it offers the only chance of peace. Persuasive as that might sound, the Afghan people have not been part of a peace process in which one side seeks peace while the other seeks victory, and the terms of peace appear forced from outside in favour of one side. Its prospects therefore are not bright. At its core are two incompatible visions of Afghanistan and a disruptive Pakistani agenda to which new layers have been added to keep Afghanistan destabilized for its ingrained security and regional interests.

This chapter critically examines the US-Taliban Agreement, Pakistan's deep involvement in Afghanistan and the Afghan peace process, the prospects of the intra-Afghan talks expected to begin any day, and the possible impact of a flawed peace process driven by US, Pakistani and other foreign interests, on Afghanistan's future.

Context

Over six months after the landmark February 29, 2020, signing of the US-Taliban Agreement or 'deal' in Doha, Qatar, on a timetable for the withdrawal of US troops from Afghanistan and Taliban assurances against terrorism against the USA and its allies, followed up by four fresh rounds of diplomacy by US Special Envoy for Afghan Reconciliation, Ambassador Zalmay Khalilzad, in the midst of the global COVID-19 pandemic in April, May June and July, that took him to Doha, Kabul, Rawalpindi/Islamabad, Delhi and Tashkent, and a special Loya Jirgah convened by President Ghani on August 7-9, 2020, prospects that intra-Afghan talks on a permanent ceasefire and a roadmap for Afghanistan that form part of the so-called Afghan 'peace' process, that had been originally scheduled to start on March 10, 2020 but held up on account of various disagreements,[1] seem finally ready to commence.

Pakistan is commonly credited as having played a critical role in the process by bringing the Taliban into direct talks with the USA, although the crucial breakthrough was provided by President Trump's unilateral decision to withdraw US troops from Afghanistan with an eye on his re-election in the US Presidential elections scheduled for November 2020. That decision removed, in principle, the most important Taliban precondition for a resolution to the conflict on the latter's terms. The Afghan government with whom the USA has a strategic partnership has had very little say in the process.

Pakistan has been able to insert itself into the process as the 'gatekeeper' of the Taliban since its emergence in Pakistan in the mid-1990s. It has also played a prominent role behind the scenes guiding the Taliban during the talks, and is expected to continue to play a dominating role in the intra-Afghan talks between the 'Afghan sides' and the Taliban that are expected to follow.

The association of Pakistan with the Afghan peace process is not without its ironies. However favourable may have been its role in Afghanistan during the struggle against the Soviets, for most Afghans its role in Afghanistan today is the anti-thesis of peace. It is associated, rather, with political interference and tutelage, quest for strategic depth, destabilization, fundamentalist violence, cross-border terrorism, and a proxy war in Afghanistan. Peace, that every Afghan yearns for, is therefore viewed with as much foreboding as hope.

Nevertheless, as the principal player in the process behind both the Taliban and USA, best illustrated by its arrest and incarceration of Mullah Baradar in February 2010 for talking to the Afghan government, and his release last year to head talks with the USA, Pakistan's s role in the peace process, although duplicitous, cannot be ignored.

The US-Taliban Agreement

At the end of 18 months of shuttle diplomacy in the Gulf, South Asia and Europe and nine rounds of direct talks with the Taliban in Doha, Qatar, partially facilitated by Pakistan, the USA and the Taliban, represented by US Special Envoy for Afghan Reconciliation Zalmay Khalilzad and senior Taliban leader, Mullah Abdul Ghani 'Baradar', respectively, signed an 'Agreement for Bringing Peace to Afghanistan between the Islamic Emirate of Afghanistan *which is not recognized by the United States as a state and is known as the Taliban* (italics for emphasis) and the United States of America' in a ceremony in Doha on February 29, 2020[2] in the presence of US Secretary of State, Mike Pompeo, Taliban negotiators, and representatives from several countries (including India), and well-wishers of Afghanistan although not the Afghan government.

The agreement consists of four parts; the first two comprising 'Guarantees and enforcement mechanisms that will prevent the use of the soil of Afghanistan by any group or individual *against the security of the United States and its allies*' and 'Guarantees, enforcement mechanisms, and announcement of a *timeline for the withdrawal of all foreign forces from Afghanistan*' (in that order in the preamble, and reversed in its operational section); and following the announcement of the first two parts, the third and fourth parts dealing with 'intra-Afghan negotiations between the Taliban and '*Afghan sides*' starting March 10, 2020, that will include as an agenda item 'a permanent and comprehensive ceasefire...which will be *announced along with the completion and agreement over the future political roadmap of Afghanistan*' italics for emphasis). Formally, the 'four parts above are interrelated' though 'each will be implemented in accordance with its *own agreed timeline and agreed terms*'. 'Agreement on the first two parts' will '*pave the way* for the last two parts...(which) are interconnected'.

The key elements of the US-Taliban 'deal' on troop withdrawal are well known and hardly bear repetition but to recapitulate for ready reference, Part I, its core, applying to the USA, consists of a drawdown of US troops from their level at the time of the Agreement of 13,000 to 8,600 and the closure of five US military bases in 135 days, i.e., by mid-July 2020; and the remaining US troops in 14 months, i.e., by April 2021, in return for Taliban commitments that Afghan 'soil' 'under their control' would not be used by 'groups or individuals including Al Qai'da', to 'threaten the security of the USA and its allies" (contained in Part II of the Agreement).

Part I of the Agreement also contains provisions for 'working with relevant sides' for the release of 5,000 Taliban and 1,000 prisoners 'of the other side' by March 10, disagreements over which have held up the start of the intra-Afghan talks; and the lifting of UN sanctions against the Taliban by May 29, and of US sanctions by August 27, respectively.

While the US troop withdrawal and other commitments have been proceeding on schedule and there is speculation they may even be speeded up, the issue of prisoner releases has not yet been completed even after the decision by the Loya Jirgah to release 400 high-value Taliban prisoners convicted of serious terrorist and other crimes.

US-Afghan 'Joint Declaration'

The Afghan government was absent from the ceremony marking the US-Taliban agreement, but in Kabul, President Ashraf Ghani and US Secretary for Defence, Mark Esper, issued a separate Joint Declaration[3] at a Press Conference outlining a four-stage process for a 'comprehensive and sustainable peace agreement' culminating in a 'permanent and comprehensive ceasefire'. Unlike the US-Taliban Agreement that is signed between a State and a non-State actor (the Taliban), the Joint Declaration is a document involving two states (although their legal solemnity relative to each other is worth analyzing).

The Declaration 'notes' and acknowledges the US-Taliban Agreement on most counts, notably US troop withdrawal and lifting of sanctions against the Taliban (in Part II), with some notable differences. It reaffirms the US commitment to seek funding on a yearly basis for the 'training, equipping, advising and sustaining' of the ANDSF so that Afghanistan can 'independently secure and defend itself against internal and external threats', and front-loads counter-terrorism cooperation at the top of the Declaration (Part I) followed by the section on troop withdrawals.

Significantly, unlike the provisions on security in the US-Taliban Agreement that are general and purely preventive in nature, the provisions on counter-terrorism in the 'Joint Declaration' are stronger and oriented towards joint action against 'Al Qaeda, ISIS-K and other *international* terrorist groups and individuals' though it too limits its concerns and actions to those that threaten 'the USA and its allies' omitting mention of cross-border regional outfits.

The Declaration also contains a specific clause committing the USA to 'facilitating discussions between Afghanistan and Pakistan to work out arrangements to ensure that neither country's security is threatened by actions from the territory of the other side'.

The two documents also differ on the provision for prisoner releases that had held up the start of intra-Afghan talks but with the decision of the Loya Jirgah to release them now seem on the way to resolution[4] although new hurdles have also come up. Significantly, in neither of the two documents is the issue of prisoner releases made a pre-condition for the start of intra-Afghan talks though the Taliban made it so with the tacit support of the USA.

Implications and Consequences

The Agreement is seriously imbalanced and weighted in favour of the Taliban and does not augur well for the peace process and long-term peace in Afghanistan.

First, the Agreement and process leading to it, has significantly enhanced the standing of the Taliban at the expense of the authority and legitimacy of the constitutional government of Afghanistan and the post-Bonn democratic Islamic dispensation already undermined by several acts of omission and commission on the part of the US.[5] While the Afghan Government that represents the Afghan state at the United Nations and is universally recognized does not even find proforma mention in the Agreement,[6] the signing of the Agreement between the USA and 'the Islamic Emirate of Afghanistan' amounts to a semi-recognition of a non-state actor as a government in waiting, notwithstanding the repetitive phrase '*which is not recognized by the United States as a state and is known as the Taliban*'. The lifting of US and UN sanctions against the Taliban, that includes the Haqqani Network, a US-designated terrorist group that a former US Joint Chief of Staff once described as a "veritable arm of the Pakistani ISI", will also sanitize and legitimize an organization that is deeply involved in continuing acts of terrorism in Afghanistan amongst other transnational crimes.

It is therefore not surprising that the Taliban have celebrated the Agreement as a 'victory' both in terms of substance and symbolism.

This may have been unavoidable in the face of Taliban intransigence and inflexibility and US determination to leave the Afghan battlefield, but it begs the question how the Taliban would be willing to share power with a negotiating partner on the opposite side that is it not even willing to recognize it as legitimate or even name. It lends credence to the suspicion that the Taliban are merely using the peace process to grab power.

Second, although originally the two parts of the process were supposed to be part of a composite package in which 'nothing was agreed until everything was', the de facto decoupling of the withdrawal of US troops from the intra-Afghan talks, in which (although 'inter-related' and 'inter-connected'), *'each (of the four parts) will be implemented with its own agreed timeline and agreed terms'*, means that the intra-Afghan talks on a permanent ceasefire and political settlement will proceed with a constantly declining US troop presence according to a fixed timeline and will not be able to act as a security provider and a check on unreasonable demands during the course of negotiations that will surely stretch well beyond the due date of the US troop withdrawal.

Third, although the US-Afghan Joint Declaration provides for funding for training, equipping, advising and sustaining of the ANDSF, and a good office role for the USA for talks on reciprocal security concerns between Afghanistan and Pakistan, the USA cannot be unaware that its repositioning from a strategic partner of the Afghan government to a 'neutral' good offices role, will tilt the military balance on the battlefield, and political balance on the negotiating table against the '*Afghan sides*' without any corresponding cuts on the capacity of the Taliban and their mentors to operate from their bases in Pakistan. In addition, there is a nagging suspicion that between the Republic and the Taliban, the USA has repositioned itself closer to the latter. The ability of the ANDSF to defend Afghanistan even in these circumstances should however not be under-estimated.

Fourth, and most worrying for ordinary Afghans, in addition to military vulnerability and diplomatic disadvantage, with the announcement of the permanent and comprehensive ceasefire left until the '*completion and agreement over the future political roadmap of Afghanistan*', the threat of violence and terrorism will remain hanging over their heads during the process of negotiations until an agreement is reached, like the proverbial sword of Damocles. They will in effect be negotiating with a gun on their heads.

Finally, weak as they are in an area of vital interest to the USA, the counter-terrorism focus of the Agreement on 'international' terrorist groups and individuals' 'against the USA and its allies' leaves Afghanistan and the region vulnerable to regional and cross-border terrorist groups like the Islamic State of Khorasan Province (ISKP), Al Qaeda in the Indian subcontinent (AQIS), the Lashkar-e-Taiba (LeT) and other Pak-based terrorist groups with cross-border and regional agendas and international links even as the recent (11th) report of the UN Security Council Monitoring Committee on terrorism in Afghanistan[7] reveals that the Al Qaeda continues to enjoy close operational and other ties with the Taliban and remains embedded and active in Afghanistan, and that groups like the Haqqani Network, ISKP and LeT enjoy tactical alliances and division of labour and responsibility that will keep terrorism alive in the region for the foreseeable future. Assuming that the Taliban interest in an Islamic 'Emirate' is limited to Afghanistan as they avow and that they are not interested in any wider 'jihad', the prime beneficiaries of this deal will be sponsors of terrorism in the region.

Whether these imbalances and biases in favour of the Taliban are the product of a weak American hand in the negotiations or a deliberate attempt to structure the intra-Afghan talks in favour of the Taliban (and indirectly, Pakistan), or both, is for the reader to decide. A long list of former US ambassadors to Afghanistan, scholars and others have warned against a premature withdrawal of US troops before a political settlement is reached describing it in unflattering terms including a "surrender"[8] and invoking fears of civil war and chaos in which terrorism would thrive. Everything in favour of the Taliban in the intra-Afghan equations and negotiations will also work to the advantage of Pakistan.

Pakistan's Interests in Afghanistan

Pakistan's role in the Afghan peace process has to be seen in relation to its larger objectives in Afghanistan, the instruments that it has as its disposal in order to realize these objectives and their relationship with its regional ambitions including its revanchist agenda vis-à-vis India, and its larger geo-political interests, in particular vis-à-vis the USA and China.

Barring changes in instrumentality and context, fundamentally, these remain the same as they have been since it began to play a major role in Afghanistan's affairs promoting political Islam in Afghanistan even before the Soviet intervention in Afghanistan in 1979 gave it the opportunity of playing a more direct military role in supporting and arming the Afghan Mujahideen.

Broadly, Pakistani motivations in Afghanistan can be grouped into three sets of interests: those related to its historic desire since its creation in 1947 to convert the Durand Line that was designed as a line delineating spheres of influence between British India and Afghanistan in 1893 into a formal boundary between Afghanistan and Pakistan (typically emphasized by Afghan analysts); its chronic attempts to use Afghanistan as a weapon for what it regards as its unfinished agenda of Partition with India with regard to the status of the Indian territory of Jammu & Kashmir combined with a paranoia over a potential Indo-Afghan alliance against Pakistan (favoured most by Western observers); and those that relate to its use of major powers, especially the USA and increasingly China, for economic or regional objectives (usually highlighted by regional players like Iran[9] and India amongst others). In fact, most analysts generally agree that all three are intertwined in differing degrees.

Together with the outsized role Pakistan (especially the ISI) has played in Afghanistan since the period of Soviet intervention as (i) a front-line state for the USA in its proxy war against the Soviet Union, and as a conduit for arms, staging ground and 'handlers' for the Afghan Mujahideen, (ii) their formative role and influence in domestic Afghan politics through their favoured groups and leaders (notably Hekmatyar during the Mujahideen period); (iii) host country for up to 3-4 million Afghan refugees in Pakistan at various times, (iv) the emergence of the Taliban as a phenomenon from madrassas in Pakistan in the mid-1990s, and finally (v) their influence on the Taliban government from 1996-2001, they have led to a conditioned reflex on the part of the Pakistani political and especially military establishment to treat Afghanistan as its fiefdom in which it could decide the limits of Afghan autonomy.

This proprietary attitude on the part of Pakistan towards Afghanistan has manifested itself in attempts to keep the latter dependent on the former, exercise political tutelage over Afghanistan and generally treat it as a 'client' state; deny or restrict space for Afghanistan to pursue its age-old relationship with India (including staffing of ministries by Indian-trained personnel, military training in India, etc.); formalize the Durand Line as the boundary between Afghanistan and Pakistan; use Afghanistan for strategic depth against India; leverage the USA to pursue its interests in Afghanistan and the region; and promote radicalism and terrorism from Kashmir to Central Asia as an instrument of its foreign policy.

Role of Pakistan in the Peace Process: The Past

These obsessions and reflexes also drive its interest in the Afghan peace process in the past and now.

Both President Karzai and President Ghani made several efforts to initiate direct, indirect, bilateral (through Pakistan) or internationally-assisted talks with the Taliban as part of a peace and reconciliation process during their terms, without success. These included overtures by President Karzai in 2007 following the regrouping and resurgence of the Taliban as a militant-terrorist force after the USA had diverted its attention to Iraq in 2004, and again during and after his Presidential re-election campaign in 2009-10 (when he proposed a Peace Loya Jirgah in June 2010 and set up a high peace council for Afghan reconciliation); and a sustained effort following the London conference on Afghanistan where a 'peace and reconciliation' process advanced by the UK with Pakistani backing that President Karzai insisted that should be 'Afghan-led', was inscribed into the Afghan agenda. This effort, with its ups and downs lasted until 2013 and included a detailed 'roadmap' for power-sharing bearing a strong British-Pakistani imprint, while members of the international community also pushed for the opening of a Taliban office in Doha, Qatar.

Each of these failed either because the Taliban did not respond, as in 2007 and 2009; or was sabotaged by Pakistan, as it happened when Mullah Baradar was trapped and arrested in a joint US-Pakistani operation laid by Pakistani Intelligence in February 2010 when engaged in secret talks with the Afghan government; and a number of other occasions where a Pakistani hand has been suspected;[10] or by Taliban intransigence and over-reach (such as its refusal to deal with the Afghan government which it dismisses as 'puppets' of the USA), as it happened after the opening of a Taliban office for the peace process in Doha when President Karzai angrily objected to it after the Taliban insisted on flying the flag of the Islamic Emirate and projecting itself as a government-in-exile in June 2013.

Implicitly acknowledging that past efforts to kick-start peace talks with the Taliban had failed because President Karzai had given up or avoided involving Pakistan and its army, President Ghani made near abject efforts to reach out to Pakistan and its military after his election in September 2014, with visits to Pakistan, Saudi Arabia and China (pointedly avoiding India), with the express purpose of roping in the Pakistani Army in the effort.

Although circumstances in Pakistan seemed propitious, with the Pakistani Army launching its own military operations against the Tehrik-e-Taliban Pakistan (TTP), Zarb-e-Azb, in North Waziristan earlier in 2014, a number of daring and savage attacks against high-value Pakistani military targets including a Pakistani Army School[11] that raised hopes of a change in Pakistani attitudes towards its support for terrorism, a flurry of high-level government and military visits between Afghanistan and Pakistan amidst unilateral gestures on the part of President Ghani and his then National Security Advisor (and now Foreign Minister), Hanif Atmar, towards Pakistan[12] as expressions of Afghan good faith and expectations of a quid pro quo on direct talks with the Taliban facilitated by the Pakistani Army, all these overtures came to naught.

As bomb blasts and insecurity in Afghanistan continued to grow through 2015-16 without any concrete action against the Taliban on the part of Pakistan or the promised talks with the Taliban, Afghan-Pakistan relations began to sour again; and when Mullah Omar's death under mysterious circumstances as far back as in 2013 was finally revealed and admitted in the midst of their first official talks in Murree in 2015 followed by a rash of deadly attacks in Afghanistan, President Ghani declared that Pakistan was engaged in an 'undeclared war' against Afghanistan.[13]

One plausible reason for Pakistani failure to cooperate when everything else pointed towards a possible change in approach could be the signing of the US-Afghan Bilateral Security Agreement held back by President Karzai and a slowed withdrawal of troops under President Obama's 'surge and drawdown' in 2014 in response to increased Taliban violence and fears of instability in Afghanistan.

Then came President Trump's South Asia strategy in August 2017 that authorized a robust military strategy against the Taliban led by the ANDSF with little scope for negotiations, and bluntly identified Pakistan as the problem in Afghanistan (as President Obama had done during his campaign trail but not followed through clearly) giving a larger role for India, vitiating Afghanistan-Pakistan relations further. However, when even that did not succeed in curbing violence, President Ghani made one last offer trying to build on the 2018 Eid ceasefire with a call for 'unconditional 'talks and a seven-stage plan for peace in 2018.[14] Once again, the Taliban failed to respond.

These failed attempts reveal first, that the route to the Taliban lay through the Pakistani Army, and no 'peace' process regardless of its objectives could succeed bypassing the latter; second, that Pakistan would not negotiate with or deliver any results to the Afghan government or authorities without the USA as the principal interlocutor from which it could extract concessions for its 'cooperation'; and third, that keeping Afghanistan destabilized is part of the Pakistani agenda.

Role of Pakistan in the Peace Process: Present

Newer developments, fears and perceived opportunities confirm these observations. The most obvious among them is the opportunity Pakistan sees to exploit Afghan war fatigue in the West, and the fortuitous effort led by the President Trump himself[15] (but also Russia and China for their own reasons), to see coalition troops out of Afghanistan, to (i) regain strategic depth, influence and control in Afghanistan that was lost with the ouster of the Taliban in 2001 and the gradual realization by the USA that Pakistan was playing a double game in Afghanistan, (ii) free itself of the grip of the Financial Action Task Force (FATF) over its role in international terrorist financing and access IMF and other loans for its struggling economy, and (iii) revive efforts to internationalize the issue of J&K after its change of status in August 2019. Pakistan has made several efforts up to the level of Prime Minister Imran Khan to use its cooperation with the USA on Afghanistan to seek US censure or mediation on Kashmir, without success.[16]

A less obvious but worrying factor that Pakistan would rather not acknowledge is the fear that restiveness in the Pashtun areas of Pakistan manifested in two contrasting movements, an extremist, militant and terrorist movement and the TTP, that has from time to time been targeted by the Pakistani state and Army, but at other times been useful for its ends in Afghanistan;[17] and more recently, the popular, pacifist movement for peace, dignity and opposition to the Pakistani military's use of the Pashtun people as fodder for extremism and destabilization of the region represented by the Pashtun Tahafuz Movement (PTM) and its charismatic leaders, might spill over into a revival of sentiments for Pashtunistan.

Pakistan will do everything possible to prevent sympathy and support for the PTM from spilling over into Afghanistan (which briefly had its own version of a peace movement against the excesses of the Afghan Taliban and Afghan state forces in the Helmand Peace Initiative) leading to any kind of irredentist movement among Pashtuns on both sides of the Durand Line. This has included measures such as fencing the Durand Line since 2017 to reinforce its status as a de facto boundary, frequent border closures, and periodic cross-border shelling and rocket attacks leading to exchanges of fire between the Pakistani and Afghan security forces at the border as has taken place in July in Kunar and Spin-Boldak.

So far, instability and violence in Afghanistan has prevented this. But such a possibility, particularly if peace returns to Afghanistan, is something that the Pakistani Army cannot countenance. This is a compelling reason for Pakistan to continue to promote conflict in Afghanistan so that the Pashtuns of Afghanistan are kept distracted.

A byproduct of this fear of Pashtun consolidation is that Pakistani agencies also feel the need to reach out to non-Pashtun ethnicities in Afghanistan as a hedge against such an eventuality. While overtures are already being made, the Afghan peace process provides a ringside seat for it in this.

Another constant concern that Pakistan cannot escape is that their chosen instruments of destabilization and influence in Afghanistan may depart from their set agenda given half an opportunity, and work against them. This was true of the Afghan Mujahiddeen in the 1990s, most of whom (other than Jalaluddin Haqqani and Gulbuddin Hekmatyar) turned against Pakistan once the Soviets left, and remain so for the Afghan Taliban.

The cases of Mullah Zaeef,[18] the former Taliban ambassador to Pakistan and stringent critic of Pakistan's handling of the Taliban, Mullah Baradar in 2010, Mullah Baradar (illustrated earlier) and Mullah Akhtar Mansour, the then Taliban second-in-command who was killed in a US drone attack crossing over from Iran into Balochistan in May 2016 with a Pakistani passport in his possession on a suspected Pakistani Intelligence tip, are well known; but there are media and Intelligence reports of efforts by others, including those that have played a prominent role in the peace process, chafing against the tutelage and clutches of the ISI or seeking to wean themselves away from Pakistan as far back as 2001-02, when according to one credible report[19] several influential Taliban leaders including Mullah Baradar and the Taliban Defence Minister amongst other prominent Taliban offered to surrender to the post-Bonn interim administration of Karzai in return for a normal life in Afghanistan with the knowledge of Mullah Omar.

As a result, Pakistani agencies have not only maintained tight control over the Taliban, especially leaders based in Pakistan, but also nurtured alternatives in case elements of the Taliban display too much independence of their mentors in Pakistan. Their most favoured instrument is of course the Haqqani Network, now under Sirajuddin Haqqani, but there is enough evidence and literature[20] now, including in the report of the UN Security Council Monitoring Committee referred to above,[21] of shadowy links and a far too neat division of labour and responsibility for attacks between the Taliban, especially the Haqqani Network (and other hardline elements that may or may not be at a tangent with the leadership and Taliban negotiators in Doha), and the Al Qaeda (who may now be embedded amongst the Taliban as a 'surrogate' force),[22] the ISKP, the Lashkar-e-Taiba and the Al Qaeda in the Indian subcontinent (AQIS) amongst others, notwithstanding contradictions and periodic clashes amongst some of them.

A number of such commanders and operatives have also recently been killed or arrested in joint US-Afghan, ANDSF[23] or NDS[24] operations in Afghanistan, such as the AQIS Chief Asim Umar in September 2019, the arrest of the 'Emir' of the ISKP, Aslam Farooqi, in April, and the death of another ISKP leader involved in the attack on the Sikh gurudwara amongst others, Sanaullah,[25] in May this year.

Given the mounting evidence and literature on the subject, it is possible to discern a common mastermind at work directing their operations and providing for alternatives and fallbacks, in case the Taliban get too independent of their handlers if and when they come to positions of power in Afghanistan as part of the peace process. In view of the common ties each of these are known to have with Pakistani Intelligence agencies, it is not difficult to guess who that could be. On the other hand, the reported leadership tussles and rifts between different factions within the Taliban, including between Mullah Umar's son, Mullah Yaqub Mullah Akhtar Mansour (earlier), and others now as COVID-19 has reportedly afflicted the seniormost ranks of the Taliban[26] also call into question Pakistan's ability to maintain full control over Taliban factions and elements that it has nurtured or relied on at different times.

Each of the above factors has played a role in shaping Pakistan's essentially dual strategy in Afghanistan: to install a client regime in Afghanistan through the negotiating table or the battlefield, and if that is not possible, to keep Afghanistan destabilized through factionalism, ethnic conflicts, extremism and terrorism so that it cannot ever be a threat to Pakistan. Typically, since even their chosen instruments of tutelage have not always played according to plan, the two strategies are pursued together.

Intra-Afghan Talks

Notwithstanding the above, now that the intra-Afghan talks are around the corner, what are the prospects of their success? Several scenarios can be visualized. First, since the first hurdle to get the talks started seem to be overcome with the prisoner release reaching a critical threshold, the best-case scenario that could potentially end in a power-sharing arrangement and bring peace to Afghanistan would, of course, be the best for Afghanistan and the world at large as it would enable the world to engage with Afghanistan as a single entity in which all political forces can compete peacefully.

However, the prospect of this happening rests on six assumptions: that the two sides will negotiate in good faith; that it will be possible to reconcile the deep differences between Taliban ideology and objectives and that of traditional power brokers and democratic Islamic republican forces of post-Bonn Afghanistan; that the Taliban and post-Bonn Afghanistan are prepared to share power based on compromises on their core values; that both sides will be able to rein in factional differences and individual ambitions; that Pakistan is prepared to settle for peace in Afghanistan; and that the USA actually has a vision for peace in Afghanistan that envisages power-sharing between the two sides.

Each of these is questionable, and nothing from our understanding of the peace process analyzed so far is encouraging. Theoretically, with its leverage on the Taliban, Pakistan could do a lot to moderate its positions on issues of ideology and power-sharing, but it is unlikely that it will play such a role. On the contrary, learning from past overtures on both the Afghan sides to seek some reconciliation, it would appear that, if anything, their role would be to harden these demands. Foremost among the irreconcilables is an almost unbridgeable gap between the Taliban vision of an Islamic Emirate and the post-Bonn Islamic Republic reflected in deep divisions on the 2004 constitution including democracy, civic freedoms such as freedom of expression and free media, rights and advancement of women, governing structures, etc. Though the Taliban seem to have the upper hand now, resistance on the part of Afghan democratic forces and ethnic groupings to renewed Taliban rule and excesses should not be under-estimated.

Under the circumstances, three sets of scenarios seem more likely. The first is that talks commence in Doha once remaining obstacles are overcome, and the two sides hold two or three exploratory rounds that could serve as opening positions and confidence-building measures until the US elections before talks recommence in right earnest.

The second is that differences over details, large and small, erupt and result in divisions between and within delegations that, coupled with Taliban and Pakistani moves, could stalemate the talks or worse, slide down a slippery slope into failure, political turmoil, return to hostilities and military operations, internecine conflicts and clashes on both sides, or even a total breakdown of order with an even more lethal cocktail of extremist and terrorist organizations in the fray than was the case during the intra-Mujahideen conflict of the early 1990s that led to the birth of the Taliban as a conservative, repressive but temporarily stabilizing force.

The third could be an attempted Taliban military take-over with covert (or overt) support of Pakistan, and a blind eye on the part of the USA or that behind a facade of acting as an honest broker, the USA may actually work to bring the Taliban into power as its preferred choice. Although the Ghani-Abdullah agreement to work together may stave that off, this may already be happening. The USA seems to have accepted that peace will come to Afghanistan on Pakistani and Taliban terms, not those of the Afghan people. Every act of Special Envoy Khalilzad support by the US State Department since direct talks with the Taliban were opened over 18 months ago has privileged the Taliban. None of these augur well for peace in Afghanistan.

Recent developments, such as (i) the obviously ghost-written Sirajuddin Haqqani Op-Ed in the *New York Times* that was an unabashed attempt to whitewash the leader of an acknowledged terrorist outfit as a reasonable figure for a potential leadership position in the government; (ii) the Trump–Baradar telephone conversation of March 3, 2020[27] in which he referred to the Taliban as "powerful people...fighting for your soil"; (iii) Secretary Pompeo's threat to withhold US$ 1 bn in aid this year and another 1 bn next year in the midst of the COVID pandemic that was expected to hit Afghanistan hard; and (iv) Khalilzad's blunt message to India in May-June to talk to the Taliban to address its concerns that was both a blatant attempt to divide Indian loyalties and weaken India's support for the Afghan government and democratic forces and push them towards starting talks on Taliban terms so that the way to the US exit could be cleared, and a subtle message to India that the USA was determined to bring the Taliban into the power structure whether Afghan sides agreed to talk or not, all point in the direction of a Taliban-heavy dispensation in Kabul at a minimum.

In any of these scenarios, the intra-Afghan talks, far from acting as a peace process, will serve Pakistan's destabilization agenda in Afghanistan and set in motion the seeds of another civil war. While the USA has retained the right to correct its policies if the Taliban do not uphold their side of the deal, only time will tell whether the USA is being irresponsible in pulling out of Afghanistan in a haste without creating conditions for both sides to negotiate and share power in good faith, and leave Afghanistan contested and in Pakistani hands once again as it did in the 1990s or exercise its parallel commitments to the Afghan government to strengthen the capacity of the Afghan government and security forces to resist Taliban violence and terrorism and play a positive role in bringing about a fair peace that accommodates the interests of all sides.

Meanwhile, with US-China relations deteriorating post-COVID-19, new forces have also been set in motion in Asia that could impact on the situation in Afghanistan unpredictably. China has already been actively involved in efforts to bring about reconciliation between the Afghan government and the Taliban in trilateral, quadrilateral and other formats involving the Afghan sides, Pakistan, the USA and most recently, Russia, in the past. But recent developments such as the India-China border stand-off in Ladakh, plans to formalize the China-Iran Comprehensive Strategic Partnership with a wide-ranging US$ 400 billion road map for investments over 25 years that includes port access and security-related cooperation, and its most recent initiative in convening a meeting of Foreign Ministers of China, Pakistan, Nepal and Afghanistan ostensibly to deal with

COVID-19 but also deeper and longer term strategic objectives, presage much greater activism in the wider region from Iran across the Pamirs, Hindu Kush, Karakoram, Kunlun and Himalayan ranges to Xinjiang and Tibet that could have fateful implications for Afghanistan as well.

NOTES

1. Not the least, a dispute between the principal contenders, President Ashraf Ghani and Dr. Abdullah Abdullah, on the results of the September 29, 2019, Presidential election results, an 'inclusive' negotiating team and leadership on the Afghan side for the talks, and disagreements and haggling over the issue of prisoner releases demanded by the Taliban amongst other issues, including serious terrorist attacks against minorities and women, and US threats of aid cuts on political grounds in the midst of the looming COVID pandemic that was expected to affect Afghanistan badly.
2. "Joint statement on the signing of the US-Taliban agreement," Office of the Spokesperson, US Department of State, March 9, 2020, https://www.state.gov/joint-statement-on-the-signing-of-the-u-s-taliban-agreement-2/; https://www.state.gov/wp-content/uploads/2020/02/Agreement-For-Bringing-Peace-to-Afghanistan-02.29.20.pdf
3. "Joint Declaration between the Islamic Republic of Afghanistan and the United States of America for Bringing Peace to Afghanistan," US Department of State, February 29, 2020, https://www.state.gov/wp-content/uploads/2020/02/02.29.20-US-Afghanistan-Joint-Declaration.pdf
4. In point of fact, while the US-Taliban Agreement commits the USA to 'work with all sides' to release 5,000 Taliban prisoners from Afghan jails in return for an estimated 1,000 Afghan soldiers held captive by the Taliban as a 'confidence building measure by March 10, 2020, the US-Afghan Joint Declaration merely commits the Afghan government to 'participate in a U.S.-facilitated discussion with Taliban representatives...to determine the feasibility of releasing significant numbers of prisoners on both sides' with the help of the ICRC.
5. Such as keeping the elected Afghan government out of the negotiations and not always being fully transparent about it in its briefings, and announcing the US-Taliban 'deal' just three weeks before the September 29 elections (and scheduling the first round of intra-Afghan talks two days before it) signalling the inconsequentiality of the democratic process and the will of the people.
6. This would hold true even though the government was not formally sworn in until March 7.
7. https://www.undocs.org/S/2020/415
8. https://www.washingtonpost.com/opinions/i-was-ambassador-to-afghanistan-this-deal-is-a-surrender/2019/01/29/8700ed68-2409-11e9-ad53-824486280311_story.html?output Type =amp; https://www.atlanticcouncil.org/blogs/new-atlanticist/us-taliban-negotiations-how-to-avoid-rushing-to-failure/
9. See Farzad Ramezani Bonesh, *Asia Times*, May 11, 2020. 'Pakistan's Approach to the Peace Process'; https://asiatimes.com/2020/05/pakistans-approach-to-afghan-peace-process/
10. Such as the killing of Ustad Burhanuddin Rabbani in a suicide bomb attack in an attempt to meet a Taliban emissary in 2011 and another that left the then NDS Chief, Assadullah Khalid, seriously injured in 2013, as also the placement of an imposter in place of Mullah Akhtar Mansour to meet US officials in a secret operation in 2010.
11. Tthat included attacks on a Pakistani naval air base in Karachi in June 2014, an airbase in

Quetta in August 2014 and an Army School in Peshawar in December 2014 on top of an earlier attack on the Pakistani Army Headquarters in Rawalpindi in 2009.

12. Including the signing of an MoU on Intelligence cooperation, arrests of suspects of the Army Public School massacre on Intelligence provided by Pakistan, operations against TTP leaders and elements sheltering in Afghanistan, and the handing over of a leading TTP commander, Latifullah Mehsud, to Pakistan, and relations with India being put on hold during this process amongst other gestures.
13. Ahmed Bilal Khalil, The Tangled History of the Afghanistan-India-Pakistan Triangle', *The Diplomat,* December 16, 2016.
14. https://tolonews.com/Peace-converted.pdf https://tolonews.com/Peace-converted.pdf
15. Flip flops in US policy towards Pakistan, Afghanistan and the region as a whole including Iran, as well as the increasing role that a rising and assertive China, its all-weather ally, is playing in Pakistan through the CPEC and the port of Gwadar, as also in Afghanistan, have also shaped Pakistan's tactical positions on Afghanistan for better or for worse.
16. https://www.dw.com/en/convincing-trump-on-kashmir-pakistani-pm-khans-toughest-diplomatic-test/a-50548589
17. Kunwar Khuldun Ahmad, *The Diplomat*, October 8, 2019, https://thediplomat.com/2019/10/the-return-of-the-pakistani-taliban/
18. Abdul Salam Zaeef, '*My Life with the Taliban*', Hachette India, 2010.
19. Anand Gopal, 'Flash from the Past: Missed Opportunities for Reconciliation', Afghan Analysts Network, 15 November 2010.
20. Antonio Giustozzi - Taliban and Islamic State: https://www.crpaweb.org/single-post/2017/12/15/Enemies-or-Jihad-Brothers-Relations-Between-Taliban-and-Islamic-State
    Obaid Ali - Still Under IS's Black Flag: Qari Hekmat's ISKP island in Jawzjan https://www.afghanistan-analysts.org/still-under-the-iss-black-flag-qari-hekmats-iskp-island-in-jawzjan-after-his-death-by-drone/
    Borhan Osman - ISKP's Battle of Minds - https://www.afghanistan-analysts.org/iskps-battle-for-minds-what-are-their-main-messages-and-who-do-they-attract/
    Kabir Taneja - The Fall of ISIS and its implications for South Asia – https://www.orfonline.org/research/the-fall-of-isis-and-its-implications-for-south-asia/
21. https://www.undocs.org/S/2020/415, [ibid].
22. Javid Ahmad: https://thehill.com/opinion/international/502358-the-talibans-emerging-tactical-terror-alliances?rnd=1591911424
23. Afghan National Defence and Security Forces consisting of the Afghan National Army and the Afghan National Police.
24. National Directorate of Security, Afghanistan's primary Intelligence agency.
25. https://timesofindia.indiatimes.com/india/death-of-key-iskp-leader-exposes-pak-isis-links-with-lashkar-other-terror-outfits/articleshow/75605140.cms
26. https://foreignpolicy.com/2020/05/29/taliban-leadership-disarray-coronavirus-covid-peace-talks/
27. https://tolonews.com/afghanistan/trump-holds-phone-call-talibans-mullah-baradar-mujahid

20

Afghanistan 2019-2020

Lt. Gen. (Retd.) Ravi Sawhney and Amb. Amar Sinha (Retd)

Introduction

2019 in Afghanistan was a year of wait and transition, dominated by the ongoing 'peace talks' between the USA and the Taliban. There was a flurry of international activity around these talks as well as the Presidential elections slated for late spring/early summer. The Presidential elections, due in mid-year, faced uncertainty due to the Doha talks. These US-Taliban negotiations were essentially bilateral with the Afghan government, and others, including NATO allies, kept out of the loop. Speculation regarding a possible 'interim' government was commonplace. Pakistani leadership contributed to the confusion by suggesting the Pak model of interim administration to oversee the election, which drew a sharp rebuke from the Afghans. It was however clear that the Afghan legitimate government awaiting a fresh mandate was being undermined by the USA through prioritization of the Taliban. In a closed-door briefing in Washington DC in March 2019, the visiting Afghan NSA, evidently piqued, suggested that the US Chief Negotiator harboured ambitions to be a "viceroy".[1] This led to his year-long boycott by all American officials creating an awkward situation for both sides. Thus, most of the 2019 developments reached denouement only in 2020.

The year 2019 was more violent than usual in the country. Usually, the new year dawns peacefully in Afghanistan, with the Taliban on winter break, planning and replenishing for the spring offensive in late March/April: and in Pakistan it is usually family time. However, 2019 was different as Taliban looked for battlefield gains while the talks were on. They also wanted to give a message to the world that peace would continue to elude Afghanistan as long as the Taliban remained out of the power structure. Their attacks would be brutal and deadlier each time the US negotiator visited Kabul, or when talks hit a roadblock in Doha. Little respect for religion or humanity was displayed; with Taliban's targets going beyond security forces to wedding halls, mosques, gurudwaras, hospitals and maternity wards homing on to the civilians, particularly ethnic minorities. Additionally, the Taliban and their handlers, conveniently used the cover of a relatively new phenomenon—the ISIS-K aka ISKP (Islamic State of Khorasan province)—which claimed credit for those attacks that Taliban's code of war ostensibly prohibits. Taliban thus wanted to appear in comparison as the lesser evil and worthy of engagement by the USA and other regional powers.

According to a **June 2020 report of the US Congressional Research Service**[2] "2019 was a violent year in Afghanistan: The United Nations reports that over 10,000 civilians were killed or injured in fighting in 2019, down slightly from 2018. The conflict also involved an array of other armed groups, including active affiliates of both Al Qaeda (AQ) and the Islamic State (IS, also known as ISIS, ISIL, or Da'esh). According to the UN Mission in Afghanistan (UNAMA) IS-K or ISKP was responsible for 157 terror attacks in 2019. On the other hand, US operations intensified in 2019 and more munitions were dropped in 2019 than in any other year since at least 2010. According to Al Jazeera, quoting a US Air Force Central Command report, US forces dropped a record 7,423 munitions in 2019.[3] According to media reports, the USA also conducted strikes in 27 of Afghanistan's 34 provinces in the first two months of 2020 alone, while by some measures, the Taliban were in control of, or contesting, more territory in 2019 than at any point since 2001.

US Policy

Since 2001, Afghanistan has been an important element of the USA's global war on terror. Perhaps no other country, barring Pakistan, affects Afghanistan to such an extent. However, both countries do so in very different ways. While the architect of 9/11, Osama bin Laden, was eliminated in his hiding place in Pakistan, and the AQ substantially degraded, a range of designated terror groups continued to thrive in the ecosystem created by the Taliban. Taliban's claimed jihad is supposed to rid Afghanistan of all foreign troops. It would therefore be appropriate to look at the evolving US policy in the face of developments in Afghanistan/Pakistan. For some time now it was becoming clear that 'everyone was tired of this endless war', as articulated by President Trump, and his democratic rival, Biden. Bringing the boys back home was President Trump's poll promise that needed redemption as per the US electoral calendar.

Despite his 'original instinct to pull out the troops', President Trump had announced an ambitious South Asia Strategy on 21 August 2017 at Fort Myer.[4] Some of the key elements of his pronouncement were:

(a) At the core was a shift from a time-based approach to one based on conditions to ensure an honourable and enduring outcome. It recognized the results of rapid exit as predictable and unacceptable.

(b) Categorization of the Taliban regime as one that gave comfort and shelter to terrorists, and of the terrorists taking innocent lives as "thugs, criminals and predators".

(c) Strategy, not guided by arbitrary timetables, was aimed at stopping resurgence of safe havens, in the Af-Pak region. Political settlement after effective military effort could include elements of the Taliban though it was not a certainty. Included in the strategy was a commitment to support the Afghan government and the Afghan military but eventually Afghans had to take ownership of their future.

(d) Another element of the new strategy was a fresh approach to Pakistan, which precluded silence on Pakistan's safe havens for terrorist organizations, the Taliban, and other groups that pose a threat to the region and beyond. President Trump accused Pakistan of giving safe havens to the 'agents of chaos, violence and terror" and warned that Pakistan "has much to lose by continuing to harbour criminals and terrorists".

(e) Publicly castigating Pakistan for harbouring the same organizations "that try to kill Americans" every day despite receiving "billions and billions of dollars", President Trump demanded a change: "It was time for Pakistan to demonstrate its commitment to civilization, order, and to peace".

(f) Yet another part of the South Asia strategy was the USA's strategic partnership with India, and its role in stability in Afghanistan, especially in the areas of economic assistance and development.

(g) Easing of earlier rules of engagement and greater delegated authority to the US commander in the field to fully and swiftly wage battle with a clear mission to defeat the enemy. (Note the emphasis on intention to defeat).

Casting aside the earlier reticence of the US policy–makers, President Trump went further on 1 January 2018 when he tweeted, "The United States has foolishly given Pakistan more than 33 billion dollars in aid over the last 15 years, and they have given us nothing but lies and deceit, thinking of our leaders as fools. They give safe haven to the terrorists we hunt in Afghanistan, with little help. No more!"[5]

This had left Pakistan stunned, and Afghans elated. Finally, someone was calling out Pakistan for its duplicitous policy despite being a major non-NATO ally of the USA. President Trump had echoed what every Afghan (and Indian) knew, and had regularly drawn the world's attention to the roots of the problem besetting the region.

The U-turn in USA Policy

President Trump's 'original instincts', however, overtook his new policy within a year. In a U-turn, the USA decided to directly engage with the Taliban: a step justified by the US desire to bring its longest war to a close. A prominent Afghan-American, Ambassador Zalmay Khalilzad, was appointed the Special Representative and chief negotiator by autumn of 2018 to engage the Taliban leadership in Doha. He did so on a continuous basis exuding a sense of urgency. The timelines under discussion affected the Presidential election schedule in Afghanistan. So dramatic was the shift in policy and accompanying narrative, and so uncertain its outcome that it acted as a dampener on Afghan enthusiasm for elections.

Elections in Afghanistan and Government Formation

The election announcement was delayed until April 2019, and the initial date fixed in July was soon pushed back to late September to await an outcome from Doha. While over a dozen candidates and presidential teams were in the fray, the delays and the shifting sands of Afghan politics had left them in disarray. The inept handling of the 2018 Parliamentary elections, and the ensuing allegations of corruption and manipulation, had created serious doubts about the competence and independence of the Election Commission. Its credibility had sunk so low that it necessitated a complete overhaul of the Commission at a late hour. Reconstituting a brand new Election Commission, just before Presidential elections, proved to be a challenge as all contenders had to sign off on its composition to ensure impartiality. Analysts were critical of the two leading contenders who, despite their 2014 agreement governing the National Unity Government (NUG), had failed to reform the Election Commission, or bring about other constitutional changes.

The election campaign remained subdued and lacklustre against the backdrop of the fraught security situation and uncertainty relating to the Doha talks. Unlike in 2014, this time the Taliban publicly vowed to disrupt elections[6] and attacked a few political rallies, including that of President Ghani who was seeking re-election. Attacks were also launched at events of Dr. Abdullah as well as on the office of Amrullah Saleh, the running mate of President Ghani. Like in 2014, once again, the *Battle Royale* had pitted President Ghani against his erstwhile Chief Executive, Dr. Abdullah.

There were serious discordant voices within Afghan political circles, including former President Karzai, who called for stopping of the elections, days before polling day, and focussing on peace instead.[7] In early September, there were signs of a breakthrough in Doha though these hopes were dashed when President Trump tweeted sudden calling off the talks.[8] It soon became clear that the Taliban had refused to travel to Camp David for a signing ceremony hosted by President Trump where the Afghan President was also to be present. Taliban insisted that the deal be inked in Doha before any such high-level interaction. They were either apprehensive of American intentions or of being subjected to new pressures for softening their stance. In the meanwhile, many Afghan political leaders demanded a halt to the elections while wanting all focus to shift towards peace talks with Taliban, arguing that the election would lead the country towards a deeper political and social crisis. Indeed, had the deal been signed in early September, the intra-afghan negotiations would have started on 25 September rendering polls set for three days later meaningless. This however did not happen.

The election took place on September 28 but the turnout was disappointing with just about 2 of the nearly 10 million registered voters turning out to vote.[9] The polling day was marred by 260 security incidents of which 90 directly targeted polling centres according to *Tolo News*. Over 20 police officers and nine civilians lost their lives, with hundreds injured. It not only turned out to be the bloodiest, but also an election with perhaps the lowest turnout in Afghanistan's recent history. Amidst widespread allegations of fraud, both front-runners declared victory soon after the voting. The Independent Election Commission was inundated with questions and allegations of serious fraud. The stage was set for another political impasse and an extended period of political uncertainty.

After several months of scrutiny, and eliminating fraudulent votes, the IEC, on the basis of around 1 million valid votes, declared President Ghani as the victor on 18 February 2020. He had won over 50 per cent of the votes, crossing the threshold by around 11,000 votes, in what was a very close contest. A second round run-off was avoided. However, Abdullah and his supporters rejected Ghani's narrow majority count as fraudulent and sought to establish themselves as a separate government, with both Ghani and Abdullah holding separate inauguration ceremonies on March 9, 2020. This led the Taliban, and a few nations, to raise questions on the legitimacy of the mandate of the new government.

In the meanwhile, on the US-Taliban track, negotiations had restarted in December and on 14 February 2020, it was announced that a deal was ready for signature. Incidentally, the first draft of the deal was finalized as early as in March 2019. The US-Taliban agreement on Bringing Peace to Afghanistan[10] was formally signed on 29 February in Doha and laid down definite timelines including commencement of the intra-afghan negotiations on 10 March after release of up to 5,000 Taliban prisoners. It also envisaged a seven-day reduction in violence to enable such a release, and begin the process of US troop withdrawal over the next 135 days. The two parallel tracks, of US negotiations with Taliban and Afghan political processes, with conflicting calendars, were creating a piquant situation. It took weeks of negotiations and mediation by Khalilzad and others, and a public threat by Secretary of State Pompeo of withholding the USD 1 bn US assistance, before a compromise could be reached. Promisingly, unlike 2014, besides US negotiators, prominent Afghan leaders played an important role in coming up with an Afghan solution. Public patience was running low at the political impasse and Afghans wished to move to stage two of the peace process.

A political agreement signed on May 17, 2020,[11] created a High Council for National Reconciliation, with Abdullah as its chairman, to lead negotiations with the Taliban. The negotiating team and a newly-formed Ministry of Peace and Reconciliation was to function under this authority. The agreement also stipulated that Abdullah would nominate 50 per cent of the cabinet nominees and some other high-level appointments, besides conferring the rank of Field Marshal on Vice President Dostum. The agreement, inter-alia, called for holding the long-delayed provincial and district elections, as well as municipal elections, which have never been held. While the agreement ended the immediate political impasse, according to analysts, its ambiguities may plant the seeds of future conflict and, more importantly, that "it did not remove the underlying causes of the crisis, notably the polarization caused by the current political system." *(Source: Congressional Research Service)*

US-Taliban Agreement

After negotiations lasting eighteen months, the USA and the Taliban signed a peace agreement on February 29, providing for withdrawal of all foreign forces from Afghanistan within 14 months, subject to the Taliban keeping their commitment of not allowing the use of Afghan soil to threaten the USA and its allies; engaging in intra-Afghan negotiations (which were to start on March 10 between the Taliban and "Afghan sides") to finalize a permanent ceasefire and the future political roadmap of Afghanistan; release of all prisoners by both sides (release of up to 5,000 Taliban prisoners held by the Afghan government and 1,000 prisoners held by the Taliban by March 10) and lifting of US and UN sanctions against the Taliban. US Secretary of State Pompeo informed the US Congress of two secret annexures dealing with implementation and protection of US soldiers.[12] In a separate US-Afghan government joint declaration[13] issued simultaneously, the USA reaffirmed its commitment to support the Afghan security forces and the Afghan government, took note of the US-Taliban agreement, and expressed readiness to participate in intra-Afghan negotiations. President Trump had a long telephonic talk with the Taliban leader, Mullah Baradar, within days of signing of the agreement as a sign of his personal commitment. The UNSC unanimously endorsed a US-sponsored resolution, welcoming the "significant steps towards ending the war and opening the door to intra-Afghan negotiations"[14] enabled by the US-Taliban agreement. Interestingly, a day before the US-Taliban agreement was inked, the USA and Russia had, in a joint statement, rejected the possibility of the Islamic Emirate coming back to Afghanistan. This statement became public nearly a week later.[15]

One-Sided Deal

The agreement has received mixed appraisal with many analysts describing it as one sided, paving the way for withdrawal of US forces in return for a vague commitment by the Taliban not to allow the use of Afghan soil to threaten the USA and its allies, without any guarantee of peace in Afghanistan. Because of their family and ideological ties with Al Qaeda, and other Pakistan-based terror groups, serious doubts remain over Taliban's ability and willingness to sever links with them. Taliban's commitment to power sharing, constitutional governance and respecting the rights and liberties that the Afghans have come to enjoy, is seen as highly suspect. Significantly, the agreement lays down deadlines for action on all items except for successful conclusion of intra-Afghan negotiations that would lead to a ceasefire and evolve the future political framework. In a media chat, President Trump acknowledged that the Taliban could possibly seize power after the USA leaves, adding that US forces could not remain in Afghanistan indefinitely and eventually they (Afghanistan) will have to protect themselves.[16]

What is in Store for Afghanistan?

The agreement to bring peace to Afghanistan, erroneously called Afghan Peace Agreement, increasingly resembles a stillborn baby refusing to kick or wail. As this is being written, there are indications that the Afghan government may relent and release the last 400 prisoners. This has led the Taliban to announce a three-day ceasefire for Bakrid (Eid-ul-Adha) with hints that this may be extended if all prisoners are released. Despite many flaws in the Agreement, it is the closest Afghanistan has come to start intra-Afghan negotiations. Afghans are clear-headed about the long road ahead with only promises to go by for now. Despite this, the national mood overwhelmingly favours giving it a good shot.[17] They are willing to take the first step on a journey in search of 'honourable and just peace', cessation of hostilities, ceasefire and an end to the endless cycle of violence. It is still not clear if the Taliban (as a whole) are willing to peacefully reintegrate in a power sharing agreement. Quite a few Taliban voices still demand a monopoly on power and re-establishment of the Islamic Emirate.

In the interim, the Taliban continues to attack every fibre of Afghan society. Worrying reports have emerged that the recently-released prisoners are back in the battlefield. Within two days of signing the agreement, the Taliban announced ending the seven days' period of reduction of violence observed by them before the deal was concluded, and resumed attacks on Afghan forces. Violence picked up substantially. A Reuters report, based on data obtained from a Western military source, claimed that Taliban attacks increased by 70 per cent between March 1 and April 15 compared to the same period a year ago.[18] This creates a delicate situation that could easily slip out of control, even though some of the more heinous attacks have been claimed by other groups operating under new flags and symbols.

The continuing violence also provides an opportunity to the 'spoilers' to derail the peace talks. Elements within the Taliban may not wish to lose influence and access to resources, which will inevitably happen once the intra-Afghan negotiations succeed. Entities supporting the Taliban, and other shades of terrorism, cannot be happy at the prospect of their decades-long efforts coming to naught. A peaceful Afghanistan, where a reformed Taliban eschews violence and settles for an equitable power sharing arrangement, does not serve their larger strategic purpose. It is reasonable to assume that they would push the Taliban negotiators towards maximalist demands, even risking a breakdown. No outcome may be preferable from their perspective than an outcome that is reasonable and good for Afghanistan.

Pakistan's Role

Any analysis of the Afghanistan situation cannot ignore the Pakistani role. US-Pakistan relations have been marked by wild swings and 2019 was no different. Lady Luck smiled again on them in 2019, with a change in US policy. From public accusations and castigation, and scaling back of aid, the USA acknowledged the Pakistani role in facilitating the deal between it and the Taliban. Pakistan was consulted and also leaned on to nudge the Taliban towards a deal. The second-highest Taliban official, and one of the co-founders of the Movement, Mullah Baradar, was released from Pakistani prison to take charge of the Doha office. Despite public denials by Pakistan, as host and home, they wield the strongest control over the Taliban making them, arguably, the most important actor in Afghanistan. However, its self-serving policies have left the Pakistani reputation in tatters. The relentless search for "strategic depth" has brought the Pakistani leadership to believe that their objectives can only be achieved through a 'pliable' government in Kabul. They see the Taliban's return to Kabul as redemption of their decades-long policy, and thus the 29 February deal was a moment of triumph for many Pakistanis, as it was for most terrorist groups around the world. International recognition, and power, is what all terror groups seek, and here was the Taliban getting it on a platter! Pakistan knows well enough that any government in Kabul that presides over a stable country would resist their hegemonic designs. Therefore, despite the rhetoric of a peaceful Afghanistan, a degree of turmoil therein suits them. These considerations will continue to guide their policy, notwithstanding the fate of the US-Taliban deal. They will continue to use proxies to destabilize any government in Kabul.

Beyond the diplomatic exigency of seeking Pakistani cooperation, required for the Doha negotiations, US agencies continued to highlight Pakistan's double game.

The US State Department's counter-terrorism report of 2019 included a stinging indictment, "Pakistan remained a safe harbour for other regionally focused terrorist groups. It allowed groups targeting Afghanistan, including the Afghan Taliban and affiliated Haqqani Network, as well as groups targeting India, including Lashkar–e- Taiba and its affiliated front organizations, and Jaish-e-Mohammed (JeM), to operate from its territory...", and an acknowledgement, "Pakistan, however, did make some positive contributions to the Afghanistan peace process, such as encouraging Taliban's reduction in violence. Pakistan made some progress towards meeting the Action Plan requirements for the FATF, allowing it to avoid being blacklisted, but did not complete all Action Plan items in 2019".[19]

Another quarterly report by the Inspector General of the US Department of Defence to Congress (19 May 2020) has noted continued Pakistani support for violence by the hard-line Taliban movement in Afghanistan. The report also observes continuity in Islamabad's quest for what it has long been defined as its interests in Afghanistan. This report assumes significance as it also covers the period beyond the US-Taliban agreement and notes that Islamabad had celebrated the February 29 deal and highlighted its role in making it possible. However, based on US intel reports, it significantly notes that "Pakistan continues to harbour the Taliban and associated militant groups in Pakistan, such as the Haqqani Network, which maintains the ability to conduct attacks against Afghan interests".[20] And that Pakistan "refrained from applying coercive pressure that would threaten its relationship with the Afghan Taliban. Thus Pakistan pressure is modulated which does not mark a change in its policies". Thus, it is clear that Pakistan wants to have the cake and eat it too.[21]

The peaceful Pashtun Tahafuz Movement in Pakistan, which has found sympathy, and support in Afghanistan has added to Pakistan's real and imagined worries. This has the potential of straining Pakistani relations with the Taliban. Iran's outreach breaks the Taliban coherence, and is a challenge to Pakistan according to author and IR expert, Avinash Paliwal.

In the wake of the August 2019 Indian decision on reorganization of the state of J&K, the Taliban spokesman was quick to reject the Pakistani Foreign Minister's attempt to create its linkage with the ongoing peace process. Pakistan will continue to resuscitate its old narrative that 'the road to Kabul runs through Kashmir' rather than recognizing that the buck stops in Rawalpindi. Thus, it is expected that Pakistan would create new leverages in case the Taliban shows too much independence.

Conclusion

In many quarters, it has been assumed that the Taliban is coming back to take over Kabul soon, so a hedging policy may become an urgent requirement. This line of argument has misread Afghan tiredness with war, and their willingness to get the Taliban back in the fold, as an acceptance of the ideology of the Taliban. If at all, the past decades, and continuing violence, have made the Afghans treasure the gains since 2001 even more. The ability of Afghan society to embrace the erstwhile hardliners was on display in the return of Gulbudin Hekmatyar. However, much of the analysis has created a wrong binary—Emirate vs. the Republic. These are not two sides of the same coin.

While the Taliban has not been particularly forthcoming about its vision of the future, some glimpses have filtered through their statements to the media. The Taliban spokesman, Suhail Shaheen, struck a conciliatory and reassuring note on January 30 when his audio message to the AP spoke of the Taliban wanting to live alongside their countrymen "in an inclusive Afghan world". Similarly, the deputy leader of the Taliban, Sirajuddin Haqqani (leader of the proscribed Haqqani Network) in a signed opinion piece in the *New York Times* on 20 February, 2020 titled 'What We, The Taliban Want' (believed to be ghost written, a week before the Doha deal) tried to allay fears of the global community when he stated that "We (Taliban) acknowledge the importance of maintaining friendly relations with all countries and take their concerns seriously. Afghanistan cannot afford to live in isolation. The new Afghanistan will be a responsible member of the international community". Simultaneously, he reassured his fellow Afghans by stating that the Taliban would like an "inclusive society" where the "rights of the women that are granted by Islam—from the right to education and the right to work—are protected, and where merit is the basis for equal opportunity".[22] Despite the deputy leader of Taliban writing, "I am convinced that the killing and the maiming must stop", the situation on the ground tells a totally different story. Moderate statements have dried up while high levels of violence, constant blame game against the Kabul Government, and characterisation of the Afghan security forces as the enemy are the norm. The continuation of 'jihad' now, after the deal, has little justification.

It is useful to note what one of the leading experts on the region, Marvin G. Weinbaum, posted on his Facebook on 9 June 2020:

> "Some clarity over the Taliban strategy was achieved with a statement this past week by Sirajuddin Haqqani, the group's deputy leader. While asserting that negotiating for peace is a core component of the Taliban's philosophy, he expressed the group's unwillingness to abandon the path of jihad. His mixed message was delivered along with film footage showing the training of suicide bombers in an undisclosed location. The Taliban's pursuit of peaceful diplomacy alongside military power is understandable. Through using political means, the Taliban has acquired a once unimagined international legitimacy, negotiated the departure of foreign forces, and secured the release of many battle-hardened Taliban fighters—all without having to seriously compromise".

His conclusions that "The Taliban's military and diplomatic strategies are intended to work in tandem, one leveraging the other. Each has as its ultimate goal the Taliban's recovery of an emirate lost in 2001. Adversaries can pretend otherwise, but they do so at their peril" are worrying and cannot be overlooked easily.[23]

Thus, the jury is still out on which way Afghanistan will go. Will it be a déjà vu, 40 years after the exit of one super power? Or will Afghanistan see a period of peace and prosperity? The writers would like to bet on the latter, however, it is time the Taliban show signs of change. Therein hangs the fate of Afghanistan.

NOTES

1. https://www.business-standard.com/article/pti-stories/us-state-department-summons-visiting-afghan-nsa-in-rare-rebuke-119031500132_1.html
2. Congressional Research Service : https://crsreports.congress.gov/R/45122
3. https://www.aljazeera.com/news/2020/01/record-7423-bombs-dropped-afghanistan-2019-report-200128142958633.html#:~:text=The%20US%20has%20dropped%207%
4. https://www.whitehouse.gov/briefings-statements/remarks-president-trump-strategy-afghanistan-south-asia/
5. https://twitter.com/realDonaldTrump/status/947802588174577664 and https://www.bbc.com/news/world-us-canada-42536209
6. https://www.washingtonpost.com/world/asia_pacific/taliban-threatens-to-disrupt-afghan-elections-dismisses-september-polls-as-ploy/2019/08/06/26c2103a
7. http://www.1tvnews.af/en/news/afghanistan/39555-karzai-urges-afghan-government-to-postpone-election-focus-on-peace
8. https://www.bbc.com/news/world-us-canada-49642655
9. https://www.firstpost.com/world/afghanistan-presidential-election-2019-sharp-drop-in-voter-turnout-as-only-20-vote-7-million-had-voted-in-2014-7421521.html
10. https://www.state.gov/wp-content/uploads/2020/02/Agreement-For-Bringing-Peace
11. https://www.aljazeera.com/news/2020/05/afghanistan-ghani-abdullah-sign-power-sharing-deal-200517105526348.html
12. https://www.politico.com/news/2020/03/02/secret-documents-trump-afghanistan-119035
13. https://www.state.gov/wp-content/uploads/2020/02/02.29.20-US-Afghanistan-Joint-Declaration.pdf
14. https://www.un.org/press/en/2020/sc14139.doc.htm
15. https://www.state.gov/joint-statement-on-the-signing-of-the-u-s-taliban-agreement/
16. https://www.aljazeera.com/news/2020/03/trump-taliban-possibly-seize-power-troops-leave-200306160431549.html
17. https://www.pajhwok.com/en/2020/01/27/most-afghans-want-peace-taliban-stress-ceasefire
18. https://www.reuters.com/article/health-coronavirus-afghanistan-taliban/taliban-increase-attacks-on-afghan-forces-since-signing-us-deal-data-idUSL4N2C7026
19. US State Dept's Country reports on terrorism 2019" https://www.state.gov/reports/country-reports-on-terrorism-2019/
20. https://media.defense.gov/2020/May/19/2002302407/-1/-1/1/LEAD%20INSPECTOR%20GENERAL%20FOR%20OPERATION%20FREEDOM'S%20SENTINEL.PDF
21. Ibid.
22. https://www.nytimes.com/2020/02/20/opinion/taliban-afghanistan-war-haqqani.html
23. Facebook page of Prof. Marvin Weinbaum https://www.facebook.com/marvin.weinbaum

21

Conclusion: The Road Ahead

Tilak Devasher

Writing in *Pakistan Insights 2019*, I had posed the question: Where would Pakistan be a year from now? What would be the status of Indo-Pak relations during this period? Allowing for the caveat that 'crystal-ball gazing in the case of Pakistan and Indo-Pak relations is always fraught with risk', I had cautioned, 'Despite this, at the time of writing, the portents for either Pakistan or Indo-Pak relations are not very positive.'

My prognosis for Pakistan was that it would continue to be in dire economic straits, if not worse; the IMF bail-out would be like putting Pakistan on a ventilator, keeping it going but without the heft to implement structural changes needed to resuscitate the economy on a long-term basis; while the China Pakistan Economic Corridor (CPEC) would continue, the Chinese would increasingly find Pakistan's inability to re-pay loans and interest to be a major constraint; politically, having 'selected' Imran Khan as a replacement for Nawaz Sharif, it was unlikely that the army would pull the rug from under his feet soon. Hence, civil-military relations in the short-term were likely to be smoother than they had been for a long time with the caveat that Imran Khan did not start getting ideas of being the effective chief executive of Pakistan and started performing, especially in the economic sphere.

It is a matter of some satisfaction that most of the prognosis has come to pass.

How will the next year be for Pakistan and Indo-Pak Relations?

The one difference between 2019 and 2020 is the on-going COVID-19 pandemic and how it has crippled the world, with Pakistan being no exception. The full consequences of its lingering impact are working themselves out and at the time of writing, it is indeed difficult to assess or predict when it will peter out and with what consequences.

Having said that, Imran Khan's political fortunes are unlikely to be very different from his first two years. Given his thin coalition majority in parliament, his government can easily be destabilized should the army so desire by working on the smaller parties. However, it is unlikely that it will resort to this as long as he lets them run the defence and security policies and does not get ideas of being an executive PM. In addition, the army would expect him to perform on the economic front, something that he has not done adequately so far. Thus, civil-military relations are likely to be 'on the same page' though such a mantra is actually indicative of the erosion of civil authority rather than being an element of stability.

The opposition for most of 2019-20 was unable to pose much of a threat to the government while it continued to reel under Imran Khan's accountability onslaught. Maulana Fazlur Rahman of the Jamiat Ulema-e-Islam (F) did try and dislodge Imran Khan in 2019 through an 'Azadi march' that fizzled out since the other opposition parties were not on board. However, at the time of going to print, the Opposition has got its act together, set up the Pakistan Democratic Movement (PDM) and called for Imran Khan to step down and go in for fresh elections. Nawaz Sharif from London has upped the ante by directly targeting the Establishment calling it 'a state above the state'. A series of rallies have been planned in all the four provinces between October and December culminating in a march on Islamabad in January 2021. The outcome of the agitation would depend on the PDM maintaining unity and generating and sustaining enough momentum to rattle the government. Equally, a lot would depend on the attitude of the Establishment.

The Pashtun rights movement led by the Pashtun Tahaffuz Movement (PTM) is likely to grow and continue to catch the imagination of the Pashtuns and of the other oppressed nationalities like the Baloch and the Sindhis. Despite censorship and intimidation, the movement would continue to agitate for the missing Pashtun youth and protest against the Pashtuns being used as cannon fodder for foreign policy objectives. It is equally likely that the Army would continue to be sceptical of any rights movement, no matter how genuine it is.

Balochistan would continue to simmer even as the army's repression moves up several notches to protect the CPEC and Gwadar port. The number of missing persons and cases of tortured dead bodies of the Baloch surfacing periodically are likely to rise.

Economically, a lot would depend on the impact of COVID-19 and how Pakistan is able to tackle the downslide in economic parameters. The reality is that Pakistan's economy was already tanking prior to COVID-19. The pandemic has further adversely impacted it and so the economy will continue its downward slide with the tough IMF bailout conditions nowhere near being met, especially the unrealistic revenue target that was much too ambitious to begin with. Quite likely, the IMF loan may have to be readjusted given the changed reality. Under the circumstances, it is unlikely that Pakistan would be able to tackle its long-term structural problems such as low tax-to-GDP ratio, low savings rate, low investment-to-GDP ratio, circular debt, etc. Neither is it likely to enhance spending on socio-economic development given the large outlays for debt-servicing and defence.

Pakistan has been on the Financial Action Task Force (FATF)'s grey list since June 2018 for its failure to curb terror financing and money laundering. Despite being on the grey list for over two years, it has not been able to fulfil all the action points it was mandated to do. It is likely to languish on the list though it is doubtful if it will be pushed on to the Black List.

Beyond the day-to-day issues, there are the serious long-term challenges that Pakistan faces—Water, Education, Economy and Population—collectively that I had termed as the WEEP factors.[1] These will continue to be neglected to Pakistan's detriment. Of these, the most critical continues to be the declining water availability that is likely to make Pakistan an absolute water-scarce country by 2025 and the fact that almost 50 per cent of Pakistan's children are out of primary schools.

Foreign policy is likely to pose an even bigger challenge in the year ahead primarily due to the changing nature of geo-politics and question marks over Pakistan's ability to assess the developing situation. The immediate focus would continue to be getting bilateral and multilateral financial aid for the sinking economy despite protestations that Pakistan would not beg for money.

The China-Pakistan Economic Corridor (CPEC) would continue to be the pivot for relations with China. Despite Imran Khan's known hostility to the project while he was in the opposition, he is by now committed to it. However, as the bills start coming in for payment, Pakistan will realise the true cost of the projects. Moreover, the hostility of the Baloch to the project could see intensification. Pakistan may seek to fish in the troubled waters of the tense India-China relations and enter the fray to try and seek territorial gains. This could well prove a costly mistake for it.

Pakistan's relations with the USA are evenly poised. The initial hostility of President Trump was tempered due to the USA's need to get Pakistan to facilitate an exit deal with the Taliban from Afghanistan. Having achieved its limited objective, the USA is likely to pull out most, if not all, of its troops during the year. This will once again downgrade Pakistan's importance except if, in the interim, Pakistan manages to get the Taliban installed in Kabul. How the relations pan out in the year ahead would also depend in a large measure on the results of the November 2020 US presidential elections. Pakistan would be hoping for a victory of the Democrats.

Having facilitated the US-Taliban deal signed on 29 February 2020, Pakistan would be hoping that it would eventually lead to the return of the Taliban to power in Kabul. A lot would depend on the way the intra-Afghan dialogue proceeds and if the Ghani government is able to maintain unity or elements of it split, making side deals with the Taliban. All sides would watch the US elections closely and its aftermath to see which way the new US government would tilt.

With the Islamic world, Pakistan would have to be nimble enough to navigate between Saudi Arabia and Iran and between the Arab and non-Arab states striving for leadership of the Islamic world. By aligning itself with Turkey, Malaysia and Iran, Pakistan is in danger of losing the support of its greatest benefactor, Saudi Arabia, which has frequently bailed it out financially, in terms of deferred payment for energy and for providing employment to millions of its workers. What will continue to rankle Pakistan is the lack of interest shown by Saudi Arabia and the UAE on Kashmir.

The revision of the temporary Article 370 and Article 35-A pertaining to Jammu and Kashmir is something that caught Pakistan by surprise and its consequences would continue to reverberate for a long time. The feeling in Pakistan is that it has lost its pivot—the *Nazaria-i-Pakistan* or the Ideology of Pakistan of which Kashmir was the central issue, apart from Islam. With the basis of Pakistani nationalism knocked out, Pakistan and Imran Khan are running helter-skelter trying to find a suitable narrative in order to garner international support on Kashmir. Not surprisingly, therefore, Imran Khan launched a personal tirade against PM Modi, the BJP and the RSS and is likely to continue this during the year ahead. Indo-Pak relations are perhaps at their lowest ebb and likely to remain in cold storage for some time to come.

NOTES

1. Please see the author's '*Pakistan: Courting the Abyss*'.

Index